Formal Assessment

THE BRITISH TRADITION

Upper Saddle River, New Jersey
Glenview, Illinois
Needham, Massachusetts

ACKNOWLEDGEMENTS

Grateful acknowledgment is made to the following for copyrighted material:

Henry Holt and Company, Inc.
"Loveliest of Trees" by A. E. Housman from THE COLLECTED POEMS OF A. E. HOUSEMAN. Copyright © 1965 by Holt, Rinehart and Winston.

Alfred A. Knopf, Inc.
From "A Dill Pickle" by Katherine Mansfield from THE SHORT STORIES OF KATHERINE MANSFIELD. Copyright © 1920, 1922, 1923, 1924, 1926, 1937 by Alfred A. Knopf, Inc.

Oxford University Press
"Sunday Morning" by Louis MacNeice from THE COLLECTED POEMS OF LOUIS MACNEICE, edited by E. R. Dodds. Copyright © 1966 by The Estate of Louis MacNeice. From "Shore Woman" from WINTERING OUT by Seamus Heaney. Copyright © 1072 by Seamus Heaney.

Note: Every effort has been made to locate the copyright owner of material reprinted in this book. Omissions brought to our attention will be corrected in subsequent printings.

ISBN 0-13-058381-2

4 5 6 7 8 9 10   05 04 03

CONTENTS

"The Seafarer," translated by Burton Raffel
"The Wanderer," translated by Charles Kennedy
"The Wife's Lament," translated by Ann Stanford

Selection Test

Critical Reading

On the line, write the letter of the one best answer.

_____ 1. The phrase "summer's sentinel," meaning a cuckoo, is an example of
    a. a kenning.   c. a scop.
    b. a predicate.   d. an exile.

_____ 2. What does the author of "The Wanderer" seem to miss most?
    a. material possessions   c. adventure
    b. religion   d. companionship

_____ 3. During this time in history, many groups of people left or were sent from their homes. Knowing this helps the reader understand why
    a. each person was sent away.
    b. each person was lonely.
    c. the theme of "exile" was so common.
    d. the lyric poem was popular.

_____ 4. Which of the following best describes the speaker's message at the end of "The Seafarer"?
    a. Life at sea is both exhilarating and wearisome.
    b. Gifts of gold for heaven will not redeem a sinful soul.
    c. Those who walk with God shall be rewarded.
    d. The earth no longer flourishes in glory.

_____ 5. Read this sentence from "The Wife's Lament":

> Be he outlawed far in a strange folk-land—that my beloved sits under a rocky cliff rimed with frost a lord dreary in spirit.

What words or phrases help you to recognize the historical context of the line?
    a. rocky cliff
    b. outlawed; strange folk-land
    c. dreary in spirit
    d. my beloved

_____ 6. The main theme of "The Wanderer" involves the
    a. value of friendship.   c. importance of traditions.
    b. need for safety.   d. pain of homelessness.

_____ 7. In "The Wife's Lament," the wife assumes her husband is now
    a. on an exciting adventure and does not think of her.
    b. on his way home for a reconciliation.
    c. married to someone else.
    d. melancholy, as she is.

_____ 8. Which of the following characteristics of Anglo-Saxon poetry is illustrated by "The Seafarer"?
   a. celebration of heroic achievements
   b. use of caesura
   c. rhymed couplets
   d. Caedmonian verse

_____ 9. The first part of "The Seafarer" is the story of
   a. a man's life on the sea.
   b. a sailor's conversion to Christianity.
   c. an exile's lament for his country.
   d. an ocean storm off the coast of England.

_____ 10. The purpose of a caesura in a line of Anglo-Saxon poetry is to
   a. remind a scop what to say.
   b. provide a metaphorical name for something.
   c. indicate a pause for breath.
   d. mark the four beats in the line.

_____ 11. What initiated the wife's exile in "The Wife's Lament"?
   a. her husband's long absence
   b. a plot by her husband's kinsmen
   c. her traveling in spite of her husband's wishes
   d. the lord of that region issuing a formal decree

_____ 12. When reading Anglo-Saxon poetry, how does recognizing historical context help a reader understand why certain things occur?
   a. It gives the reader clues about the situation in the time period in which it was written.
   b. It helps readers restate in their own words what the poem says.
   c. It requires readers to use a dictionary to find the meaning of complicated words.
   d. It shows the reader how important correct spelling and grammar is.

_____ 13. What is the reason, despite all the hardships he's suffered, that the narrator in "The Seafarer" continues to follow the life of the sea?
   a. weary fatalism   c. religious vision
   b. passionate curiosity   d. material need

_____ 14. In "The Wanderer," which of the following pairs best represents the contrast of tone between the poet's dreams and his present circumstances?
   a. hopeful/somber   c. rapturous/grieving
   b. mournful/longing   d. melancholy/depressed

_____ 15. Which element in "The Seafarer" is most characteristic of lyric poetry?
   a. regular rhythm and rhyme
   b. strong reliance on figurative language
   c. intense personal emotion
   d. narrative structure

Vocabulary and Grammar

On the line, write the letter of the one best answer.

_____ 16. Which is the best meaning of the italicized word in this sentence?

   The Wander's _eagerness_ to work again was overwhelming.

   a. enthusiasm   c. sorrow
   b. irritation   d. fear

____ 17. Which words are the compound predicate in this excerpt?

> A brother / Opens his palms and pours down gold / On his kinsman's grave

    a. "opens his palms and pours down gold"
    b. "brother, opens his palms"
    c. "pours down gold"
    d. "pours down gold, on his kinsman's grave"

____ 18. Which is the best meaning of the italicized word in the phrase "Are *fervent* with life"?
    a. frightful   c. cautious
    b. cowardly   d. passionate

____ 19. The wife in "The Wife's Lament" describes her life with her husband as "*Blithe* was our bearing." According to this statement, her life with her husband was _____.
    a. joyless   c. lonely
    b. cheerful   d. cruel

____ 20. Which sentence contains a compound predicate?
    a. "I grieved each dawn / wondered where my lord my first on earth might be."
    b. "I had few loved ones in this land / or faithful friends."
    c. "I am all longing."
    d. "The valleys are dark the hills high / the yard overgrown bitter with briars/a joyless dwelling."

Essay Questions

21. One way to understand a piece of literature is to look at it in its historical context. In an essay, tell how knowing the historical context helps you better understand the poetry in this section. Use examples from the selections to illustrate this historical connection.

22. A fundamental Anglo-Saxon belief is that human life is shaped by fate. How is this belief reflected in the poems in this section? Answer this question in an essay, giving examples from one or more of the poems to support your explanation.

23. Most of the poems and stories of the Anglo-Saxon period were passed along by the oral tradition. In an essay, tell how the use of features such as the kenning and caesura may have helped maintain this oral tradition. Illustrate your explanation with examples from the selections.

from *Tristia* by Ovid
"Far Corners of Earth" by Tu Fu

Selection Test

Critical Reading

On the line, write the letter of the one best answer.

_____ 1. What does the following excerpt suggest about Ovid's real wishes?

> O harsh Lachesis, who gave me, born under a star that's unlucky, / The threads of a life that were not shorter than those which are mine.

    a. He wishes he had never been born.
    b. He wishes he had died at a younger age.
    c. He wishes revenge upon Lachesis.
    d. He wishes he could escape from the city.

_____ 2. How does Ovid's inability to communicate with the people around him affect his feelings about his exile?
    a. It reminds him of his crimes before Caesar.
    b. It reinforces his feelings of isolation.
    c. It relieves him of the necessity of talking with the barbarians.
    d. It increases his desire to write.

_____ 3. Why was Ovid sent into exile?
    a. for offending Caesar
    b. for attempting to assassinate Caesar
    c. for flirting with Caesar's wife
    d. for plotting with the barbarians against Caesar

_____ 4. Judging from the selections, which aspect of exile is hardest on Ovid and Tu Fu?
    a. the constant danger of their surroundings
    b. the boring monotony of their days
    c. isolation from things with which they are familiar
    d. suffering the displeasure of their rulers

_____ 5. To what does Ovid compare the length of his exile?
    a. the ice on the river Danube
    b. the siege of Troy
    c. the war between the Romans and the barbarians
    d. the distance to the horizon

_____ 6. With whom does Ovid sympathize as helpless victims of unceasing violence?
    a. Greek colonizers
    b. local farmers
    c. Persian tailors
    d. merchants

____ 7. Which of the following lines comes closest to expressing the tedious monotony of Ovid's life in exile?

    a. "Since I've been here in the Pontus the Danube has frozen thrice over, / The waves of the Euxine ocean have hardened as well three times."

    b. "Under his helmet the shepherd blows on straws joined with pitch-gum / And instead of a wolf the trembling sheep stand in dread of war."

    c. "The summer solstice deprives me of nothing at all from the nighttime / Nor does the winter solstice make shorter each of my days."

    d. "And as it happens, they think I am crazy when to their jabber / I nod my head to say 'yes' and shake it to signify 'no.' "

____ 8. Which of the following details distinguishes Ovid's situation from Tu Fu's?

    a. While Ovid is forced to stay in one place, Tu Fu is allowed to wander.

    b. Tu Fu reveals the reason for his exile, while Ovid does not.

    c. Tu Fu is accompanied by his family, while Ovid is completely alone.

    d. Ovid is already an old man, while Tu Fu is still quite young.

____ 9. Which of the following lines best sums up the meaning of exile for Tu Fu?

    a. "mountains looming, impassable"

    b. "year after year, nothing familiar"

    c. "my heart already broken in quiet times"

    d. "each day wandering a new waste of highway"

____ 10. Which word best describes Tu Fu's poem?

    a. wearisome

    b. loquacious

    c. elongated

    d. economical

Essay Questions

11. Tu Fu and Ovid suffer from exile in similar ways. Using details from both selections, write an essay explaining why exile should be such a terrible form of punishment. Go on to make a judgment as to which poem gives a more effective description of exile and why.

12. The image of clouds in Tu Fu's "Far Corners of Earth" carries both a literal and symbolic meaning. Write an essay discussing the dual meaning of this and other concrete images in the poem. How do the various images contribute to the mood and the meaning of the poem?

13. Ovid was a satirist whose attentions were not always welcome by the targets of his criticism. Based on this selection, write an essay speculating on how Ovid might have offended his ruler. Which passages in *Tristia* criticize aspects of the local society? Describe the tone of Ovid's criticisms and suggest why he included those passages here.

Part Test, Unit 1, Part 1: Earthly Exile, Heavenly Home

Critical Reading

The questions below are based on the following selection.

This excerpt is taken from "The Husband's Message," a lyric written in response to "The Wife's Lament."

In the hold of a ship, o'er the salt sea-streams,

Where my liege lord sent me oft I have sailed.

Now in a bark's bosom here am I borne.

Now shalt thou learn of my lord's loyal love;

[5] His enduring affection I dare to affirm.

    Lady ring-laden, he bade me implore thee,

Who carved this wood, that thou call to mind

The pledges you plighted before you were parted,

While still in the same land together you shared

[10] A lordly home and the rapture of love,

Before a feud drove him far from his folk.

He it is bids me eagerly urge

When from the hill slope, out of the wood,

Thou hearest the cuckoo plaintively calling,

[15] Haste thee to ship on the tossing sea.

Let no living man, then, delay thee in sailing,

Stay thee in leaving or stop thee in flight.

    Spread thy sail on the home of the sea-mew,

Take seat in thy galley, and steer away south

[20] To where o'er the sea-lane thy lover awaits.

No greater bliss could his heart engage

In all the world —'twas his word to me—

If God the Almighty would grant you two

To dwell together and deal out gifts,

[25] To tried retainers, of treasure and rings.

On the line, write the letter of the one best answer.

_____ 1. In "The Husband's Message," the husband of the title is
    a. the poem's speaker.
    b. the "you" referred to in lines 8–9 and 23.
    c. the "liege lord" referred to in line 2.
    d. a common seaman.

____ 2. Which of the following is not a likely aspect of the husband's mood?
    a. anxiety   c. eagerness
    b. resentment   d. loneliness

____ 3. Anglo-Saxon lyrics developed from _____.
    a. Norse songs   c. Medieval manuscripts
    b. translations   d. the oral tradition

____ 4. Which of the following aspects of the poem would be *least* likely to be clarified by considering the work's historical context?
    a. the use of the word *rapture*
    b. the implications of the phrase *the tossing sea*
    c. the identity of the speaker
    d. the nature of the husband's faith in God

____ 5. Every line in the selection contains an example of a(n) _____.
    a. kenning   c. allegory
    b. caesura   d. metaphor

____ 6. Why are the wife and husband separated?
    a. He has embarked on a voyage of discovery.
    b. She was unwilling to travel with him.
    c. She must tend the "lordly home."
    d. He is fighting in a foreign war.

____ 7. Which of the following images is unrelated to the husband's feelings of love and expectation?
    a. a cuckoo's call   c. a sail
    b. a ship's hold   d. treasure and rings

____ 8. Which of the following is not a central part of the husband's message to his wife?
    a. a request to carve him a ring
    b. an affirmation of his love for her
    c. a request to remember her marriage vows
    d. an invitation to sail to him in the future

____ 9. A lyric poem expresses
    a. a poet's most beautiful ideas.
    b. some of the poet's political viewpoints.
    c. the speaker's intense love for a subject.
    d. the thoughts and feelings of a single speaker.

____ 10. Which one of the following phrases is a kenning?
    a. liege lord
    b. lady ring-laden
    c. salt sea-streams
    d. the tossing sea

Vocabulary and Grammar

On the line, write the letter of the one best answer.

____ 11. Which one of the following sentences contains a compound predicate?
    a. Storms beat on the rocky cliffs and were echoed by icy-feathered terns and the eagle's screams.
    b. This tale is true, and mine.
    c. The only sound was the roaring sea, the freezing waves.
    d. The salt waves tossing and the towering sea!

_____ 12. A sentence with a compound predicate contains
  a. one verb and one subject.
  b. more than one verb and more than one subject.
  c. two verbs.
  d. more than one verb.

_____ 13. Which of the following is the most accurate definition of _grievous_?
  a. Sorrow
  b. To feel deep sadness
  c. Hard to bear
  d. In a way that is difficult to bear

_____ 14. Which one of the following sentences contains a compound predicate?
  a. Night would blacken; it would snow from the north.
  b. The time for journeys would come and my soul called me eagerly out, sent me over the horizon, seeking foreigners' homes.
  c. But there isn't a man on earth so proud, so born to greatness, so bold with his youth, grown so brave, or so graced by God, that he feels no fear as the sails unfurl.
  d. No harps ring in his heart, no rewards, no passion for women, no worldly pleasures, nothing.

_____ 15. Given the meanings of the related words _grieve_ and _grievous_, what is the most appropriate antonym for the word _grief_?
  a. woe   c. relaxation
  b. joyousness   d. misery

Essay Questions

16. A reader meets the speaker of "The Seafarer" in the poem's very first line. Based on information you find in the poem, write a description of this person—including his age, appearance, and personality—as you picture him. Support your description with words or phrases from the poem.

17. In lines 25–26 of "The Wife's Lament," the speaker asserts that she must "bear the anger" of her beloved "far and near." In a short essay, explain what she means by this statement. Cite passages from the poem to help clarify your explanation.

18. The seafarer, the wanderer, and the wife alike are clearly "mindful of misery" brought on by exile. In an essay, explain why exile was such a consuming, difficult situation for an individual in the Middle Ages. Would exile be any different for an individual today? Why or why not? Use references to one or more of the texts to support your ideas.

from *Beowulf*, translated by Burton Raffel

Selection Test

Critical Reading

On the line, write the letter of the one best answer.

_____ 1. How can the reader tell that *Beowulf* is a legendary story?
   a. It takes place a long time ago.
   b. The story involves warriors and battles.
   c. The hero is described as someone greater than all other men.
   d. The people in the story are called Geats and Danes.

_____ 2. Why does Beowulf sail with his chosen companions to Hrothgar's kingdom?
   a. to bring home treasures from that rich kingdom
   b. to help Hrothgar by destroying a monster
   c. to win glory by slaying a fire-breathing dragon
   d. to take over Higlac's throne

_____ 3. Which of the following lines from *Beowulf* contains an example of kenning?
   a. " 'Higlac is my cousin and my king; the days / Of my youth have been filled with glory.' "
   b. "Their guide reined in his horse, pointing / To that hall, built by Hrothgar for the best / And bravest of his men . . ."
   c. "The high hall rang, its roof boards swayed, / And Danes shook with terror."
   d. " '. . . I have come so far, / Oh shelterer of warriors and your people's loved friend, / That this one favor you should not refuse me . . .' "

_____ 4. From which fact can the reader infer that Beowulf is honorable?
   a. Beowulf refuses to use weapons because Grendel uses none.
   b. Higlac is Beowulf's cousin.
   c. Beowulf is the strongest of the Geats.
   d. Beowulf vows to ambush Grendel and destroy the monster.

_____ 5. What does this line mean?

   the monster's thoughts were as quick as his greed or his claws

   a. He is hungry.
   b. He has intelligence.
   c. He has sharp claws.
   d. He is not trustworthy.

_____ 6. At the end of the battle, the poet attributes Grendel's defeat to
   a. Beowulf's strength.
   b. Grendel's evil.
   c. God's power.
   d. Hrothgar's luck.

_____ 7. Which of the following best summarizes the theme of Beowulf?
   a. Might makes right.
   b. Brains are superior to brawn.
   c. Wickedness cannot be defeated.
   d. Valor will triumph.

_____ 8. Which is the best paraphrase of the following passage from the poem?

> So the living sorrow of Healfdane's son / Simmered, bitter and fresh, and no wisdom / Or strength could break it: that agony hung / On king and people alike . . .

   a. Hrothgar felt a strong and unending sorrow that he had no power to overcome. It affected both him and his subjects.
   b. The king was in agony and out of his mind because of what his people had done to him.
   c. Grendel was furious at the Danes and so he inflicted great pain on the king and his people.
   d. Hrothgar felt an endless sorrow he couldn't get rid of.

_____ 9. Wiglaf thinks he and his comrades should help Beowulf fight the dragon because
   a. Beowulf is too old and sick to fight.
   b. it will increase Beowulf's chance of victory.
   c. then Beowulf's comrades can claim the monster's treasure.
   d. in the past they had promised to repay Beowulf's kindness with their lives.

_____ 10. When the dying Beowulf gives Wiglaf his gold necklace, the gesture means that
   a. Beowulf has captured the monster's treasure.
   b. Beowulf wants Wiglaf to kill his comrades.
   c. Beowulf recognizes Wiglaf's superior strength in battle.
   d. Beowulf is passing on the rulership of Geatland to Wiglaf.

_____ 11. Which of the following lines from Beowulf contains an example of a caesura?
   a. ". . . Hidden evil before hidden evil."
   b. ". . . Burns like a torch. No one knows its bottom . . ."
   c. ". . . And golden cups and the glorious banner . . ."
   d. ". . . And struck at the dragon's scaly hide."

_____ 12. Which is the best paraphrase for this passage from the selection?

> —Then the sword / Melted, blood-soaked, dripping down / Like water, disappearing like ice when the world's / Eternal Lord loosens invisible / Fetters and unwinds icicles and frost . . .

   a. God made the bloody sword turn to dripping icicles and frost.
   b. Beowulf loosened his grip on the bloody sword and it disappeared into the water.
   c. Beowulf's bloody sword became liquid the way ice and frost do when God warms and melts them.
   d. God made the sword melt and freed Beowulf from the magic fetters that bound him.

_____ 13. Why is it ironic that after his death the Geats build a tower to memorialize Beowulf?
   a. Beowulf requested that the tower be built.
   b. The treasure is left in the tower.
   c. Beowulf's body has been cremated.
   d. Most of the Geats had deserted him in battle.

_____ 14. Which phrase best paraphrases the underlined words in this quotation from the poem?

> . . . they could hack at Grendel / From every side, trying to open / A path for his evil soul, but their points Could not hurt him.

   a. to kill him   c. to turn his soul to God
   b. to drive him out of the hall   d. to help him escape

_____ 15. When used to describe Beowulf, the phrase "noble protector of all seamen" is an example of
   a. a caesura.   c. a kenning.
   b. a wyrd.   d. an alliteration.

Vocabulary and Grammar

On the line, write the letter of the one best answer.

____ 16. Grendel's arm hanging in the banquet hall of the Danes might be described as _____ for the evil he had done.
   a. writhing
   b. solace
   c. reparation
   d. massive

____ 17. When Beowulf requests that he alone "May purge all evil from this hall," what does he mean by *purge*?
   a. drive out
   b. overcome
   c. cleanse
   d. bury

____ 18. Which of the following passages contains an appositive phrase?
   a. "A powerful monster, living down / In the darkness, growled in pain, impatient / As day after day the music rang / Loud in that hall. . . ."
   b. " . . . sailors / Have brought us stories of Herot, the best / Of all mead-halls, deserted and useless . . ."
   c. ". . . He was spawned in that slime, / Conceived by a pair of those monsters born / Of Cain, . . ."
   d. And sometimes they sacrificed to the old stone gods, / Made heathen vows, hoping for Hell's / Support, . . ."

____ 19. Which words from the following passage form an appositive phrase?

   . . . A deer, / Hunted through the woods by packs of hounds, / A stag with great horns, though driven through the forest / From faraway places, prefers to die / On those shores, . . .

   a. "A deer,"
   b. "Hunted through the woods"
   c. "A stag with great horns"
   d. "though driven through the forest"

____ 20. Which of these words best fits the image of the dragon presented in this quotation?

   . . . The dragon / Coiled and uncoiled, its heart urging it / Into battle . . .

   a. writhing
   b. purging
   c. massive
   d. loathsome

Essay Questions

21. Many critics and teachers believe that *Beowulf* contains themes that are relevant to modern life. Do you agree or disagree? Explain your answer in an essay.

22. The pagan Germans, Greeks, and other ancient peoples believed that fame and glory are the only things that will survive a human being's death. What evidence do you find in this poem of the importance placed on a person's public reputation? Write an essay in which you use examples from the poem to support your answer.

23. The hero of an epic poem normally embodies the ideals of conduct that are most valued by the culture in which the epic was composed. Write an essay in which you show how Beowulf embodies the ideals of conduct in the Anglo-Saxon culture. You should mention at least four of Beowulf's virtues. For each one, cite the part or parts of the epic where the virtue is displayed.

"The Prologue" from *Gilgamesh*, translated by David Ferry
from the *Iliad* by Homer

Selection Test

Critical Reading

On the line, write the letter of the one best answer.

_____ 1. According to the prologue to *Gilgamesh*, who, or what, is Uruk?
   a. Gilgamesh's father
   b. Gilgamesh's enemy
   c. Gilgamesh's city
   d. Gilgamesh's sword

_____ 2. According to the prologue, who is responsible for writing down the story of Gilgamesh?
   a. Lady Wildcow Ninsun
   b. Anu and Ishtar
   c. Gilgamesh himself
   d. Utnapishtim

_____ 3. Which designations are *not* used to describe Gilgamesh in the prologue?
   a. the Wild Ox
   b. the Terrible King
   c. the Web
   d. Shadow of Darkness

_____ 4. What does the line "who knew the way things were before the Flood" suggest about Gilgamesh?
   a. He is very old.
   b. He was present at the creation of the world.
   c. He owns many old books.
   d. He possesses secret knowledge.

_____ 5. Which one flaw is suggested in the otherwise heroic description of Gilgamesh contained in the prologue?
   a. He is part man.
   b. He is overly boastful.
   c. He is too trusting.
   d. He is two-thirds a god.

_____ 6. According to the *Iliad*, what does Achilleus risk by his refusal to honor Hektor's corpse?
   a. inflaming Hektor's army against the Greeks
   b. inciting Hektor's family to revenge
   c. incurring the wrath of the gods
   d. dissatisfying Athene

_____ 7. According to the *Iliad*, where is the weak point in Hektor's armor through which Achilleus strikes his fatal blow?
   a. the heel
   b. the back
   c. the front of the knee
   d. the throat

8. In the *Iliad*, how many times had Hektor run away before to avoid fighting Achilleus?
   a. once
   b. three times
   c. four times
   d. never

9. According to the *Iliad*, which of the following quotations best illustrates Achilleus's hatred for Hektor?
   a. "I must take you now, or I must be taken."
   b. "There can be no love between you and me, nor shall there be oaths between us."
   c. "On you the dogs and the vultures shall feed and foully rip you."
   d. "Die: and I will take my own death at whatever time Zeus and the rest of the immortals choose to accomplish it."

10. What role did trickery play in the *Iliad* in Achilleus's victory over Hektor?
   a. Hektor was tricked into fighting by a goddess disguised as his brother.
   b. A goddess drugged Hektor, tricking him into throwing his spear at a false image of Achilleus.
   c. Achilleus pretended to be hurt in order to trick Hektor into laying down his spear.
   d. Achilleus attacked Hektor from behind after hiding inside a wooden horse.

Essay Questions

11. Both Gilgamesh and Achilleus are described as part god, part human. Choose one hero, and in an essay, explain which of his abilities or personality traits derive from his human side and which from his divine nature. Use specific details from the text to support your analysis.

12. In ancient times, the stories of epic heroes conveyed important lessons to an audience of ordinary people. Using examples from either selection, write an essay describing the possible connections between the fantastic feats of the heroes and the everyday life of the people. Make a judgment as to whether the values and behaviors exhibited by the heroes are still relevant to contemporary life.

13. The fight between Achilleus and Hektor is one of the most dramatic scenes in the *Iliad*. Likewise, the prologue to *Gilgamesh* succeeds in creating a definite sense of expectation. In an essay, explain which details and techniques are used to achieve the sense of tension and anticipation in these selections. Compare one of the selections to a contemporary film or book that builds the same sort of excitement.

Part Test, Unit 1, Part 2: Focus on Literary Forms—The Epic

Critical Reading

The questions on page 15 are based on the following selection.

This excerpt is taken from the very beginning of the epic poem Beowulf—just before the speaker first describes the monster Grendel lurking outside Hrothgar's banquet hall.

> Then Beo was king in that Danish castle,
>
> Shild's son ruling as long as his father
>
> And as loved, a famous lord of men.
>
> And he in turn gave his people a son,
>
> [5] The great Healfdane, a fierce fighter
>
> Who led the Danes to the end of his long
>
> Life and left them with four children,
>
> Three princes to guide them in battle, Hergar
>
> And Hrothgar and Halga the Good, and one daughter,
>
> [10] Yrs, who was given to Onela, king
>
> Of the Swedes, and became his wife and their queen.
>
> Then Hrothgar, taking the throne, led
>
> The Danes to such glory that comrades and kinsmen
>
> [15] Swore by his sword, and young men swelled
>
> His armies, and he thought of greatness and resolved
>
> To build a hall that would hold his mighty
>
> Band and reach higher toward Heaven than anything
>
> That had ever been known to the sons of men.
>
> [20] And in that hall he'd divide the spoils
>
> Of their victories, to old and young what they'd earned
>
> In battle, but leaving the common pastures
>
> Untouched, and taking no lives. The work
>
> Was ordered, the timbers tied and shaped
>
> [25] By the hosts that Hrothgar ruled. It was quickly
>
> Ready, that most beautiful of dwellings, built
>
> As he'd wanted, and then he whose word was obeyed
>
> All over the earth named it Herot.
>
> His boast come true he commanded a banquet,
>
> [30] Opened out his treasure-full hands.
>
> That towering place, gabled and huge,

Stood waiting for time to pass, for war

To begin, for flames to leap as high

As the feud that would light them, and for Herot to burn.

On the line, write the letter of the one best answer.

_____ 1. Shild was _____.
a. Beo's son
b. Healfdane's contemporary
c. Beo's father
d. Hrothgar's lord

_____ 2. Lines 15–18 are a good illustration of Hrothgar's considerable _____.
a. humor
b. ambition
c. sensitivity
d. valiance

_____ 3. Many works of epic literature were developed
a. by Danish people.
b. orally.
c. in mead halls.
d. by scribes and scholars.

_____ 4. Which of the following is the most accurate paraphrase of the sentence in lines 1–3?
a. Beo's popularity—and the length of his reign—as king of Denmark equaled those of his father, Shild.
b. Beo was king of Denmark for as long as Shild's son had been king.
c. Shild was a famous lord of men and a beloved king of Denmark, just like his son Beo.
d. Beo's castle was the place where beloved Shild had also ruled as king of Denmark.

_____ 5. An epic is a long narrative poem that
a. expresses the thoughts and feelings of a single speaker.
b. celebrates God.
c. dramatizes history.
d. celebrates the deeds of a legendary or heroic figure.

_____ 6. Lines 12–19 give the reader a vivid indication of Hrothgar's
a. aesthetic sense.
b. military prowess.
c. political power and influence.
d. domestic needs.

_____ 7. When paraphrasing, a reader
a. focuses on key ideas and details.
b. contrasts ideas in a long, involved sentence.
c. analyzes the speaker's tone of voice.
d. includes all details in the original sentence.

_____ 8. Hrothgar's reputation was made
a. in Herot.
b. on the battlefield.
c. as a seaman.
d. as an architect.

_____ 9. What does the speaker accomplish in lines 1–11?
a. The speaker explains the history of Denmark.
b. The speaker characterizes Beowulf's future enemies.
c. The speaker celebrates military victory.
d. The speaker establishes the distinguished genealogy of Hrothgar.

_____ 10. What is ironic about lines 30–34?
a. War ruins beauty and culture.
b. The speaker compares fire and a feud.
c. After describing the construction of the magnificent Herot, the speaker foreshadows its destruction.
d. Hrothgar is shown to be an unsteady ruler.

Vocabulary and Grammar

On the line, write the letter of the one best answer.

____ 11. Which one of the following contains an appositive phrase?
    a. "The corners of the earth were made lovely with trees . . ."
    b. "Till the monster stirred, that demon, that fiend, Grendel . . ."
    c. "The high hall rang, its roof boards swayed, and Danes shook with terror . . ."
    d. "The living sorrow of Healfdane's son . . ."

____ 12. Appositives and appositive phrases are nouns or pronouns with modifiers that
    a. identify, explain, or rename nouns or pronouns.
    b. modify the subject of a sentence.
    c. function similarly to verbals.
    d. provide incidental information about characters and setting.

____ 13. Based on your understanding of the meaning of the Latin root *–sol-*, which of the following is not built upon this root?
    a. solstice   c. console
    b. solace   d. consolation

____ 14. Which of the following contains an appositive or appositive phrase?
    a. "Stalked Hrothgar's warriors, old and young . . ."
    b. "Protected by God—God, whose love Grendel could not know . . ."
    c. "Glittering at the top of their golden helmets wild boar heads gleamed . . ."
    d. "Herot stood empty, and stayed deserted for years, twelve winters of grief for Hrothgar, king of the Danes . . ."

____ 15. Which of the following contains an appositive or appositive phrase?
    a. "Your prince, Healfdane's son, protector of this people . . ."
    b. ". . . a king, before, but now a beaten warrior."
    c. ". . . your country is cursed with some strange, vicious creature that hunts only at night and that no one has seen . . ."
    d. "I'll guide you myself—and my men will guard your ship, keep it safe here on our shores . . ."

Essay Questions

16. When he first meets Hrothgar, Beowulf boasts of his skill as a warrior. What do these claims tell you about his character? Write an essay detailing what you learn about Beowulf's character from his speech to the king.

17. In the battle between the epic hero Beowulf and the monster Grendel a reader finds not only a dazzling scene packed with action, but also a symbolic battle. Based on details you find in the selection, write an essay in which you explain the opposing forces Beowulf and Grendel may represent. What universal battle might their own fight symbolize?

18. The early Middle Ages are sometimes called the Dark Ages by historians. Write an essay in which you give your opinion of the appropriateness of the expression as a description of the Anglo-Saxon period. Look through the selections to find examples to support your opinion.

Name _____ Date _____

from *A History of the English Church and People* by Bede
from *The Anglo-Saxon Chronicle,* translated by Anne Savage

Selection Test

Critical Reading

On the line, write the letter of the one best answer.

____ 1. Bede's main purpose in writing *A History of the English Church and People* was to
   a. describe Britain's geography.
   b. provide a factual narrative of past events in Britain.
   c. delineate the languages and nations within Britain.
   d. compare Britain and Ireland.

____ 2. Considering the time in which he wrote, which source would probably have provided Bede with the most reliable information that Britain had "twenty-eight noble cities"?
   a. personal experience   c. records from a monastic library
   b. testimony from sailors   d. accounts in letters

____ 3. From his phrase "all are united in their study of God's truth," what can be inferred about Bede's attitude toward the English Church?
   a. He believed in its teachings.   c. He questioned its sovereignty.
   b. He was aware of its influence.   d. He reluctantly obeyed its mandates.

____ 4. Bede's account suggests that Britain had
   a. an ideal climate.   c. abundant natural resources.
   b. a powerful navy.   d. a unified government.

____ 5. Which of the following lines probably reflects the greatest degree of historical accuracy?
   a. " 'Go and settle there if you wish; should you meet resistance, we will come to your help.' "
   b. "Ireland is broader than Britain, and its mild and healthy climate is superior."
   c. " . . . it is said that some Picts from Scythia put to sea in a few long ships and were driven by storms around the coasts of Britain . . . "
   d. "On the opposite side of Britain, which lies open to the boundless ocean, lie the isles of the Orcades."

____ 6. According to Bede's account, in which of the following ways are the four British nations different?
   a. They worship differently.   c. They speak different languages.
   b. Not all study the scriptures in Latin. d. They have very different climates.

____ 7. Which of the following seems to lend the greatest credibility to Bede's work?
   a. the large amount of specific, factual information
   b. his personal observations on climate
   c. the references to religion in Britain
   d. his descriptions of different customs

____ 8. The line "almost everything in this isle enjoys immunity to poison" suggests that Bede
   a. had a very high opinion of Ireland. c. traveled frequently to Ireland.
   b. originally lived in Ireland.   d. preferred Britain to Ireland.

____ 9. In writing *A History of the English Church and People*, Bede was not completely scholarly or accurate because he
   a. made extensive use of the limited resources of his time.
   b. sometimes accepted unlikely tales as truth.
   c. relied heavily on his own observations.
   d. did not cite his sources.

____ 10. Find the main (independent) clause in this sentence from *The Anglo-Saxon Chronicle*.

> As it fell out, at a certain time in the same year, six ships came to the Isle of Wight and did much evil there, both in Devon and everywhere along the sea-coast.

   a. "As it fell out, at a certain time in the same year"
   b. "six ships came to the Isle of Wight and did much evil there"
   c. "and did much evil there"
   d. "both in Devon and everywhere along the seacoast"

____ 11. Which of the following sentences from *The Anglo-Saxon Chronicle* betrays a bias on the part of the writer?
   a. "As it fell out, at a certain time in the same year, six ships came to the Isle of Wight and did much evil there, both in Devon and everywhere along the seacoast."
   b. "Then king Alfred commanded longships to be built against the ash-ships."
   c. "The same summer no less than twenty ships perished with men and all along the south coast."
   d. "When he meant to leave there, he had it announced to the army that they would all leave together."

____ 12. Break the following sentence down. Then decide which choice presents the main (independent) clause.

> When writing supposedly historical accounts, authors present their facts as completely as possible, unencumbered by bias, prejudice, or exaggeration.

   a. When writing supposedly historical accounts, authors present their facts
   b. When writing supposedly historical accounts, authors present their facts as completely as possible
   c. authors present their facts
   d. present their facts as completely as possible

____ 13. Which of the following sentences is unbiased?
   a. Edward went on a rampage and brutally murdered many of the Danish force's soldiers.
   b. Edward became king after the noble king Alfred died.
   c. King Edward ruled with great wisdom and fairness.
   d. Edward was Alfred's son.

____ 14. The following sentence is from *The Anglo-Saxon Chronicle*. Break the sentence down and decide which option best gives the main points.

> Aethelwald lured the East Anglian force into breaking the peace, so that they ravaged over the land of Mercia, until they came to Cricklade, went over the Thames there, siezed all they could carry off both in and around Braydon and then went home-ward again.

   a. Aethelwald tricked the soldiers so that they broke the peace; they ravaged the land; they seized all they could carry; they went home.
   b. Aethelwald persuaded many soldiers to cross the Thames and ravage Braydon before returning home with what they'd stolen.

c. The soldiers ravaged over the land of Mercia and crossed the Thames River at Cricklade.

d. After peace was declared, Aethelwald and his soldiers were greedy; they ravaged the land of Mercia and all the towns along the Thames.

Vocabulary and Grammar

On the line, write the letter of the one best answer.

_____ 15. Which of the following quotations from Bede's account is a compound sentence?
a. "The original inhabitants of the island were the Britons, from whom it takes its name. . . ."
b. "There is also much black jet of fine quality, which sparkles in firelight."
c. "Ireland is the largest island after Britain, and lies to the west."
d. "Ireland is broader than Britain, and its mild and healthy climate is superior."

_____ 16. According to *The Anglo-Saxon Chronicle*, Aethelwald took over the manors at Wimbourne and _____ the gates against King Edward's army.
a. ravaged
b. stranded
c. barricaded
d. hallowed

_____ 17. If a place has been *ravaged*, it is _____.
a. holy
b. protected
c. stranded
d. ruined

_____ 18. A compound sentence always contains
a. one independent clause and one dependent clause.
b. a conjunction.
c. at least two independent clauses.
d. a semicolon.

_____ 19. An adjective that might be used to describe *promontories* is _____.
a. loud
b. high
c. broken
d. holy

_____ 20. Which of the following can be used to join two independent clauses in a compound sentence?
a. a period or comma
b. a colon
c. a conjunction or a semicolon
d. a subject or a predicate

Essay Questions

21. The two passages in this selection tell a great deal about the now-distant past. What are some of the things we can learn from the events of the past? Write about some examples of historical literature or documents that affect the way people live today.

22. Research materials for people writing in Bede's time were restricted to information from the oral tradition, manuscripts in monastic libraries, and records of such events as planting crops and other community events. In an essay, discuss why such resources might make it difficult to get a completely accurate account of the past.

23. Bede was not only a respected historian, but also a man fascinated by science and the natural world. Write an essay showing how Bede's interest in science is revealed in the excerpt from *A History of the English Church and People*.

The Prologue from *The Canterbury Tales* by Geoffrey Chaucer

Selection Test

Critical Reading

On the line, write the letter of the one best answer.

_____ 1. Chaucer uses the pilgrimage primarily as a device to
   a. emphasize the characters' religious aspirations.
   b. frame the stories told by individual characters.
   c. describe the rigors of medieval life.
   d. create a vivid and realistic setting.

_____ 2. The narrator is portrayed as
   a. stern and judgmental.   c. robust and merry.
   b. sophisticated and worldly.   d. naive and observant.

_____ 3. The narrator says he plans to "give account of all their words and dealings, / Using their very phrases as they fell." For which kind of characterization would an author provide such details?
   a. direct characterization   c. direct and indirect characterization
   b. indirect characterization   d. dramatic characterization

_____ 4. Which best describes Chaucer's attitude toward the Nun?
   a. amused tolerance   c. marked scorn
   b. polite detachment   d. weary reproachfulness

_____ 5. Using the *who, what, where, when, why,* and *how* questioning strategy, write the letter of the phrase that best summarizes the meaning of the following passage.

> He was an easy man in penance-giving / Where he could hope to make a decent living; / It's a sure sign whenever gifts are given / To a poor Order that a man's well shriven, / And should he give enough he knew in verity / The penitent repented in sincerity.

   a. He gave out easy penances and absolution in exchange for gifts.
   b. He gave out easy penances in exchange for gifts wherever he thought he could get gifts out of the confessors.
   c. He gave out easy penances and absolution in exchange for gifts wherever he thought he could get gifts out of the confessors. He knew that if he exacted a large enough price for the sin that the penitent person would truly feel sorry for what he'd done.
   d. He gave out easy penances and absolution in exchange for gifts wherever he thought he could get gifts out of the confessors. He knew that if he exacted a large enough price for the sin that the penitent person would truly feel sorry for what he'd done. In fact, whenever a poor group of friars receives gifts you can be sure that someone has just received absolution for his sins.

_____ 6. What can the reader infer about the Friar from these lines?

> But anywhere a profit might accrue / Courteous he was and lowly of service too.

   a. He helps others make money.   c. He has aspirations to be a merchant.
   b. He is humble and servile.   d. He will use people for money.

_____ 7. Whom do the pilgrims agree to set up as judge over themselves?
- a. the narrator
- b. the Host
- c. the Oxford Cleric
- d. the Sergeant at the Law

_____ 8. Chaucer describes the Pardoner's hair as "rat-tails" primarily to
- a. furnish realistic detail.
- b. provide comic relief.
- c. suggest the Pardoner's obsession with current fashions.
- d. imply moral corruption.

_____ 9. What do the following lines suggest about the woman from Bath?

> In all the parish not a dame dared stir / Towards the altar steps in front of her

- a. She is a religious fanatic.
- b. She abhors the Christian church.
- c. She is selfish and arrogant.
- d. She disdains the company of women.

_____ 10. Chaucer calls the Franklin's girdle "white as morning milk" to
- a. reiterate the Franklin's obsession with food.
- b. emphasize the Franklin's personal cleanliness.
- c. symbolize the Franklin's purity of heart.
- d. show the Franklin's weakness for fancy clothes.

_____ 11. Using the _who, what, where, when, why,_ and _how_ questioning strategy to understand the following passage, write the letter of the phrase that best summarizes its meaning.

> Whatever money from his friends he took / He spent on learning or another book / And prayed for them most earnestly, returning / Thanks to them thus for paying for his learning.

- a. He stole his friends' money, spent it on books, and then prayed his friends would return.
- b. Whatever money he borrowed from his friends he spent on his studies and books, prayed for more books, and then sent his friends thank-you notes for paying for his learning.
- c. Whatever money he could get from his friends he spent on his studies and books, prayed for his books, and then returned thanks to his friends for paying for his learning.
- d. Whatever money he borrowed from his friends he spent on his studies and books and then prayed earnestly for his friends as a way of giving them thanks.

_____ 12. Which of the following is _not_ an example of direct characterization?
- a. "He was an honest worker, good and true . . . "
- b. " . . . His mighty mouth was like a furnace door."
- c. "Children were afraid when he appeared."
- d. "He wore a fustian tunic stained and dark . . . "

_____ 13. By positioning his description of the Miller almost immediately after that of the Plowman, Chaucer accentuates
- a. the virtues of the Plowman.
- b. the buffoonishness and criminality of the Miller.
- c. the kinship between these two laborers.
- d. the virtues of the Plowman as well as the buffoonishness and criminality of the Miller.

_____ 14. What theme does Chaucer convey in "The Prologue" to _The Canterbury Tales_?
- a. the conflicts inherent in society
- b. the basic evil of mankind
- c. the infinite variety of human nature
- d. the pitfalls of sensual pleasure

Vocabulary and Grammar

On the line, write the letter of the one best answer.

____ 15. In standing by to carve meat for his father at the table, the young Squire is showing himself to be _____.
  a. garnished
  b. prevaricating
  c. solicitous
  d. sanguine

____ 16. Writers use the past perfect tense to indicate an action or a condition
  a. was done perfectly.
  b. that ended before another past action began.
  c. that started in the past but has continued to the present.
  d. that ended after another past action began.

____ 17. The word *commission* means to
  a. go on a mission with someone.
  b. found a religious outpost.
  c. give authorization.
  d. plunge ahead.

____ 18. What verb tense is Chaucer using in the underlined portion of the following passage?

> This noble example to his sheep he gave, / First following the word before he taught it, / And it was from the gospel he <u>had caught</u> it.

  a. present tense
  b. past tense
  c. past perfect tense
  d. past progressive tense

____ 19. Identify the verb tense Chaucer uses in the underlined portion of the following passage.

> He lisped a little out of wantonness / To make his English sweet upon his tongue. / When he <u>had played</u> his harp, or having sung, / His eyes would twinkle in his head as bright / As any star upon a frosty night.

  a. past
  b. past perfect
  c. past progressive
  d. present perfect

____ 20. Which word or phrase is most nearly the same in meaning as *avouches*?
  a. stands up for
  b. agrees
  c. says doubtfully
  d. asserts positively

Essay Questions

21. In "The Prologue" to *The Canterbury Tales*, Chaucer's narrator introduces many different characters traveling to Canterbury. Choose one of these characters and write an essay explaining the nature of his or her personality and what the key details and statements reveal about this individual's personality.

22. Consider the many characterizations of the men and women associated with the church. From these portraits, what conclusion might you draw about Chaucer's attitude toward the church and/or religious practitioners? Write an essay in which you present your conclusion and support it with evidence from "The Prologue."

23. Although the narrator provides many details about the other pilgrims going to Canterbury, he says little about himself. The reader is left to infer the narrator's character from what most impresses the narrator as worthy of reporting, what the narrator accepts as true—that is, how discerning he is—and from what little he says directly to the reader about himself and his manner of storytelling. Write an essay in which you explain the nature of the narrator's personality, supporting your ideas with evidence from the text.

"The Nun's Priest's Tale" and **"The Pardoner's Tale"**
from *The Canterbury Tales* by Geoffrey Chaucer

Selection Test

Critical Reading

On the line, write the letter of the one best answer.

____ 1. In "The Nun's Priest's Tale" by Geoffrey Chaucer, which character trait almost leads to Chanticleer's downfall?
   a. respect for family
   b. taste for romance
   c. tendency to boast
   d. fear of battle

____ 2. The narrator of "The Nun's Priest's Tale" portrays himself as a man who
   a. dislikes and mistrusts women.
   b. admires rhetorical skill.
   c. seeks only to entertain.
   d. invents fictional tales.

____ 3. Chanticleer tells Pertelote several stories to prove that
   a. dreams can be prophetic.
   b. murder never goes unpunished.
   c. dreams can be confusing.
   d. history offers valuable lessons.

____ 4. In what respect does Chanticleer's relationship with Pertelote follow the rules of courtly love?
   a. She offers a token of her love.
   b. He is totally devoted to her.
   c. They refrain from touching.
   d. He admires her from afar.

____ 5. Which passage creates the impression that Chanticleer's struggle with the fox is an epic battle?
   a. " . . . And off he bore him to the woods, the brute, / And for the moment there was no pursuit."
   b. "Sure never such a cry or lamentation / Was made by ladies of high Trojan station . . ."
   c. " 'Never again, for all your flattering lies, / You'll coax a song to make me blink my eyes . . .' "
   d. " '. . . Do what you like, the cock is mine for good; / I'll eat him there in spite of every one.' "

____ 6. The moral of "The Nun's Priest's Tale" is
   a. beware of flattery.
   b. dreams are unreliable.
   c. women are treacherous.
   d. murder will out.

____ 7. Which of the following words most closely means the same thing as the word *deferred* in this context?

   > He woke and told his friend what had occurred / And begged him that the journey be deferred / At least a day, implored him not to start.

   a. postponed
   b. stopped
   c. blocked
   d. rerouted

____ 8. In "The Pardoner's Tale" the three rioters are sure that they can destroy Death, and yet they fail to see that they are falling into his trap. This is an example of _____.
   a. irony
   b. heroism
   c. hedonism
   d. flattery

____ 9. What becomes clearer when rereading the following passage from "The Pardoner's Tale"?

> . . . if it be your design/To find out Death, turn up this crooked way/Towards that grove. If left him there today/Under a tree, and there you'll find him waiting.

    a. There is a hooded figure near the grove awaiting the three rioters.
    b. The plague will get the three rioters because there is a graveyard near the grove.
    c. The man is directing the three rioters towards their own death.
    d. The three rioters will be victorious over Death because they are not afraid of him.

____ 10. The moral of "The Paronder's Tale" is
    a. Friends should never be trusted.   c. A promise is a promise.
    b. Greed is the source of evil.   d. Old men are unreliable.

____ 11. Which of the following best describes the three rioters?
    a. prating, kindly, old
    b. hoary, arrogant, insincere
    c. earnest, brave, handsome
    d. prating, arrogant, greedy

____ 12. One of the ways Chaucer creates an effective *exeplum* in "The Pardoner's Tale" is by
    a. using rhyme and meter.
    b. making it very long.
    c. giving clear characterization of the people in the story.
    d. using simplified language.

____ 13. How do two of the rioters decide to increase their share of the gold?
    a. poison the other rioter upon his return
    b. stab the other rioter upon his return
    c. turn the third rioter in to the priest
    d. find the original owner of the gold and rob him for more.

____ 14. Who is (or are) the real traitor(s) in the "The Pardoner's Tale"?
    a. the three rioters
    b. Death
    c. the old man
    d. the plague

Vocabulary and Grammar

On the line, write the letter of the one best answer.

____ 15. The word most nearly opposite in meaning to *timorous* is _____.
    a. shy   c. loud
    b. discreet   d. assertive

____ 16. When _____ saw the fox run away with Chanticleer in his teeth, they suddenly became terribly afraid that they had lost _____ and let out a great cry of lament.
    a. they; them
    b. she; him
    c. they; him
    d. she; them

____ 17. The objective case is used when a pronoun
    a. is the predicate noun.
    b. receives the action of the verb.
    c. is the subject or predicate noun.
    d. receives the action of the verb or is the object of a preposition.

_____ 18. The word *pallor* means extreme _____.
   a. paleness
   b. anger
   c. sorrow
   d. friendliness

_____ 19. What word does the adjective clause modify in the following sentence?

   The old man who was building the wall around the ancient city was nearly seventy years old.

   a. man
   b. wall
   c. city
   d. old

_____ 20. The word most nearly opposite in meaning to *hoary* is _____.
   a. contemporary
   b. honest
   c. senior
   d. young

Essay Questions

21. Do you find the use of animals as characters in "The Nun's Priest's Tale" effective? Would your appreciation of the tale change if all the characters were human? Explain your answer.

22. Consider how the fox captures Chanticleer and how Chanticleer outwits the fox. Then write a moral to "The Nun's Priest's Tale" based on what you learn from these incidents. Support your moral with incidents and examples from the text.

23. Who is the old man in the "The Pardoner's Tale"? Is he a spy for Death? Is he an innocent bystander? Is he Death itself? Write an essay in which you assert your position. Use examples from the text to support your position.

Name _____ Date _____

"Elizabeth II: A New Queen," *The London Times*

Selection Test

Critical Reading

On the line, write the letter of the one best answer.

_____ 1. According to the article, which qualities will be most useful to Elizabeth in her role as queen?
    a. a superior education   c. high seriousness and commitment to duty
    b. youthful vigor and vitality   d. family support

_____ 2. Why did Elizabeth cancel all of her engagements shortly after her marriage?
    a. She had fallen ill.
    b. She was pregnant with her first child.
    c. She and her husband had separated.
    d. She had gotten tired of public life.

_____ 3. Why should "constitutional history" have been an important subject in the education of the future queen?
    a. The monarch's ceremonial duties demand a thorough knowledge of tradition and precedent.
    b. The monarch serves in parliament as arbiter of constitutional issues.
    c. The monarch must appoint judges, who in turn must interpret the constitution.
    d. The monarch must report to the people once a year on changes in the constitution.

_____ 4. What role did Elizabeth's wedding play in public life?
    a. It caused controversy because her husband was considered to be better qualified to be monarch than she was.
    b. It reassured the public that the royal line would be continued.
    c. It provoked a "baby boom" among married people in England.
    d. It provided a "flash of color" in the hard and dreary lives of the people.

_____ 5. What seems to be the underlying purpose of the newspaper account?
    a. to acquaint people with Elizabeth's good qualities
    b. to introduce Elizabeth to a public that knows little about her
    c. to assure people of Elizabeth's fitness to be queen
    d. to announce Elizabeth's succession to the throne

_____ 6. Why was Elizabeth *not* expected to succeed to the throne?
    a. Her older brother was first in line for the throne.
    b. Women are generally not allowed to serve as monarch.
    c. At birth she was not a direct descendant of the king.
    d. As a young lady she seemed incapable of fulfilling public duties.

_____ 7. How did the King whom Elizabeth succeeded die?
    a. on a hunting trip   c. while sipping tea in his private apartment
    b. during a state visit to France   d. in his sleep

_____ 8. Which of Elizabeth's personality traits did the prime minister especially praise upon the occasion of her marriage?
    a. generosity, flamboyance, and a sense of grandeur
    b. graciousness, understanding, and simplicity
    c. royal bearing and innate nobility
    d. reticence, modesty, and beauty

_____ 9. How did Elizabeth overcome the shyness she exhibited as a young girl?
a. by speaking continuously on radio
b. by participating in amateur theatrical productions
c. by traveling alone to all parts of the world
d. by attending public school

_____ 10. Which phrase best sums up the function of the monarchy as described in the article?
a. to represent the nation to foreign dignitaries
b. to provide the nation with leadership and moral guidance
c. to distract people from their daily lives
d. to encourage a sense of community among the people

Essay Questions

11. Write an essay describing Elizabeth's qualifications to be queen. Use details from the article to describe Elizabeth's duties and her preparation for them. Judging from the article, which personality traits seem most important to being queen and which ones least important?

12. Many years have passed since Elizabeth first ascended to the throne. In that time the monarchy's role in forging a national identity has been compromised by scandals and increased attention to the personal weaknesses of the royal family. Write an essay arguing for or against the idea that in today's world the ceremonial role of the royal family has become irrelevant and even detrimental to the life of the country.

13. The respectful tone of the newspaper biography of Elizabeth II is hardly imaginable today, given the frenzied attention the media pays to modern celebrities. Write an essay exploring the link between royalty, celebrity, and the media. Compare the coverage of Elizabeth's coronation in 1952 to some recent coverage of the royal family or another celebrity with which you are familiar. How would the article be different if written today? What role has the media played in enhancing or detracting from the image of the royal family?

Part Test, Unit 1, Part 3: A National Spirit

Critical Reading

The questions on page 29 are based on the following selection.

This passage is from "The Pardoner's Tale" in Geoffrey Chaucer's Canterbury Tales. *The Pardoner entertains the others with a tale involving three "rioters" who intend to take revenge against Death for taking the life of one of their friends. In this part of the tale, a boy and then the proprietor of a pub speak to the rioters about the recent death and burial of their friend.*

"He was a friend of yours in days of old,

And suddenly last night, the man was slain,

Upon his bench, face up, dead drunk again.

There came a privy thief, they call him Death,

[5] Who kills us all round here, and in a breath

He speared him through the heart, he never stirred.

And then Death went his way without a word.

He's killed a thousand in the present plague,

And, sir, it doesn't do to be too vague

[10] If you should meet him; you had best be wary.

Be on your guard with such an adversary,

Be primed to meet him everywhere you go,

That's what my mother said. It's all I know."

The publican joined in with, "By St. Mary.

[15] What the child says is right; you'd best be wary,

This very year he killed, in a large village

A mile away, man, woman, serf at tillage,

Page in the household, children—all there were.

Yes, I imagine that he lives round there. . . ."

[20] The rioter said, "Is he so fierce to meet?

I'll search for him, by Jesus, street by street.

God's blessed bones! I'll register a vow!

Here, chaps! The three of us together now,

Hold up your hands, like me, and we'll be brothers

[25] In this affair, and each defend the others,

And we will kill this traitor Death, I say!

Away with him as he has made away

With all our friends. God's dignity! To-night!"

On the line, write the letter of the one best answer.

_____ 1. What do the three rioters pledge to do?
   a. kill several people in a town a mile away
   b. search for Death
   c. defend each other and kill Death
   d. be wary in the presence of Death

_____ 2. What is the best description of the boy's attitude toward Death?
   a. respectful
   b. self-assured
   c. terrified
   d. indifferent

_____ 3. Who in this passage is indirectly characterized as being rash?
   a. the rioter
   b. the boy
   c. Death
   d. the publican

_____ 4. Context clues can help you determine that the word *page* in line 18 means _____.
   a. sheet of paper
   b. announcement
   c. alarm
   d. servant

_____ 5. Which of the following quotations might in context be considered mock-heroic?
   a. "There came a privy thief . . ." (l. 4)
   b. ". . . you had best be wary." (l. 10)
   c. "'. . . I'll register a vow!'" (l. 22)
   d. "'I imagine that he lives round there . . .'"

_____ 6. Analyzing the sentence in lines 4–6 will help you determine that
   a. the *who* is Death and a rioter and the *what* is the killing of the rioter.
   b. the *who* is a rioter and the *what* is Death.
   c. the *who* is the boy and the *what* is the killing of the rioter.
   d. the *who* is Death and the *what* is death.

_____ 7. In what sense is the rioters' plan foolish?
   a. They don't know where Death is.
   b. Death has already killed more than a thousand people in the area.
   c. Death is not mortal.
   d. Death carries a spear.

_____ 8. What conclusion can you draw from the identity of Death's victims?
   a. Death claims only those who defy him.
   b. Death takes the lives of powerless people.
   c. Death prefers sinners.
   d. Death has the power to take the lives of everybody.

_____ 9. By using context clues, you can infer that the word *primed* in line 12 means _____.
   a. first   c. pleased
   b. confident   d. prepared

_____ 10. In line 19, Chaucer _____ characterizes the publican as naive.
   a. symbolically   c. poetically
   b. indirectly   d. directly

Vocabulary and Grammar

On the line, write the letter of the one best answer.

____ 11. Which of the following is a compound sentence?
    a. "The force had not, by the grace of God, utterly broken down the English. . . ."
    b. "As it fell out, at a certain time in the same year, six ships came to the Isle of Wight and did much evil there, both in Devon and everywhere along the sea-coast."
    c. "They were nearly twice as long as the others; some had sixty oars, some more."
    d. "At the present time there are in Britain, in harmony with the five books of the divine law, five languages and four nations—English, British, Scots, and Picts."

____ 12. Which of the following sentences contains examples of both past and past-perfect tenses?
    a. "When they had spread northwards . . ., it is said that some Picts from Scythia put to sea . . ."
    b. "It seems a reasonable thing to say what their condition was . . ."
    c. "He often sat at table in the chair of honor, above all nations, when in Prussia."
    d. "Another nun, the chaplain at her cell, was riding with her, and three Priests as well."

____ 13. When singing, Chanticleer takes pains to close his eyes in "concentration," meaning
    a. pertaining to a common center.
    b. the action of focusing on a common center.
    c. caused by a common center.
    d. judged to have a common center.

____ 14. Which of the following sentences does not contain a pronoun in the objective case?
    a. "No singer could approach him in technique. . . ."
    b. "'. . . Whither so fast away? / Are you afraid of me, that am your friend?'"
    c. "All that he sang came welling from his soul / And how he put his voice under control!"
    d. "O Chanticleer, accursed be that morrow / That brought thee to the yard from thy high beams!"

____ 15. Which of the following sentences contains an error involving pronoun case?
    a. Courteous she was, discreet and debonair.
    b. Such a joy it was to hear them sing.
    c. And Pertelote whom heard him roar and scream was quite aghast.
    d. Repletion never left her in disquiet.

Essay Questions

16. Based on your reading of Bede's *A History of the English Church and People* write an essay in which you explain why you would—or would not—enjoy making a time-travel visit to the Britain portrayed in Bede's work. Include quotations from Bede that especially influence your thoughts.

17. Write an essay analyzing the "Prologue" or "The Nun's Priest's Tale" from *The Canterbury Tales*. In your essay, explain how Chaucer contributes to Britain's sense of its own identity in his time. Consider not only the characters he portrays, but the assumptions he makes about his audience—what he thinks most of his readers know or believe.

18. *The Anglo-Saxon Chronicle* was pieced together from fragments of oral and recorded history. In an essay, speculate on the lives and world view of the Anglo-Saxons, based on the subjects they chose to document.

from *Sir Gawain and the Green Knight,* translated by Marie Borroff
from *Morte d'Arthur* by Sir Thomas Malory

Selection Test

Critical Reading

On the line, write the letter of the one best answer.

____ 1. Which statement would you include in a summary of the first section of *Sir Gawain and the Green Knight*?
a. The Green Knight has a beard.
b. The Green Knight arrives at King Arthur's court in the middle of a New Year's Eve feast.
c. Sir Gawain flinches when the Green Knight swings his ax.
d. King Arthur is amazed by the Green Knight but he does not show it.

____ 2. Which of the following events from *Sir Gawain and the Green Knight* conveys a sense of the supernatural?
a. The Green Knight challenges King Arthur's knights.
b. Sir Gawain arrives at the Green Castle and finds it hideous.
c. The Green Knight does not die from Sir Gawain's blow.
d. The Green Knight only scratches Sir Gawain with his ax.

____ 3. Which of the following primary plot elements characteristic of medieval romances is missing from the excerpt from *Sir Gawain and the Green Knight*?
a. castle life   c. chivalry
b. adventure   d. a damsel in distress

____ 4. In *Sir Gawain and the Green Knight,* why does Sir Gawain volunteer to fight the Green Knight?
a. He wants to protect the honor of his king and fellow knights.
b. He wants to settle an old dispute he has with the Green Knight.
c. He wants to protect the queen.
d. He wants to prove that the Green Knight is not real.

____ 5. Which of the following events in *Sir Gawain and the Green Knight* represents a deviation from the ideals of chivalry?
a. King Arthur accepts the Green Knight's challenge.
b. Sir Gawain keeps the magic girdle.
c. Sir Gawain takes the Green Knight's ax.
d. The Green Knight reminds Sir Gawain of his promise.

____ 6. Which character could you leave out of a summary of *Sir Gawain and the Green Knight*?
a. King Arthur
b. the lady of the castle near the Green Chapel
c. the lord of the castle near the Green Chapel
d. Guenevere

____ 7. Sir Gawain's main internal conflict in *Sir Gawain and the Green Knight* involves his guilt over
a. accepting the lady's gift.   c. violating the chivalric code.
b. disappointing King Arthur.   d. accepting the knight's challenge.

_____ 8. Which saying best paraphrases what the Green Knight says to Sir Gawain at the end of *Sir Gawain and the Green Knight*?
   a. Live by the sword and die by the sword.
   b. Admit your mistakes and move on.
   c. A leopard never changes his spots.
   d. The best is yet to come.

_____ 9. The central theme of *Morte d'Arthur* involves the
   a. consequences of greed.
   b. nobility of war.
   c. principles of chivalry.
   d. perils of battle.

_____ 10. Which of the following parts of *Morte d'Arthur* involves an element of the supernatural?
   a. King Arthur's campaign against Sir Lancelot
   b. the death of Sir Lucan the Butler
   c. Sir Bedivere's decision to stay with the hermit
   d. the catching of King Arthur's sword

_____ 11. In *Morte d'Arthur*, why does Sir Gawain suggest that King Arthur sign a month-long treaty with Sir Mordred?
   a. Sir Gawain knows that Arthur and his men are overmatched.
   b. Sir Gawain thinks that they should compromise about the rule of England.
   c. Sir Gawain is convinced that Sir Mordred's wrath will die down in that time.
   d. King Arthur needs time to confer and plan the battle with his knights.

_____ 12. The battle between King Arthur and Sir Mordred in *Morte d'Arthur* is similar to other legends of the Middle Ages because
   a. it is historically accurate.
   b. is not realistic.
   c. its heroes fight nobly.
   d. it presents death solely in an idealized, spiritual manner.

_____ 13. In *Morte d'Arthur*, which personal characteristic motivates Sir Bedivere to disobey King Arthur's order to throw the king's sword into the lake?
   a. evil   c. common sense
   b. ambition   d. greed

_____ 14. In *Morte d'Arthur*, the black hoods worn by the ladies who come to take King Arthur away on the barge are used to symbolize _____.
   a. defeat   c. illness
   b. death   d. magic

_____ 15. Which statement would you *not* include in a summary of *Morte d'Arthur*?
   a. King Arthur has a dream in which he is warned to delay his battle with Mordred.
   b. Sir Bedivere reluctantly throws King Arthur's sword into the lake.
   c. Both King Arthur and Mordred tell their men to charge if they see a sword drawn.
   d. The hermit who buries King Arthur was once the Bishop of Canterbury.

Vocabulary and Grammar

On the line, write the letter of the one best answer.

_____ 16. In *Sir Gawain and the Green Knight*, Sir Gawain feigned courage because he did not want to appear fearful. The word *feigned* means _____.
   a. doubted the meaning of   c. inferred the existence of
   b. put on a show of   d. demanded more from

____ 17. Choose the pair that completes these lines from *Sir Gawain and the Green Knight.*

> Had I been a bit _____, a buffet, perhaps,
> I could have dealt _____:

   a. busiest, most directly
   b. busier, most directly
   c. busier, more directly
   d. busiest, most directly

____ 18. Which of these lines from *Sir Gawain and the Green Knight* contains the comparative form of a word?

   a. " 'I am the weakest, well I know, and of wit feeblest;' "
   b. " 'That no host under heaven is hardier of will,' "
   c. " 'Stoutest under steel-gear on the steeds to ride,' "
   d. " 'She made trial of a man most faultless by far' "

____ 19. Which is the most appropriate word to describe what the hermit did to King Arthur in *Morte d'Arthur*?

   a. rejected
   b. emancipated
   c. instructed
   d. interred

____ 20. Which word is most nearly opposite in meaning to *righteous*?

   a. honorable
   b. immortal
   c. unethical
   d. reliable

Essay Questions

21. Medieval romances often blend realistic details, magical or supernatural happenings, and religious sentiment. Write an essay in which you show how this blend of different elements is found in *Sir Gawain and the Green Knight* and *Morte d'Arthur.* Cite at least one example of vivid realism, one of magic or the supernatural, and one of religious sentiment in each section.

22. *Sir Gawain and the Green Knight* and *Morte d'Arthur* were written by two different people. Do you think the portrait of King Arthur is consistent in these two stories? Write an essay in which you analyze the character of King Arthur as he is portrayed in these two stories. Cite examples from the texts to back up your observations. Then compare the two Arthurs.

23. *Sir Gawain and the Green Knight* and *Morte d'Arthur* are two of the best-known chivalric romances of the Middle Ages. Write an essay in which you explain, first, what chivalry is and, second, how its ideals and code of conduct are represented in the poems. Refer, not only to the character and conduct of Gawain and Arthur, but also to those of other characters. Make note of the impulses and interests with which chivalry conflicts in these romances, and the ways in which the romance resolves these conflicts.

Letters of Margaret Paston "Lord Randall," "The Twa Corbies,"
"Get Up and Bar the Door," and "Barbara Allan," Anonymous

Selection Test

Critical Reading

On the line, write the letter of the one best answer.

_____ 1. Both the letters and the ballads in this selection reveal information about medieval life, but only the letter
   a. follows a specific form.
   b. tells about the difficulties of medieval life.
   c. reveals the author's thoughts and feelings.
   d. contains a narrative.

_____ 2. Margaret Paston's letters reveal that
   a. many of the Pastons' tenants supported the Duke of Suffolk's actions.
   b. the Duke of Suffolk arrested people who helped defend the Pastons' property.
   c. the Duke's men refused to rob or deface the church.
   d. Sir John Paston moved his family to London after the Duke threatened to take over Hellesdon.

_____ 3. In Margaret Paston's letter to her son, she appeals to him to
   a. organize the defense of Caister.
   b. negotiate with Fastolf of Cowhawe to regain Caister.
   c. meet her in Caister to plan the defense of the castle.
   d. bring supplies into Caister for the tenants.

_____ 4. In the ballad "Lord Randall," Lord Randall's mother realizes that her son has been poisoned when he tells her that
   a. his dogs became swollen and died.
   b. he and his dogs ate the same food.
   c. he ate eels boiled in broth.
   d. his true love cooked his dinner.

_____ 5. Which of the following is the best modern English version of these lines from "The Twa Corbies"?

   O'er his white banes, when they are bare, / The wind sall blaw for evermair.

   a. Over his white bones, when they are bare,
      The wind will blow from everywhere.
   b. Over his white bones, when they are bare,
      The wind shall blow forevermore.
   c. Over his white bones, when they are bare,
      The wind's always blowing through the air.
   d. Over his wide bones, when they are bare,
      The wind shall blow from here to there.

_____ 6. Which of the following elements lends mystery to "The Twa Corbies"?
   a. The knight's name is never revealed to the reader.
   b. The ravens' plans for the knight's body are revealed.
   c. There is no mention of how the knight died.
   d. The story is presented from the ravens' point of view.

_____ 7. Which of the following ideas is central to the meaning of "The Twa Corbies"?
   a. the cruelty of animals
   b. the importance of companions
   c. the brevity of life
   d. the selfishness of people

_____ 8. Which elements of a ballad are present in "The Twa Corbies"?
   a. a greeting and a closing   c. individual authors
   b. repetition   d. dialogue and rhyme

_____ 9. Which modern English word has the same meaning as the italicized word in this excerpt from "The Twa Corbies"?

   The tane unto the *tither* did say

   a. tiller   c. other
   b. river   d. thither

_____ 10. Which of the following best summarizes the theme of "Get Up and Bar the Door"?
   a. loyalty to one's spouse
   b. the value of silence
   c. people's pettiness
   d. distrust of strangers

_____ 11. In "Get Up and Bar the Door," variations of the line "get up and bar the door" in that ballad act almost as a _____.
   a. stanza
   b. refrain
   c. main idea
   d. quatrain

_____ 12. What do the words in italics mean in the following lines?

   And I'll pike out his bonny blue *e'en*. (from "The Twa Corbies")
   Will ye kiss my wife before my *een*? (from "Get Up and Bar the Door")

   a. eyes   c. even
   b. one   d. knee

_____ 13. Which of the following best states the theme of "Barbara Allan"?
   a. the harshness of life
   b. the sorrow of neglected love
   c. the justice of death
   d. the depth of a mother's love

_____ 14. In "Barbara Allan" from Barbara Allan's reaction to the death of John Graeme, the reader can infer that she feels an enormous sense of _____.
   a. hopelessness   c. remorse
   b. love   d. vindication

_____ 15. In "Barbara Allan" which of the following actions performed by Barbara Allan makes clear her intentions at the end of the ballad?
   a. listening to the death bell
   b. drawing back the curtain in the sick room
   c. departing from the sick room
   d. requesting that a narrow bed be made

Vocabulary and Grammar

On the line, write the letter of the one best answer.

____ 16. An appropriate word to describe what the Duke of Suffolk's men did to Hellesdon is
_____.
   a. enquired
   b. exiled
   c. ransacked
   d. emaciated

____ 17. Which of the following excerpts from "Lord Randall" contains an example of direct address?
   a. "'O yes! I am poison'd; . . .'"
   b. "'For I'm weary wi' hunting, and fain wald lie down.'"
   c. "'I dined wi' my true-love; . . .'"
   d. "'O where hae ye been, Lord Randall, my son?'"

____ 18. Which line from "Get Up and Bar the Door" contains an instance of direct address?
   a. "Tho muckle thought the goodwife to hersel, . . ."
   b. "Now whether is this a rich man's house, . . ."
   c. "'My hand is in my hussyfskap, . . .'"
   d. "'Goodman, you've spoken the foremost word; . . .'"

____ 19. The word *succor* means _____.
   a. succeed
   b. help
   c. secure
   d. tolerate

____ 20. Which phrase is most nearly the same in meaning as *asunder*?
   a. under the ground
   b. into parts and pieces
   c. very quickly
   d. in a calm manner

Essay Questions

21. Ballads are meant to be sung. Choose any two of the following ballads: "The Twa Corbies," "Get Up and Bar the Door," and "Barbara Allan." Write an essay in which you explain how their structure, style, and content are largely determined by the fact that they were originally composed to be sung.

22. Trust is an important element in the ballads "Lord Randall" and "Barbara Allan." Write an essay that explains how trust or a lack of trust leads to death for Lord Randall and for Barbara Allan. In your essay, analyze how each character's feelings of trust change over the course of the ballad.

23. Reading Margaret Paston's letters is one way to learn about the Middle Ages, but is it the most effective way? Write an essay in which you describe the advantages and disadvantages of learning about history through personal letters. Include in your essay a discussion of how bias affects the way events are portrayed in personal letters.

"How Siegfried Was Slain" from *The Nibelungenlied*, translated by A. T. Hatto

Selection Test

Critical Reading

On the line, write the letter of the one best answer.

_____ 1. Which of the following lines spoken by Siegfried best shows his lack of insight?
   a. "'Unless we hunters are better looked after, I'll not be a companion of the hunt.'"
   b. "'There is no need for the doer of the deed to weep when the damage is done.'"
   c. "'If I had the strength I would have good reason to complain.'"
   d. "'Your kinsmen without exception wish me well, nor have I deserved otherwise of them.'"

_____ 2. Which of the following best states the theme of this selection from *The Nibelungenlied*?
   a Noble men are not suspicious-minded, and so can be destroyed by the treachery of the weak.
   b. Worldly achievements will not bring happiness.
   c. Peaceful relations can only be kept through cooperation.
   d. Dishonesty will ultimately lead to self-destruction.

_____ 3. Kriemhild does not warn Siegfried that she has betrayed his secret weakness because
   a. she wishes to destroy him.
   b. she fears she will lose his love.
   c. she hopes to prevent war between him and her family.
   d. she does not realize what she has done.

_____ 4. What does the line "The hunt was over, yet not entirely so" foreshadow?
   a. Siegfried will be killed by Hagen.
   b. The hunting ritual will not be complete.
   c. Not all the animals will be killed.
   d. Kriemhild will seek revenge from the hunters.

_____ 5. Siegfried ignores Kriemhild's warnings of danger because his character is _____.
   a. loyal
   b. hateful
   c. trusting
   d. proud

_____ 6. What flaw in Siegfried's character does Hagen exploit to murder him?
   a. pride in his hunting skills
   b. loyalty to the king
   c. inability to resist a challenge
   d. affection for his wife

_____ 7. Why is it ironic that Siegfried's weapons are tipped with heads so large "that any beast they pierced must inevitably soon die"?
   a. Siegfried will kill no more animals with his weapons.
   b. Siegfried will be killed by one of his own weapons.
   c. Siegfried is the only man strong enough to use his weapons.
   d. Siegfried's life cannot be saved by his weapons.

____ 8. Like *Beowulf* and the Arthurian legends, *The Nibelungenlied* expresses the ethic of a warrior-society. What aspect of such an ethic does Hagen betray when he kills Siegfried?
   a. Fight fairly.
   b. Seek self-knowledge.
   c. Hunt the strongest opponents.
   d. Confront fear.

____ 9. Besides Brunhild's desire for revenge, what additional motive might the murderers have?
   a. disgust at Siegfried's arrogance
   b. anger at Siegfried's treachery
   c. fear of Siegfried's political power
   d. jealousy of Siegfried's superiority

____ 10. The dying Siegfried asks Hagen to take care of Kriemhild. What does this tact suggest about the values of their society?
   a. Ties of blood could count for more than moral judgment.
   b. Forcing someone to care for one's widow was a warrior's supreme revenge.
   c. Forgiving one's enemies at death was all-important.
   d. Honor counted for little when death was near.

Essay Questions

11. Siegfried's character is a particularly good example of a "tragic hero." A tragic hero has been defined as a person with many superior qualities and one fatal flaw. Show how this definition applies to Siegfried.

12. The narrative in this selection makes consistent use of omens and foreshadowing. In an essay, discuss the use of these devices, explaining which details serve as omens or foreshadowings of which events. How do these details affect the overall mood or theme of the selection?

13. In order to survive as long as they have, epic tales such as *The Nibelungenlied* must address universal human emotions and situations. Write an essay analyzing the role of the following four basic conditions in the story of Siegfried's death: love, honor, betrayal, revenge. How is each category represented in the tale? Make a judgment about which of the four is most important to the story. Go on to argue whether or not human nature has changed since the composition of this tale.

Part Test, Unit 1, Part 4: Perils and Adventures

Critical Reading

The questions on pages 40 and 41 are based on the following selection.

This selection is a modern English version of the anonymous ballad "Sir Patrick Spens."

The king sits in Dumferling town,
    Drinking the blood-red wine:
"O where will I get a good sailor,
    To sail this ship of mine?"

[5] Up and spoke an ancient knight,
    Sat at the king's right knee:
"Sir Patrick Spens is the best sailor,
    That sails upon the sea."

The king has written a broad letter,
[10]   And signed it with his hand,
And sent it to Sir Patrick Spens,
    Was walking on the sand.

The first line that Sir Patrick read,
    A loud laugh laughed he;
[15] The next line that Sir Patrick read,
    The tear blinded his eye.

"O who is this has done this deed,
    This ill deed done to me,
To send me out this time of the year,
[20]   To sail upon the sea!

"Make haste, make haste, my merry men all
    Our good ship sails the morn:"
"O say not so, my master dear,
    For I fear a deadly storm.

[25] "Late, late yesterday evening I saw the new moon,
    With the old moon in her arm,
And I fear, I fear, my dear master,
    That we will come to harm."

O our Scots nobles were right loath

[30]   To wet their cork-heeled shoes,

But long before the play were played,

    Their hats they swam above.

O long, long may their ladies sit,

    With their fans into their hand,

[35] Or ever they see Sir Patrick Spens

    Come sailing to the land.

O long, long may the ladies stand,

    With their gold combs in their hair,

Waiting for their own dear lords,

[40]   For they'll see them no more.

Halfway over, halfway over to Aberdour,

    It's fifty fathoms deep

And there lies good Sir Patrick Spens,

    With the Scots lords at his feet.

On the line, write the letter of the one best answer.

_____   1. What problem does the king face at the beginning of the ballad?
          a. finding a good ship
          b. finding a good sailor to sail his ship
          c. convincing Sir Patrick Spens to sail for him
          d. getting a message to Sir Patrick Spens

_____   2. Why might the king's wine be described as "blood-red"?
          a. It is the only kind of wine the king enjoys.
          b. It is wine of extremely high quality.
          c. The king's decisions sometimes cause bloodshed.
          d. It is the most precise description of the wine's color.

_____   3. How many characters are directly quoted in this folk ballad?
          a. four   c. three
          b. two   d. five

_____   4. Which of the following is the best summary of the first stanza?
          a. The Scottish king seeks a good sailor for his ship.
          b. As he sits and drinks wine, the king thinks about his needs.
          c. The Scottish king and an elderly knight discuss good sailors.
          d. The king asks for a good sailor to sail his ship.

_____ 5. Why does Sir Patrick Spens view the king's request as an "ill deed"?
   a. Sailing will place Sir Patrick Spens in grave peril.
   b. The king is not Sir Patrick Spens's ruler.
   c. Sir Patrick Spens's sailing skills have eroded over the years.
   d. He believes that the king is evil.

_____ 6. Which of the following elements is not present in this folk ballad?
   a. dialogue   c. simile
   b. repetition   d. narrative

_____ 7. Why does one of Sir Patrick Spens's sailors think the voyage is ill-fated?
   a. He is superstitious.
   b. He is unimpressed with the sturdiness of the king's ship.
   c. He senses that the king's letter was forged.
   d. He saw an omen in the sky the previous day.

_____ 8. What happens to the Scots lords who dislike the idea of getting their "cork-heeled shoes" wet?
   a. They elect not to sail.   c. They are fired by Sir Patrick Spens.
   b. They drown.   d. They live out their lives in another kingdom.

_____ 9. Sir Patrick's response to the king's letter shows the value his society put on
   a. willingness to rise to any challenge.   c. unquestioning obedience to the king.
   b. great deeds of seafaring.   d. religious devotion.

_____ 10. Which of the following best captures the ballad-writer's attitude towards the code of chivalry?
   a. The code is _____ unreasonable; blindly following it leads to needless destruction.
   b. The code is noble; it holds society together even in dangerous times.
   c. Kings thoughtlessly abuse the loyalty of those tied to them by the code.
   d. The code is stern and may lead to unreasonable acts; those who are faithful to it whatever the cost have a kind of tragic glory.

Vocabulary and Grammar

On the line, write the letter of the one best answer.

_____ 11. Which of the following is the comparative form of an adjective?
   a. sharper   c. sternly
   b. faithful   d. fairest

_____ 12. Which of the following lines contains direct address?
   a. "'By God, I rejoice / That your fist shall fetch this favor . . .'"
   b. "'Would you grant me the grace,' said Gawain to the king . . ."
   c. "'Goodman, you've spoken the foremost word . . .'"
   d. "'Alas,' said Sir Bedivere, 'that was my lord King Arthur . . .'"

_____ 13. Write the letter of the word closest in meaning to that of the italicized word in the following sentence.

   [He] withdrew the ax *adroitly* before it did damage.

   a. thoroughly   c. smoothly
   b. physically   d. skillfully

_____ 14. Words such as *certain, certify, certificate,* and *certainly* are based on the Latin root –*cert*-, meaning _____.
   a. document   c. agreement
   b. sure   d. doubt

_____ 15. What is the correct superlative form of the adverb *discourteously*?
  a. more discourteously
  b. discourteouslier
  c. most discourteously
  d. discourteouslyest

Essay Questions

16. Choose one of the four folk ballads ("Lord Randall," "Get Up and Bar the Door," "The Twa Corbies," or "Barbara Allan"). Write an essay that explains the events in the ballad, noting any details that are implied but not directly stated. Point out any literary techniques—such as rhyme, dialogue, repetition—that heighten the dramatic effect of the ballad.

17. Modern ideas of the law can be quite different from both the ideals and the realities of the Middle Ages. Write an essay on this contrast. First, describe how the law works—or doesn't work—in the Pastons' quarrel with the Duke of Suffolk. Then, describe the obligations and actions that tie Sir Gawain to the Green Knight. Contrast both the Paston's situation and Gawain's situation with the way in which the law protects and obligates citizens in the modern world.

18. Arguably the ideals of chivalry were impossible for real men to live up to. Choose one of the selections—such as *Morte d'Arthur*, "The Twa Corbies," *Sir Gawain and the Green Knight*, or *The Nibelungenlied*—in which chivalry fails—either in the sense that someone fails to live up to its ideals, or in the sense that following the ideal leads to disaster. Write an essay in which you explain the "failure" of chivalry in detail. Explain whether the piece shows that death in the service of an ideal is a noble thing, or a wasteful, sad thing.

Sonnets 1, 35, and 75 by Edmund Spenser
Sonnets 31 and 39 by Sir Philip Sidney

Selection Test

Critical Reading

On the line, write the letter of the one best answer.

____ 1. Which is the best paraphrase for the following lines from Sonnet 1?

> Those lamping eyes will deign sometimes to look
> And read the sorrows of my dying spright
> Written with tears in heart's close bleeding book.

   a. Those eyes that look like large lamps sometimes look like blood and tears.
   b. Those eyes sometimes look and see my sad spirit, tearful and full of sorrow.
   c. Those eyes see my sorrowful nymph-like self, covering my books with blood and tears.
   d. Those lamps that are like eyes sometimes give the illusion that the book in the corner is covered with blood and tears.

____ 2. The message that the speaker of Sonnet 75 wishes to convey to his love is that
   a. he will love her for eternity.
   b. his verse will immortalize their love.
   c. the pleasure of love is worth its suffering.
   d. the pleasures of love must end with death.

____ 3. One way to identify the form of a Spenserian sonnet is by its
   a. unrhymed iambic pentameter.
   b. four beat line and *aabb* rhyme scheme.
   c. *abab bcbc cdcd ee* rhyme scheme.
   d. *ababbcbcc* rhyme scheme.

____ 4. How does a Spenserian sonnet differ from a Petrarchan sonnet?
   a. The Spenserian sonnet contains a different number of lines.
   b. Spenser's sonnets were written as part of a sequence.
   c. The Spenserian sonnet sometimes has no break between the octave and the sestet.
   d. The Spenserian sonnet deals with love and the natural world.

____ 5. Which of the following best describes the meaning conveyed by these lines from Spenser's Sonnet 1?

> Leaves, lines, and rhymes, seek her to please alone, / Whom if ye please, I care for other none.

   a. If she likes the poem, then I shall write another.
   b. I don't care if anyone else likes the poem if she is pleased by it.
   c. If the poem pleases her, then I shall never love another woman.
   d. I try to please her, since I love only her.

© Prentice-Hall, Inc.

____ 6. In these lines from Spenser's Sonnet 35, what is the speaker claiming?

> Yet are mine eyes so filled with the store / Of that fair sight, that nothing else they brook

    a. I have such an abundance that I don't need anything else.
    b. My eyes are so filled with the sight of my beloved that I can't bear to look at anything else.
    c. Her overwhelming beauty is like nothing else in nature.
    d. Her fair eyes remind me of the beauties of nature.

____ 7. The image of pages ". . . in love's soft bands, / Like captives trembling at the victor's sight" from Spenser's Sonnet 1 reinforces the theme that
    a. his poetry is not worthy of her.
    b. his beloved has won the argument between them.
    c. his beloved is cruel.
    d. like the pages, he too is a hopeless captive at the mercy of his beloved.

____ 8. The following lines come from Spenser's Sonnet 1:

> that angel's blessed look,/My soul's long lacked food, my heaven's bliss

Restating these lines in simpler words is an example of
    a. recognizing historical context
    b. paraphrasing
    c. predicting
    d. recognizing speaker's situation

____ 9. The unifying theme of Sonnet 31 and Sonnet 39 is
    a. natural beauty.   c. relief from pain.
    b. hopeless love.   d. endless suffering.

____ 10. Which of the following is a characteristic of Sidney's Sonnets 31 and 39?
    a. The speaker is engaged in an internal conflict.
    b. A heavenly body stimulates the speaker's thoughts.
    c. The speaker accepts that his love is lost.
    d. The speaker sees Stella's image in his sleep.

____ 11. In Sonnet 31, Sidney uses the moon to
    a. explain life on earth.   c. emphasize his power.
    b. reflect his own feelings.   d. symbolize all people.

____ 12. In the line "Is constant love deemed there but want of wit?" from Sonnet 31, Sidney is suggesting that
    a. true love leads to unhappiness.   c. love and intelligence are similar.
    b. no love can live forever.   d. only fools can hope to find true love.

____ 13. Sidney's Sonnets 31 and 39 illustrate what characteristic of the sonnet sequence?
    a. The poet is scorned by his lover.
    b. Relationships are presented in a true-to-life way.
    c. The heavens are employed symbolically.
    d. The ultimate outcome is left unresolved.

____ 14. Which of the following is the best paraphrase of these lines from Sidney's Sonnet 31?

> What, may it be that even in heavenly place / That busy archer his sharp arrows tries?

    a. Is it true that they practice archery in heaven?
    b. What kind of sharp arrows fly in heaven?
    c. Is it true that people fall in love in heaven?
    d. Does an archer fix his arrows in heaven?

___ 15. In Sidney's Sonnet 39, the speaker asks sleep to "make in me those civil wars to cease." Which of the following best describes the "civil wars" the speaker suffers?
   a. the inner turmoil caused by love
   b. the quarrel between the speaker and his beloved
   c. the anger the speaker feels toward society
   d. Stella's love for another man

Vocabulary and Grammar

On the line, write the letter of the one best answer.

___ 16. The word *deign* means ___ .
   a. to lower oneself   c. to govern
   b. to make plans   d. to heal

___ 17. Which phrase or sentence shows correct capitalization of a proper noun?
   a. "With how sad steps, O Moon, thou climb'st the skies!"
   b. "The Baiting place of wit, the balm of woe . . ."
   c. "When Ye behold that angel's blessed look . . ."
   d. "In their amazement like Narcissus Vain . . ."

___ 18. Which of the following is always a proper noun?
   a. Helicon   c. Love
   b. Death   d. Balm

___ 19. Which word or phrase is closest in meaning to the word *wan*?
   a. wit   c. pale
   b. to grow weak   d. soothing

___ 20. According to Sidney in Sonnet 39, sleep is a ___ for sorrow.
   a. languor   c. spright
   b. balm   d. deign

Essay Questions

21. Spenser and Sidney use a variety of images in their sonnets to convey the theme of hopeless and painful love. Choose two or three images from the sonnets, and write an essay explaining how each image contributes to this theme. For example, in Sonnet 39 Sidney uses the image of "fierce darts" thrown by Despair to describe the pain the lover feels.

22. The common practice in sonnet sequences of the time was to portray the beloved lady as extraordinarily beautiful but unreachable, while the lover was portrayed as remaining faithful to his beloved even though he endured an agony of love. Write an essay discussing these conventions in the sonnets you have read. How do Spenser and Sidney depict themselves in the different sonnets? How do they characterize their beloveds? Use specific examples that reflect these conventions.

23. The three sonnets from Spenser's sonnet sequence each describe some aspect of the speaker's love for his lady, but each focuses on a different aspect or expression of that love. Write an essay discussing these sonnets. What is the subject of each? What are the dominant images? What is the overall impression these three sonnets considered together convey about the speaker, his beloved, and their relationship?

Sonnets 29, 106, 116, and 130 by William Shakespeare

Selection Test

Critical Reading

On the line, write the letter of the one best answer.

____ 1. In Sonnet 29, the speaker changes from
 a. fearful to confident.
 b. hopeful to resigned.
 c. bitter to defiant.
 d. despondent to thankful.

____ 2. In Sonnet 29, what is emphasized about the speaker in Shakespeare's three-quatrain form?
 a. his jealousy   c. his self-pity
 b. his feelings of love   d. his sense of hope

____ 3. In Sonnet 106, "all you prefiguring" means
 a. ancestors' understanding.
 b. current writers' answering.
 c. past writers' foreshadowing.
 d. readers' guessing.

____ 4. Which of the following phrases from Sonnet 106 best supports Shakespeare's purpose for writing the sonnet?
 a. "So all their praises are but prophecies"
 b. "Of this our time"
 c. "In praise of ladies dead"
 d. "I see their antique pen would have express'd"

____ 5. Which of the following best describes the theme of Sonnet 116?
 a. True love is transient.
 b. True love never dies.
 c. Love guides its lovers.
 d. All love changes.

____ 6. In Sonnet 116, Shakespeare describes love as ____ .
 a. fickle   c. humorous
 b. unique   d. long-lasting

____ 7. Which saying best describes the theme of Sonnet 130?
 a. Love conquers all.   c. Love is blind.
 b. Truth is beauty.   d. Beauty is skin deep.

____ 8. The tone of Shakespeare's Sonnet 130 is both
 a. serious and bleak.
 b. cheerful and optimistic.
 c. hopeful and exaggerated.
 d. lighthearted and realistic.

____ 9. In each self-contained quatrain in Sonnet 130, the speaker ____ the features of his beloved.
 a. praises   c. compares to nature
 b. examines   d. berates

_____ 10. What frequent characteristic of a Shakespearean sonnet is exemplified by Sonnets 29, 106, 116, and 130?
   a. a conclusion presented in the final couplet
   b. a hopeful and uplifting tone
   c. an idealized view of love and life
   d. an inconsistent rhyme scheme

_____ 11. Unlike the Petrarchan or Spenserian sonnet form, the Shakespearean sonnet form
   a. contains three quatrains and a couplet.
   b. is written in iambic pentameter.
   c. contains an initial octave and final sestet.
   d. concludes with an alexandrine.

_____ 12. The form of the sonnet influences its contents by
   a. shortening thoughts to fit quatrains and couplets.
   b. using chronological order.
   c. following a rhyme scheme.
   d. using the Petrarchan structure.

_____ 13. Which of the following is a characteristic of a Shakespearean sonnet?
   a. six iambic feet to the line
   b. a rhyme scheme of _abab cdcd efef gg_
   c. four quatrains
   d. groupings of eight and six lines

_____ 14. You can relate structure to theme by thinking of a sonnet as
   a. a fortune cookie.
   b. a gemstone in an elegant case.
   c. a symphony.
   d. a tote bag.

Vocabulary and Grammar

On the line, write the letter of the one best answer.

_____ 15. Which word is most nearly the same in meaning as _sullen_?
   a. bright
   b. dull
   c. dismal
   d. shy

_____ 16. The word _scope_ means _____ .
   a. record
   b. range
   c. obstacle
   d. prediction

_____ 17. By merely coloring his hair, he completely _____ his appearance.
   a. prefigures
   b. remedies
   c. alters
   d. impedes

_____ 18. Participles are verb forms usually ending in _____ .
   a. _-ly_
   b. _-ment_
   c. _-ness_
   d. _-ing_ or _-ed_

_____ 19. Find all of the participles used as adjectives and the nouns they modify in the following passage:

> Of this our time, all you prefiguring; / And, for they look'd but with divining eyes, / They had not skill enough your worth to sing: / For we, which now behold these present days, / Have eyes to wonder, but lack tongues to praise.

a. Adjective: *prefiguring*, noun: *time*
b. Adjective: *worth*, noun: *sing*; adjective: *present*, noun: *days*
c. Adjective: *wonder*, noun: *eyes*; adjective: *praise*, noun: *tongues*
d. Adjective: *divining*, noun: *eyes*

_____ 20. Which words are participles that can be used as adjectives in the blanks of this sentence?

> Poets are known for their _____ hearts and _____ souls.

a. searching; tortured
b. warm; colorful
c. big; sensitive
d. expansive; tragic

Essay Questions

21. Although love is the basic theme of Sonnets 29, 106, 116, and 130, it is treated differently in each one. In an essay, discuss the different treatments of love in these sonnets. Which sonnet do you think presents the truest depiction of love? Why? Support your arguments with examples.

22. Sonnets 29 ("When in disgrace . . .") and 130 ("My mistress' eyes . . .") have ending couplets that differ in their meaning and function. Sonnet 29 ends with the lines "For thy sweet love remembered such wealth brings / That then I scorn to change my state with kings." The closing lines of Sonnet 130 are "And yet, by heaven, I think my love as rare / As any she belied with false compare." Write an essay that explains how each couplet relates to the rest of its sonnet. How are these couplets different in this relationship? How effective is each couplet as an ending to its sonnet?

23. The idea of time plays a role in the themes of both Sonnet 103 ("When in the chronicle . . .") and Sonnet 116 ("Let me not to the marriage . . . "). In an essay, contrast the very different concepts of time presented in these sonnets. What is the relationship of time to beauty in each poem? Use examples from the poems to support your ideas.

Sonnets 18 and 28 by Petrarch
Sonnets 69 and 89 by Pablo Neruda

Selection Test

Critical Reading

On the line, write the letter of the one best answer.

_____ 1. Which of the following lines suggests the poet's willingness to share his love with the world?
  a. "And still a watchful glance around me throw, / Anxious to shun the print of human tread"
  b. "so that my shadow can travel along in your hair, / so that everything can learn the reason for my song"
  c. "That well I deem each mountain, wood and plain, / And river knows, what I from man conceal"
  d. "since then you are, I am, we are, / and through love I will be, you will be, we'll be"

_____ 2. Which of the following images does Neruda use in both Sonnet 69 and Sonnet 89?
  a. hands, a rose, fog   c. cobbles, wheat, the sea
  b. wheat, wind, light   d. sand, light, the moon

_____ 3. Which of the following statements best summarizes the main idea of Petrarch's Sonnet 18?
  a. The beauty of the poet's lover is beyond his ability to describe it.
  b. Beauty is in the eye of the beholder.
  c. The beauty of the poet's lover is matched only by the poet's ability to write poems.
  d. Love is the most beautiful of all emotions.

_____ 4. Which of the following statements is true about Petrarch's Sonnet 28?
  a. It contains 16 lines, not 14 as in his other sonnets.
  b. It is the only sonnet in which he uses the name "Laura."
  c. The object of his love is never mentioned.
  d. The image of the river stands for the object of the poet's love.

_____ 5. In Sonnet 89, what effect does Neruda say his lover had on him?
  a. She saved his life.   c. She exposed him to true beauty.
  b. She changed his destiny.   d. She taught him the meaning of love.

_____ 6. In Neruda's Sonnet 69, what is the significance of the fact that others cannot perceive the "light" the poet sees in his lover's hand?
  a. Their love is a secret.
  b. The lover possesses great inner beauty.
  c. Their love was never consummated.
  d. Neruda's friends disapprove of his lover.

_____ 7. In what sense is Petrarch insincere in Sonnet 18?
  a. Though professing his desire to be alone, he really craves the attention of other people.
  b. While asserting he wants to keep his love a secret, he nevertheless tells many friends about it.
  c. While failing to describe his lover's beauty, he still manages to flatter her.
  d. Despite denying the power of his own poetry, he actually praises himself in the last lines.

8. Which word best describes the mood of Petrarch's Sonnet 28?
   a. forlorn
   b. jovial
   c. flustered
   d. contemptuous

9. In which sonnet does the poet imagine his lover's life after his own death?
   a. Neruda's Sonnet 69
   b. Neruda's Sonnet 89
   c. Petrarch's Sonnet 18
   d. Petrarch's Sonnet 28

10. To whom does Petrarch confess his woes in Sonnet 28?
    a. a priest
    b. his lover
    c. all mankind
    d. the natural world around him

Essay Questions

11. Write an essay comparing the images of love created by Petrarch and Neruda. Use details from the sonnets to describe the poets' different approaches to love. Go on to compare one of the sonnets to a modern day love song or poem with which you are familiar. How does the example you chose differ from Petrarch's or Neruda's poetry?

12. Both Neruda and Petrarch employ nature imagery in their sonnets. Write an essay explaining how this imagery contributes to the main themes of two or more of the sonnets.

13. American actress Mae West once said, "Love conquers all things except poverty and toothache." Write an essay relating this quotation to the sonnets written by either Neruda or Petrarch. What was West saying about love? How does the poet you chose express the same idea?

Part Test, Unit 2, Part 1: Lovers and Their Lines

Critical Reading

The questions below are based on the following selection.

Sonnet 26

by Edmund Spenser

Sweet is the rose, but grows upon a briar;

Sweet is the juniper, but sharp his bough;

Sweet is the eglantine, but pricketh near;

Sweet is the fir bloom, but his branches rough;

[5] Sweet is the cypress, but his rynd is tough;

Sweet is the nut, but bitter is his pill;

Sweet is the broom flower, but yet sour enough;

And sweet is moly, but his root is ill.

So every sweet with sour is tempered still,

[10] That maketh it be coveted the more:

For easy things that may be got at will,

Most sorts of men do set but little store.

Why then should I account of little pain,

That endless pleasure shall unto me gain.

On the line, write the letter of the one best answer.

_____ 1. According to the speaker, what is the effect of tempering "every sweet with sour"?
  a. The sweet becomes an object of scorn.
  b. The sweet becomes more desirable.
  c. The sour dominates the sweet.
  d. The sweet and the sour render each other neutral.

_____ 2. Which of the following senses is not important to the poem's imagery?
  a. taste   c. smell
  b. hearing   d. touch

_____ 3. Which of the following is not a feature of a Spenserian sonnet?
  a. fourteen lines in iambic pentameter
  b. a single theme
  c. an octave and a sestet
  d. the rhyme scheme *abababab cdecde*

_____ 4. In this poem, Spenser's subject is
  a. the relationship between plants and flowers.
  b. the avoidance of envy.
  c. the relationship between pain and pleasure.
  d. love of God.

_____ 5. With what does the speaker equate the sweetness of various plants and flowers?
   a. "Most sorts of men"
   b. "endless pleasure"
   c. "a briar"
   d. "easy things"

_____ 6. Which is the best contemporary English paraphrase of Spenser's words in lines 11–12?
   a. Most people do not value highly things that they can get easily.
   b. Most people value highly things that they can get easily.
   c. Most people feel that the most valuable things cannot be bought.
   d. Things that one gets after much toil are difficult to appreciate.

_____ 7. Which group of lines is an example of a thought's spanning more than one poetic line?
   a. lines 1–11
   b. lines 13–14
   c. lines 8–14
   d. lines 12–13

_____ 8. Which of the following is not a helpful strategy for reading Sonnet 26?
   a. listening
   b. considering the characteristics of the time period
   c. distinguishing fact from opinion
   d. identifying the poem's speaker

_____ 9. To what personal experience might lines 13–14 refer?
   a. a political victory
   b. a heroic battle
   c. a religious conversion
   d. a love affair

_____ 10. Which is the best assessment of the speaker's experiences?
   a. The speaker has felt a great deal of pain in his life.
   b. The speaker believes that the pain he has felt is not especially significant.
   c. The speaker believes that others' pain is more important than his own.
   d. The speaker has never felt pain in his life.

Vocabulary and Grammar

On the line, write the letter of the one best answer.

_____ 11. Which passage contains an error in the capitalization of proper nouns?
   a. "And happy rhymes bathed in the sacred brook of helicon whence she derived is . . ."
   b. "Whom if ye please, I care for other none"
   c. "In their amazement like Narcissus vain"
   d. "And in the heavens write your glorious name"

_____ 12. Which line contains a participle used as an adjective?
   a. "A chamber deaf to noise, and blind to light"
   b. "My soul's long lacked food, my heaven's bliss"
   c. "When in the chronicle of wasted time"
   d. "And all their shows but shadows, saving she"

_____ 13. Words such as _chronicle, chronological,_ and _chronic_ derive from the Greek word meaning ____.
   a. history   c. numbers
   b. time   d. paper

_____ 14. The word *languished* is what form of the verb *languish*?
   a. present perfect
   b. present participle
   c. past perfect
   d. past participle

_____ 15. A *sullen* mood or atmosphere might also be called _____.
   a. dismal
   b. disassociated
   c. destroyed
   d. sensitive

Essay Questions

16. The word *friendship* can refer to a casual relationship or to one of great depth, mutual re-spect, and understanding—even one based on romantic love. From the poems in Part 1 of this unit, choose what you consider to be the most interesting example of friendship. Write the first draft of an essay in which you detail the author's presentation of this friendship and explain why you find it most interesting.

17. Nature is often used as a symbol in literature. Choose the selection that you believe most effectively presents nature symbolically. For example, you might choose a sonnet of Spenser, Sidney, or Shakespeare, or "The Passionate Shepherd to His Love." Write an essay in which you analyze the effectiveness of the writer's presentation of nature.

18. Choose a single poem and study it until you feel you understand it thoroughly. Then write an essay in which you closely analyze the poet's use of imagery and explain how it con-tributes to the poem's total effect.

from *Utopia* by Sir Thomas More
Elizabeth's Speech Before Her Troops by Queen Elizabeth I

Selection Test

Critical Reading

On the line, write the letter of the one best answer.

____ 1. According to More, what traits in a king do his subjects ultimately hate and scorn?
  a. wickedness and selfishness
  b. sloth or pride
  c. disorder or boldness
  d. dissatisfaction and fraud

____ 2. What kind of leadership seems the most detestable to More?
  a. leadership based on pride, disorder, and scorn
  b. leadership based on hatred
  c. leadership based on contempt, mismanagement, and impoverishment
  d. leadership as an outgrowth of crime

____ 3. What does More mean by the following sentence?

  He is a poor physician who cannot cure a disease except by throwing his patient into another.

  a. It is a bad ruler who solves the problems of his kingdom by sacrificing his own people.
  b. Bad rulers tend to cope poorly during crises of disease.
  c. Bad rulers, like poor physicians, use unorthodox methods to solve their problems.
  d. Fabricius is a bad ruler because he mistreats his people.

____ 4. According to More, what constitutes generosity of heroic proportions in a monarch?
  a. resisting the seizure of property
  b. scorning poverty
  c. reigning over rich and happy subjects
  d. taking care of his subjects before himself

____ 5. How does More think poverty plays a role in the downfall of a king?
  a. Poverty often leads to the bankruptcy of the court.
  b. Impoverished subjects are unhappy and more likely to rise up against the king.
  c. Poverty can lead to the kind of widespread crime that disables the court.
  d. The impoverished can so lower the spirit of a king that he quits his kingdom.

____ 6. Summarizing long, difficult sentences you read mainly involves
  a. restating the main idea.
  b. restating both the main and supporting ideas.
  c. paraphrasing the conclusion.
  d. identifying supporting ideas as they relate to the conclusion.

____ 7. What key way does More expect a king to show the courage of a hero?
  a. by tending to his people's happiness over his own
  b. by maintaining the peace
  c. by governing poor subjects
  d. by curbing crime and governing free people

____ 8. How might you best summarize this complex sentence from Queen Elizabeth's speech?

> My loving people, we have been persuaded by some, that are careful of our safety, to take heed how we commit ourselves to armed multitudes, for fear of treachery. . . .

    a. Advisers warn the queen to go among her troops carefully, for fear of traitors among the soldiers.
    b. Those who worry about the kingdom's safety fear treachery above all else.
    c. The queen has been convinced that it is important to remain committed to the army.
    d. The queen has been warned that fear of treachery will mean the outbreak of war.

____ 9. In her "Speech Before Defeating the Spanish Armada," what most dramatically illustrates Queen Elizabeth's heroism?
    a. her admission that she "is a weak and feeble woman"
    b. her assurance that she will pay rewards to her people
    c. her declared loyalty to her subjects
    d. her resolve to die for her kingdom

____ 10. To what is Elizabeth referring when she claims to have the heart of a king?
    a. She possesses the kind of compassion for her subjects that a king possesses.
    b. She loves her beloved with the strength of a king.
    c. Although she is "a weak and feeble" woman, she has the soul and determination of a king.
    d. She knows that she will die like a king.

____ 11. Which of these quotations from her speech shows that Elizabeth trusts her people?
    a. "I have placed my chiefest strength and safeguard in the loyal hearts . . . of my subjects."
    b. ". . . to lay down . . . for my kingdom . . . my honor and my blood . . ."
    c. "I myself will take up arms . . ."
    d. ". . . you have deserved rewards and crowns . . ."

____ 12. What is the main idea in this passage from Elizabeth's speech?

> . . . rather than any dishonor grow by me, I myself will take up arms. . . .

    a. Elizabeth vows to give in to her enemies should she be dishonored.
    b. The queen will not be responsible for war.
    c. Elizabeth will go to war herself before dishonoring her kingdom.
    d. If Elizabeth dishonors her kingdom, she pledges to go to war.

____ 13. What do you think Elizabeth means by "the enemies of my God"?
    a. foes of the kingdom   c. opposers of her religion
    b. traitors to her father   d. opposers of her Catholicism

____ 14. According to Elizabeth, what makes her subjects worthy for battle?
    a. their behavior in the camp and their courage in the field
    b. their obedience and nobility
    c. their virtues in the field and valor in the camp
    d. their strength and loyal hearts

Vocabulary and Grammar

On the line, write the letter of the one best answer.

____ 15. A monarch whose aim is the complete ____ of his subjects' holdings is no prince of the people.
    a. sloth   c. treachery
    b. impoverishment   d. confiscation

____ 16. A complex sentence contains a main clause and
  a. one other independent clause.
  b. one or more subordinate clauses.
  c. one or more nonrestrictive clauses.
  d. just one dependent clause.

____ 17. Which word is most nearly the same in meaning as *abrogated*?
  a. censored
  b. abridged
  c. impaired
  d. abolished

____ 18. When Elizabeth said that the lieutenant general should act in her stead at wartime, she meant he should
  a. have her horse at the ready.
  b. take on the role of monarch when war breaks out.
  c. represent her on the battlefield.
  d. take on the role of prince when war breaks out.

____ 19. How might you best combine these two simple sentences into a complex sentence?

  Elizabeth had a sad childhood. She grew up to have a colorful personality.

  a. Elizabeth had a sad childhood but a colorful personality.
  b. Elizabeth had a sad childhood and grew up to have a colorful personality.
  c. Although Elizabeth had a sad childhood, she grew up to have a colorful personality.
  d. Elizabeth grew up to have a colorful personality despite the fact that she had a sad childhood.

____ 20. How might you best combine these three simple sentences into a complex sentence?

  His enemy initially came to his aid. He reflected a moment. The soldier chose to kill his enemy.

  a. His enemy initially came to his aid, so after reflecting a moment, the soldier chose to kill his enemy.
  b. Although his enemy initially came to his aid, after he reflected a moment, the soldier chose to kill his enemy.
  c. When his enemy initially came to his aid, he reflected a moment, and chose to kill his enemy.
  d. Because his enemy initially came to his aid, he reflected a moment, and chose to kill his enemy.

Essay Questions

21. Elizabeth I was very popular with her subjects, who generally trusted her leadership. Suppose that you were a subject of Elizabeth's and were present for her rallying speech. Write an essay describing how her speech made you feel. What would your reaction have been? Why?

22. Both Sir Thomas More and Elizabeth I had strong ideas about the leadership qualities monarchs should have. Whose ideas about leadership, More's or the queen's, do you think are the most on target? Write an essay in which you argue for your choice. How realistic do the ideas seem? How detailed? Support your points with details from the selections.

23. Sir Thomas More invented the word *utopia* as a title for his book. In Latin, the new word meant "no place." Write an essay in which you connect this word to More's ideas. From what you have read of his book, why do you think he chose this title? What does the word *utopia* mean today? Why do you suppose More felt he needed to invent a new word for the title of his book?

from The King James Bible

Selection Test

Critical Reading

On the line, write the letter of the one best answer.

_____ 1. Which is the main idea of Psalm 23?
   a. The Lord protects all living creatures.
   b. If one believes in the Lord, there is nothing to fear.
   c. Life is everlasting under the Lord's eye.
   d. Goodness and mercy are shown only to those who believe in the Lord.

_____ 2. Which of the following was most likely the purpose of Psalm 23?
   a. to portray events in the Holy Land
   b. to tell of historical events
   c. to describe people's reliance upon animals
   d. to be used as a hymn for public worship

_____ 3. Which kind of figurative language is used in this first line of Psalm 23?

   The Lord is my shepherd; I shall not want.

   a. hyperbole   c. metaphor
   b. simile   d. personification

_____ 4. Psalm 23 can be characterized as lyrical because it
   a. expresses the feelings and observations of a single speaker.
   b. tells a story from which a moral can be drawn.
   c. has no consistent rhyme scheme.
   d. can be accompanied by music.

_____ 5. You can infer that the phrase "I will dwell in the house of the Lord forever" in Psalm 23, means that
   a. I will never die.
   b. When I die, I will be buried in the Lord's temple.
   c. My spirit will be with the Lord for eternity.
   d. The Lord will protect me from my enemies.

_____ 6. In "The Sermon on the Mount," Jesus is explaining why
   a. people cannot change their condition in life.
   b. God takes care of the things in nature.
   c. people should trust in God to care for their worldly needs.
   d. food and clothing are necessary.

_____ 7. The word that best describes "The Sermon on the Mount" is _____.
   a. speech   c. dialogue
   b. poem   d. lyric

_____ 8. In "The Sermon on the Mount," Jesus is explaining that people should
   a. serve God alone and not pursue worldly wealth.
   b. take care what they eat and drink.
   c. consider themselves equal to all of nature.
   d. consider the glory of Solomon.

_____ 9. What does Jesus mean in "The Sermon on the Mount" when he says the following?

Is not the life more than meat, and the body than raiment?

a. Stylish clothing is not essential for survival.
b. Food and clothing are of secondary importance.
c. Life is dependent upon physical necessities.
d. Meat is not important to the diet.

_____ 10. Which phrase best summarizes the inferred meaning of this sentence from "The Sermon on the Mount"?

Which of you by taking thought can add one cubit unto his stature?

a. You have to accept what you are.
b. Thinking about it will not make you taller.
c. Worrying cannot change things.
d. You should not concern yourself with the things of this world.

_____ 11. "The Parable of the Prodigal Son" is most importantly about
a. greed.   c. charity.
b. forgiveness.   d. sibling rivalry.

_____ 12. The main lesson of "The Parable of the Prodigal Son" revolves around the behavior of the
a. elder son.   c. younger son.
b. servants.   d. father.

_____ 13. In "The Parable of the Prodigal Son," how does the father feel toward the son who stayed home?
a. He loves him as much as he loves his prodigal son.
b. He is angry that his son won't join the feasting.
c. He feels that his son has been guilty of breaking his commandments.
d. He feels his son is unworthy.

_____ 14. "The Parable of the Prodigal Son" can be described as a story because it
a. conveys a moral or religious message.
b. contains figurative language.
c. can be set to music.
d. is a narrative of events.

_____ 15. The prodigal son wants to become one of his father's hired servants because
a. he wants to earn his inheritance back.
b. he wants to help his brother.
c. he is homesick.
d. he is starving and wants to earn food.

_____ 16. By the way that the father treated his prodigal son, you can infer that the father was
a. angry that his son had returned penniless.
b. hoping to hire his son as a servant.
c. happy that his son had returned.
d. hoping the prodigal son would take his brother's place.

Vocabulary and Grammar

On the line, write the letter of the one best answer.

_____ 17. Which word or phrase is most nearly the same in meaning as _transgressed_?
a. crisscrossed an area   c. violated a law
b. made a mistake   d. changed

_____ 18. Which of the following contains an infinitive phrase?
   a. "or else he will hold to the one, and despise the other . . ."
   b. "and he began to be in want. . . ."
   c. "And the younger of them said to his father . . ."
   d. "And he went and joined himself to a citizen . . . of that country. . . ."

_____ 19. The infinitive phrase in ". . . and am no more worthy to be called thy son" is a(n) _____ that _____ .
   a. adjective; modifies "son"
   b. noun; is the subject of the sentence
   c. noun; is a direct object
   d. adverb; modifies "worthy"

_____ 20. The son believed he had never _____ any of his father's rules.
   a. entreated   c. despised
   b. transgressed   d. expended

Essay Questions

21. Psalm 23 explains the relationship between God and human beings. The language in the psalm requires the reader to make inferences about that relationship. In an essay, explain the relationship that is being described. What are the main comparisons that convey it? Make specific references to the psalm to support your position.

22. "The Parable of the Prodigal Son" is about the forgiveness of a father for his son who has gone astray. The parable can also be understood to reflect the relationship between God and human beings. Write an essay from this perspective in which you explain what this relationship is. What do you think is the role of the son who remained faithful?

23. Animals and animal imagery play a prominent role in the three selections from The King James Bible. In an essay, discuss how animals help convey the point of each of the selections. What does each of the animals symbolize? Use specific examples to make your points.

from *A Man for All Seasons* by Robert Bolt

Selection Test

Critical Reading

On the line, write the letter of the one best answer.

_____ 1. Which of the following quotations best expresses the threat Henry is making to More for failing to support his divorce?
    a. "Thomas, you understand me; we will stay here together and make music."
    b. "And thank God I have a friend for my Chancellor. Readier to be friends, I trust, than he was to be Chancellor."
    c. "I was right to break him; he was all pride, Thomas; a proud man; pride right through."
    d. ". . . there is a mass that follows me because it follows anything that moves—and there is you."

_____ 2. From which book of the Bible does the following quote come?

    Thou shalt not uncover the nakedness of thy brother's wife.

    a. Deuteronomy   c. Leviticus
    b. Pentateuch   d. Kings I

_____ 3. Which word best sums up Henry's relationship with the Catholic Church?
    a. cooperative   c. disproportionate
    b. antagonistic   d. conciliatory

_____ 4. Henry's insistence on divorcing Catherine despite the Pope's objection can be best attributed to his
    a. unbridled vanity.   c. idle nature.
    b. political daring.   d. lust for power.

_____ 5. What two personal interests does Henry reveal in this selection?
    a. music and sailing   c. sailing and writing
    b. hunting and cooking   d. hunting and music

_____ 6. What "duty" does Henry cite in justifying his desire to divorce Catherine?
    a. to follow his heart's desire
    b. to create a more just church
    c. to leave a son as heir to the throne
    d. to protect his brother's widow

_____ 7. Why does Henry mention the name of Wolsley during his conversation with More?
    a. to give an example of how generous the king can be
    b. to threaten More with his replacement as chancellor
    c. to entice More with the prospect of becoming prime minister
    d. to remind More of what happens to people who oppose the king

_____ 8. Which reason best explains Henry's efforts to enlist More's support?
    a. More can convince the Pope to approve Henry's divorce.
    b. More's honest support would help ease Henry's conscience.
    c. He needs More in order to win the support of Lord Cromwell.
    d. More's support would provide Henry the pretext for creating a new church.

_____ 9. Which line most clearly expresses More's opposition to Henry?

    a. "I am sick to think how much I must displease Your Grace."

    b. "There is my right arm. Take your dagger and saw it from my shoulder, and I will laugh and be thankful, if by that means I can come with Your Grace with a clear conscience."

    c. "As I think of it I see so clearly that I can not come with Your Grace that my endeavor is not to think of it at all."

    d. "Your Grace is unjust. I am Your Grace's loyal minister."

_____ 10. What relationship was Catherine to Henry before their marriage?

    a. sister-in-law   c. niece

    b. second cousin   d. no relation

Essay Questions

11. Henry implies that he would prefer to live a quiet life away from court in pursuit of his personal interests, rather than dealing with the headaches of being a monarch. Write an essay explaining why a ruler with Henry's absolute power might feel that way. What are the pros and cons of Henry's situation? Make a judgment about how sincere Henry is in his desire to retreat from power. Support your judgment with excerpts from the selection.

12. The practice of absolute power depends on people's blind faith in authority, that is, in their willingness to carry out any order, no matter how outrageous. Write an essay exploring how this expectation unfolds in the relationship between More and Henry. Why does More's opposition threaten the survival of the monarchy as Henry knew it?

13. For all his absolute power as monarch, Henry strained to convince More and others of his right to divorce Catherine. Write an essay speculating on why Henry should feel the need to persuade his followers that his conduct is right. Identify the constraints, both real and imagined, that Henry faced in the practice of his power.

Part Test, Unit 2, Part 2:
The Story of Britain—The Influence of the Monarchy

Critical Reading

The questions below are based on the following selection.

This selection is "I Corinthians 13" from the King James Bible—a letter in which Paul advises the Corinthians on the importance of charity.

Though I speak with the tongues of men and of angels, and have not charity, I am become as sounding brass, or a tinkling cymbal. And though I have the gift of prophecy, and understand all mysteries, and all knowledge; and though I have all faith, so that I could remove mountains, and have not charity, I am nothing. And though I bestow all my goods to feed the poor, and though I give my body to be burned, and have not charity, it profiteth me nothing. Charity suffereth long, and is kind; charity envieth not; charity vaunteth not itself, is not puffed up, doth not behave itself unseemly, seeketh not her own, is not easily provoked, thinketh no evil; rejoiceth not in iniquity, but rejoiceth in the truth; beareth all things, believeth all things, hopeth all things, endureth all things. Charity never faileth: but whether there be prophecies, they shall fail; whether there be tongues, they shall cease; whether there be knowledge, it shall vanish away. For we know in part, and we prophesy in part. But when that which is perfect is come, then that which is in part shall be done away. When I was a child, I spake as a child, I understood as a child. I thought as a child: but when I became a man, I put away childish things. For now we see through a glass darkly; but then face to face: now I know in part; but then shall I know even as also I am known. And now abideth faith, hope, charity, these three; but the greatest of these is charity.

On the line, write the letter of the one best answer.

_____ 1. What analogy does Paul use to clarify his main point?
   a. He compares himself to a prophecy.
   b. He compares himself to mountains.
   c. He compares himself to a cymbal.
   d. He compares himself to angels.

_____ 2. A good restatement of the second sentence is:
   a. A person lacking charity is worthless despite having total knowledge, the ability to tell the future, complete understanding of life's secrets, and power.
   b. Knowledge, understanding, and visionary powers are inadequate without faith.
   c. Moving mountains is impossible without charity.
   d. An extraordinarily eloquent person lacking charity is inadequate.

_____ 3. A speech offering religious or moral instruction is _____.
   a. a psalm
   b. a sermon
   c. an anecdote
   d. a parable

_____ 4. A good way to clarify a long or difficult sentence is to
   a. summarize its main idea.
   b. listen to the way it sounds.
   c. make inferences about the writer's tone.
   d. compare and contrast attitudes.

5. According to Paul's fourth sentence, which of the following is something that charity does?
   a. envies
   b. rejoices in iniquity
   c. seeks her own
   d. suffers

6. From context clues in the next-to-last sentence, you can infer that the clause "we see through a glass darkly" means that
   a. we see pessimistically.
   b. we cannot see at all.
   c. we see poorly.
   d. we see face to face.

7. What is the chief lesson Paul intended to teach?
   a. Adults must think differently than children.
   b. Charity is the most important virtue to practice.
   c. Charity rejoices in the truth.
   d. Faith, hope, and charity are of equal value to human beings.

8. Paul writes that he possesses all but which of the following?
   a. profits from charity
   b. faith that can remove mountains
   c. the ability to speak with the tongues of men and of angels
   d. the gift of prophecy

9. Paul encourages the Corinthians
   a. to think as children again.
   b. to speak prophecies.
   c. to think as adults.
   d. to understand all mysteries.

10. According to the next-to-last sentence, what will change in the future about the way Paul knows?
    a. He will know in part.
    b. He will know as a child.
    c. He will know as he is known.
    d. He will know as an adult.

Vocabulary and Grammar

The two questions below consist of a related pair of words in CAPITAL LETTERS, followed by four other pairs of words. Choose the pair that best expresses a relationship similar to that expressed in the capitalized words. Write the correct letter on the line.

11. FRAUDULENT : VALID ::
    a. feeble : young
    b. compassionate : unmerciful
    c. forfeited : ceded
    d. sloth : industry

12. BETRAYAL : TREACHERY ::
    a. stature : shape
    b. subsequent : previous
    c. confiscation : release
    d. morality : righteousness

On the line, write the letter of the one best answer.

____ 13. Which sentence does *not* contain an infinitive phrase?
   a. "No man can serve two masters; for either he will hate the one, and love the other; or else he will hold to the one, and despise the other."
   b. "He maketh me to lie down in green pastures."
   c. "I am no more worthy to be called thy son."
   d. "He began to be in want."

____ 14. Which of the following is a complex sentence?
   a. "Bring forth the best robe and put it on him."
   b. "Consider the lilies of the field, how they grow; they toil not, neither do they spin."
   c. "Though I walk through the valley of the shadow of death, I will fear no evil."
   d. "Thou preparest a table before me in the presence of mine enemies."

____ 15. Which word in the following sentence is modified by the infinitive phrase?

   He sent him into his fields to feed swine.

   a. He
   b. sent
   c. him
   d. fields

Essay Questions

16. Psalm 23 is sometimes read during funeral services. Write an essay in which you analyze why these verses from the King James Bible might offer consolation to people who have recently lost a loved one.

17. Though both parables and sermons are intended to instruct the listener or reader, they use different methods to achieve this end. In an essay, compare and contrast the ways in which "The Sermon on the Mount" and "The Parable of the Prodigal Son" instruct their audiences.

18. Sir Thomas More's *Utopia* was published in 1516. After rereading the excerpt several times and inferring meanings, write an essay in which you provide a clear, thorough explanation of possible social and political conditions in England in the early 1500's.

The Tragedy of Macbeth, **Act I,** by William Shakespeare

Selection Test

Critical Reading

On the line, write the letter of the one best answer.

_____ 1. What is the central theme of Act I of *The Tragedy of Macbeth*?
a. the price of fame
c. betrayal
b. the supernatural
d. loyalty in battle

_____ 2. *The Tragedy of Macbeth* and other Elizabethan plays represented a radical shift in English drama because they were
a. not about religious themes.
b. based upon ancient myths.
c. tragedies.
d. performed by both men and women.

_____ 3. Based upon the information in Act I, what appears to be Macbeth's character flaw?
a. an obsessive need to be loved
b. cowardice
c. a desire for power
d. slow-wittedness

_____ 4. During the Elizabethan period, theater companies began to
a. travel more.
b. use actors who were usually members of the nobility.
c. use permanent performance spaces.
d. cast men to play women and women to play men.

_____ 5. What important role do the witches play in Act I?
a. They help define the setting.
b. They provide historical background.
c. They help describe other characters.
d. They foreshadow events.

_____ 6. Based upon the information in Act I, what can you infer about King Duncan?
a. He is a weak leader.
b. He is a shrewd military planner.
c. He is reluctant to join his men in battle.
d. He places a high value on bravery and loyalty.

_____ 7. Which of the following best describes Macbeth's feelings about the possible assassination of King Duncan?
a. great confidence
b. tortured ambivalence
c. determined ambition
d. relentless guilt

_____ 8. Why does Lady Macbeth think Macbeth has a poor chance of achieving power?
a. He is not ruthless enough.
b. He lacks sufficient ambition.
c. He is too loyal to King Duncan.
d. He does not have the wit to devise a workable plan.

_____ 9. What do stage directions give the reader?
   a. definitions of certain text terms
   b. information about what is taking place on the stage
   c. information about the characters' backgrounds
   d. historical information about the play

_____ 10. Throughout Act I, Macbeth's plans and actions seem to be motivated most of all by
   a. his lust for wealth.   c. his wife's encouragement.
   b. the support of the witches.   d. the advice of Banquo.

_____ 11. Which of the following is an example of a stage direction?
   a. ALL. Fair is foul, and foul is fair. / Hover through the fog and filthy air.
   b. [*Thunder and lightning. Enter* THREE WITCHES.]
   c. 3. **Anon:** At once.
   d. FIRST WITCH. I come, Graymalkin.[1]

_____ 12. Elizabethan tragedies were modeled on plays from
   a. France.
   b. Eastern Europe in the Middle Ages.
   c. ancient Greece and Rome.
   d. early South American civilizations.

_____ 13. The annotations in *The Tragedy of Macbeth*, Act I, are a helpful aid for
   a. figuring out what characters are physically doing on stage.
   b. clarifying unfamiliar language.
   c. understanding theme.
   d. following the plot structure of the play.

_____ 14. In what way is Lady Macbeth stronger than her husband?
   a. She is harsher with the servants.
   b. She is better able to pretend she loves King Duncan.
   c. She stands firm when Macbeth begins to waver in his deadly purpose.
   d. She understands the witches' prophesies.

_____ 15. Which would be true if you were watching a play at the Globe Theater back in Shakespeare's day?
   a. The stage lighting would come from candles.
   b. The play would most likely be about a religious subject.
   c. The illusions of time and space would come from the words of the play.
   d. The audience would number about 15,000 people per performance.

Vocabulary and Grammar

On the line, write the letter of the one best answer.

_____ 16. Which of the following quotes from *The Tragedy of Macbeth* contains a linking verb?
   a. "A sailor's wife had chestnuts in her lap, / And mounched, and mounched, and mounched."
   b. "So fair and foul a day I have not seen."
   c. "Stay, you imperfect speakers, tell me more . . ."
   d. "What bloody man is that?"

_____ 17. Which of the following sentences contains an action verb?
   a. "The witches were on the path ahead."
   b. "Macbeth seemed transfixed by them."
   c. "Banquo called out to them."
   d. "What are these / So withered, and so wild in their attire, / That they look not like th' inhabitants of th' earth, and yet are on 't?"

____ 18. *Imperial* and *sovereign* are examples of
  a. words about political relationships.
  b. action verbs.
  c. words about Shakespeare.
  d. linking verbs.

____ 19. The soldier who sold secrets to the enemy army was imprisoned for ____ .
  a. valor
  b. liege
  c. sovereign
  d. treason

____ 20. Macbeth shows great ____ in battle.
  a. valor
  b. treason
  c. desperation
  d. perturbation

Essay Questions

21. Throughout Shakespeare's plays, you will see stage directions such as [Aside] and [Alarum within]. Choose several of these stage directions and explain what they mean. How do they help you understand *The Tragedy of Macbeth*, Act I? Give examples to support your answer.

22. The following lines are spoken by Lady Macbeth in *The Tragedy of Macbeth*, Act I, Scene v:

Come, you spirits / That tend on mortal thoughts, unsex me here, / And fill me, from the crown to the toe, top-full / of direst cruelty!

Write an essay in which you first explain the meaning of these lines and then relate them to the character of Lady Macbeth as she is depicted in Act I.

23. When the characters of Banquo and Macbeth are introduced in Act I, they appear quite similar in rank, loyalties, and character. However, as the act progresses, the two characters begin to diverge. Write an essay comparing and contrasting Macbeth and Banquo in this act. How do they seem alike? At what point do they first diverge? Give illustrations of their similarities and differences from Act I to support your position.

The Tragedy of Macbeth, **Act II**, by William Shakespeare

Selection Test

Critical Reading

On the line, write the letter of the one best answer.

_____ 1. What is the central idea of Shakespeare's *The Tragedy of Macbeth*, Act II?
  a. Ambition leads to madness.
  b. Tragedy befalls even honest men.
  c. A murderer must live with his conscience.
  d. Crime does not pay.

_____ 2. For which of the following reasons did Shakespeare probably choose to write *The Tragedy of Macbeth* in blank verse?
  a. to create a rhythmic effect
  b. to create an effect of natural speech
  c. to contrast with other metrical patterns
  d. to depart from conventional iambic pentameter

_____ 3. In Scene ii, Lady Macbeth's purpose in drugging the servants is
  a. so they will commit King Duncan's murder.
  b. so they will sleep through King Duncan's murder.
  c. to erase their memory of the night.
  d. to kill them for their knowledge of the crime.

_____ 4. Which of the following characterizes the line "This night's great business into my dispatch" as blank verse?
  a. It has ten syllables with the stress falling on every second syllable.
  b. It is written in iambic hexameter.
  c. It pauses in three places to help prevent a singsong rhythm.
  d. It has ten syllables and a varied pattern of stressed and unstressed syllables.

_____ 5. Which of the following symbols in Scene ii signals that the murder has been accomplished?
  a. the knocking at the south entry
  b. the words spoken by Malcolm and Donalbain
  c. the owl's scream and the crickets' cries
  d. the voice Macbeth hears

_____ 6. Macbeth declares he will "sleep no more" because he believes
  a. he will now become a fugitive.
  b. his conscience will never let him rest.
  c. he will not have sweet dreams.
  d. he will soon die.

_____ 7. What does Macbeth really mean when he indicates that the blood on his hands will redden all the seas?
  a. It is a comment on his profound guilt.
  b. Lady Macbeth will not be able to wash off the blood.
  c. It is a comment on his fear of being found out.
  d. He is afraid to wash the blood off his hands.

_____ 8. In the Old Man's dialogue in Scene iv, which of the following symbolizes King Duncan?
    a. a mousing owl   c. a horse
    b. darkness   d. a falcon

_____ 9. In the following quotation from Banquo, what does he say the purpose of meeting should be?

> And when we have our naked frailties hid, / That suffer in exposure, let us meet / And question this most bloody piece of work, / To know it further. Fears and scruples shake us.

    a. To know the bloody piece of work further
    b. To get shelter from the exposure suffered
    c. To shake their fears and scruples
    d. To hide their naked frailties

_____ 10. When Lady Macbeth says "My hands are of your color, but I shame / To wear a heart so white" she means that
    a. her hands are red with King Duncan's blood and she is ashamed.
    b. her hands are red with King Duncan's blood and she is afraid.
    c. her hands are red with King Duncan's blood, but, unlike her husband, she is not afraid.
    d. she will have to live with the murder of King Duncan for the rest of her life.

_____ 11. Why do you suppose Shakespeare made Banquo the last person Macbeth sees before he murders King Duncan?
    a. Banquo, who is loyal to the king, represents Macbeth's last chance to do what is right and call off his murderous plan.
    b. Banquo and Macbeth have both heard the witches' prophesies and Banquo probably knows what Macbeth is about to do.
    c. Shakespeare needed a bit of comic relief in the scene.
    d. Shakespeare needed to introduce the character of Fleance, who accompanies Banquo in the scene.

_____ 12. What reason does Lady Macbeth give for not killing King Duncan herself?
    a. She says that she is a woman and incapable.
    b. She says the witches' prophesy forbids it.
    c. She says the king looked like her father as he slept.
    d. She says that her husband must do it to prove his strength.

_____ 13. Unrhymed iambic pentameter is also called
    a. blank verse.   c. dialogue.
    b. a metric foot.   d. trochee.

_____ 14. To make sense of blank verse, you must
    a. read up to each line break and analyze before going on.
    b. read and analyze each full sentence, no matter where the line breaks.
    c. read each word as a separate thought.
    d. pay little attention to punctuation.

Vocabulary and Grammar

On the line, write the letter of the one best answer.

_____ 15. Which of the following sentences is correct?
    a. Lie down that dagger.   c. The dagger lie on the table.
    b. Lay down that dagger.   d. Macbeth has gone to lay down.

_____ 16. To creep through the castle without awakening anyone, Macbeth's footsteps must be _____ .
    a. imperial
    b. multitudinous
    c. palpable
    d. stealthy

_____ 17. The servants had _____ the table for supper.
    a. lie
    b. laid
    c. lain
    d. lay

_____ 18. As soon as Macbeth commits murder, the weight of his conscience becomes _____ .
    a. stealthy
    b. multitudinous
    c. palpable
    d. augmented

_____ 19. Banquo wants to _____ King Duncan, but Macbeth would rather take the king's place.
    a. entreat
    b. elucidate
    c. confound
    d. augment

_____ 20. How long the porter had _____ in bed is impossible to say.
    a. laid
    b. lay
    c. lain
    d. lied

Essay Questions

21. It is clear from Acts I and II that Macbeth has a vivid and often quite accurate imagination. Write an essay explaining how Macbeth's imagination works in Act II. What things does he imagine? How does his imagination affect his actions? Use examples from Act II to support your ideas.

22. The following lines are spoken by Macbeth in Act II, Scene ii:

Methought I heard a voice cry 'Sleep no more! / Macbeth does murder sleep'—the innocent sleep, / Sleep that knits up the raveled sleave of care, / The death of each day's life, sore labor's bath, / Balm of hurt minds, great nature's second course, / Chief nourisher in life's feast . . .

In an essay, discuss the meaning of these lines for Macbeth. Why do you think Shakespeare chose to portray Macbeth as so conscience-stricken by his deed? How would the story be different if Macbeth's actions caused him no moral suffering?

23. Contrast is one of the most effective devices a writer can use to add vividness to the depiction of characters. Write an essay in which you explain how the characterizations of Macbeth and Lady Macbeth are enhanced by contrast in the scenes that precede and follow the murder of Duncan in Act II.

The Tragedy of Macbeth, Act III, by William Shakespeare

Selection Test

Critical Reading

On the line, write the letter of the one best answer.

_____ 1. To persuade the two murderers to agree to kill Banquo, Macbeth tells them
a. he will make them officials of the court.
b. they will be given a large sum of money and a place to live.
c. that Banquo has been the cause of all their misery.
d. that they will be immune from imprisonment forever.

_____ 2. In Scene ii, what is the connotation of the word *scorpions* in this line?

O, full of scorpions is my mind, dear wife

a. thoughts   c. superstitions
b. doubts   d. horrors

_____ 3. Act III of Macbeth serves mainly to
a. introduce the play's climax.
b. expose Macbeth's mounting troubles.
c. introduce important new characters.
d. resolve the play's central conflicts.

_____ 4. What is the cause of Macbeth's irrational behavior at the banquet?
a. too much to drink   c. a sudden illness
b. a lack of sleep   d. his guilty conscience

_____ 5. When Macbeth says to Lady Macbeth in Scene iv, "We are yet but young in deed," he means that they are
a. just learning how to rule. c. new to the ways of crime.
b. a young king and queen.   d. innocent of crime.

_____ 6. Macbeth's guilt causing him to imagine he sees Banquo's ghost at the banquet is an example of
a. external conflict.   c. theme.
b. internal conflict.   d. poetic license.

_____ 7. By the end of Act III, how has Macbeth changed since the beginning of the play?
a. He is now quick to use treachery to suit his ends.
b. He now enjoys the respect of his comrades.
c. He is now comfortable with the witches' prophecies.
d. He now has confidence in his ability to rule.

_____ 8. Why does Macbeth send along a third murderer to join the first two in killing Banquo?
a. Macbeth has become terribly suspicious and trusts no one; he sends the third murderer to make certain the job gets done.
b. The third murderer had his own reasons for wanting Banquo dead and asked to be sent.
c. Macbeth knows that Fleance is strong and quick; he feels a third murderer will be needed.
d. The first and second murderers are employed by Banquo.

_____ 9. When Lady Macbeth claims "Nought's had, all's spent, / Where our desire is got without content . . ." she means that
   a. she and Macbeth have quarreled.
   b. she and Macbeth have risked everything but have gained no happiness because they are living in fear.
   c. she regrets the killing of Duncan.
   d. she does not want Macbeth to have Banquo killed.

_____ 10. In Scene i, Macbeth is glad that Banquo will not be returning to the palace until nightfall because
   a. Macbeth wants Banquo to arrive late to the banquet.
   b. Banquo is the guest of honor at the banquet.
   c. Macbeth wants Banquo killed under cover of darkness.
   d. Macbeth hopes that Banquo will become lost.

_____ 11. When Act III begins, Banquo says that he knows
   a. he will one day be king.
   b. Macbeth killed Duncan.
   c. Macbeth plans to kill him.
   d. he will not be attending the banquet that evening.

_____ 12. When Macbeth says "Upon my head they placed a fruitless crown / And put a barren scepter in my gripe . . ." he means
   a. he is powerless.
   b. he will be prosecuted for his crimes.
   c. he and Lady Macbeth want many children.
   d. he has no male heir.

_____ 13. Which of the following is an external conflict?
   a. Before Macbeth kills King Duncan, he imagines he sees a dagger floating in the air in front of him.
   b. Macbeth regrets killing King Duncan, although he would do it again if necessary.
   c. Macbeth wants Banquo dead, so he hires men to murder him.
   d. At the banquet, Macbeth's guilty conscience conjures up an image of the dead Banquo.

_____ 14. Why does Macbeth fear Banquo?
   a. Banquo is loyal to the true king.
   b. He knows that Banquo wants to kill him.
   c. Banquo wants to steal the crown away from him.
   d. Banquo has a male heir.

_____ 15. In a play, the rising action consists of the events that lead up to the
   a. last line in the scene.
   b. climax.
   c. external conflict.
   d. internal conflict.

Vocabulary and Grammar

On the line, write the letter of the one best answer.

_____ 16. In which of the following sentences do the subject and verb agree?
   a. Lady Macbeth, mistress of many servants, are on the way to the banquet hall.
   b. When Banquo and Fleance approached the palace, Banquo were killed.
   c. Fleance escape.
   d. When he first enters the banquet hall, Macbeth appears jocund.

____ 17. Macbeth fears Banquo's ____ heart.
   a. jocund
   b. dauntless
   c. infirm
   d. broken

____ 18. At the banquet, Lady Macbeth encourages her husband to be ____ .
   a. jocund
   b. indissoluble
   c. infirm
   d. passionate

____ 19. There is none but ____ / Whose being I do fear . . ."
   a. they
   b. he
   c. himself
   d. them

____ 20. Banquo's allegiance to King Duncan was ____ .
   a. jocund
   b. infirm
   c. indissoluble
   d. malicious

Essay Questions

21. In Shakespeare's plays, soliloquies reveal a character's true thoughts and feelings and often indicate how circumstances are developing for the character. Write an essay in which you explain what the following soliloquy reveals about Lady Macbeth's situation and state of mind in Act III, Scene ii.

   Nought's had, all's spent, / Where our desire is got without content: / 'Tis safer to be that which we destroy / Than be destruction dwell in doubtful joy.

22. In some ways, the murder of Banquo represents an act of betrayal even more foul than that of Duncan. Write an essay discussing this statement. In what ways are the murders similar? In what ways do they differ? What changes does the plot to murder Banquo reveal in Macbeth?

23. In Act III, Scene ii, Macbeth says that he and his wife must make their faces *vizards*, or masks, to their hearts. *The Tragedy of Macbeth* contains many instances in which the characters mask their thoughts, feelings, or desires. Write an essay about the theme of "masks"—betrayal, falsehood, and concealment—in Act III of the play. Which characters use them? What do they conceal and why? Are the masks necessarily evil? Use examples from the text to illustrate your points.

The Tragedy of Macbeth, **Act IV,** by William Shakespeare

Selection Test

Critical Reading

On the line, write the letter of the one best answer.

____ 1. A major purpose of Act IV is to foreshadow events related to
    a. Lady Macbeth's fate.   c. Macbeth's downfall.
    b. Macduff's family.   d. Malcolm's future.

____ 2. When the witch says, "Something wicked this way comes," you know that
    a. the apparitions are about to appear.
    b. even the witches now consider Macbeth evil.
    c. the witches' "master" is approaching.
    d. the witches are afraid of Macbeth.

____ 3. After visiting the witches, why does Macbeth initially change his mind and decide not to have Macduff killed?
    a. He knows Macduff has fled to England.
    b. He is reassured by the third apparition.
    c. He believes the witches will protect Macduff.
    d. He decides instead to kill Macduff's wife.

____ 4. Which of the following best describes how Shakespeare portrays Macduff's son in Act IV?
    a. shy and confused
    b. cheerful and naive
    c. fearful and timid
    d. questioning and courageous

____ 5. In Scene iii, what finally convinces Malcolm that Macduff is loyal?
    a. Macduff's reaction to the murder of his family
    b. Macduff's noble despair for his country
    c. Macduff's professed hatred for Macbeth
    d. Macduff's attempts to refute Malcolm's claims of character flaws

____ 6. Which of the following lines spoken by Malcolm best conveys how he really feels about Scotland?
    a. ". . . yet my poor country / Shall have more vices than it had before . . ."
    b. ". . . were I King, / I should cut off the nobles for their lands . . ."
    c. ". . . It weeps, it bleeds, and each new day a gash / Is added to her wounds."
    d. "If such a one be fit to govern, speak: / I am as I have spoken."

____ 7. The end of Act IV foreshadows an important conflict between
    a. Macbeth and Macduff.
    b. Malcolm and Ross.
    c. Macbeth and his wife.
    d. Macduff and Malcolm.

____ 8. In Elizabethan theater, ____ was especially important because there were no elaborate special effects, lighting, or sets.
    a. blank verse   c. stage makeup
    b. imagery   d. costuming

_____ 9. In Act IV, Macbeth visits the witches because he thinks that
  a. their evil doings can help him maintain his power.
  b. they can turn back the hands of time.
  c. by killing them, he can escape his fate.
  d. they can rid him of Banquo's ghost.

_____ 10. What is imagery?
  a. blank verse
  b. Shakespearean language
  c. language that writers use to re-create sensory experiences
  d. very formal language

_____ 11. Which senses do the following lines appeal to?

> This avarice / Sticks deeper, grows with more pernicious root / Than summer-seeming lust, and it hath been / The sword of our slain kings.

  a. hearing and touch   c. sight and smell
  b. taste and sight   d. sight and touch

_____ 12. Which sense does the following quotation appeal to?

> This tyrant, whose sole name blisters our tongues, / Was once thought honest.

  a. taste   c. touch
  b. sight   d. smell

_____ 13. One of the images that runs throughout the whole play is that of
  a. ships at sea.   c. brotherly love.
  b. battle armor.   d. blood.

_____ 14. Which of your senses does the following quote appeal to?

> Nay, had I pow'r, I should / Pour the sweet milk of concord into hell, / Uproar the universal peace, confound / All unity on earth.

  a. taste, touch, and hearing c. smell and touch
  b. sight, hearing, and smell d. taste

Vocabulary and Grammar

On the line, write the letter of the one best answer.

_____ 15. Macbeth's evil deeds have a _____ effect on Scotland.
  a. credulous   c. sundry
  b. judicious   d. pernicious

_____ 16. There is plenty of truth in the three _____ prophecies.
  a. witch's   c. witch'
  b. witches'   d. witches

_____ 17. The witches add wool of bat, tongue of dog, and other _____ ingredients to their caldron.
  a. credulous   c. avarice
  b. judicious   d. sundry

_____ 18. The first _____ contribution to the caldron is the venom of a sleeping toad.
  a. witch's   c. witch'
  b. witches'   d. witches

_____ 19. In Act IV, the _____ introduce Macbeth to apparitions who tell him more prophesies.
  a. witch's   c. witch'
  b. witches'   d. witches

____ 20. "But for your husband, / He is noble, wise, ____ , and best knows / The fits o' th' seasons . . ."
a. judicious
c. credulous
b. pernicious
d. sundry

Essay Questions

21. It might be said that with every act in *The Tragedy of Macbeth*, Macbeth becomes more evil. In Act I, Macbeth hears the witches' prophecies and considers doing evil; in Act II, he kills King Duncan; and in Act III, he kills his comrade Banquo. In an essay, discuss Macbeth's crime in Act IV. Why does Macbeth commit it? How is it different from the crimes Macbeth commits in the previous acts? Support your points with details from Act IV.

22. Macbeth appears only in the first of the three scenes in Act IV, yet his presence is strongly felt in Scenes ii and iii. Write an essay explaining how that presence is felt. How are the feelings of Lady Macduff produced by that "felt presence"? How does it affect the meeting between Malcolm and Macduff?

23. Critics sometimes suggest that the fourth acts of Shakespeare's plays represent a letdown in dramatic tension between the rising action of the earlier acts and the culminating events of the fifth act. Write an essay in which you evaluate each of the three scenes in Act IV of Macbeth for dramatic effectiveness and contribution to plot development.

Name _____ Date _____

The Tragedy of Macbeth, **Act V,** by William Shakespeare

Selection Test

Critical Reading

On the line, write the letter of the one best answer.

____ 1. What is the main message of *The Tragedy of Macbeth*, Act V, Scene i, which includes Lady Macbeth's sleepwalking scene?
   a. Illness comes to evil people.
   b. A guilty conscience is not easily mended.
   c. Wives should be forgiven for their husbands' misdeeds.
   d. One is doomed to relive evil deeds.

____ 2. In Scene iii, what does Macbeth's behavior toward the servant who comes to deliver a message ultimately show about Macbeth's character?
   a. He has grown brutal.
   b. He has remained honorable.
   c. He has grown timid.
   d. He has begun to lack confidence.

____ 3. When Macbeth reveals in Scene v that he has grown impervious to fear and horror, he is underscoring the play's theme of the
   a. destructiveness of blind ambition.
   b. conflict between love and ambition.
   c. betrayal of friends and family.
   d. senselessness of battle and the brevity of life.

____ 4. At what point does Macbeth first begin to realize that he has been tricked by the prophecies?
   a. when he confronts and kills Young Siward
   b. when he learns that Birnam Wood is moving toward the castle
   c. when he is told that Lady Macbeth is dead
   d. when Macduff reveals the details of how he was born

____ 5. In Act V, in what way does Macbeth revert to his former self?
   a. He laments the death of his wife.
   b. He treats his followers with respect.
   c. He fights with courage and skill.
   d. He places Scotland's interests before his own.

____ 6. Why does Shakespeare have Macbeth display certain admirable traits at the end of the play?
   a. to reinforce the idea that Macbeth is a victim of his tragic flaw
   b. so the audience will realize that Macbeth was deceived by the witches
   c. to make Macbeth's death seem less tragic
   d. so the audience will no longer consider Macbeth a villain.

____ 7. In Act V, which of the following represents the resolution of the plot?
   a. Lady Macbeth dies.
   b. Macbeth kills Young Siward.
   c. Macbeth vows to fight.
   d. Macduff kills Macbeth.

8. When the doctor watches Lady Macbeth sleepwalking, he
   a. prescribes her a potion.
   b. tells Lady Macbeth's servant to make certain she gets back to bed.
   c. goes after her to awaken her gently.
   d. is completely baffled.

9. You can infer that the doctors in Shakespeare's time knew very little about

   I. psychology.
   II. emotional distress.
   III. the mind-body connection.

   a. I and II   c. I and III
   b. II and III   d. I, II, and III

10. When the doctor tells the waiting-gentlewoman to take from Lady Macbeth "the means of all annoyance," it is because he fears that Lady Macbeth might
    a. be upset when she finds out she's been sleepwalking.
    b. be guilty of a crime of treason.
    c. plan to leave Dunsinane.
    d. try to kill herself.

11. When Macbeth says "Out, out, brief candle!" the word *candle* refers to
    a. the blood on his hands.
    b. life.
    c. death.
    d. his crown.

12. In Act V, Scene i, you can tell that the waiting-gentlewoman is
    a. afraid of the doctor.
    b. angry about the death of King Duncan.
    c. loyal to Lady Macbeth.
    d. disloyal to Macbeth and his wife.

13. Lady Macbeth kills herself because
    a. she cannot bear her guilt.
    b. her husband is about to be dethroned.
    c. she has gone insane.
    d. she is about to be attacked by Malcolm's forces.

14. At the end of the play, how does Macbeth's courage in battle affect the reader?
    a. It brings the reader full circle by once again pointing up an aspect of his noble nature.
    b. It brings up a new side of Macbeth, one of bravery in the face of adversity.
    c. It shows that Macbeth is courageous only in desperation.
    d. It shows Macbeth's hatred for Malcolm and Macduff.

Vocabulary and Grammar

On the line, write the letter of the one best answer.

15. Which of the following sentences has a correct pronoun and antecedent?
    a. When Macbeth finds out Lady Macbeth is dead, she continues to fight.
    b. Although Macbeth grieves for Lady Macbeth, her response is that she would have died soon anyway.
    c. Macbeth hears of his wife's death, which makes him very sad, but he continues to fight.
    d. Lady Macbeth is dead, but he can't give up.

_____ 16. The trees of Birnham Wood moving toward Dunsinane are _____ of Macbeth's downfall.
   a. clamorous
   b. developments
   c. harbingers
   d. perturbations

_____ 17. "Life's but a walking shadow, a poor player / That struts and frets _____ hour upon the stage / And then is heard no more."
   a. its
   b. his
   c. a poor player's
   d. their

_____ 18. The servant and the doctor hide _____ in the shadows when Lady Macbeth comes by, sleepwalking.
   a. themselves
   b. himself
   c. herself
   d. oneself

_____ 19. Lady Macbeth's guilt causes her a great _____ of spirit.
   a. harbinger
   b. perturbation
   c. development
   d. fortification

_____ 20. The witches dance wildly around their caldron in a _____ frenzy.
   a. clamorous
   b. pristine
   c. perturbed
   d. virtuous

Essay Questions

21. In stories, plays, or films, it is always satisfying when villains get what they deserve in the end. In an essay, discuss whether this is the case with Macbeth and Lady Macbeth or whether they might have gotten off too easily. Do you think their fate would have been the same if they'd committed the same deeds today? Use events in the play to support your argument.

22. Early in Act V, Lady Macbeth's doctor says, "Unnatural deeds / Do breed unnatural troubles." Write an essay in which you explain how this remark may be applied to Lady Macbeth's condition at this point and to the general situation in Macbeth's realm.

23. The following excerpt from *The Tragedy of Macbeth* is one of the most quoted passages ever written in the English language.

Tomorrow, and tomorrow, and tomorrow / Creeps in this petty pace from day to day, / To the last syllable of recorded time; / And all our yesterdays have lighted fools / The way to dusty death. Out, out brief candle! / Life's but a walking shadow, a poor player / That struts and frets his hour upon the stage / And then is heard no more. It is a tale / Told by an idiot, full of sound and fury / Signifying nothing.

Write an essay explaining what you think this passage means. How does it relate to Macbeth's situation? Why do you think it has fascinated readers throughout the centuries?

Name _____ Date _____

from *Oedipus the King* by Sophocles

Selection Test

Critical Reading

On the line, write the letter of the one best answer.

____ 1. Which quotation best illustrates Oedipus's sense of duty as king?
    a. "I Oedipus whom all men call the Great."
    b. "I pity you children. You have come full of longing."
    c. "My spirit groans for city and myself and you at once."
    d. "I would be very hard should I not pity suppliants such as these."

____ 2. Why does the priest call Oedipus the "savior" of Thebes?
    a. Oedipus promises to cleanse the city of the plague.
    b. Oedipus freed the city from the power of the Sphinx.
    c. Oedipus saved the city from the evil reign of King Laius.
    d. Oedipus captured and killed Jocasta.

____ 3. Why didn't the people of Thebes try to solve King Laius's murder at the time it was committed?
    a. They were beset by other problems.
    b. They were afraid of Oedipus.
    c. They were glad Laius was dead.
    d. They had helped murder him.

____ 4. Which of the following lines spoken by Oedipus best portrays his tragic situation?
    a. "And justly you will see in me an ally, a champion of my country and the God."
    b. "God will decide if we prosper or remain in sorrow."
    c. "How could a robber dare a deed like this were he not helped with money from the city, money and treachery?"
    d. "When I drive pollution from the land I will not serve a distant friend's advantage, but act in my own interest."

____ 5. Who informs Oedipus of the god's pronouncement?
    a. the priest   c. Creon
    b. Jocasta   d. Laius

____ 6. Who is Cadmus?
    a. the father of the Sphinx
    b. the brother of King Laius
    c. the legendary founder of Thebes
    d. the god who foretells Oedipus's tragedy

____ 7. Which word best describes Oedipus's attitude to the suppliants who come to beg his favor?
    a. arrogant   c. aloof
    b. attentive   d. sympathetic

____ 8. Which episode is best considered the turning point in Oedipus's journey from successful king to tragic hero?
    a. when the priest calls Oedipus the "savior" of Thebes
    b. when Creon relays the message from the oracle
    c. when the suppliants beg Oedipus to eliminate the plague from the city
    d. when Oedipus kills the Sphinx

9. Which of the following statements best expresses the central theme of *Oedipus the King*?
     a. Without knowing the past, one is condemned to repeat it.
     b. Life is a difficult and cruel struggle of self-discovery.
     c. In the end, one loves one's desires and not what is desired.
     d. People are in full control of their destinies.

___ 10. Which word does *not* describe Oedipus's character?
     a. quick-tempered
     b. responsible
     c. resolute
     d. indifferent

Essay Questions

11. At the end of *Oedipus the King,* the chorus sums up the action with lines that mean "no one should be counted happy until freed by death from pain and sorrow." Write an essay explaining the connection between this statement and Oedipus's life. Describe Sophocles's outlook on life based on the selection and this final line.

12. One of the great paradoxes of Oedipus's story rests in the combined effect of fate and free will. Using examples from the selection, write an essay defining these two categories. Go on to make a judgment as to which one most determines Oedipus's life. What lessons can be learned from Oedipus's struggles?

13. Much of Oedipus's tragedy can be traced to the fact that he is unsure of his true identity. In an essay, explain how this fact contributes to the central message of the play. Relate his situation to one you are familiar with from contemporary films, books, or your own life. Argue for or against the idea that someone in Oedipus's situation should be held responsible for his actions.

Part Test, Unit 2, Part 3: Focus on Literary Forms—Drama

Critical Reading

The questions below are based on the following selection.

This selection is from The Tragical History of the Life and Death of Doctor Faustus *by Christopher Marlowe. Early in the play, Dr. Faustus, the main character, contracts his soul to Lucifer (also known as Mephistophilis) for special powers of the mind. Now facing perpetual damnation at midnight, he makes a desperate attempt to repent and save his soul.*

FAUST. Stand still, you ever-moving spheres of heaven,
That time may cease and midnight never come;
Fair Nature's eye, rise, rise again, and make
Perpetual day; or let this hour be but
A year, a month, a week, a natural day,
That Faustus may repent and save his soul! . . .
Mountains and hills, come, come and fall on me
And hide me from the heavy wrath of God. . . .

[*The watch strikes.*]

Ah, half the hour is past; 'will all be past anon.
O God,
If thou wilt not have mercy on my soul,
Yet for Christ's sake whose blood hath ransomed me
Impose some end to my incessant pain:
Let Faustus live in hell a thousand years,
A hundred thousand, and at last be saved!
O, no end is limited to damnèd souls!
Why wert thou not a creature wanting soul?
Or why is this immortal that thou hast? . . .
Cursed be the parents that engendered me!
No, Faustus, curse thyself, curse Lucifer
That hath deprived thee of the joys of heaven.

[*The clock strikes twelve.*]

It strikes, it strikes! Now, body, turn to air
Or Lucifer will bear thee quick to hell!

[*Thunder and lightning.*]

O soul, be changed to little water drops
And fall into the ocean, ne'er be found.
My God, my God, look not so fierce on me!

[*Enter* DEVILS.]

Adders and serpents, let me breathe awhile!
Ugly hell, gape not—come not, Lucifer—
I'll burn my books—ah, Mephistophilis!

[*Exit* DEVILS *with* FAUSTUS.]

On the line, write the letter of the one best answer.

_____ 1. To whom or what does Faust speak in the first two lines?
    a. himself
    c. the stars, planets, and moon
    b. Mephistophilis
    d. the gods

_____ 2. What does Faust mean by the phrase "fair nature's eye" in line 3?
    a. the sun
    c. time
    b. God
    d. the moon

_____ 3. This scene from Marlowe's Elizabethan drama is written in _____.
    a. prose
    c. blank verse
    b. free verse
    d. couplets

_____ 4. Which two of the reader's senses are most engaged by this passage?
    a. taste and touch
    c. smell and taste
    b. sight and hearing
    d. sight and smell

_____ 5. What is the meaning of Faust's question, "Why wert thou not a creature wanting soul"?
    a. He wonders why God has no soul.
    b. He questions whether any of God's creatures possess more soul than he.
    c. He considers himself more fortunate than a soulless creature.
    d. He would have preferred to be born a soulless creature rather than a human being.

_____ 6. In order to read Marlowe's scene for meaning, you need to focus on sentences rather than lines. Which one of these lines contains a complete thought?
    a. A year, a month, a week, a natural day
    b. Ah, half the hour is past; 'twill all be past anon
    c. Yet for Christ's sake whose blood hath ransomed me
    d. Or Lucifer will bear thee quick to hell

_____ 7. With what or whom is Faust primarily in conflict in this scene?
    a. God
    c. devils
    b. Lucifer
    d. himself

_____ 8. Reading between the lines helps you understand that in this scene Faust feels which one of the following emotions?
    a. confidence
    c. regret
    b. gratefulness
    d. pride

_____ 9. Which of the following is not the object of Faust's curses?
    a. Lucifer
    c. himself
    b. God
    d. his parents

_____ 10. The imagery in this scene is primarily related to
    a. human physiology.
    c. machines.
    b. the natural world.
    d. magic.

Vocabulary and Grammar

On the line, write the letter of the one best answer.

_____ 11. When Macbeth says that he sees the dagger in *palpable* form, he means that it is
    a. only a vision.
    b. not within reach.
    c. sharp.
    d. capable of being touched or felt.

____ 12. What is the best definition for *judicious* in the following passage?

> [Macbeth] is noble, wise, judicious, and best knows
> The fits o' th' seasons . . .

    a. showing poor judgment
    b. showing cowardice
    c. showing good judgment
    d. showing intelligence

____ 13. Early in Act III, Macbeth refers to the *dauntless* temper of Banquo's mind and claims that "'tis much he dares." In this context, the word *dauntless* means ____.
    a. incapable of being intimidated
    b. nervous and confused
    c. cautious
    d. diseased

The two questions below consist of a related pair of words in CAPITAL LETTERS, followed by four other pairs of words. Choose the pair that best expresses a relationship similar to that expressed in each capitalized pair of words. Write the correct letter on the line.

____ 14. IMPERIAL : EMPIRE ::
    a. regal : velvet   c. familial : family
    b. king : princely   d. rule : authority

____ 15. EQUIVOCATE : MISLEAD ::
    a. oath : swear   c. sundry : various
    b. enlarge : augment   d. lie : aver

On the line, write the letter of the one best answer.

____ 16. Which line contains a linking verb?
    a. "Nor would we deign him burial of his men."
    b. "The victory fell on us."
    c. "What bloody man is that?"
    d. "Ten thousand dollar to our general use."

____ 17. Which sentence contains incorrect agreement between a subject and verb?
    a. "So are he mine, and in such bloody distance that every minute of his being thrusts against my near'st of life."
    b. "Your spirits shine through you."
    c. "Treason has done his worst."
    d. "Things bad begun make strong themselves by ill."

____ 18. Which of the following is a singular possessive noun?
    a. men's   c. traitors'
    b. witches'   d. murderer's

____ 19. What is the antecedent of the pronoun *his* in the following speech?

> This guest of summer,
> The temple-haunting martlet, does approve
> By his loved mansionry that the heaven's breath
> Smells wooingly here.

    a. this   c. martlet
    b. guest   d. mansionry

____ 20. What is the subject of the following sentence?

> O, full of scorpions is my mind, dear wife!

    a. scorpions
    b. my
    c. mind
    d. wife

Essay Questions

21. As in most of Shakespeare's tragedies, several characters in *The Tragedy of Macbeth* die for different reasons and by various means. Write an obituary for one of the important characters—Macbeth, Lady Macbeth, Banquo, or Duncan—that dies during the play. In the obituary, summarize the person's life, indicate the cause or manner of death, and indicate key personality traits.

22. King Duncan is integral to the plot of *The Tragedy of Macbeth*. Reread the king's speeches in the play's early scenes and think about Shakespeare's portrayal of this character. In an essay, analyze Duncan's character traits and explain the importance of these traits in relation to the meaning of the play as a whole.

23. *The Tragedy of Macbeth* is a Shakespearean tragedy that is especially rich in imagery. Choose an important soliloquy from the play and analyze the imagery Shakespeare uses to create a certain effect.

24. Choose two important characters from the play and review their speeches and scenes. In an essay, compare and contrast the personality traits of these characters. You might choose Macbeth, Lady Macbeth, Banquo, Macduff, and/or Duncan.

25. There is considerable talk—and a handful of scenes, most notably featuring the witches—involving supernatural forces in *The Tragedy of Macbeth*. In an essay, explain the role of the witches and their prophecies in the tragedy's unfolding plot and themes.

Name _____ Date _____

Critical Reading

On the line, write the letter of the one best answer.

_____ 1. What is the message of "Holy Sonnet 10?"
  a. Death can never triumph because faith grants eternal life.
  b. Death is meant only to bring pleasure to humankind.
  c. Were it not for death, humans could never appreciate life.
  d. Death is part of life and is both good and evil.

_____ 2. "Holy Sonnet 10" can be considered a metaphysical conceit because
  a. the poem is a self-contradiction that reveals a kind of truth.
  b. philosophical and religious issues are set up in opposition to one another.
  c. it uses the image of death to make a point about life.
  d. an idea is debated by likening it to an arrogant but finally powerless tyrant.

_____ 3. Why is the seemingly contradictory phrase "Death, thou shalt die" actually true within the context of "Holy Sonnet 10?"
  a. The speaker believes he can kill Death.
  b. After death, a Christian awakes to eternal life.
  c. It is impossible for Death to do anything except die.
  d. Death can have no physical existence.

_____ 4. Which of the following pairs are the subjects of John Donne's "Song"?
  a. love and faith   c. love and death
  b. faith and death   d. faith and immortality

_____ 5. In "Song," the lines "Yesternight the sun went hence, / And yet is here today" are an example of
  a. a metaphysical conceit.   c. irony.
  b. an allusion.   d. a paradox.

_____ 6. Which of the following is the best interpretation of these lines from "Song"?

> When thou weep'st, unkindly kind,
> My life's blood doth decay.

  a. Although I have tried to keep it secret, you know I am dying.
  b. You cry because you love me, but your tears make me suffer.
  c. You are false-hearted, and your supposedly kind tears are meant to hide your true feelings.
  d. There is no kindness in this life, for we are both dying.

_____ 7. Which of the following excerpts from "A Valediction: Forbidding Mourning" is the best example of a metaphysical conceit?
  a. "So let us melt, and make no noise, / No tear-floods, nor sigh-tempests move, / 'Twere profanation of our joys / To tell the laity our love."
  b. "But we by a love so much refined, / That our selves know not what it is . . . "
  c. "Our two souls therefore, which are one, / Though I must go, endure not yet / A breach, but an expansion, / Like gold to airy thinness beat."
  d. "If they be two, they are two so / As stiff twin compasses are two; / Thy soul the fixed foot, makes no show / To move, but doth, if th'other do."

8. In "A Valediction: Forbidding Mourning," what do you recognize to be the speaker's motivation in the following lines?

> Our two souls therefore, which are one,/ Though I must go, endure not yet/ A breach, but an expansion.

   a. to tell his beloved that they will never meet again
   b. to assure his beloved that the distance will make their love grow
   c. to warn his beloved that careless thoughts might destroy his love
   d. to emphasize the distance that will be between them.

9. What can you infer about the speaker's situation from these final lines from "A Valediction: Forbidding Mourning"?

> Thy firmness makes my circle just,
> And makes me end where I begun.

   a. The speaker and his lover are bound, though they may be apart.
   b. The speaker feels he is going around in circles to attract his lover.
   c. The relationship between the speaker and his lover seems to go over the same ground again and again.
   d. The strength of the speaker's love keeps him prisoner.

10. In "Meditation 17," God is presented as being analogous to
    a. a child.
    b. a publisher.
    c. a bell.
    d. a preacher.

11. Which of the following excerpts from "Meditation 17" expresses the major theme of the poem?
    a. "Tribulation is treasure in the nature of it, but it is not current money in the use of it . . . "
    b. "The bell doth toll for him that thinks it doth . . . "
    c. "Any man's death diminishes me because I am involved in mankind . . . "
    d. "The church is catholic, universal, so are all her actions . . . "

12. In "Meditation 17," what is meant by the statement "when one man dies, one chapter is not torn out of the book, but translated into a better language . . . "?
    a. When we die, we do not cease to exist but instead achieve eternal life.
    b. Through our deaths, others learn how to live better lives.
    c. The church records both the lives and deaths of its members.
    d. If a written record is left of our lives, our lives will have been worthwhile.

13. What conclusion can you draw about the speaker's motive for writing "Meditation 17"?
    a. The speaker believes that people should try to avoid any suffering.
    b. The speaker wants to convey the importance of suffering and death in the spiritual experience.
    c. The speaker does not think that he himself will ever die.
    d. The speaker is being paid by the church to make this statement.

14. According to the argument Donne puts forth in "Meditation 17," how can one be affected by another's death?
    a. All human beings fear death.
    b. Death is powerful and saps strength from all who observe it.
    c. It is obligatory to mourn each time someone dies.
    d. Human beings are necessarily involved with one another.

Vocabulary and Grammar

On the line, write the letter of the one best answer.

____ 15. Which word best characterizes a situation in which a woman claims a neighbor's dog destroyed her garden and sues the neighbor?
a. profanation   b. breach   c. contention   d. covetousness

____ 16. Which of the following words means the opposite of *covetousness*?
a. jealousy   b. generosity   c. avarice   d. devotion

____ 17. Which word best characterizes the townspeople who are members of a church's congregation?
a. translators   b. laity   c. piety   d. affliction

____ 18. Which of the following sentences best changes the active voice of this statement into the passive voice?

> Affliction makes us more aware of death.

a. Affliction is making us more aware of death.
b. Death is made more aware to us by affliction.
c. We are made more aware of death by affliction.
d. More awareness of death is made by affliction.

____ 19. In which of the following excerpts does Donne use both the passive and active voices?
a. ". . . this bell calls us all; but how much more me, who am brought so near the door by this sickness."
b. "Truly it were an excusable covetousness if we did; for affliction is a treasure, and scarce any man hath enough of it."
c. "For those whom thou think'st thou doth overthrow, / Die not . . . "
d. ". . . when one man dies, one chapter is not torn out of the book, but translated into a better language . . . "

____ 20. Which of the following excerpts contains an example of the passive voice?
a. "So let us melt, and make no noise, / No tear-floods, nor sigh-tempests move . . . "
b. "Death be not proud, though some have called thee / Mighty and dreadful . . . "
c. "Perchance he for whom this bell tolls may be so ill as that he knows not it tolls for him."
d. ". . . some pieces are translated by age . . ."

Essay Questions

21. Both "A Valediction: Forbidding Mourning" and "Song" deal with the separation of the speaker and his beloved. Both poems also give a strong sense of the nature of the love that exists between the speaker and his beloved. Write an essay that discusses the characteristics of that love. What is special about it? Cite details from either one or both of the poems to support your points.

22. Although "Meditation 17" is not a poem, it uses the paradoxes and conceits that characterize metaphysical poetry. In an essay, discuss one paradox and two conceits found in "Meditation 17." What is the apparent contradiction in the paradox, and what is the sense behind it? How are the conceits appropriate even though the things being compared are very different?

23. It could be said that the use of conceits and paradoxes is particularly appropriate to religious writings and to love poetry. Write an essay giving general definitions of conceits and paradoxes. Then explain why you think their use is appropriate to these two forms of writing. Support your ideas with examples from the works of Donne.

"On My First Son," "Song: To Celia," and "Still to Be Neat"
by Ben Jonson

Selection Test

Critical Reading

On the line, write the letter of the one best answer.

_____ 1. What is the theme of "On My First Son"?
   a. the death of a child
   b. the responsibilities of fatherhood
   c. the birth of a child
   d. the purpose of suffering

_____ 2. What is the speaker expressing in these lines from "On My First Son"?

   . . . For why / Will man lament the state he should envy? / To have so soon scaped
   world's, and flesh's rage, / And, if no other misery, yet age?

   a. a conviction that early death is preferable to life
   b. confusion and anger about the value of life
   c. concern about loving life too much
   d. fury that life leads only to misery and old age

_____ 3. In "On My First Son," what is the "best piece of poetry" referred to in the lines
   ". . . say here doth lie / Ben Jonson his best piece of poetry"?
   a. the poem "On My First Son" itself
   b. Jonson's son
   c. Jonson's early writings
   d. the epitaph on Jonson's grave

_____ 4. An epigram is characterized by
   a. parallelism, clarity, brevity, and rhyme.
   b. parallelism, wit, brevity, and humor.
   c. truthfulness, permanence, and serious subject matter.
   d. permanence, brevity, clarity, and wit.

_____ 5. Which of the following epitaphs can be considered epigrammatic?
   a. Rest in peace
   b. First in war, first in peace, first in the hearts of his countrymen
   c. How great thou art
   d. Here doth lie Ben Jonson his best piece of poetry

_____ 6. The theme of "Song: To Celia" is the
   a. tragic course of romantic love.
   b. healing qualities of love.
   c. sensuous pleasures of love.
   d. futility of earthly love.

_____ 7. Jonson's probable purpose in writing "Song: To Celia" was to
   a. describe Celia's physical beauty.
   b. lament his lost love.
   c. depict an amorous courtship.
   d. reveal the silliness of lovers.

© Prentice-Hall, Inc.   First Son/To Celia/Neat   **89**

_____ 8. Which of the following best describes the speaker's view of Celia in "Song: To Celia"?
  a. realistic   c. humorous
  b. critical   d. idealistic

_____ 9. Which of the following is true of *all* epigrams?
  a. They contain a hidden truth.
  b. They always violate common sense.
  c. They confuse the reader.
  d. They are love poems.

_____ 10. What is the speaker saying in the following passage?

> Or leave a kiss but in the cup, / And I'll not look for wine. / The thirst that from the soul doth rise, / Doth ask a drink divine: / But might I of Jove's nectar sup, / I would not change for thine.

  a. His lady's kiss is the nectar of Jove.
  b. Only the nectar of Jove will satisfy his thirst.
  c. He would not trade the kiss his lady left in the cup for the nectar of Jove.
  d. The wine in his lady's cup is like the nectar of Jove.

_____ 11. The *thirst* that the speaker refers to in the passage "The thirst that from the soul doth rise," is
  a. his desire for wine.
  b. his desire for his lady's love.
  c. his desire for the nectar of Jove.
  d. his desire for a spiritual awakening.

_____ 12. What is the speaker saying in the following excerpt?

> I sent thee late a rosy wreath, / Not so much honoring thee, / As giving it a hope, that there / It could not withered be. / But thou thereon did'st only breathe, / And sent'st it back to me; / Since when it grows and smells, I swear, / Not of itself, but thee.

  a. He was late in sending his lady flowers.
  b. He sent his lady a wreath to honor her.
  c. He hoped she would accept his gift.
  d. He thinks the wreath has acquired some of his lady's characteristics.

_____ 13. What can you hypothesize about the speaker in "Song: To Celia"?
  a. He wishes to please his lady.
  b. He unrealistically idealizes his lady.
  c. He loves flowers.
  d. He is fearful his lady will return the wreath.

_____ 14. What might you hypothesize about the speaker in this excerpt?

> Still to be powdered, still perfumed; / Lady, it is to be presumed, / Though art's hid causes are not found / All is not sweet, all is not sound.

  a. He probably prefers a more natural appearance.
  b. He is in love with the lady whom he addresses.
  c. He is in love with another woman.
  d. He considers women's attitudes toward grooming as mysterious.

_____ 15. "Still to Be Neat" can be considered epigrammatic because it
  a. consists of brief, rhyming lines.
  b. expresses an idea in a memorable fashion.
  c. can be used as an inscription.
  d. can be set to music.

Vocabulary and Grammar

On the line, write the letter of the one best answer.

____ 16. Which of the following archaic words belongs in the line "Seven years thou _____ lent to me . . . "?
   a. wast   c. doth
   b. hast   d. wert

____ 17. Which meaning does the line "Drink to me only with thine eyes" express?
   a. Drink to me and to no one else.
   b. Use just your eyes to drink to me.
   c. Drink to me with your eyes and no one else's.
   d. Drink to me and do nothing else.

____ 18. Which of the following sentences expresses the idea: "Harvey has just one pair of boots, which were a gift from his uncle"?
   a. Harvey received his only pair of boots from his uncle.
   b. Harvey received his pair of boots from his only uncle.
   c. Harvey was the only person in the family to receive a pair of boots from his uncle.
   d. Harvey's pair of boots was the only gift he received from his uncle.

____ 19. Which of the following groups of archaic words fit the blanks in the lines "_____ art a monument without a tomb, / And art alive still, while _____ book _____ live"?
   a. thy; thou; dost   c. thou; thy; dost
   b. thou; thy; doth   d. thou; thy, hast

____ 20. Which of the following lines includes an incorrect use of an archaic word?
   a. "Farewell, thou child of my right hand and joy . . . "
   b. "Seven years thou wert lent to me . . . "
   c. "The thirst that from the soul doth rise . . . "
   d. "For a good poet's made not born / And such wert thou."

Essay Questions

21. Even though Jonson clearly intended each of the poems in this selection to be read by others, he addressed each poem directly to one person. Write an essay discussing how writing in the second person, rather than in the third person, affects the language and the content of the poems. Consider the following questions as you outline your essay: To whom is each poem addressed? What words, phrases, or images might be different if the poem were addressed to the world rather than directly to that person? Support your analysis with specific examples from one or more of the poems.

22. Ben Jonson is noted for his superb poetic craftsmanship, which attracted and influenced young writers of the time. He believed that good poetry was not simply a matter of "nature" or talent, but of work as well. He wrote, "For though the poet's matter nature be, / His art doth give the fashion. And that he / Who casts to write a living line, must sweat." Think about the craftsmanship in Jonson's poems, and write an essay discussing it. What specific characteristics of his work are evidence of his "sweat"? Use examples from one or more of the poems to support your ideas.

23. When Ben Jonson lost his first son, he could have written a long, formal poem of praise and mourning, as other poets had done in honor of the dead. Instead, he chose to write an epigram, a brief, informal poem. Write an essay discussing your ideas about why Jonson chose to write an epigram rather than a longer poem. How is an epigram suitable as a poem of mourning? Would a longer poem have better expressed Jonson's grief? Support your ideas with details from the poem.

Name _____ Date _____

"To His Coy Mistress" by Andrew Marvell
"To the Virgins, to Make Much of Time" by Robert Herrick
"Song" by Sir John Suckling

Selection Test

Critical Reading

On the line, write the letter of the one best answer.

_____ 1. Which of the following lines from "To His Coy Mistress" best expresses the *carpe diem* theme?
    a. "Had we but world enough, and time, / This coyness lady were no crime."
    b. "Thus, though we cannot make our sun / Stand still, yet we will make him run."
    c. ". . . I would / Love you ten years before the Flood . . . "
    d. "And the last age should show your heart. / For, lady, you deserve this state, / Nor would I love at lower rate."

_____ 2. In "To His Coy Mistress," to what does Marvell allude in the line "Time's winged chariot hurrying near"?
    a. a gathering of angels   c. the approach of death
    b. his love's acceptance of him   d. unwanted attentions from his rival

_____ 3. In "To His Coy Mistress," the lines "The grave's a fine and private place, / But none I think do there embrace" are an expression of which attitude toward death?
    a. acceptance of death's inevitability but disbelief in any comfort of eternal life
    b. denial that life and love end with death
    c. desire for death and rejection of earthly passions and pains
    d. belief in the enjoyment of earthly pleasures combined with anticipation of life after death

_____ 4. At times, the speaker in "To His Coy Mistress" displays tongue-in-cheek humor. Which of these lines best shows that humor?
    a. "And tear our pleasures with rough strife / Thorough the iron gates of life . . ."
    b. "But at my back I always hear / Time's winged chariot hurrying near . . . "
    c. "The grave's a fine and private place, / But none I think do there embrace."
    d. "And yonder all before us lie / Deserts of vast eternity."

_____ 5. Hidden quatrains, such as those in "To His Coy Mistress," are
    a. four lines with an *abab* rhyme scheme.
    b. any four lines that depart from the poem's rhyme scheme.
    c. four-line stanzas that stand apart from the rest of the poem.
    d. two couplets joined by one idea, word picture, or comparison.

_____ 6. Which of the following lines from "To the Virgins, to Make Much of Time" best expresses the *carpe diem* theme?
    a. "For, having lost but once your prime, / You may forever tarry."
    b. "That age is best which is the first . . ."
    c. "Then be not coy, but use your time . . ."
    d. "The glorious lamp of heaven, the sun, / The higher he's a-getting . . ."

_____ 7. The rosebuds in the first line of "To the Virgins, to Make Much of Time" are a symbol of
    a. the beauty of nature.   c. the joys of youth.
    b. early childhood.   d. love and marriage.

8. What does the flower symbolize in these lines from "To the Virgins, to Make Much of Time"?

> And this same flower that smiles today
> Tomorrow will be dying.

   a. the length of human life
   b. a prosperous garden
   c. the innocence of life
   d. disappointment in love

9. Which word from "To the Virgins, to Make Much of Time" symbolizes passion and energy?
   a. lamp
   b. blood
   c. race
   d. smiles

10. What is the theme of Sir John Suckling's "Song"?
   a. Women are fickle in matters of the heart.
   b. Don't waste your time on an unrequited love.
   c. Loving takes place in the imagination only.
   d. The moodiness of a lover can cause suffering.

11. In the poem "Song," the attitude of the speaker toward his subject can best be described as
   a. condescending.
   b. mildly rebuking.
   c. admiring.
   d. slightly sarcastic.

12. Which of the following lines from "Song" is the best expression of the *carpe diem* theme?
   a. "Will, when speaking well can't win her, / Saying nothing do't?"
   b. "Why so dull and mute, young sinner?"
   c. "Will, when looking well can't move her, / Looking ill prevail?"
   d. "Quit, quit, for shame; this will not move, / This cannot take her."

13. Which word best expresses the speaker's attitude in these lines from "Song"?

> If of herself she will not love, / Nothing can make her: / The devil take her!

   a. commitment
   b. betrayal
   c. impatience
   d. despair

Vocabulary and Grammar

On the line, write the letter of the one best answer.

14. The root word *prime* comes from a Latin word meaning _____.
   a. first in importance or first in time
   b. the best or most accomplished
   c. the biggest or largest part
   d. the whole thing

15. Which phrase has nearly the same meaning as *amorous*?
   a. full of love
   b. weak and very tired
   c. reluctant to make a commitment
   d. shy and withdrawn

16. Which of the following words means the opposite of *wan*?
   a. exhausted
   b. sickly
   c. shy
   d. strong

_____ 17. What does the word *coy* mean?
   a. slow to fall in love
   b. quick to make decisions
   c. slow to make a commitment
   d. quick to fall in love

_____ 18. Which of the italicized words is the superlative form of an irregular adjective?
   a. John had *better* luck than Andrew in his relationship.
   b. Of the three men, Andujar had the *worst* difficulties in his relationships.
   c. Claire had a *greater* fear of making a commitment than Helene did.
   d. Julie was *taller* than the other three women.

_____ 19. Which of the italicized words is the comparative form of an irregular adjective?
   a. Marvell had a *shorter* life than Herrick did.
   b. Was the seventeenth century a *more turbulent* period than the eighteenth century?
   c. Suckling accomplished more in *less* time than many poets.
   d. Suckling may have lived the *most tragic* life of the three.

_____ 20. Which of the following is *not* the superlative form of an irregular adjective?
   a. coldest
   b. furthest
   c. best
   d. most

Essay Questions

21. The poems "To His Coy Mistress" by Andrew Marvell, "To the Virgins, to Make Much of Time" by Robert Herrick, and "Song" by Sir John Suckling all address the theme of *carpe diem*. Choose one or more of these poems and write an essay in which you discuss the handling of this theme by each poet. What advice does he give? How does he urge this listener to "seize the day"? Give examples from the poem or poems you discuss to support your comparison.

22. Marvell, Herrick, and Suckling were masters of the English language and fond of witty word play. Were these poets able to display their wit and ease with language in these poems? Choose one poem and, in an essay explain how the poet used wit, puns, put-downs, and other kinds of word play. Can you find examples of ways in which the poet verbally "clowns around"? Do you think the poet enjoyed writing the poem?

23. Poets often use images to express ideas that might be more difficult to express if stated directly. Choose one or more of the three poems and discuss the use of images by the poet(s). Does the poet use images? What kinds of images does he use? Are the images easy to understand and effective in communicating emotions and ideas? Give examples to support your response.

"Freeze Tag" by Suzanne Vega
"New Beginning" by Tracy Chapman

Selection Test

Critical Reading

On the line, write the letter of the one best answer.

_____ 1. Which statement is true about the singer in "New Beginning"?
   a. The singer hates the world and would like to end it.
   b. The singer loves life and wants to make it better.
   c. The singer wants to be left alone.
   d. The singer wants to punish people for hurting others.

_____ 2. Why does the singer in "New Beginning" believe "it's time to start all over"?
   a. The world has wasted its natural resources.
   b. The world is filled with suffering and pain.
   c. The world is overpopulated.
   d. Too many people have died because of hunger.

_____ 3. Which statement best expresses the principle for which the singer is arguing in "New Beginning"?
   a. People should live in peace and unity.
   b. Different races of people must learn to leave each other alone.
   c. Society would be better off without guns.
   d. People should ignore bad things in life and appreciate the good.

_____ 4. Which of the following problems does the singer explicitly mention in "New Beginning"?
   a. overpopulation   c. separation
   b. hunger   d. pollution

_____ 5. Which phrase best describes the singer's character in "New Beginning"?
   a. angry and pessimistic
   b. hopeful and full of love for life
   c. sensitive and withdrawn
   d. cautiously optimistic

_____ 6. Which two concepts form the central metaphor of "Freeze Tag"?
   a. movies/game
   b. cold/play
   c. winter/childlike
   d. immobile/fake

_____ 7. Which typical playground game or equipment is *not* mentioned in "Freeze Tag"?
   a. hide-and-seek   c. teeter-totter
   b. slides   d. tag

_____ 8. By setting the song "Freeze Tag" in a playground, Vega suggests that
   a. adults often treat their feelings like children's games.
   b. children deal with relationships more honestly than adults.
   c. children have the same problems as adults.
   d. some people never grow up.

© Prentice-Hall, Inc.

Freeze Tag/New Beginning   **95**

Unit 3: A Turbulent Time (1625–1798)

_____ 9. "Freeze Tag" is primarily about
         a. an estranged mother–daughter relationship.
         b. a failing relationship.
         c. kids fighting on a playground.
         d. two kids falling in love.

_____ 10. What do the figures of "Dietrich" and "Dean" symbolize for the singer in "Freeze Tag"?
         a. Old movies give the most realistic picture of love.
         b. People who hide their feelings never get hurt.
         c. Women are more honest than men.
         d. Some people act out roles rather than behaving honestly.

Essay Questions

11. Spanish-American philosopher George Santayana said, "Those who cannot remember the past are condemned to repeat it." Write an essay relating this quotation to "New Beginning." Would Chapman agree or disagree with Santayana? Explain how Chapman's or Santayana's approach would work when applied to some contemporary problem with which you are familiar.

12. The song "Freeze Tag" is a model of sustained metaphor. In an essay, describe the many layers of meaning in this song. Discuss how the everyday details of the song help to express a larger, spiritual meaning, and identify what that meaning is.

13. Chapman's song in part describes an ideal situation, where change can be achieved based simply on the desire to do so. Vega, in contrast, describes in part the difficulty of making changes. Choose one or both of these songs and write an essay discussing their points of view. Analyze the attitudes of one or both of the songwriters to the past and its influence on the present. Do you think a person really can control time in a way that addresses the problems in these songs?

Part Test, Unit 3, Part 1: The War Against Time

Critical Reading

The questions below are based on the following selection.

This selection is John Donne's "Holy Sonnet 14." Donne addresses a "three-personed God," a reference to the Trinity—the Father, the Son, and the Holy Ghost.

Holy Sonnet 14 by John Donne

Batter my heart, three-personed God; for You

As yet but knock, breathe, shine, and seek to mend;

That I may rise, and stand, o'erthrow me, and bend

Your force, to break, blow, burn and make me new.

[5] I, like an usurped town, to another due,

Labor to admit You, but O, to no end,

Reason Your viceroy in me, me should defend,

But is captived, and proves weak or untrue.

Yet dearly I love You, and would be loved fain,

[10] But am betrothed unto Your enemy.

Divorce me, untie, or break that knot again;

Take me to You, imprison me, for I,

Except You enthral me, never shall be free,

Nor ever chaste, except You ravish me.

On the line, write the letter of the one best answer.

_____ 1. So that the speaker of the poem may rise and stand, he asks God to do all of the following *except*
   a. knock him.
   b. batter him.
   c. o'erthrow him.
   d. burn him.

_____ 2. In line 2, why does the speaker complain of God's gentleness?
   a. He wants to display his toughness.
   b. He feels that his faith is too strong.
   c. His resistance requires God to be more forceful.
   d. Irrational thoughts have taken him over.

_____ 3. Like many other of Donne's poetical works, this selection is an example of
   a. free verse.
   b. narrative poetry.
   c. epic poetry.
   d. metaphysical poetry.

© Prentice-Hall, Inc.

_____ 4. The rhythms and sentence patterns of the poem's first four lines signal the speaker's
     a. relaxed approach to prayer.
     b. passionate attitude about religious faith.
     c. reluctance to address topics directly.
     d. conventional attitudes about God.

_____ 5. According to lines 9–10, what is the speaker's present condition?
     a. He is angry at God.
     b. He is wedded to sin.
     c. He is wedded to his faith in God.
     d. He is exhausted by his love.

_____ 6. Which is the best description of the poem's tone?
     a. gentle   c. urgent
     b. respectful   d. pastoral

_____ 7. Lines 3, 13, and 14 are notable for
     a. the paradoxes they contain.
     b. their approximate rhymes.
     c. their formal language.
     d. the epigrams they contain.

_____ 8. Which is the best explanation of the meaning of line 14?
     a. Chastity is unrelated to spirituality.
     b. Human beings must find balance in their lives.
     c. God can redeem only those who are chaste.
     d. Being ravished—or transformed—by God would be cleansing.

_____ 9. Donne's speaker makes an important comparison between
     a. a viceroy and God.
     b. himself and a "usurped town."
     c. God and a flame.
     d. himself and Satan.

_____ 10. In sum, what does the speaker of this poem desire?
     a. sin
     b. kindness
     c. marriage
     d. salvation

Vocabulary and Grammar

The three questions below consist of a related pair of words in CAPITAL LETTERS, followed by four other pairs of words. Choose the pair that best expresses a relationship _similar_ to that expressed by the words in capital letters.

_____ 11. TREPIDATION : CALMNESS ::
     a. piety : faithlessness
     b. tremulous : placid
     c. coyness : commitment
     d. tribulation : recourse

_____ 12. CONTENTION : DISPUTE ::
     a. affliction : hardship
     b. treasure : worth
     c. diminish : increase
     d. divine : splendor

____ 13. LOVE : AMOROUS ::
        a. goodness : gentleness
        b. romantic : love
        c. evil : malevolent
        d. fury : deceitful

On the line, write the letter of the one best answer.

____ 14. Which line is written in the passive voice?
        a. Tribulation is treasure in the nature of it.
        b. Rest in soft peace.
        c. I sent thee late a rosy wreath.
        d. When one man dies, one chapter is not torn out of the book, but translated into a better language.

____ 15. Which line contains an adjective in its irregular comparative form?
        a. Sweetest love, I do not go for weariness of thee.
        b. Perchance I may think myself so much better than I am as that they who are about me and see my state may have caused it to toll for me.
        c. At my back I always hear Time's winged chariot hurrying near.
        d. We get nearer and nearer our home.

Essay Questions

16. Although most often portrayed in serious, heartfelt terms, the subject of romantic love can also have its amusing—even ridiculous—side. Choose a poem that laughs at certain aspects of love and / or lovers. In an essay, identify what the poet is making fun of and describe how he accomplishes this. You might look at Jonson's "Song: To Celia" or Suckling's "Song."

17. In an essay, compare and contrast Ben Jonson's "On My First Son" and Robert Herrick's "To the Virgins, to Make Much of Time." Pay special attention to the two poets' styles, and explain how their stylistic devices—such as tone, rhyme, rhythm, and imagery—relate to their subjects.

18. For centuries poets and other writers have engaged the thorny topic of the passage of time and the brevity of human beauty, youth, and life itself. For example, Marvell's "To His Coy Mistress" and Herrick's "To the Virgins, to Make Much of Time" both promote the idea of *carpe diem* ("seize the day"); John Donne more directly confronts death in "Holy Sonnet 10." Write an essay in which you explain how one of these poets addresses the theme of life's relation to death in an especially meaningful or interesting way.

Poetry of John Milton

Selection Test

Critical Reading

On the line, write the letter of the one best answer.

_____ 1. What is the theme of this excerpt from *Paradise Lost*?
   a. service to God
   b. good and evil
   c. consequences of rebellion
   d. historical relationships

_____ 2. Milton's epic poem *Paradise Lost* expresses values of seventeenth-century Christian England in that it reflects a prevalent belief in
   a. Greek and Roman classical gods.
   b. earthly angels.
   c. serpents and sea monsters.
   d. Heaven and Hell.

_____ 3. Which of the following describes the style in which *Paradise Lost* is written?
   a. unrhymed iambic pentameter
   b. rhymed couplets
   c. quatrains of varying rhyme schemes
   d. run-on lines

_____ 4. What is the main clause in the following lines from *Paradise Lost*?

   And chiefly thou O Spirit, that dost prefer / Before all temples the upright heart and pure, / Instruct me, for thou know'st . . .

   a. that dost prefer
   b. for thou know'st
   c. And chiefly thou O Spirit
   d. Instruct me

_____ 5. The lines "With loss of Eden, till one greater Man / Restore us, and regain the blissful seat" allude to the
   a. power of God.
   b. punishment of Satan.
   c. coming of Christ.
   d. joy of the angels.

_____ 6. Which of the following lines referring to Satan best expresses the conflict between Satan and God?
   a. ". . . the thought / Both of lost happiness and lasting pain / Torments him . . ."
   b. "He trusted to have equaled the Most High . . . "
   c. ". . . he views / The dismal situation waste and wild . . . "
   d. "He soon discerns . . . / One next himself in power, and next in crime . . ."

_____ 7. By combining Hebrew and Classical (Greek and Roman) elements in *Paradise Lost*, Milton conveys the message that
   a. people throughout history have been concerned with similar themes.
   b. seventeenth-century readers were highly educated.
   c. Christian values are superior to Hebrew and Classical values.
   d. the battles of these earlier cultures were not fought in vain.

_____ 8. The word *light* in the line "When I Consider How My Light Is Spent" refers to the poet's
   a. talent.
   b. eyesight.
   c. failure.
   d. patience.

_____ 9. What is the theme of Sonnet XIX?
   a. One does not have to labor or accomplish great things to serve God.
   b. God's angels serve those who cannot serve themselves.
   c. Those who have lost the ability to exercise their talents must wait.
   d. Idleness due to an infirmity is not a sin.

_____ 10. Which of the following best describes the change in tone between the octave and the sestet of Sonnet XIX?
   a. from angry to tranquil
   b. from disturbed to accepting
   c. from suspicious to resigned
   d. from resentful to joyous

_____ 11. What is the main clause in the following lines from "Paradise Lost"?

   "Fallen cherub, to be weak is miserable,/ Doing or suffering . . .

   a. Fallen cherub
   b. to be weak
   c. to be weak is miserable
   d. Doing or suffering

_____ 12. In Sonnet VII, which of the following attitudes of the speaker is reflected in these lines?

   That I to manhood am arrived so near,
   And inward ripeness doth much less appear

   a. disgust that his vitality is fading
   b. regret at his lack of maturity
   c. shame at his insufficient talent
   d. anger that he is not the best poet in England

_____ 13. What is the rhyme scheme of the first two stanzas (octave) of Sonnet VII?
   a. _abab abab_   c. _abba abba_
   b. _abab cdcd_   d. _abba cddc_

_____ 14. One of the central ideas of Sonnet VII is that
   a. people are in charge of their fate.
   b. human destiny is mostly in the hands of fate.
   c. people are obliged to use their talents.
   d. maturity is determined by God and must be accepted.

_____ 15. When you encounter complex sentences, you can break them down to find the main clause, which
   a. supports the main idea.
   b. clarifies the sentence.
   c. does not stand by itself.
   d. stands by itself.

Vocabulary and Grammar

On the line, write the letter of the one best answer.

_____ 16. Which phrase has nearly the same meaning as _illumine_?
   a. light up
   b. go beyond
   c. be stubborn
   d. use trickery

_____ 17. Which of the following words or phrases is most nearly opposite in meaning to *transgress*?
   a. justify an action
   b. leave in one place
   c. violate a law
   d. obey

_____ 18. What does the word *ignominy* mean?
   a. praise
   b. honor
   c. dishonor
   d. trick

_____ 19. In which sentence is the word *who* used correctly?
   a. Satan, to who all the fallen angels looked for leadership, waited.
   b. Beelzebub, who was second in command, sat near Satan.
   c. Satan fled from God, about who he had learned so much.
   d. Satan, of who you may have heard, was once an angel.

_____ 20. In which sentence is the word *who* or the word *whom* used correctly?
   a. To who did Satan speak?
   b. Whom was the first angel to begin the revolt?
   c. Against whom did Satan rebel?
   d. God hurled thunderbolts at who?

Essay Questions

21. Many writers use their work as an outlet through which they can examine and come to an understanding of personal issues. Choose one or both of Milton's sonnets, the excerpt from *Paradise Lost*, or all three, and write an essay in which you explain whether or not you think Milton was working through personal issues and, if so, what conclusions he drew. For example, what were his concerns about his blindness?

22. Between 1642 and 1660, England was torn apart by civil war. There were, perhaps, no real winners or losers during this period, only survivors. Write an essay in which you discuss ways in which *Paradise Lost* reflects this turbulent time. Are there winners and losers in *Paradise Lost*? Is the victory total? Do victory and an end to war bring peace and calm?

23. The opening book of *Paradise Lost*, from which the excerpt in your textbook is taken, is considered by many readers to be the most powerful and moving of the twelve books in this epic poem. Satan, the arch-fiend, is the central character in this book, and he steals the show. Analyze the character of Satan in the excerpt from *Paradise Lost*. Does Milton make him a sympathetic character? Can you see Satan's point of view? Give examples from the text to support your response.

from "Eve's Apology in Defense of Women" by Amelia Lanier
"To Lucasta, on Going to the Wars" and **"To Althea, from Prison"**
by Richard Lovelace

Selection Test

Critical Reading

On the line, write the letter of the one best answer.

_____ 1. What does Lanier want to accomplish in her poem "Eve's Apology in Defense of Women"?
a. to reveal the unfair treatment of women in society
b. to correct a misunderstood passage in the Bible
c. to investigate the relationship between Adam and Eve
d. to retell the story of Adam and Eve in verse

_____ 2. Which of the following motives best describes Lanier's use of the Biblical story of Adam and Eve in "Eve's Apology in Defense of Women"?
a. to describe a passage in order to teach the reader something about the Bible
b. to retell a traditional story in order to entertain the reader
c. to evoke Biblical imagery to give her statement a religious tone
d. to draw on a traditional story in order to make an argument more powerful

_____ 3. Which of the following pieces of information would best help a reader to understand the pertinent historical context of "Eve's Apology in Defense of Women"?
a. The Bible was much admired in seventeenth-century England.
b. Women were second-class citizens in seventeenth-century England.
c. Oliver Cromwell enforced order with an iron hand.
d. Seventeenth-century English poets were mostly from the upper class.

_____ 4. Reformers use traditional stories in order to
a. give their ideas a religious flavor.
b. make their ideas more familiar.
c. make it appear that God is on their side.
d. popularize Bible stories and fables.

_____ 5. By basing "Eve's Apology in Defense of Women" on a Biblical story, Lanier meant her poem to be understood by
a. church officials only.
b. Puritans only.
c. everyone in the culture.
d. members of the upper class only.

_____ 6. What does Lanier mean when she writes "Yet Men will boast of Knowledge, which he took / From *Eve*'s fair hand, as from a learned book"?
a. Men possess the right to knowledge only because God took the apple from Eve and gave it to Adam.
b. Men can boast of their knowledge only because Eve lost her wisdom when she gave Adam the apple.
c. Men are boastful even though Adam originally received knowledge through Eve's actions.
d. Men now claim the exclusive right to learning and power even though Adam originally received knowledge through Eve's actions.

_____ 7. Which of the following information would best help a reader to understand the historical context of "To Lucasta, on Going to the Wars"?
   a. The Bible was much admired in seventeenth-century England.
   b. Lovelace was very handsome, and he painted pictures.
   c. Lovelace was a Royalist who supported Charles I.
   d. Seventeenth-century English poets were mostly from the upper class.

_____ 8. What does the speaker mean in the following lines?

   I could not love thee, Dear, so much, / Loved I not honor more.

   a. Love and honor are the same thing.
   b. Lucasta has hurt his pride and he cannot love her any more.
   c. His love for Lucasta is greater than his love of honor.
   d. He would be unworthy of love if honor meant nothing to him.

_____ 9. What is the theme of Lovelace's poem "To Lucasta, on Going to the Wars"?
   a. Romantic love will always endure.
   b. Love for country is the highest love.
   c. Youthful lovers should remain chaste.
   d. Honor creates inconstancy in love.

_____ 10. By using the word _nunnery_ in reference to his loved one, in "To Lucasta, on Going to the Wars," the speaker creates the impression that she is
   a. chaste.   c. cold.
   b. religious.   d. coy.

_____ 11. Which of the following words best describes the speaker's attitude about his imprisonment in "To Althea, from Prison"?
   a. despairing   c. solitary
   b. defiant   d. cowardly

_____ 12. Which of the following is the central idea of Lovelace's poem "To Althea, from Prison"?
   a. Lovers must endure separation.
   b. Innocent minds are free.
   c. One can become drunk on liberty.
   d. True lovers cannot be imprisoned.

_____ 13. Which of the following words best describes the tone of "To Althea, from Prison"?
   a. lamenting   c. ethereal
   b. resentful   d. uplifting

_____ 14. Which of the following actions would be the most helpful to a reader who wanted to use historical context to understand a piece of seventeenth-century writing?
   a. reading an encyclopedia article about the author
   b. researching the impact of the piece on twentieth-century literature
   c. researching the historical period in which the piece was written
   d. researching the use of the author's theme in works from other times and places

Vocabulary and Grammar

On the line, write the letter of the one best answer.

_____ 15. What does the word _discretion_ mean?
   a. power of free decision
   b. ability to be generous
   c. failure to observe terms
   d. wisdom to make good choices

_____ 16. Which of the following means the opposite of *inconstancy*?
   a. drunkenness
   b. silence
   c. greediness
   d. dependability

_____ 17. If you *breach* a contract you
   a. sign and date it.
   b. study it carefully.
   c. break its terms.
   d. give it to a lawyer.

_____ 18. Which of the following pairs of phrases or words are *not* correlative conjunctions?
   a. not so . . . as
   b. but . . . no
   c. neither . . . nor
   d. both . . . and

_____ 19. Which of the following sentences contains a correlative conjunction?
   a. Lovelace was not the only Royalist who wanted the king restored.
   b. Other groups also had revolutionary ideas.
   c. When Lovelace was young he was both handsome and wealthy.
   d. England was at war with Spain.

_____ 20. Which of the following sentences does *not* contain a pair of correlative conjunctions?
   a. Lanier's poem is not only thought provoking, it is powerful.
   b. Eve neither begs nor pleads to make her case.
   c. She persuades by using images that are both vivid and provocative.
   d. You can either read Lanier's poetry or have it read to you.

Essay Questions

21. England in the seventeenth century was marked by turbulent events and social upheaval. In an essay, describe the historical context of one or both of Lovelace's poems "To Lucasta, on Going to the Wars" and "To Althea, from Prison." How does Lovelace respond to events in his lifetime with his poetry?

22. Amelia Lanier's poem "Eve's Apology in Defense of Women" uses a traditional Bible story as a way to show the unfair relationship between men and women in society. Discuss Lanier's argument in an essay. Does she succeed in making her point? How does she think Eve was treated? What does the treatment of Eve say about the treatment of women in society? Use specific lines or phrases from the poem to support your arguments.

23. "To Lucasta, on Going to the Wars" and "To Althea, from Prison" are love poems. Both poems, however, present love in a wider context of life. Analyze either one or both of Lovelace's poems by writing an essay in which you explain how Lovelace relates love to other responsibilities and concerns. What values do you think Lovelace holds in highest regard?

Part Test, Unit 3, Part 2: The Story of Britain—A Nation Divided

Critical Reading

The questions below are based on the following selection.

Sonnet XVIII, "On the Late Massacre in Piemont" by John Milton

Avenge, O Lord, thy slaughtered saints, whose bones

Lie scattered on the Alpine mountains cold,

Even them who kept thy truth so pure of old

When all our fathers worshiped stocks and stones,

[5] Forget not; in thy book record their groans

Who were thy sheep, and in their ancient fold

Slain by the bloody Piemontese, that rolled

Mother with infant down the rocks. Their moans

The vales redoubled to the hills, and they

[10] To heaven. Their martyred blood and ashes sow

O'er all the Italian fields, where still doth sway

The triple tyrant, that from these may grow

A hundred fold, who, having learnt thy way,

Early may fly the Babylonian woe.

On the line, write the letter of the one best answer.

_____ 1. To whom is this poem addressed?
   a. the Piemontese
   b. God
   c. slaughtered saints
   d. Italian patriots

_____ 2. A reader might infer that the slain "saints" died
   a. in Babylon.
   b. for political reasons.
   c. from hypothermia.
   d. for religious reasons.

_____ 3. The rhyme scheme of this poem identifies it as
   a. an Italian sonnet.
   b. a narrative poem.
   c. an epic poem.
   d. a Shakespearean sonnet.

_____ 4. Which of the following lines is a main clause?
   a. "Even them who kept thy truth so pure of old"
   b. "When all our fathers worshiped stocks and stones"
   c. "Their martyred blood and ashes sow"
   d. "The triple tyrant, that from these may grow / A hundred fold, who, having learnt thy way"

_____ 5. With what metaphor does Milton further describe the "slaughtered saints" of line 1?
   a. sheep
   b. fathers
   c. vales
   d. ashes

_____ 6. Which phrase allows a reader to infer that the Piemontese preyed on their countrymen?
   a. "thy slaughtered saints"
   b. "all our fathers"
   c. "Their martyred blood"
   d. "in their ancient fold"

_____ 7. Which phrase provides a transition from the octave to the sestet of the poem?
   a. "that rolled"
   b. "Forget not"
   c. "Their moans"
   d. "and they"

_____ 8. What is distinctive about the image featured in the beginning of line 8?
   a. It uses personification.
   b. It is specific instead of general.
   c. It is violent.
   d. It is unconscionable.

_____ 9. What does the speaker wish will happen after the blood and ashes of the slain are sown "o'er the Italian fields"?
   a. New saints will be born and flourish there.
   b. The triple tyrant will continue to rule.
   c. The living will learn from the mistakes of the dead.
   d. The Piemontese will flee.

_____ 10. How many sentences appear in the poem's sestet?
   a. one
   b. two
   c. three
   d. none

Vocabulary and Grammar

On the line, write the letter of the one best answer.

_____ 11. The word _illumine_, which Milton uses in the excerpt below, is formed from the Latin word meaning

   What in me is dark
   Illumine, what is low raise and support . . .

   a. daring.   c. lamp.
   b. opacity.   d. reduction.

_____ 12. What is the best synonym for _semblance_ as it appears in the following passage?

   My hasting days fly on with full career,
   But my late spring no bud or blossoms showeth.
   Perhaps my semblance might deceive the truth,
   That I to manhood am arrived so near . . .

   a. intelligence   c. image
   b. emotion   d. trickery

____ 13. What is the best definition of *tempestuous* as it appears in the following excerpt?

> There the companions of his fall, o'erwhelmed
> With floods and whirlwinds of tempestuous fire,
> He soon discerns . . .

    a. turbulent
    b. rapid
    c. mild
    d. angry

____ 14. Which line contains a pair of correlative conjunctions connecting two words or groups of words?
    a. "We know right well he did discretion lack."
    b. "He was lord and king of all the earth before poor Eve had either life or breath."
    c. "He never sought her weakness to reprove with those sharp words which he of God did hear."
    d. "Men will boast of knowledge, which he took from Eve's fair hand, as from a learned book."

____ 15. In which line is there an error in the use of *who* or *whom*?
    a. "Who first seduced them to that foul revolt?"
    b. "Be it so, who now is sovereign can dispose and bid what shall be right."
    c. "O how . . . changed from him, who in the happy realms of light clothed with transcendent brightness didst outshine myriads though bright."
    d. "Farthest from him is best, who reason hath equaled."

Essay Questions

16. Attempting to comfort a loved one left behind is a difficult task—and a popular subject for poets. Read "To Lucasta, on Going to the Wars" carefully several times. Then think about what thoughts and feelings you would have if you were the recipient of this poem. In an essay, write why you would or would not be comforted by the poem—and why. Use quotations from the poem to support your ideas.

17. If poetry is an apt literary form for expressing grief about a subject, it is also an excellent form for bestowing praise. In an essay, explain how Richard Lovelace treats each of these topics in a single poem, "To Althea, from Prison." Make reference to specific lines in which the poet expresses praise or grief.

18. For centuries poets, artists, philosophers, and scientists have explored the question of free will as it applies to human beings. How much of our behavior and experience happens as a result of our own will, and how much (if any) is determined for us? Read either of the Milton sonnets carefully in light of these questions. In an essay, analyze how the speaker of the poem would respond to the question of free will in humans.

Name _____ Date _____

from *The Diary* by Samuel Pepys
from *A Journal of the Plague Year* by Daniel Defoe

Selection Test

Critical Reading

On the line, write the letter of the one best answer.

____ 1. In the selections from *The Diary*, which emotions predominate in Pepys's descriptions of the people of London whom he hears about or passes on his walks through the city?
   a. anger and impatience
   b. scorn and disgust
   c. fascination and curiosity
   d. pity and compassion

____ 2. As evident in "The Plague" and "The Fire of London," Pepys's style in *The Diary* is to
   a. make broad generalizations.
   b. note details and examples.
   c. develop abstract concepts.
   d. collect facts and figures.

____ 3. The main idea of the second of Pepys's "Plague" entries is that
   a. the day has been both good and bad.
   b. death has come very close to him.
   c. his money and family have been spared.
   d. strong laws can control the plague.

____ 4. What conclusion can you draw from Pepys's statement that some people "will (because they are forbid) come in crowds along with the dead corps to see them buried"?
   a. Some people are curious enough to risk infection themselves.
   b. Some people are so despondent that they hope to become infected.
   c. Some people come to see their friends and relatives buried.
   d. Some people are foolish enough to disobey the law and risk arrest.

____ 5. From which of the following passages from *The Diary* can you draw the conclusion that the people of London believed the fire could not be stopped?
   a. "spare no houses, but . . . pull down before the fire every way."
   b. "Good hopes there was of stopping it at the Three Cranes above. . . ."
   c. "nobody . . . endeavoring to quench it, but to remove their goods . . ."
   d. "nor any sleep all this night to me nor my poor wife."

____ 6. In his diary entries, Pepys implies that he is
   a. a home-loving family man.
   b. a responsible public servant.
   c. an astute social critic.
   d. a pleasure-loving aristocrat.

____ 7. Which of the following lines from *The Diary* best supports the idea that Pepys is recognized as a man of influence and status in London?
   a. "So I made myself ready presently, and walked to the Tower, and there got up upon one of the high places . . ."
   b. "I to Paul's Wharf, where I had appointed a boat to attend me . . ."
   c. "I find Sir W. Rider tired with being called up all night, and receiving things from several friends."
   d. ". . . and the King commanded me to go to my Lord Mayor from him . . ."

Unit 3: A Turbulent Time (1625–1798)

_____ 8. To make his account of the plague believable, Defoe includes many
   a. numbers and measures.
   c. signs and symptoms.
   b. similes and metaphors.
   d. names and quotations.

_____ 9. A central idea of the excerpt from _A Journal of the Plague Year_ is
   a. the rules forbidding people to visit burial pits are cruel and unnecessary.
   b. the plague has made the usual rituals of civilized society meaningless.
   c. the people of London have become hardened and apathetic.
   d. the authorities have been callous in their treatment of mourners.

_____ 10. In describing the narrator's exchange with the sexton in lines such as "'T is a speaking sight . . . and has a voice with it, and a loud one, to call us all to repentance,'" Defoe makes the scene seem like an authentic eyewitness account by
   a. mimicking the man's speech.
   c. mentioning the man's position.
   b. personifying the burial pit.
   d. using a common expression.

_____ 11. What conclusion can you draw from the statement by Defoe's narrator that the pit was expected to last a month but instead was filled in two weeks?
   a. Some people who were expected to die from the plague recovered.
   b. The buriers used too much earth to cover the bodies.
   c. People were dying more rapidly than anyone had expected.
   d. The pit wasn't as deep as it was supposed to be.

_____ 12. Pepys's and Defoe's accounts of the plague are similar in that both writers mention
   a. religious meanings they perceive.
   b. ordinary pleasures they enjoy.
   c. important people they encounter.
   d. concrete details they observe.

_____ 13. Which of the following best contrasts the way in which Pepys and Defoe's narrator present themselves to the reader?
   a. Defoe's narrator portrays himself as an objective eyewitness, while Pepys offers his emotions and opinions.
   b. Defoe's narrator is vague and squeamish about unpleasant details, while Pepys relates them unflinchingly.
   c. Defoe's narrator is concerned with the effects of the plague on individuals, while Pepys focuses on the whole city.
   d. Defoe's narrator tells how he bent an official rule, while Pepys shows himself helping to make such a rule.

_____ 14. One way in which Pepys's account of the plague may be more credible than Defoe's is that, unlike Defoe, Pepys
   a. names people and tells how he knows them.
   b. cites dates and discusses actual places.
   c. conveys his fears and says that he is sad.
   d. uses the city streets as vantage points.

Vocabulary and Grammar

On the line, write the letter of the one best answer.

_____ 15. Ague, a fever accompanied by chills and sweating, was one of the early symptoms of the plague. When Pepys writes that he has "_apprehensions_ of an ague," he means that
   a. he feels angry because he may get sick with the plague.
   b. he thinks that he is already sick with the plague.
   c. he feels hopeful that he will not get sick with the plague.
   d. he is afraid that he will get sick, infect his family, and die.

_____ 16. Which of the following sentences contains a gerund?
   a. People were crowding around the pits to see plague victims buried.
   b. Watching the fire made Pepys fear his own house would burn.
   c. People were saving their possessions and not quenching the fire.
   d. Hoping to die, the man threw himself into the burial pit.

_____ 17. When Pepys describes the fire as "lamentable," he means that
   a. it is extremely distressing.
   b. it is moving very fast.
   c. it is burning very hot.
   d. it may cause an explosion.

_____ 18. Which of the following passages from _The Diary_ and _A Journal of the Plague Year_ does _not_ contain a gerund?
   a. "a horrid noise the flames made, and the cracking of houses at their ruin . . ."
   b. "their dearest relations were perhaps dying, or just dead . . . "
   c. "what covering they had fell from them . . . "
   d. "the buriers had covered the bodies so immediately with throwing in earth . . . "

_____ 19. Which of the following passages from _A Journal of the Plague Year_ contains a gerund?
   a. "the voice of mourning was truly heard in the streets."
   b. "the plague was long a-coming to our parish . . . "
   c. "they were making preparations to bury the whole parish . . . "
   d. "I stood wavering for a good while . . . "

_____ 20. When Defoe writes that "coffins were not to be had for the _prodigious_ numbers that fell in such a calamity as this," he means that
   a. it was not considered sanitary to bury plague victims in coffins.
   b. burying plague victims in coffins would expose the coffin-makers to infection.
   c. there were more dead people than the coffins needed to bury them.
   d. there was not enough wood to build coffins for plague victims.

Essay Questions

21. Both _The Diary_ and _A Journal of the Plague Year_ provide many details about everyday life in London during the plague. Write an essay in which you describe what it might have been like to live in London during the plague and, based on the two excerpts, draw your own conclusions about life during the plague. If you were to walk down a London street in 1665, what might you see, hear, and smell? How might the plague cause you to change your daily routine? Support your description with details from one or both of the excerpts.

22. A diarist can structure his or her entries in any number of ways—examples are a simple chronological description of a day, the diarist's reflections, or memories of the event. Write an essay comparing and contrasting the structures of _The Diary_ and _A Journal of the Plague Year_. Do these authors describe events in chronological order? Do they give background information? Do they reflect on the meaning of the events that they recount? Do they include vivid images? Use details from the excerpts to support your answer.

23. Pepys and Defoe each write accounts of historical events. However, a diary reveals not only details about the events, but also details about the diarist's personality and character. Write an essay in which you discuss either one or both of the central characters in each passage. What is the motivation of each character for the things that he does? How does each character feel about the plague? How does each behave during a crisis? Use details from one or both of the excerpts to support your answer.

© Prentice-Hall, Inc.

The Diary/Plague Year **111**

Unit 3: A Turbulent Time (1625–1798)

Name _____ Date _____

from Gulliver's Travels by Jonathan Swift

Selection Test

Critical Reading

On the line, write the letter of the one best answer.

_____ 1. In the story of how the dispute arose between the Big-Endians and the Little-Endians, the chief objects of Swift's satire are
    a. triviality and pettiness.
    b. ignorance and superstition.
    c. arrogance and pomposity.
    d. religion and principle.

_____ 2. The Lilliputian wars are a satire on
    a. political institutions.
    b. table manners.
    c. religious conflict.
    d. political fighting.

_____ 3. What do both Gulliver's pocket perspective-glass and his spectacles most likely symbolize in this excerpt from "A Voyage to Lilliput"?
    a. imperfect vision
    b. inaccurate perception
    c. increased insight
    d. intellectual armor

_____ 4. After Gulliver brings the enemy ships to the Lilliputian prince, the prince's request prompts Gulliver to make the generalization that all rulers are
    a. greedy.
    b. fickle.
    c. stupid.
    d. petty.

_____ 5. In "A Voyage to Lilliput," what is Swift implying when he quotes the Lilliputian official's description of Blefuscu as "the other great empire of the universe"?
    a. that France is really the greater country
    b. that Britain has a narrow view of the world
    c. that Britain has too high an opinion of France
    d. that France is a threat to Britain's security

_____ 6. The fact that Gulliver apologizes to readers for the king of Brobdingnag's narrow-mindedness shows that Gulliver is
    a. narrow-minded himself.
    b. gracious about his host's good intentions.
    c. willing to accept the flaws of others.
    d. trying to make readers identify with the king.

_____ 7. What generalization does the King of Brobdingnag imply about British professionals such as priests, soldiers, judges, and senators?
    a. They spend all their time gambling.
    b. They do not care about their careers.
    c. They spend all their time fighting.
    d. They do not deserve their positions.

_____ 8. When the king of Brobdingnag tells Gulliver he "knew no reason why those who entertain opinions prejudicial to the public should be obliged to change or should not be obliged to conceal them," Swift is actually satirizing
    a. the hypocrisy of the right to freedom of speech.
    b. crime in England.
    c. the English judicial system.
    d. rich people's prejudices against the poor.

_____ 9. Gulliver's stories about his country's greatness convince the king of Brobdingnag that the English as a group are

    a. very small.   c. selfish idiots.

    b. hateful vermin.   d. rich and powerful.

_____ 10. According to the king of Brobdingnag the qualifications necessary to be an English legislator are

    a. pride and arrogance.

    b. wit and ingenuity.

    c. an appreciation of the arts and nature.

    d. ignorance, idleness, and vice.

_____ 11. What is the target of Swift's satire when he has Gulliver offer the king of Brobdingnag the technology to make gunpowder and the king refuses?

    a. the inhumanity of modern warfare

    b. the inability of rulers to accept change

    c. the folly of the religious schism in Europe

    d. the wisdom of European rulers

_____ 12. Whom or what might Swift be satirizing with the line "And it would be hard indeed if so remote a prince's notions of virtue and vice were to be offered as a standard for all mankind"?

    a. the king of France

    b. the king of Blefuscu

    c. the king of England

    d. Lilliputian politics as a whole

_____ 13. In contrast to Gulliver's likely view of similar elements in Lilliputian society, the King of Brobdingnag views

    a. British disputes as meaningful.

    b. British titles as significant.

    c. British weapons as dangerous.

    d. British factions as important.

_____ 14. What theme do "A Voyage to Lilliput" and "A Voyage to Brobdingnag" together convey?

    a. People tend to think that their own disputes are more important than those of others.

    b. People who travel widely have a more objective view of themselves and their countries.

    c. People too often compare themselves to others and as a result feel a false superiority.

    d. People tend to be suspicious of foreigners no matter how wise or reasonable the foreigners are.

Vocabulary and Grammar

On the line, write the letter of the one best answer.

_____ 15. If a person is _habituated_ to a certain situation, he or she

    a. has bad habits.

    b. is trying to change the situation.

    c. helped to create the situation.

    d. is used to the situation.

_____ 16. Which of the following words is closest in meaning to _schism_?

    a. battle   c. division

    b. debate   d. problem

_____ 17. If a person *conjectures* about the weather, he or she is
  a. predicting.
  b. warning.
  c. complaining.
  d. guessing.

_____ 18. Which of the following sentences uses the preposition *among* correctly?
  a. There was a conversation among Gulliver and the king of Brobdingnag.
  b. Among the two countries, war was an ongoing fact of life.
  c. There was animosity among Gulliver and the Lilliputian king.
  d. Among many of the people of Lilliput, Gulliver was considered a hero.

_____ 19. In which of the following sentences could you use *between* to fill in the blank?
  a. Swift was a popular satirist _____ the English.
  b. There was a special bond _____ Swift and the members of the Scriblerus Club.
  c. _____ other things, Swift was an accomplished scholar.
  d. Swift was _____ those who felt that unbridled violence was a negative force.

_____ 20. Which of the following sentences uses the preposition *between* correctly?
  a. There was much amazement about Gulliver between the Lilliputians.
  b. Between clergymen, the practice of writing satire was rare.
  c. Swift saw a connection between narrow-mindedness and corruption.
  d. He advocated broad-mindedness between all people.

Essay Questions

21. Satire can be directed at different kinds of objects—society, politics, human nature, institutions, for example. Write an essay in which you explain the target of Swift's satire in one or both of the excerpts from *Gulliver's Travels*.

22. Jonathan Swift's early ambition was toward a life in politics, but, not receiving the support he needed to follow that ambition, he embarked upon a career in the church. It is no surprise, then, that politics and religion figure prominently in his work. Write an essay exploring the importance of both church and state in *Gulliver's Travels* and how the treatment of both institutions may be rooted in Swift's experience. Use examples from one or both of the excerpts.

23. Jonathan Swift was a man who had little tolerance for fanaticism of any kind. He disliked the human tendencies toward selfishness and pride, but he maintained lifelong admiration for the attributes of individual human beings. Find examples from one or both of the selections that illustrate Swift's impatience with human folly and his admiration for the individual spirit.

from *An Essay on Man* and from *The Rape of the Lock*
by Alexander Pope

Selection Test

Critical Reading

On the line, write the letter of the one best answer.

Unit 3: A Turbulent Time (1625–1798)

_____ 1. A central idea of the excerpt from *An Essay on Man* is that human beings
   a. control their minds but not their hearts.
   b. have many powers but also many weaknesses.
   c. try too hard to be completely rational.
   d. resemble beasts more than angels.

_____ 2. Pope's images in this excerpt from *An Essay on Man* suggest the view that intellect and emotion are
   a. fundamentally similar.
   b. equally valuable.
   c. mutually complementary.
   d. strongly opposing.

_____ 3. When Pope refers to "a middle state," he is referring most likely to a state between
   a. birth and death.
   b. god and animal.
   c. knowledge and doubt.
   d. Heaven and Hell.

_____ 4. Which of the following is a characteristic of a true epic reflected in *The Rape of the Lock?*
   a. a sarcastic tone
   b. an elevated style
   c. a serious subject
   d. an ironic theme

_____ 5. Belinda's cards are the mock-epic substitute for
   a. admirers.
   b. rivals.
   c. soldiers.
   d. enemies.

_____ 6. Which of the following lines from *The Rape of the Lock* could have been found in a true epic?
   a. "For lo! the board with cups and spoons is crowned . . . "
   b. ". . . Descend, and sit on each important card . . . "
   c. ". . . With singing, laughing, ogling, and all that."
   d. ". . . (But airy substance soon unites again)."

_____ 7. What activity is Pope most likely referring to in these lines?

   A third interprets motions, looks, and eyes; / At every word a reputation dies.

   a. judicial decisions
   b. slanderous gossip
   c. news reporting
   d. idle conversation

_____ 8. Which of the following characterizes a true epic and is seen in *The Rape of the Lock*?
   a. everyday details
   b. humorous contrasts
   c. heroic acts
   d. impossible events

_____ 9. Alexander Pope's purpose for writing *The Rape of the Lock* was to
   a. show Belinda as a shallow person.
   b. expose the absurdity of the card game called omber.
   c. poke fun at the spoiled upper classes.
   d. speak out against the rich, and in favor of the poor.

_____ 10. A central theme of *The Rape of the Lock* is the
   a. pettiness of the nobility.
   b. naivete of the very young.
   c. watchfulness of the angels.
   d. tragedy of romantic love.

_____ 11. In *The Rape of the Lock*, when the baron cries out that the glorious prize is his, he refers to
   a. the hairs he has snipped from Belinda's head.
   b. the game of omber he has won.
   c. Clarissa's hand in marriage.
   d. a pair of scissors.

_____ 12. In *The Rape of the Lock*, with what weapon does Belinda defeat the baron?
   a. a pair of scissors
   b. a cup of coffee
   c. a large pinch of snuff
   d. a candleholder

_____ 13. Which of the following best describes the overall feeling that Pope meant to convey in *The Rape of the Lock*?
   a. satiric but angry
   b. bitterly disappointed
   c. pitying
   d. affectionately mocking

_____ 14. Which of the following statements best describes the point Pope makes in *The Rape of the Lock*?
   a. When all is said and done, the rich don't get along with each other all that well.
   b. The rich are not as intelligent as the poor.
   c. The rich have too much time on their hands and not enough to think about.
   d. The rich enjoy gossiping and attending card parties.

Vocabulary and Grammar

On the line, write the letter of the one best answer.

_____ 15. The word *desist* means to
   a. hurry.
   b. stop.
   c. argue.
   d. annoy.

____ 16. Which phrase has nearly the same meaning as *stoic*?
- a. subtly sad
- b. deeply sorrowful
- c. quietly furious
- d. steadfastly emotionless

____ 17. The word *plebeian* relates to ____.
- a. the beggars
- b. the aristocracy
- c. the lower class
- d. the upper class

____ 18. Which of the following is *not* an example of inverted word order?
- a. "The nymph exulting fills with shouts the sky. . . ."
- b. "Of broken troops an easy conquest find."
- c. "On one nice trick depends the general fate."
- d. "At this, the blood the virgin's cheek forsook. . . ."

____ 19. Inverted word order is a change in
- a. subject-verb agreement.
- b. subject-verb-complement order.
- c. subject-adjective order.
- d. verb-complement-adverb order.

____ 20. Which of the following is *not* a reason to use inverted word order?
- a. to achieve regular rhyme
- b. to emphasize key words
- c. to make the language seem more formal
- d. to place strong rhyme words at the end of a line

Essay Questions

21. *The Rape of the Lock* is based upon an actual incident that took place in London during Alexander Pope's lifetime. Pope was careful to keep the tone of the poem light. His aim was not to brutalize the upper class for their pretensions but rather to point those pretensions out and perhaps to get members of the upper class to laugh along with him. Give examples that demonstrate the light nature of the poem. How do the examples reveal the author's purpose?

22. Because of his Catholic religion, Alexander Pope was deprived of certain basic rights. He could not attend a university, vote, hold office, or live within the city limits of London. Pope also suffered from a crippling childhood disease and persistent ill health. Write an essay on how the isolating circumstances of Pope's life might have influenced his work. Use examples from one or both of the works of Pope that you have read to illustrate your point of view.

23. The twentieth-century poet Edith Sitwell calls Alexander Pope "perhaps the most flawless artist our race has yet produced." Great art is universal—meaning that it maintains its appeal for people throughout time by addressing certain truths about what it means to be human. Choose one or both of the works in the textbook and write an essay that explains what universal truths are contained in the passage or passages you select.

Name _____ Date _____

**from *The Preface to A Dictionary of the English Language* and
from *A Dictionary of the English Language* by Samuel Johnson
from *The Life of Samuel Johnson* by James Boswell**

Selection Test

Critical Reading

On the line, write the letter of the one best answer.

____ 1. Johnson's tone in "The Preface" is
    a. confident and proud.
    b. angry and embittered.
    c. relieved and detached.
    d. weary and resigned.

____ 2. Which of the following is one of Johnson's themes in this excerpt from "The Preface"?
    a. If he hadn't written it, no one else would have.
    b. If he is not praised, it is entirely his fault.
    c. If he hasn't succeeded, neither has anyone else.
    d. If he had known how much effort it would take, he would not have attempted it.

____ 3. In the excerpt from "The Preface," Johnson indirectly compares the English language to a
    a. kind patron.   c. growing tree.
    b. cruel tyrant.   d. runaway child.

____ 4. An appropriate purpose for reading "The Preface" to Johnson's dictionary would be to find out
    a. how he acted when he first met people.
    b. why he wrote the dictionary.
    c. the cause of his childhood illnesses.
    d. how many words his dictionary contains.

____ 5. Which of the following entries from Johnson's *Dictionary* has most changed its meaning from his time to the present?

    athle' tick. Strong of body; vigorous; lusty; robust.

        Science distinguishes a man of honor from one of those *athletick* brutes, whom undeservedly we call heroes. Dryden.

    ha' tchet-face. An ugly face; such, I suppose, as might be hewn out of a block by a hatchet.

        An ape his own dear image will embrace;
        An ugly beau adores a *hatchet-face.* Dryden.

    mo' dern. In Shakespeare, vulgar; mean; common.

        We have our philosophical persons to make *modern* and familiar things supernatural and causeless. Shakespeare.

    you' ngster, you' nker. A young person. In contempt.

    a. athletick
    b. hatchet-face
    c. modern
    d. youngster

6. What does the phrase "in contempt" in the definition of *youngster* refer to?
   a. Johnson's opinion of young people
   b. word meaning
   c. word derivation
   d. word usage

7. What was Johnson's main reason for including quotations from eminent authors in the dictionary?
   a. to demonstrate correct usage
   b. to amuse his readers
   c. to display the origins of the entry word
   d. to educate readers about quality literature

8. What do these dictionary entries reveal about Samuel Johnson's character?
   a. his vast knowledge of literature
   b. his contempt for lower-class speech
   c. his dislike of picturesque slang
   d. his anger at the corruption of idioms

9. An appropriate purpose for reading these entries would be to find out
   a. the modern usage of old English words.
   b. how to pronounce difficult English words.
   c. why Johnson wrote the dictionary.
   d. the rules of English grammar.

10. Which of the following is a strength in Johnson that Boswell praises above others?
   a. poetic genius
   b. depth of knowledge
   c. mental agility
   d. unfailing politeness

11. The attitude that dominates Boswell's descriptions of Johnson is
   a. deep reverence.
   b. complacent superiority.
   c. cold scrutiny.
   d. casual detachment.

12. Boswell comes away from his first meeting with Dr. Johnson feeling
   a. flattered and accepted.
   b. shattered and disillusioned.
   c. angered and deceived.
   d. humiliated and awestruck.

13. Johnson's first impression of Boswell was most likely of a person who was too
   a. fawning and servile.
   b. confident and assured.
   c. humble and modest.
   d. critical and judgmental.

14. A predominant theme in Boswell's descriptions of both Johnson's character and their first meeting is
   a. the intensity of Johnson's faith, charity, and religious devotion.
   b. the brilliance of Johnson's conversation, wit, and writing.
   c. the strength of Johnson's spirit through sadness, poverty, and illness.
   d. the harshness of Johnson's insults, retorts, and rejoinders.

15. Which of these is the most important reason for setting purposes before reading?
   a. to provide a focus and thus avoid being overwhelmed
   b. to collect the largest number of facts possible
   c. to increase your powers of concentration
   d. to concentrate on your personal areas of interest

Vocabulary and Grammar

On the line, write the letter of the one best answer.

____ 16. The ____, as sole legislator, issued a(n) ____ censoring the press.
    a. propagator, abasement
    b. propagator, adulteration
    c. dictator, caprice
    d. dictator, edict

____ 17. Which of the following words is the best synonym for *risible*?
    a. hostile
    b. laughable
    c. soaring
    d. despicable

____ 18. Which of the following words means the opposite of *malignity*?
    a. health
    b. tumor
    c. menace
    d. kindness

____ 19. Which of the following sentences contains a parenthetical expression with correct punctuation?
    a. That, Sir, I find is what a very great many of your countrymen cannot help.
    b. That, Sir, I find, is what a very great many of your countrymen cannot help.
    c. That, Sir I find, is what a very great many of your countrymen cannot help.
    d. That Sir I find is what a very great many of your countrymen cannot help.

____ 20. Which of the following sentences contains a parenthetical expression with correct punctuation?
    a. Man is, in general, made up of contradictory qualities.
    b. When a butcher tells you that his heart bleeds for his country, he has, in fact no uneasy feeling.
    c. But, however that might be this speech was somewhat unlucky.
    d. And in truth had not my ardor been uncommonly strong, so rough a reception might had deterred me forever from making any further attempts.

Essay Questions

21. Write an essay comparing Johnson's dictionary with a modern dictionary. Evaluate Johnson's contribution to the science of lexicography, the making of dictionaries. To what extent did he achieve the purposes he aspired to in "The Preface"?

22. Boswell describes Johnson as a man "of contradictory qualities. . . . At different times, he seemed a different man, in some respects. . . ." Create a written portrait of Johnson in which you present his contradictory qualities and evaluate their importance. Did his faults outweigh his virtues and achievements? Present your opinion in this essay, and cite examples from Boswell to support your answer.

23. The reader learns much about Boswell from his biography of Johnson. Write a brief character sketch of Boswell. Analyze the friendship between the two men and the influence each had on the other. Did their personal relationship compromise or enhance the biography?

"Elegy Written in a Country Churchyard" by Thomas Gray
"A Nocturnal Reverie" by Ann Finch, Countess of Winchilsea

Selection Test

Critical Reading

On the line, write the letter of the one best answer.

_____ 1. "Elegy Written in a Country Churchyard" is similar to other elegies in that it arises from
    a. the stylistic ideals of the Neoclassicists.
    b. the contemplation of the natural world.
    c. the personal experience of the poet.
    d. the traditions of the ancient Greeks.

_____ 2. Which is the best paraphrase of the following lines from "Elegy Written in a Country Churchyard"?

    On some fond breast the parting soul relies,
    Some pious drops the closing eye requires. . .

    a. Most people cry at funerals.
    b. The last thing a dying person sees is a loved one crying.
    c. Every dying person needs someone to mourn his or her passing.
    d. Death is more sorrowful for some people than for others.

_____ 3. Like the works of the Romantic poets that were to follow, Gray's "Elegy Written in a Country Churchyard" reflects a concern for
    a. all life forms.
    b. the common person.
    c. the problems caused by cities and crowds.
    d. religion.

_____ 4. A central idea of "Elegy Written in a Country Churchyard" is that
    a. the great and the lowly find equality in death.
    b. no one notices the deaths of the common people.
    c. eloquent epitaphs take away the sting of death.
    d. a country churchyard contains forgotten kings and heroes.

_____ 5. Toward the end of the poem, the poet seems to take most comfort from the thought that
    a. in another time he might have been famous.
    b. his epitaph will be more elegant than others.
    c. people may remember his habits and virtues.
    d. many in the village will mourn his death.

_____ 6. What does the poet mean in the following lines?

    Their lot forbade: nor circumscribed alone
    Their growing virtues, but their crimes confined

    a. The villagers' simple lives helped them avoid evil.
    b. The villagers' vices were the cause of their hard lives.
    c. The villagers' lives prevented them from being good.
    d. The villagers' faults were hidden by their deaths.

____ 7. In "Elegy Written in a Country Churchyard," to whom do the following lines refer?

> Each in his narrow cell forever laid,
> The rude forefathers of the hamlet sleep

    a. the townspeople asleep in their beds
    b. dead members of the community in their graves
    c. prisoners in the town jail
    d. townspeople who died in prison

____ 8. In "Elegy Written in a Country Churchyard," Gray compares the dead of the little village to famous leaders and poets in order to emphasize
    a. the many differences between them.
    b. the way in which the poor have been abused.
    c. the townspeople's lack of education.
    d. the importance of every person.

____ 9. The epitaph at the end of "Elegy Written in a Country Churchyard" is for
    a. a "hoary-headed swain."   c. a town forefather.
    b. a famous youth.   d. the speaker of the poem.

____ 10. What is a reverie?
    a. a work that mourns someone's death
    b. a fanciful, dreamlike poem
    c. a poem written in the seventeenth and eighteenth centuries
    d. a poem written in blank verse

____ 11. In "A Nocturnal Reverie," to what do the following lines refer?

> Whose stealing pace and lengthened shade we fear,
> Till torn-up forage in his teeth we hear:

    a. a horse quietly approaching through the shadows at dusk
    b. the night falling slowly over the valley
    c. a mythological unicorn
    d. the poet's fear of death

____ 12. Which is the best paraphrase of the following lines from "A Nocturnal Reverie"?

> When in some river, overhung with green,
> The waving moon and trembling leaves are seen;

    a. The moonlight, partially blocked by the trees, can be seen in the river.
    b. The overhanging branches sway between the moon and water.
    c. The breeze makes the branches tremble and the moon appear to move.
    d. The moonlight and leaves of the trees are reflected in the flowing river.

____ 13. Which is the best paraphrase of the following lines from "A Nocturnal Reverie"?

> When odors, which declined repelling day,
> Through temperate air uninterrupted stray;

    a. The sweet scents that were not detectable during the day, are, at evening, easily noticed.
    b. When the air is mild, all the repellent smells of day fade away.
    c. There is a strong, pleasant scent in the air.
    d. There is a barely detectable, but unpleasant, scent in the air.

____ 14. The speakers in "Elegy Written in a Country Churchyard" and "A Nocturnal Reverie" present themselves as somewhat
    a. self-involved.   c. proud.
    b. isolated.   d. mournful.

Vocabulary and Grammar

On the line, write the letter of the one best answer.

____ 15. Which of the following words is most nearly opposite in meaning to *jocund*?
a. hostile
b. melancholy
c. embittered
d. cheerful

____ 16. Which of the following words in closest in meaning to *penury*?
a. sadness
b. desperation
c. melancholy
d. poverty

____ 17. If a person's schedule is *circumscribed*, he or she has
a. lots of spare time.
b. no time.
c. limited time.
d. many scheduling conflicts.

____ 18. Which of the following pronouns correctly completes the line "When darkened groves ____ softest shadows wear"?
a. its
b. their
c. my
d. our

____ 19. Which of the following sentences uses correct pronoun-antecedent agreement?
a. The rose and violet give off its sweet, subtle scents.
b. Every villager will eventually have their grave in the churchyard.
c. Listen to the cows chewing on its cud.
d. All the children have their supper at the end of the day.

____ 20. Which of the following phrases does *not* use correct pronoun-antecedent agreement?
a. When nibbling sheep at large pursue their food . . .
b. When to her straggling brood the partridge calls . . .
c. Their shortlived jubilee the creature keeps . . .
d. And no fierce light disturbs, whilst it reveals . . .

Essay Questions

21. Anne Finch, Countess of Winchilsea, lived during a time when women were perceived as intellectually inferior to men. Women intellectuals were looked upon with amusement and scorn even by those members of society who considered themselves enlightened. Much of Finch's work addressed this theme, expressing sorrow at the way the world perceived the talents of women. Does Finch reveal any unhappiness or dissatisfaction in the poem "A Nocturnal Reverie"? Cite examples from the poem to support your answer.

22. The action in both Gray's "Elegy Written in a Country Churchyard" and Finch's "A Nocturnal Reverie" takes place in the evening hours. In Gray's poem, the time is dusk, when daylight has just begun to turn to darkness. Finch's poem describes early evening through deep night. Choose one or both of these poems and examine why night held such meaning for these poets. Find support for your answer in details from each work.

23. In "Elegy Written in a Country Churchyard," Thomas Gray reveals at length his strong feelings of empathy for poor farmers and their families. Regardless of his feelings, do you think Gray deliberately sets himself apart from such people? Write an essay expressing your opinion. How does the speaker's voice in the poem reveal the poet's attitude? What biographical facts about Gray can you use to support your opinion?

from *The Analects* by Confucius
from The Declaration of Independence by Thomas Jefferson

Selection Test

Critical Reading

On the line, write the letter of the one best answer.

_____ 1. What can be inferred from the Declaration of Independence about Jefferson's general attitude toward revolution and rebellion?
    a. All cases of injustice vindicate revolution and rebellion.
    b. People frequently use revolution and rebellion as their first course of action.
    c. Revolution and rebellion are methods of last resort.
    d. Revolution and rebellion are poor ways of dealing with conflict.

_____ 2. When Jefferson ends the declaration by stating his "firm reliance on the protection of divine providence," what is he suggesting?
    a. American does not need to act, since God will protect the new nation.
    b. He is secure in his belief that God will bless America's fight for independence.
    c. Americans will be rewarded in Heaven for breaking from Britain.
    d. He hopes that God will protect America's interests.

_____ 3. The major purpose of the first part of the Declaration of Independence is to
    a. establish the reasons for and justness of the break from England.
    b. prove that America is under the protection of God.
    c. emphasize the tyranny of the British king.
    d. persuade Americans that negotiations with England are still possible.

_____ 4. Jefferson's list of self-evident truths is effective because it
    a. helps his audience understand the truths.
    b. creates a connection between these truths and the colonists' attempts at reconciliation with Britain.
    c. draws his readers' attention to his personal opinions about humanity.
    d. imparts a sense of reasonableness to the beginning of his argument.

_____ 5. Jefferson uses the charged word *tyrant* to characterize the king of Britain. What emotion is Jefferson appealing to by using this word?
    a. sorrow   c. hatred
    b. scorn   d. pride

_____ 6. According to Confucius, a worthy person is one who
    a. expects a lot from others.
    b. makes no promises.
    c. considers alternate views.
    d. governs many subjects.

_____ 7. Choose the word that best completes the following sentence: According to Confucius, the health of any particular society depends on the _____ of its leader.
    a. wealth   c. friends
    b. armies   d. character

_____ 8. According to Confucius, which one quality is most important to a successful leader?
    a. intellectual ability   c. powerful personality
    b. sense of morality   d. fear of failure

9. The line "ritual performed without reverence, the forms of mourning observed without grief" is a judgment against people who are
   a. simple.
   c. phony.
   b. happy.
   d. biased.

10. Which proverb is closest in meaning to a recurrent theme in *The Analects*?
   a. It's six of one and a half-dozen of the other.
   b. A rolling stone gathers no moss.
   c. The early bird catches the worm.
   d. Actions speak louder than words.

Essay Questions

11. *The Analects* by Confucius are structured as a dialogue between the Master (Confucius) and his followers or pupils. In an essay, explain the effect of this structure on the reader's perception of the work. How does the dialogue form reinforce Confucius's lessons?

12. In a letter from 1811, Jefferson wrote, "I have never been able to conceive how any rational being could propose happiness to himself from the exercise of power over others." Write an essay linking this quotation to the basic principles outlined in the Declaration of Independence.

13. A prominent scholar suggests that Confucius had as his aim "to restore trust in government and to transform society into a moral community by cultivating a sense of humanity in politics and society." In an essay, briefly explain this view in terms of the selections from *The Analects*.

Unit 3: A Turbulent Time (1625–1798)

Part Test, Unit 3, Part 3: The Ties That Bind

Critical Reading

The questions below are based on the following selection.

The following selection is Robert Burns's "Afton Water." The Afton is a river in Ayrshire, a former county in southwestern Scotland. In this poem Burns uses several Scottish terms, including braes *("slopes"),* cot *("cottage"),* lea *("meadow"), and* birk *("birch").*

Flow gently, sweet Afton, among thy green braes,

Flow gently, I'll sing thee a song in thy praise;

My Mary's asleep by thy murmuring stream,

Flow gently, sweet Afton, disturb not her dream.

[5] Thou stock-dove whose echo resounds through the glen,

Ye wild whistling blackbirds in yon thorny den,

Thou green-crested lapwing, thy screaming forbear,

I charge you, disturb not my slumbering fair.

How lofty, sweet Afton, thy neighboring hills,

[10] Far marked with the courses of clear, winding rills;

There daily I wander as noon rises high,

My flocks and my Mary's sweet cot in my eye.

How pleasant thy banks and green valleys below,

Where wild in the woodlands the primroses blow;

[15] There oft as mild evening weeps over the lea,

The sweet-scented birk shades my Mary and me.

Thy crystal stream, Afton, how lovely it glides,

And winds by the cot where my Mary resides;

How wanton thy waters her snowy feet lave,

[20] As gathering sweet flowerets she stems thy clear wave.

Flow gently, sweet Afton, among thy green braes,

Flow gently, sweet river, the theme of my lays;

My Mary's asleep by thy murmuring stream,

Flow gently, sweet Afton, disturb not her dream.

On the line, write the letter of the one best answer.

_____ 1. Which is not addressed by the speaker in the first two stanzas?
a. the Afton
b. Mary
c. a lapwing
d. blackbirds

_____ 2. Which is the best description of the poem's mood?
a. gentle
b. assertive
c. pleading
d. sad

_____ 3. Preromantic poems such as "Afton Water" emphasize each of the following *except*
a. mystery
b. emotion
c. individual expression
d. reason

_____ 4. Which line allows you to draw a conclusion about the nature of Mary's relationship with the speaker?
a. "Flow gently, sweet Afton, disturb not her dream"
b. "I charge you, disturb not my slumbering fair"
c. "There daily I wander as noon rises high"
d. "As gathering sweet flowerets she stems thy clear wave"

_____ 5. What is the speaker's occupation?
a. lumberman
b. poet
c. shepherd
d. ferryman

_____ 6. Given this poem, how would you describe Burns's attitude toward nature?
a. suspicious
b. sympathetic
c. indifferent
d. rapturous

_____ 7. Given the speaker's promise in line 2, what might be deemed the most likely start of his song to the "sweet Afton"?
a. "Flow gently, I'll sing thee a song in thy praise"
b. "Thou stock-dove whose echo resounds through the glen"
c. "How lofty, sweet Afton, thy neighboring hills"
d. "How pleasant thy banks and green valleys below"

_____ 8. One of Burns's primary purposes in writing "Afton Water" was probably
a. to evoke the delights and beauty of nature and romantic love.
b. to ridicule certain annoying aspects of nature.
c. to celebrate England.
d. to persuade Mary to spend more time with him.

_____ 9. In which of the following lines does Burns not personify some aspect of nature?
a. "My Mary's asleep by thy murmuring stream"
b. "My flocks and my Mary's sweet cot in my eye"
c. "There oft as mild evening weeps over the lea"
d. "How wanton thy waters her snowy feet lave"

____ 10. In what sense is the second stanza crucial to the total effect of the poem?
   a. A song should have an even number of stanzas.
   b. Images involving the sense of hearing are vital to the poem.
   c. It is important that the speaker address something other than the water.
   d. Its suggestion of mild conflict roots the otherwise gentle song in the real world of nature.

Vocabulary and Grammar

On the line, write the letter of the one best answer.

____ 11. At one point Pepys notes that the number of deaths has *abated,* or _____.
   a. increased   c. lessened
   b. leveled off   d. stopped

____ 12. A *lamentable* fire is one that causes _____.
   a. excitement   c. water damage
   b. blame   d. distress

____ 13. Which sentence contains a gerund?
   a. Discoursing and lamenting the fire did little good.
   b. Poor Payne, my waiter, hath buried a child, and is dying himself.
   c. One of my own watermen, that carried me daily, fell sick as soon as he had landed me on Friday morning last.
   d. To the King's message he cried, like a fainting woman, "Lord! what can I do?"

____ 14. Which is a true statement?
   a. The word *among* is correctly used when referring to more than two items.
   b. The word *between* is correctly used when referring to more than two items.
   c. The word *between* is correctly used when referring to a single item.
   d. The word *among* is correctly used when referring to fewer than two items.

____ 15. How is the gerund *bringing* used in the following excerpt?

   His Majesty desired I would take some other opportunity of bringing all the rest of his enemy's ships into his ports.

   a. It is the subject of the sentence.
   b. It is the object of the preposition *of.*
   c. It is the direct object of the verb *take.*
   d. It modifies the noun *ships.*

____ 16. What is the antecedent of the pronoun *her* in the following passage?

   Save that from yonder ivy-mantled tower,
   The moping owl does to the moon complain
   Of such as, wandering near her secret bower,
   Molest her ancient solitary reign.

   a. bower
   b. tower
   c. owl
   d. moon

____ 17. Which line contains inverted word order?
   a. Thus far both armies to Belinda yield.
   b. She sees, and trembles at the approaching ill.
   c. He springs to vengeance with an eager pace.
   d. At once they gratify their scent and taste.

The three questions below consist of a related pair of words in CAPITAL LETTERS, followed by four other pairs of words. Choose the pair that best expresses a relationship similar to that expressed in the capitalized words.

____ 18. ODIOUS : UNPLEASANT ::
   a. disgusting : horrible
   b. ecstatic : happy
   c. foul : acrid
   d. drama : sensitivity

____ 19. CONJECTURE : GUESS ::
   a. expostulate : deride
   b. habituate : introduce
   c. imitate : mimic
   d. destitute : needy

____ 20. ABASEMENT : HUMBLED ::
   a. contentment : satisfied
   b. stoic : impassivity
   c. credulity : gullibility
   d. recompense : reward

Essay Questions

21. In his mock-epic, Alexander Pope uses grand, elevated poetic language to describe petty subjects. Identify one specific example of this technique in the excerpt from *The Rape of the Lock*. In an essay, explain how Pope uses this type of language to make his subject appear ridiculous.

22. Jonathan Swift ridicules various types of human vice and folly in *Gulliver's Travels*. In an essay, explain which particular aspects of society Swift reveals in this excerpt. Include a paragraph explaining whether you judge his satire to be light and good-humored or bitter and unsparing.

23. Thomas Gray's "Elegy Written in a Country Churchyard" has long been considered among the greatest elegies ever composed in the English language. In an essay, discuss whether you think the poem's speaker mourns a single individual—or something more.

24. Samuel Johnson's *A Dictionary of the English Language* (1755) became the standard dictionary for several generations—until the appearance of Noah Webster's volume in 1828. In the style of Johnson, write four or five additional entries to those that appear in the excerpt in your text. Include the word, its pronunciation, part of speech, and definition, as well as a sentence that clearly shows its meaning. You might wish to choose words that have acquired somewhat different meanings over the past two centuries.

25. Although most biographers make an earnest attempt to present information objectively, their own attitudes and feelings about their subjects are sometimes detectable in the finished biographies. Think about the relationship between James Boswell and Samuel Johnson. In an essay, discuss this biographer's attitude toward his subject. Explain whether you believe Boswell presents Johnson truly or not, and explain your response.

Name _____ Date _____

"On Spring" by Samuel Johnson
from "The Aims of the Spectator" by Joseph Addison

Selection Test

Critical Reading

On the line, write the letter of the one best answer.

_____ 1. What is Johnson's main topic of discussion in "On Spring"?
a. the quest for future happiness
b. the flowers and roses that bloom in spring
c. the value of spring in our lives
d. the men to whom spring gives no delight

_____ 2. "On Spring" is written in the following form—
a. a prose poem.   c. a dramatic monologue.
b. an essay.   d. an epic poem.

_____ 3. What does Johnson mean when he says in "On Spring" that "when a man cannot bear his own company there is something wrong"?
a. People should be able to appreciate solitude.
b. People should respect their employers.
c. People should always seek the company of others.
d. Employers should respect their employees.

_____ 4. What can you infer from this passage, in which Johnson describes a friend?

. . . he always talked of the spring as coming till it was past, and when it was once past, everyone agreed with him that it was coming

a. Johnson suggests that spring is easy to miss.
b. Johnson is condemning his friend for foolishness.
c. Johnson views his friend's behavior with humorous detachment.
d. Johnson suggests that his friend doesn't pay much attention to what others say.

_____ 5. Who does Johnson describe when he writes of "those, whom fear of any future affliction chains down to misery, must endeavor to obviate the danger"?
a. people who are hurtful of others
b. people who lead lives of courage and fortitude
c. people who dedicate themselves to helping others
d. people who live in timid fearfulness

_____ 6. Which of the following words best describes someone who, as Johnson advises, takes pleasure in nature?
a. happy   c. curious
b. serious   d. thrifty

_____ 7. What is Addison's main topic of discussion in his essay "The Aims of the Spectator"?
a. the occupations of women   c. the goals of a periodical
b. vice and folly   d. the role of philosophy

_____ 8. When Addison compares himself to Socrates you can infer that he is
a. exaggerating.   c. serious.
b. lying.   d. foolish.

_____ 9. What can you infer from Addison's statement that by reading *The Spectator* people will "distinguish themselves from the thoughtless herd of their ignorant and inattentive brethren."

    a. Addison is a snob.

    b. Addison is being humorous.

    c. Reading *The Spectator* will make one a snob.

    d. People in the eighteenth century were "ignorant and inattentive."

_____ 10. Which of the following words best describes Addison's attitude toward women's traditional pastimes and occupations?

    a. respectful

    b. accusatory

    c. critical

    d. horrified

_____ 11. A reader of Addison's essays would likely be someone who wants to

    a. learn about the world around him or her.

    b. know the weather and news from Europe.

    c. learn about the latest fashions in hairstyles.

    d. find out the latest financial news.

_____ 12. When you make inferences as you read a piece of writing, you

    a. divide the piece into four parts.

    b. reach logical conclusions about the author's meaning.

    c. note the author's political viewpoint.

    d. analyze the rhyme and meter of the piece.

_____ 13. In an essay, the thoughts and feelings that are expressed are those of the

    a. topic.

    b. author.

    c. poet.

    d. protagonist.

_____ 14. An essay is best described as a

    a. short prose piece about nature.

    b. short dramatic piece on ambition.

    c. a brief monologue on a strong emotion.

    d. a short prose piece on a specific topic.

Vocabulary and Grammar

On the line, write the letter of the one best answer.

_____ 15. What does the word *contentious* mean?

    a. invisible to the eye   c. immature

    b. very intelligent   d. argumentative

_____ 16. Which of the following means the opposite of *transient*?

    a. loud   c. permanent

    b. colorful   d. slow

_____ 17. Which of the following phrases has almost the same meaning as *speculation*?

    a. thoughtful guessing   c. inconvenient delay

    b. rambling speech   d. narrow-minded judgment

_____ 18. Which of the following words is *not* a relative pronoun?

    a. that   c. whom

    b. however   d. whose

_____ 19. Which of the following italicized phrases is an example of an adjective clause?
      a. I have often considered these poor souls *with an eye of great commiseration*
      b. the mind that lies fallow *but a single day*
      c. those whom sorrow incapacitates to enjoy *the pleasures of contemplation*
      d. I have the satisfaction of finding many *whom it can be no shame to resemble*

_____ 20. Which of these italicized phrases is *not* an adjective clause?
      a. a book *without a cover*
      b. the man *who lives upstairs*
      c. the bicycle *that he lost*
      d. a woman *whose ambitions will take her far*

Essay Questions

21. "On Spring" reflects on the wide variety of reactions people have to springtime and on the season's symbolic role as a time of hopefulness and renewal. In an essay, discuss Johnson's views on springtime. How does Johnson feel about spring? How does he think others should feel about it? Use specific details from Johnson's essay as evidence of your interpretation.

22. In "The Aims of the Spectator," Joseph Addison describes a number of different "types" of people who make up English society in the early eighteenth century. He describes regular families, wealthy gentlemen who don't need to work, tradesmen, idle gossips, and women. Choose two "types" or groups discussed in "The Aims of the Spectator"—one group that Addison seems to sympathize with and one group that he seems to criticize. Then write an essay describing how Addison believes *The Spectator* will benefit the lives of each group. How does he describe the behavior of these people? How does he think *The Spectator* will change them?

23. A scholar of Samuel Johnson's work has written that Johnson's writing shows a "keen understanding of human frailty." Write an essay in which you relate the scholar's statement to "On Spring." What human frailties does Johnson touch upon? Does he condemn these frailties or does he suggest ways to overcome them? Include evidence to support your points.

Name _____ Date _____

Selection Test

Critical Reading

On the line, write the letter of the one best answer.

_____ 1. Which of the following statements most closely matches Quindlen's own definition of "home"?
    a. "Home life as we understand it is no more natural to us than a cage is to a cocka-too." (George Bernard Shaw)
    b. "This is the true nature of home—it is the place of Peace; the shelter, not only from injury, but from all terror, doubt and division." (John Ruskin)
    c. "A home is not a mere transient shelter: its essence lies in the personalities of the people who live in it." (H. L. Mencken)
    d. "A person travels the world over in search of what he needs and returns home to find it." (George Moore)

_____ 2. Why does homelessness strike Quindlen as the world's most important problem?
    a. She was once homeless herself.
    b. She acutely senses people's need for a place of their own.
    c. Her uncle volunteers in a shelter for homeless people.
    d. Many people in New York live on the streets.

_____ 3. What does the following excerpt reveal about Quindlen's approach to the problem of homelessness?

> Here is a woman without a bureau. There is a man with no mirror, no wall to hang it on.

    a. The solution to a large problem must begin with something small.
    b. Only large social programs will solve the problem of homelessness.
    c. The government should provide not only apartments, but also furnishings to all people who are homeless.
    d. A basic human right is the right to shelter.

_____ 4. What does the homeless woman try to prove to Quindlen?
    a. She is not really homeless.
    b. She does not really live at the bus station, but in a nice house.
    c. She has maintained her dignity and deserves respect.
    d. She lost her house in a divorce.

_____ 5. Which development has most affected the concept of "home" since the days of Quindlen's grandparents?
    a. increased drug usage
    b. increased social mobility
    c. higher mortality rates
    d. more single parents

_____ 6. Where did Quindlen meet the homeless woman named Ann?
    a. at a train station
    b. in a bus terminal
    c. outside Quindlen's house
    d. at a soup kitchen

_____ 7. When a woman tells Quindlen that all she wants is "one room, painted blue," what does this symbolize for Quindlen?
   a. the woman's passion for painting
   b. the need for individuals to have a room of their own
   c. the importance of ownership and belonging
   d. the woman's deep sadness

_____ 8. Why does the homeless woman named Ann carry a picture of a house?
   a. to prove to herself she is not adrift, alone, or anonymous
   b. to fool the police into believing she has a home
   c. to remind her of her happy childhood
   d. to prove to Quindlen that she does not need a place to stay

_____ 9. What does Quindlen recommend as a means of dealing with the problem of homelessness?
   a. Society should build large apartment projects where people without homes could live for free.
   b. The general public must stop looking at homelessness as an abstract problem, and begin seeing it in terms of real individuals.
   c. Every family in America should pay for housing for one homeless person.
   d. Government must pass laws in order to help homeless people.

_____ 10. According to Quindlen, what effect does "changing an adjective into a noun" ("the poor, not poor people") have on the problem of homelessness?
   a. It enables the general public to relate to the issue, even when it does not affect them directly.
   b. It draws attention to people who are homeless, allowing social leaders to clearly see the individuals behind the generic term.
   c. It allows homeless people to organize as a group in order to attract help for people without homes.
   d. It robs homeless people of their individuality and dignity, making it easier for society to ignore their plight.

Essay Questions

11. In "Homeless," Quindlen approaches a serious social issue in an informal and personal manner. Write an essay discussing the effect such an approach has on the reader. Is Quindlen's approach appropriate or inappropriate to the subject matter? How would the effect differ if she had taken a more distanced, factual approach, such as in a government report?

12. In "Homeless," Quindlen carefully connects the ideas of "family" and "home." Write an essay examining her definition of "home." How is that definition linked to the idea of "family"? How have both concepts changed over the years, according to Quindlen?

13. Quindlen suggests an approach to dealing with the problem of homeless people without suggesting any concrete measures or social policies. In an essay, briefly describe the "personal" approach recommended by Quindlen. What ultimately is Quindlen's goal in dealing with people without homes? Go on to outline a policy based on this approach, something that might alleviate the problem of homelessness on the "global" level.

Part Test, Unit 3, Part 4: Focus on Literary Forms—The Essay

Critical Reading

The questions below are based on the following selection.

The following selection is from Joseph Addison's essay "Thoughts in Westminster Abbey." Westminster Abbey is a famous English church where English monarchs are crowned—and where English monarchs and many famous writers and statesmen are buried. This essay (in its entirety) was printed in The Spectator *on March 30, 1711.*

When I am in a serious humor, I very often walk by myself in Westminster Abbey; where the gloominess of the place, and the use to which it is applied, with the solemnity of the building, and the condition of the people who lie in it, are apt to fill the mind with a kind of melancholy, or rather thoughtfulness, that is not disagreeable. I yesterday passed a whole afternoon in the churchyard, the cloisters, and the church, amusing myself with the tombstones and inscriptions that I met with in those several regions of the dead. Most of them recorded nothing else of the buried person, but that he was born upon one day, and died upon another: the whole history of his life being comprehended in those two circumstances, that are common to all mankind. I could not but look upon these registers of existence, whether of brass or marble, as a kind of satire upon the departed persons; who had left no other memorial of them, but that they were born and that they died. They put me in mind of several persons mentioned in the battles of heroic poems, who have sounding names given them, for no other reason but that they may be killed, and are celebrated for nothing but being knocked on the head.

Upon my going into the church, I entertained myself with the digging of a grave; and saw in every shovelful of it that was thrown up, the fragment of a bone or skull intermixed with a kind of fresh moldering earth that some time or other had a place in the composition of a human body. Upon this I began to consider with myself what innumerable multitudes of people lay confused together under the pavement of that ancient cathedral; how men and women, friends and enemies, priests and soldiers, monks and prebendaries, were crumbled amongst one another, and blended together in the same common mass; how beauty, strength, and youth, with old age, weakness, and deformity, lay undistinguished in the same promiscuous heap of matter.

After having thus surveyed this great magazine of mortality, as it were, in the lump; I examined it more particularly by the accounts which I found on several of the monuments which are raised in every quarter of that ancient fabric. Some of them were covered with such extravagant epitaphs that, if it were possible for the dead person to be acquainted with them, he would blush at the praises which his friends have bestowed upon him. There are others so excessively modest, that they deliver the character of the person departed in Greek or Hebrew, and by that means are not understood once in a twelvemonth. . . .

Unit 3: A Turbulent Time (1625-1798)

On the line, write the letter of the one best answer.

_____ 1. How does Addison regard walking in Westminster Abbey?
    a. He finds it disagreeable.   c. He finds it fascinating.
    b. He finds it boring.   d. He finds it agreeable.

_____ 2. What does Addison have in common with "the people who lie in" the abbey?
    a. He has a famous name.   c. He is multilingual.
    b. He will die.   d. He has a respectable military career.

_____ 3. In the first paragraph, what connection does Addison make in his mind?
   a. He links his mood with the tombstones' appearance.
   b. He makes a connection between Westminster Abbey and the English character.
   c. He links the epitaphs' modesty with the names of several subjects of heroic poems.
   d. He connects the tombstones' design with the abbey.

_____ 4. After reading the first paragraph, you can infer that Addison is
   a. prone to reflection.
   b. hostile toward religious conformity.
   c. disrespectful of the dead.
   d. a member of the English upper classes.

_____ 5. By the phrase "these registers of existence," Addison means _____.
   a. graveyards   c. graves
   b. stonemasons   d. tombstones

_____ 6. What irony does Addison suggest in the second paragraph?
   a. One can see parts of bones or skulls in some graveyards.
   b. In this graveyard, dissimilar types of people are "blended together."
   c. The "ancient cathedral" holds both long-dead and recently deceased persons.
   d. A cathedral the size of Westminster can hold "multitudes of people."

_____ 7. Addison "tests" various ideas on all of the following topics except
   a. the value of religious faith.
   b. human pride.
   c. the impermanence of life.
   d. the humbling power of death.

_____ 8. From the second paragraph, a reader may infer that Addison's attitude toward the "blend[ing] together" of human remains is one of _____.
   a. disapproval
   b. deep pleasure
   c. keen interest
   d. resentment

_____ 9. How do the tombstones in the churchyard differ from those in the church?
   a. Those in the churchyard are larger.
   b. Those in the church are older.
   c. Those in the churchyard are older.
   d. Those in the church carry more detailed epitaphs.

_____ 10. From his comments in the third paragraph, you can infer that Addison
   a. adores extravagant epitaphs.
   b. is terrified of death.
   c. speaks fluent Greek.
   d. disapproves of extravagant epitaphs.

Vocabulary and Grammar

The questions below consist of a related pair of words in CAPITAL LETTERS, followed by four other pairs of words. Choose the pair that best expresses a relationship *similar* to that expressed in the capitalized words.

_____ 11. TRANSIENT : VISITOR ::
   a. traveling : motion
   b. constant : temporary
   c. immature : toddler
   d. scholar : knowledgeable

____ 12. CONTENTIOUS : IRRITABLE ::
  a. diversion : attention
  b. furious : angry
  c. content : quarrelsome
  d. hatred : conflict

____ 13. AFFLUENCE : POVERTY ::
  a. speculation : estimation
  b. donation : wealth
  c. propitious : inconvenient
  d. tediousness : excitement

On the line, write the letter of the one best answer.

____ 14. Which line contains an adjective clause?
  a. "This, I say, is the state of ordinary women."
  b. "I would earnestly entreat them not to stir out of their chambers till they have read this paper."
  c. "I shall spare no pains to make their instruction agreeable."
  d. "There is another set of men that I must likewise lay a claim to, whom I have lately called the blanks of society."

____ 15. What is the adjective clause in the following passage?

> I would therefore in a very particular manner recommend these my speculations to all well-regulated families that set apart an hour in every morning for tea and bread and butter.

  a. "in a very particular manner"
  b. "these my speculations to all well-regulated families"
  c. "that set apart an hour in every morning for tea and bread and butter"
  d. "for tea and bread and butter"

Essay Questions

16. Little did Joseph Addison know that his audience would include literature students nearly three hundred years in the future. In an essay, explain the specific types of people Addison names as his target audience. You might wish to speculate on the subjects in which these people might have been interested.

17. Samuel Johnson credits "a French author" with the idea that "very few men know how to take a walk." In an essay, explain what you think this statement means. Do you agree or disagree? In your opinion, how might a person take a walk "skillfully" or "knowledgeably" or "well"?

18. Offering reflections on nature's seasons has been a common topic of essayists for centuries. In an essay, identify and explain how Samuel Johnson treats this subject in a surprising or unfamiliar way.

"To a Mouse" and **"To a Louse"** by Robert Burns

"Woo'd and Married and A'" by Joanna Baillie

Selection Test

Critical Reading

On the line, write the letter of the one best answer.

_____ 1. What happens to the mouse's home in "To a Mouse"?
   a. Winter winds blow it away.
   b. The speaker's plow destroys it.
   c. The speaker's dog digs it up.
   d. It collapses under the sleet and rain.

_____ 2. Which lines from "To a Mouse" contain an example of dialect?
   a. "I'm truly sorry man's dominion"
   b. "Has broken Nature's social union,"
   c. "Has cost thee mony a weary nibble!"
   d. "In proving foresight may be vain:"

_____ 3. In "To a Mouse," the poet's attitude toward the mouse is chiefly one of ____.
   a. pity   c. respect
   b. scorn   d. disgust

_____ 4. According to the speaker in "To a Mouse," humans and mice are alike in their
   a. loneliness.
   b. willingness to steal.
   c. failure to plan for the future.
   d. vulnerability to disaster.

_____ 5. Which sentence best translates this line from "To a Mouse"?

   But, Mousie, thou art no thy lane . . .

   a. But Mousie, you are all alone.
   b. But Mousie, you are lame.
   c. But Mousie, you are not alone.
   d. But Mousie, you are not your house.

_____ 6. The central objects of the poet's scorn in "To a Louse" are
   a. religion and ritual.
   b. vanity and conceit.
   c. gossip and slander.
   d. fashion and finery.

_____ 7. Which line from "To a Louse" contains an example of dialect?
   a. "and seek your dinner / On some poor body."
   b. "dare unsettle / Your thick plantations."
   c. "a blunder free us / And foolish notion. . . ."
   d. "Detested, shunned by saunt an' sinner . . ."

_____ 8. What does the louse symbolize in "To a Louse"?
   a. illness   c. poor hygiene
   b. human flaws   d. inequality among people

_____ 9. Which statement best translates the passage?

> How dare ye set your fit upon her, / Sae fine a lady? / Gae somewhere else, and seek your dinner / On some poor body. / Swith! in some beggar's haffet squattle;

    a. This lady must have found you in a beggar's house.
    b. You should live on a beggar, not a wealthy lady.
    c. You attack wealthy and poor people both.
    d. You should not depend on others for your dinner.

_____ 10. Which strategy would be most helpful in translating the line?

> What airs in dress an' gait wad lea's us,
> And ev'n devotion!

    a. speaking words aloud, listening for similarities to standard English
    b. reading the footnote
    c. noting that apostrophes signal that a letter has been omitted
    d. looking for similarities between dialect words and standard English words

_____ 11. What is the bride's principal concern in the poem "Woo'd and Married and A'"?
    a. She is not in love with her bridegroom.
    b. She has nothing beautiful to wear.
    c. The bridegroom is too old for her.
    d. She fears a life of poverty and drudgery.

_____ 12. Which statement best describes what the bride learns in "Woo'd and Married and A'"?
    a. Marrying Johnny, who loves her, is enough.
    b. She and Johnny will have wealth eventually.
    c. Most people are poor when they first get married.
    d. She is not really too young to be married.

_____ 13. Which words best describe the character of the bridegroom in "Woo'd and Married and A'"?
    a. clever and wise
    b. foolish and poor
    c. wealthy and wise
    d. irresponsible and clever

_____ 14. Judging by the dialect in "Woo'd and Married and A'," what can you conclude about the characters?
    a. They are poor English workers.
    b. They are poor but well educated.
    c. They are poorly educated Scots.
    d. They are well educated Scots.

_____ 15. Which phrase best translates this line from "Woo'd and Married and A'"?

> Is na' she very weel aff... ?

    a. Does he think she is very well off?
    b. Does he think she is foolish?
    c. Isn't she very foolish?
    d. Isn't she very well off?

Vocabulary and Grammar

On the line, write the letter of the one best answer.

_____ 16. Which word is the closest in meaning to _dominion_?
    a. authority
    b. discipline
    c. nationality
    d. society

_____ 17. Which word means the opposite of *impudence*?
        a. rudeness
        b. shamelessness
        c. happiness
        d. courtesy

_____ 18. Which phrase is the closest in meaning to *discretion*?
        a. bad judgment
        b. good judgment
        c. lack of purpose
        d. good manners

_____ 19. Which of the lines from "To a Mouse" contains an interjection?
        a. "Thy wee bit housie, too, in ruin!"
        b. "An' cozie here, beneath the blast, / Thou thought to dwell. . . ."
        c. "But, och! I backward cast my e'e. . . ."
        d. "An' lea'e us nought but grief an' pain, / For promised joy."

_____ 20. In which of the following sentences is the interjection correctly punctuated?
        a. The mouse, poor thing, is without a home!
        b. Oh, no the winter has arrived!
        c. Alas, that mouse is afraid!
        d. The winter will be cold I fear and the wind strong!

Essay Questions

21. In the poems "To a Mouse" and "To a Louse," Burns expresses an idea by having a speaker address an animal. Write an essay in which you compare his use of the two animals. Is the speaker sympathetic to each of them? How does Burns represent each animal differently? What does each animal symbolize?

22. Joanna Baillie and Robert Burns lived at the same time and both came from Scotland, so they shared the same background and many of the same cultural experiences. Write an essay in which you compare "Woo'd and Married and A'" with "To a Mouse" and "To a Louse." Were these poems written for the same audience? Are the values expressed in the poems similar or different? Do the poets use similar or different techniques in their writing? Provide evidence from the poems to support your response.

23. Robert Burns wrote poetry that was popular in Scotland. When he died, thousands attended his funeral procession and he was named the national poet of Scotland. Write an essay in which you explain how "To a Mouse" and "To a Louse" would help Burns achieve such a reputation. How do you think the use of dialect contributed to his popularity? What would his countrypeople think of his themes and subject matter?

Name _____   Date _____

"The Lamb," "The Tyger," "Infant Sorrow," and "The Chimney Sweeper,"
by William Blake

Selection Test

Critical Reading

On the line, write the letter of the one best answer.

____ 1. Which is an abstract idea symbolized by the lamb in Blake's poem "The Lamb"?
    a. knowledge   c. innocence
    b. reason   d. ecstasy

____ 2. A central idea of "The Lamb" is the
    a. beauty of the earth.
    b. excitement of experience.
    c. vastness of the universe.
    d. kindness of the creator.

____ 3. Whom does Blake refer to as "He" in "The Lamb"?
    a. the Creator   c. the lamb
    b. the shepherd   d. the child

____ 4. Which word best describes the mood of the illustration accompanying "The Lamb"?
    a. happy   c. agitated
    b. gloomy   d. serene

____ 5. In Blake's poem "The Tyger," "the forests of the night" most clearly suggest the
    a. beauty and mystery of paradise.
    b. chaos and confusion of living.
    c. peace and relief of sleep.
    d. safety and security of childhood.

____ 6. A central image of "The Tyger" is
    a. power.   c. guilt.
    b. death.   d. peace.

____ 7. In "The Tyger," what is Blake most likely suggesting that overcame the stars?

    the stars threw down their spears, / And watered heaven with their tears,

    a. joy   c. sadness
    b. admiration   d. terror

____ 8. The images in Blake's illustrated versions of "The Lamb" and "The Tyger" can be best described as
    a. strictly classical in form.
    b. swirling through the words.
    c. sophisticated and refined.
    d. irrelevant to the poems themselves.

____ 9. Who is describing the action in "Infant Sorrow"?
    a. a mother   c. a newborn infant
    b. a father   d. an omniscient narrator

___ 10. What might the "swaddling bands" described in "Infant Sorrow" represent?
a. poverty   c. confinement
b. luxury   d. protection

___ 11. In "The Chimney Sweeper" the "coffins of black" are meant to be symbols for ___.
a. work   c. youth
b. courage   d. death

___ 12. In Blake's poem "The Chimney Sweeper," the "green plain" and "clouds" most clearly suggest
a. the roofs of houses.   c. heaven or paradise.
b. the sky.   d. the countryside.

___ 13. Which word best describes the attitude of Tom Dacre in "The Chimney Sweeper"?
a. optimistic   c. happy
b. despairing   d. fearful

___ 14. Which best describes using visuals as a key to meaning?
a. studying the use of descriptive language in a piece of writing
b. using illustrations to help understand accompanying text
c. charting details found in a piece of writing
d. analyzing and interpreting the symbols in a piece of writing

Vocabulary and Grammar

On the line, write the letter of the one best answer.

___ 15. Which word is the closest in meaning to *aspire*?
a. breath   c. strive
b. descend   d. observe

___ 16. Which phrase is the closest in meaning to *sinews*?
a. ropes and pulleys
b. mechanical power
c. muscular power
d. chemical power

___ 17. When Blake mentions the tiger's "fearful symmetry," he is referring to its
a. balanced beauty.
b. chaotic wildness.
c. colorful markings.
d. fierce disposition.

___ 18. Which sentence contains an incorrect usage of the verb *rise* or *raise*?
a. We rose late and went to the tourist bureau.
b. Banners had been risen along the sides of the boulevard.
c. As we walked, I raised the issue of money.
d. Jim responded that we'd raise the cash to get home.

___ 19. Which is the past participle form of the regular verb *raise*?
a. rose   c. raised
b. had raised   d. had risen

___ 20. Which sentence uses the verb *rise* in its past tense form?
a. The president announced that he would raise taxes.
b. The people raised an uproar of protest.
c. Public discontent rose to unprecedented levels.
d. When taxes rise, so do tempers.

Essay Questions

21. Many of William Blake's poems deal with the tragic consequences of the Industrial Revolution. Blake was particularly sensitive to the negative impact industrialization had on many people's lives. He complained of the mindless labor of factories in which workers "polish brass & iron hour after hour, laborious task, kept ignorant of its use." In an essay, discuss the ideas and images set forth in "The Chimney Sweeper." How does the poem touch on the issue of exploitation and dehumanization during the Industrial Revolution? Present evidence from the poem to back up your interpretation.

22. Blake was ignored in his own time and only came to be appreciated for his creativity over a century after his death. One twentieth-century critic has said that Blake was ignored in his own time because of the complexity of his vision. This critic has said that Blake's thinking and poetry frequently combine the "opposite sides of [the same] argument." Write an essay in which you relate the critic's statement to Blake's poems "The Lamb" and "The Tyger." What are the "opposite sides" that Blake expresses or describes in these two poems? What symbols does he use to describe these oppositions? Include evidence from the poems to support your points.

23. William Blake uses a wide range of simple and sophisticated symbols in "The Lamb," "The Tyger," "The Chimney Sweeper," and "Infant Sorrow." Write an essay in which you interpret the symbols in any two of the four poems. How do the symbols Blake uses in the two poems relate to the meaning of the poems? Why might he have chosen the symbols? Support your points with details from the poems.

Name _____ Date _____

Selection Test

Critical Reading

On the line, write the letter of the one best answer.

_____ 1. Which type of modern writing does *Frankenstein* resemble most closely?
   a. morality play
   b. familiar essay
   c. science fiction
   d. realistic novel

_____ 2. What mental state does Mary Shelley say she was in when she thought of the idea for *Frankenstein*?
   a. deep slumber
   b. daytime reverie
   c. waking dream
   d. alert vigilance

_____ 3. Which is a favorite aim of the Romantic poets that Mary Shelley also had in writing *Frankenstein*?
   a. to use the language of everyday life
   b. to find evidence of the divine in nature
   c. to depict the ways of the common people
   d. to evoke intense and vivid feelings

_____ 4. Mary Shelley's statement that because her introduction will be confined to topics related to *Frankenstein* alone, she can "scarcely accuse [herself] of a personal intrusion" implies that
   a. she respects her readers' privacy.
   b. she likes to write about herself.
   c. she is modest.
   d. *Frankenstein* is based on her personal life.

_____ 5. Which was a key element of the Gothic novel that Mary Shelley set out to employ in *Frankenstein*?
   a. the inexplicable
   b. the educational
   c. the conventional
   d. the philosophical

_____ 6. What prediction is most likely from the following details in Shelley's "Introduction to *Frankenstein*"?

> When I placed my head on my pillow, I did not sleep, nor could I be said to think. My imagination, unbidden, possessed and guided me, gifting the successive images that arose in my mind with a vividness far beyond the usual bounds of reverie.

   a. The author is going to be too upset by the dreams to write anything afterwards.
   b. The author is going to get inspiration for her story.
   c. The author will die of fright.
   d. The author will tell her friends about her dream, and they will steal her ideas.

_____ 7. Which details from Shelley's "Introduction to *Frankenstein*" would lead you to predict that she would write a successful ghost story?
   a. "I busied myself to think of a story. . . ."
   b. "Perhaps a corpse would be reanimated: galvanism."
   c. "I saw the pale student of unhallowed arts kneeling beside the thing he had put together."
   d. "The idea so possessed my mind, that a thrill of fear ran through me. . . ."

8. Shelley says her husband wrote "the most melodious verse that adorns our language." From this statement, what do you infer about Shelley's feelings for her husband?
   a. She loves him.
   b. She admires him.
   c. She resents his work.
   d. She likes to tease him.

____ 9. Which statement of Shelley's helps you to predict that the situation might lead to writing ghost stories?
   a. "In the summer of 1816, we visited Switzerland, and became the neighbors of Lord Byron."
   b. "At first we spent our pleasant hours on the lake or wandering on its shores . . . "
   c. "But it proved wet, ungenial summer, and incessant rain often confined us for days to the house. Some volumes of ghost stories, translated from the German into French, fell into our hands."
   d. "These, as he brought them successfully to us, clothed in all light and harmony of poetry, seemed to stamp as divine the glories of heaven and earth, whose influences we partook with him."

____ 10. Shelley writes that after listening to the conversation with Lord Byron about Dr. Darwin, she could not sleep and instead saw a terrifying vision. This suggests that
   a. the conversation inspired her to think of the idea for her story.
   b. she was frightened by the experiments of Dr. Darwin.
   c. the poets were the first to think of the idea for *Frankenstein*.
   d. Dr. Darwin's work was scarier than any ghost story.

____ 11. Which detail from Shelley's "Introduction to *Frankenstein*" suggests that ghost stories should encourage ethical conduct?
   a. "[He] found himself in the arms of . . . her whom he had deserted."
   b. "[His doom] was to bestow the kiss of death on all the younger sons. . . ."
   c. "I busied myself to think of a story . . . to curdle the blood. . . ."
   d. "He would hope . . . that this thing . . . would subside into dead matter. . . ."

____ 12. The poets Percy Shelley and Lord Byron had trouble writing the ghost story assignment because they were "annoyed by the platitudes of prose." What prediction might you make about Mary Shelley's story from this statement?
   a. She will write her story in poetry form.
   b. She will use Percy Shelley and Lord Byron's ideas in her own story.
   c. Her story, written in prose, will be the best story of all.
   d. Her story will not be a ghost story after all.

____ 13. Which element of the Gothic novel unites it with the Romantic tradition?
   a. ordinary happenings
   b. the supernatural
   c. personal emotions
   d. the religious

____ 14. True to the Romantic culture of her time, Mary Shelley saw Frankenstein as the product of her
   a. imagination.
   b. rational mind.
   c. education.
   d. personal experience.

Vocabulary and Grammar

On the line, write the letter of the one best answer.

____ 15. In the passage, what does the word *appendage* mean?

   . . . as my account will only appear as an *appendage* to a former production . . .

   a. introduction
   b. epilogue
   c. addition
   d. revision

____ 16. In the sentence, what does the word *phantasm* suggest?

> I saw the hideous *phantasm* of a man stretched out . . .

    a. The man is not really there.
    b. The man is actually some kind of supernatural being.
    c. The man has just died and is now a corpse.
    d. Shelley only sees the man's shadow.

____ 17. What does Mary Shelley's use of the word *incitement* in this sentence indicate?

> . . . but for [Percy Shelley's] *incitement*, [*Frankenstein*] would never have taken the form in which it was presented to the world.

    a. Percy Shelley wrote *Frankenstein* for her.
    b. Percy Shelley made fun of *Frankenstein*.
    c. Percy Shelley encouraged her to write *Frankenstein*.
    d. Percy Shelley did not want her to write *Frankenstein*.

____ 18. Which italicized words are a past participial phrase?
    a. These . . . *clothed in all the light and harmony* of poetry . . .
    b. There was "The History of the Inconstant Lover," who, when he *thought to clasp* the bride . . .
    c. found himself in the arms of the pale ghost of her whom *he had deserted*.
    d. their incidents are as fresh in my mind as if I *had read them yesterday*

____ 19. Which italicized phrase is *not* a past participial phrase?
    a. he advanced to the couch of the blooming youths, *cradled in healthy sleep.*
    b. the boys, who from that hour withered like flowers *snapped upon the stalk.*
    c. Shelley . . . commenced one *founded on the experiences of his early life.*
    d. he . . . *was obliged to despatch her to the tomb of the Capulets.* . . .

____ 20. In the sentence, what does the past participial phrase "left to itself" act as?

> He would hope that, *left to itself,* the slight spark of life which he had communicated would fade; that this thing, which had received such imperfect animation, would subside into dead matter. . . .

    a. an adjective modifying "spark of life"
    b. an adjective modifying "this thing"
    c. an adverb modifying "would subside"
    d. an adjective modifying "dead matter"

Essay Questions

21. Mary Shelley's *Frankenstein* is considered a classic example of Gothic literature. Write an essay explaining what makes *Frankenstein* Gothic. On the basis of Shelley's "Introduction to *Frankenstein,*" what characteristics of Gothic literature do you think the novel includes?

22. One theme of *Frankenstein* is the potential danger of technology used for the wrong purposes. Think of a more contemporary work, such as a novel, short story, play, or movie, that explores this theme. Write an essay comparing *Frankenstein* with the contemporary work. How is each work connected to the ethical debates and controversies of its day? Be sure to briefly explain the plot of the contemporary work that you use.

23. The Gothic novel is considered a part and product of the Romantic Age. How can this be? Reconstruct the definition of Romanticism to find the answer. Remember that Romanticism is not easily defined, nor does it take only a single form. The Gothic novel has been referred to as sensational romance. Write an essay that explains how and why the Gothic novel should be a considered part and product of the Romantic Age.

"The Oval Portrait" by Edgar Allan Poe

Selection Test

Critical Reading

On the line, write the letter of the one best answer.

_____ 1. While the narrator of "The Oval Portrait" is absorbed by the portrait, his valet is
a. reading. c. sleeping.
b. unsaddling the horses. d. closing the shutters in the chateau.

_____ 2. The narrator experiences "deep and reverent awe" in turning the light away from the painting because
a. he is overwhelmed by the girl's beauty.
b. he has never seen such marvelous technique before.
c. he senses a supernatural quality in the portrait.
d. he has mistaken the head for that of a living person.

_____ 3. What the narrator finds so amazing and then so disturbing about the portrait is
a. the overly revealing depiction of the body.
b. the absoluteness of its resemblance to life.
c. the unsuitable frame chosen for the painting.
d. the girl's impulsive movement.

_____ 4. What does the narrator's early description of the portrait symbolically express?

The arms, the bosom and even the ends of radiant hair, melted imperceptibly into the vague yet deep shadow which formed the background of the whole

a. the artist's austerity
b. the artist's self-absorption
c. the bride's fawnlike liveliness
d. the bride's death

_____ 5. The very first sentence of "The Oval Portrait" places the story in the Gothic tradition by mentioning "the fancy of Mrs. Radcliffe." Which of the characters is explicitly connected with such Gothic fancy?
a. the narrator c. the valet
b. the painter d. the bride

_____ 6. How are the narrator and the painter alike?
a. Both have a beautiful young wife.
b. Both abandon the chateau.
c. Both know and care about art.
d. Both sleep in the black-curtained bed.

_____ 7. What does the sentence suggest?

And he *would* not see that the tints which he spread upon the canvas were drawn from the cheeks of her who sat beside him

a. the bride's renewed energy
b. the artist's failure to look at the canvas carefully enough
c. the urgency of finishing the portrait before the wedding
d. the artist's obsessive self-absorption

© Prentice-Hall, Inc.

8. Poe has the narrator settle into a "remote turret" in order to
   a. show the narrator's unsociable nature.
   b. create a parallel of setting between the frame and the inner story.
   c. suggest that the narrator and the valet are in hiding.
   d. make the chateau sound uninhabited.

9. What suggests that perhaps the portrait and its history exist only in the narrator's imagination or nightmare?
   a. his "deep and reverent awe"
   b. his familiarity with art terms
   c. his "dreamy stupor"
   d. his compassion for the bride

10. The artist has one last chance to choose life over art when
    a. "the spirit of the lady again flickered up as the flame within the lamp."
    b. "the light dripped upon the pale canvas only from overhead."
    c. "some who beheld the portrait spoke of its resemblance in low words."
    d. his bride "smiled on and still on, uncomplainingly."

Essay Questions

11. Much of the description in this story works to establish a gloomy and unwholesome (Gothic) atmosphere. In an essay, explain which details you consider most important in establishing this brooding mood, concentrating on the continuity of description from the frame to the inner story. Why does Poe make a point of carrying over these particular details into the inner story?

12. Write an essay discussing how the artist's ambition to capture his wife on canvas makes him the villain of the story. How does Poe stress the artist's cruelty? Which descriptions of him and the bride especially support the theme that it is sinful to sacrifice humanity, and life itself, in striving for perfect creation?

13. In an essay, speculate on why Poe chose the frame he did, creating this particular narrator and having him tell the story in the first person. Since the valet and the wound are virtually the only individualizing details, consider why Poe included them for our sense of the narrator's identity and situation, and how they relate to the inner story.

Part Test, Unit 4, Part 1: Fantasy and Reality

Critical Reading

The questions below are based on the following selection.

This excerpt is from Mary Shelley's Frankenstein. *The young Victor Frankenstein's investigations into physiology, alchemy, and the nature of life have just culminated in an astounding success—he has brought to life a body stitched together from the parts of corpses stolen from graveyards. At the beginning of this scene, Victor has seen the monster breathe for the very first time. (The Elizabeth of whom he dreams is an impoverished orphan who was adopted by Victor Frankenstein's distinguished Swiss family. At the time of this scene, Frankenstein's mother has already died after nursing Elizabeth back to health.)*

from *Frankenstein* by Mary Shelley

The different accidents of life are not so changeable as the feelings of human nature. I had worked hard for nearly two years, for the sole purpose of infusing life into an inanimate body. For this I had deprived myself of rest and health. I had desired it with an ardor that far exceeded moderation; but now that I had finished, the beauty of the dream vanished, and breathless horror and disgust filled my heart. Unable to endure the aspect of the being I had created, I rushed out of the room, and continued a long time traversing my bedchamber, unable to compose my mind to sleep. At length lassitude succeeded to the tumult I had before endured; and I threw myself on the bed in my clothes, endeavoring to seek a few moments of forgetfulness. But it was in vain: I slept, indeed, but I was disturbed by the wildest dreams. I thought I saw Elizabeth, in the bloom of health, walking in the streets of Ingolstadt. Delighted and surprised, I embraced her; but as I imprinted the first kiss on her lips, they became livid with the hue of death; her features appeared to change, and I thought that I held the corpse of my dead mother in my arms; a shroud enveloped her form, and I saw the grave worms crawling in the folds of the flannel. I started from my sleep with horror; a cold dew covered my forehead, my teeth chattered, and every limb became convulsed: when, by the dim and yellow light of the moon, as it forced its way through the window shutters, I beheld the wretch—the miserable monster whom I had created.

On the line, write the letter of the one best answer.

_____ 1. Why does Frankenstein throw himself on the bed?
    a. to hide from the monster
    b. to get some much needed rest
    c. to escape from his problems
    d. to quiet the tumult he still feels

_____ 2. What word most accurately names Frankenstein's reaction to his success in bringing the monster to life?
    a. lassitude
    b. exhaustion
    c. disillusionment
    d. changeableness

_____ 3. What is Frankenstein's original feeling about the project of creating life? What are his feelings after he succeeds?
    a. guilt, then unhappiness
    b. gladness, then frustration
    c. fear, then triumph
    d. eagerness, then horror

_____ 4. Given what you know about the nature of Gothic literature, what do you predict will happen to Elizabeth in the course of the novel?
   a. She will marry Frankenstein, and she will discover the means to defeat the monster.
   b. She will marry Frankenstein, but Frankenstein's monster will kill her.
   c. She will marry Frankenstein; then she will persuade him of the monster's right to live in peace.
   d. She and Frankenstein will not marry, since they will discuss their feelings in depth and discover that they are not really in love.

_____ 5. Given your prior knowledge of science in the nineteenth century, which of the following most probably describes the circumstances in which Frankenstein works?
   a. Frankenstein works alone, using equipment he has acquired or constructed on his own.
   b. Frankenstein is part of a research team working on the secret of life.
   c. Frankenstein's research is funded by a top-secret government grant.
   d. Frankenstein uses the university facilities and equipment for his experiments.

_____ 6. Rephrase the following sentence to clarify details:

   Unable to endure the aspect of the being I had created, I rushed out of the room, and continued a long time traversing my bedchamber, unable to compose my mind to sleep.

   a. Frankenstein can't bear the way the monster looks, so he rushes down the long passage back to his bedroom.
   b. Frankenstein can't bear the way the monster looks, so he rushes back to his bedroom, where he paces restlessly.
   c. Frankenstein can't bear the way the monster looks at him, so he rushes back to his bedroom, where he paces restlessly.
   d. Frankenstein can't bear the way the monster looks at him, so he rushes down the long passage back to his bedroom.

_____ 7. Which of the following details contributes to the Gothic quality of this passage?
   a. Frankenstein's success as a scientist
   b. Frankenstein's romantic feelings toward Elizabeth
   c. the connection in the dream between love and death
   d. the appearance of a real monster at the end of a dream

_____ 8. Which of the following details from the passage is _not_ distinctively Gothic?
   a. the dim and yellow light of the moon through the shutters
   b. a mind in turmoil
   c. a corpse crawling with worms
   d. a person's disillusionment at his or her own success

_____ 9. Judging from this passage, the monster may be a symbol of
   a. Frankenstein's passion for knowledge and its corrupting effect on his heart.
   b. Frankenstein's love for his family and grief at the death of his mother.
   c. the power of life over death.
   d. the mystery and wonder of nature.

_____ 10. In the dream, the transformation of Elizabeth into Frankenstein's dead mother may symbolize
   a. Frankenstein's feeling that he will destroy everything he loves.
   b. Frankenstein's hidden desire to kill Elizabeth.
   c. Frankenstein's prophetic knowledge that his monster will kill Elizabeth.
   d. the fact that Elizabeth suffers from a disease.

Vocabulary and Grammar

On the line, write the letter of the one best answer.

____ 11. Just after the sun ____ in the sky, we ____ from our beds, ____ our bags to our shoulders, and walked to work.
    a. rose . . . raised . . . rose   c. raised . . . raised . . . rose
    b. rose . . . rose . . . raised   d. rose . . . raised . . . rose

____ 12. Her friends' ____ gave her the confidence to develop her ideas into a novel.
    a. discretion   c. incitement
    b. impudence   d. phantasm

____ 13. Which of the following sentences contains an interjection?
    a. Did you know the poem was written for a mouse?
    b. We yelled for them to stop, but they continued.
    c. The mouse cried out in terror.
    d. Hey! Protect the mouse from the blade of the plow.

____ 14. What is the complete past participial phrase in the following sentence: Confined to the house, we talked and told ghost stories.
    a. Confined to the house   c. we talked and told ghost stories
    b. to the house   d. and told ghost stories

The question below consists of a related pair of words in CAPITAL LETTERS followed by four lettered pairs of words. On the line, write the letter of the pair that best expresses a relationship similar to that of the pair in capital letters.

____ 15. UNGENIAL : PLEASANT ::
    a. unlikely : doubtful   c. unattractive : beautiful
    b. unfair : dishonest   d. unwillingness : eagerness

Essay Questions

16. Each of the selections in this section combines elements of fantasy with realistic details. Choose one selection that combines these elements in a way that is most interesting to you. Write an essay in which you describe this selection and why you feel it is effective in its use of fantasy and reality.

17. Some selections in this section examine dark and sinister aspects of life. For example, you might think of Mary Shelley's ideas surrounding her creation of *Frankenstein* or William Blake's poems "The Tyger" and "Infant Sorrow." Write an essay about two selections from this section that present dark views of an aspect of life. What are the themes of these selections? What details emphasize their themes?

18. To help readers find meaning in their works, poets often use symbols—words, images, and ideas that stand for something else. In an essay, examine the ways in which two selections in this section use symbolism. Describe the symbols in each work and explain what they represent. Then analyze how these symbols help you to understand the pieces.

Poetry of William Wordsworth
Selection Test

Critical Reading

On the line, write the letter of the one best answer.

____ 1. Which phrase best summarizes the predominant theme of "Lines Composed a Few Miles Above Tintern Abbey"?
   a. the wondrous and fleeting emotions of childhood
   b. the renewing and uplifting power of nature
   c. the educational and religious benefits of solitude
   d. the kind and simple ways of the common folk

____ 2. Wordsworth's image "of some hermit's cave, where by his fire / The hermit sits alone" could be said to reflect the Romantics' rejection of the Neoclassical emphasis on ____.
   a. society   c. extremity
   b. religion   d. emotion

____ 3. In "Lines Composed a Few Miles Above Tintern Abbey," Wordsworth describes his second visit to the abbey as more ____ than the first.
   a. emotional   c. depressing
   b. memorable   d. reflective

____ 4. "Lines Composed a Few Miles Above Tintern Abbey" is a poem that celebrates the power of ____.
   a. analysis   c. memory
   b. deduction   d. prophecy

____ 5. Which lines most directly express Wordsworth's interest in the discovery of the mystical or the supernatural through nature?
   a. "His little, nameless, unremembered, acts / Of kindness and of love."
   b. "I cannot paint / what then I was. The sounding cataract / Haunted me like a passion . . ."
   c. ". . . not as in the hour / Of thoughtless youth; but hearing oftentimes / The still, sad music of humanity . . ."
   d. ". . . a sense sublime / Of something . . . / Whose dwelling is the light of setting suns . . ."

____ 6. Which sentence best describes the meaning of these words from "Lines Composed a Few Miles Above Tintern Abbey"?

   I cannot paint / What then I was. . . .

   a. I cannot paint the way I could when I was young.
   b. I cannot describe what I was like when I was young.
   c. I cannot describe things the way I could when I was young.
   d. I cannot paint a picture of what I was like when I was young.

____ 7. "Lines Composed a Few Miles Above Tintern Abbey" is easy to recognize as a Romantic poem because it
   a. describes the narrator's emotions about a landscape.
   b. is about a revolution.
   c. takes place entirely outdoors.
   d. argues for the importance of the individual.

____ 8. At the end of "The World Is Too Much With Us," Wordsworth demonstrates by his example the Romantic belief in the
   a. helpful influence of formal worship.
   b. critical need for universal equality.
   c. transforming power of the mind.
   d. enduring worth of ancient literature.

____ 9. What is Wordsworth's main subject in "The World Is Too Much With Us"?
   a. the frenzied quest for wealth
   b. the decline of classical learning
   c. the rise of industrial cities
   d. the wanton destruction of nature

____ 10. Which sentence best describes how the Romantic ideal applies to these lines from "London, 1802"?

> Oh! raise us up, return to us again;
> And give us manners, virtue, freedom, power.

   a. Romantics believed humanity needed a great leader.
   b. Romantics believed in the power of the arts to improve humanity.
   c. Romantics believed the arts were better in the past, before they turned away from nature.
   d. Romantics believed humanity was better in the past, before it turned away from nature.

____ 11. Which sentence best describes the meaning of these words from "London, 1802"?

> London . . . is a fen / Of stagnant waters. . . .

   a. The Thames River has flooded.
   b. Life in London has become stale.
   c. The marshy ground around London makes life difficult.
   d. English politics have grown murky.

____ 12. Which lines best summarize the theme of the excerpt from *The Prelude*?
   a. "I lost / All feeling of conviction"
   b. "I . . . toiled, intent / To anatomize the frame of social life. . . ."
   c. "I adhered / More firmly to the old tenets. . . ."
   d. "O pleasant exercise of hope and joy!"

____ 13. Why might a Romantic poet like Wordsworth have supported the French Revolution at first?
   a. The Revolutionaries claimed to support the rights and importance of individuals.
   b. The Revolutionaries advocated a return to nature.
   c. The Revolutionaries were opposed to technology.
   d. The leaders of the Revolution were poets and writers.

____ 14. Which sentence best describes Romanticism's attitude toward emotions?
   a. They are an important part of life and an important tool for an artist.
   b. They are an important part of life but should not be emphasized in art.
   c. They will lead people toward technology and away from nature.
   d. They help people appreciate nature.

Vocabulary and Grammar

On the line, write the letter of the one best answer.

_____ 15. Which word means the opposite of *sordid*?
  a. random   c. unarmed
  b. exactly   d. clean

_____ 16. What does the word *confounded* mean?
  a. bound together   c. infernal
  b. confused or bewildered   d. established at the same time

_____ 17. Which phrase is most nearly the same in meaning as *presumption*?
  a. the desire to be first
  b. a guessing at something without having the facts
  c. a sometimes egotistical assuming of things
  d. the taking of power or high office

_____ 18. What is a participle?
  a. an adjective that is used as a verb
  b. a verb form that is used as an adjective
  c. a noun that is used as a verb
  d. a verb form that is used as a noun

_____ 19. Which italicized phrase is an example of a present participial phrase?
  a. "As if they had within some *lurking* right / To wield it . . ."
  b. "betrayed / By present objects, and by *reasonings false* . . ."
  c. "more like a man / *Flying from something that he dreads* . . ."
  d. "little lines / Of sportive wood *run wild* . . ."

_____ 20. Which italicized phrase is not an example of a present participial phrase?
  a. "Frenchmen . . . *losing sight of all* / Which they had struggled for . . ."
  b. "When most intent on *making of herself* / A prime enchantress . . ."
  c. "till, *demanding formal proof*, / . . . I lost / All feeling of conviction . . ."
  d. "These waters, *rolling from their mountain springs* . . ."

Essay Questions

21. Wordsworth and a handful of other poets began a movement known as the Romantic movement. It was a revolutionary break with the type of poetry that was being written at the time. Write an essay describing Romantic poetry. What were its most important aspects? How was it different from what went before it? Provide examples from the selections you read.

22. In "The World Is Too Much With Us," Wordsworth expressed concern for the society in which he lived. He felt it had gone astray and explained how in the poem. Write an essay discussing his concerns. What were they? How did he express them? If he were alive today, might he have the same concerns for our society?

23. In "Lines Composed a Few Miles Above Tintern Abbey," the narrator revisits the area where he grew up. In the excerpt from *The Prelude*, Wordsworth describes his attitude toward the French Revolution. Each poem describes a change that occurred over time. Write an essay comparing and contrasting the two works. In each case, what was it that changed? What attitude was expressed about the changes? How are the two works similar? How are they different?

"The Rime of the Ancient Mariner" and **"Kubla Khan"**
by Samuel Taylor Coleridge

Selection Test

Critical Reading

On the line, write the letter of the one best answer.

_____ 1. Which phrase from "The Rime of the Ancient Mariner" contains alliteration?
  a. "Was tyrannous and strong"
  b. "As green as emerald"
  c. "The ice was all around"
  d. "Hither to work us weal"

_____ 2. A central theme of "The Rime of the Ancient Mariner" is the
  a. sanctity of all wild creatures.
  b. goodness of all supernatural powers.
  c. equality of all human beings.
  d. excitement of all imaginative voyages.

_____ 3. Which line from "The Rime of the Ancient Mariner" contains alliteration, consonance, and internal rhyme?
  a. "At length did cross an Albatross . . ."
  b. "By thy long gray beard and glittering eye . . ."
  c. "In mist or cloud, on mast or shroud . . ."
  d. "The bride hath paced into the hall."

_____ 4. In which line are alliteration and variations on the o sound most evident, creating a heavy, grim tone?
  a. "And every tongue, through utter drought . . ."
  b. "And a good south wind sprung up behind . . ."
  c. "And the rain poured down from one black cloud . . ."
  d. "And the owlet whoops to the wolf below . . ."

_____ 5. Throughout his narration, the mariner maintains a tone of
  a. fresh horror and awe.
  b. pure relief and comfort.
  c. dull apathy and weariness.
  d. detached wonder and amusement.

_____ 6. The dice game between Death and Life-in-Death in "The Rime of the Ancient Mariner" suggests that
  a. sailors like to gamble.
  b. luck is all that matters.
  c. universal forces are not guided by reason.
  d. female forces are more powerful than male forces.

_____ 7. At different times throughout "The Rime of the Ancient Mariner," the albatross symbolizes
  a. luck, beauty, and relief.
  b. luck, nature, and guilt.
  c. good luck, bad luck, and friendship.
  d. storms, guilt, and beauty.

Unit 4: Rebels and Dreamers (790–1832)

____ 8. Which of these lines from "The Rime of the Ancient Mariner" contains internal rhyme?
   a. "Sweet sounds rose slowly through their mouths . . ."
   b. "They moved in tracks of shining white . . ."
   c. "Ah wretch! said they, the bird to slay . . ."
   d. "And listens like a three years' child . . ."

____ 9. Which sentence states an important theme of "Kubla Khan"?
   a. Nature has supernatural powers.
   b. There is a powerful contrast between sun and ice.
   c. Human beings need pleasure.
   d. Music calms the savage beast.

____ 10. Which is a favorite subject of the Romantics and is most evident in "Kubla Khan"?
   a. the classical and the mythological
   b. the moderate and the reasonable
   c. the faraway and the exotic
   d. the universal and the democratic

____ 11. What sound devices contribute to the poet's theme in lines like these?

   In Xanadu did Kubla Khan / A stately pleasure dome decree

   a. Blurring words create a vague, abstract feeling.
   b. Linking words create a flowing, dreamlike effect.
   c. Sharpening words create a precise, analytical tone.
   d. Separating words create a rigid, marchlike rhythm.

____ 12. In which line is alliteration the dominant sound device?
   a. "So twice five miles of fertile ground . . ."
   b. "A savage place! As holy and enchanted . . ."
   c. "Five miles meandering with a mazy motion . . ."
   d. "Through wood and dale the sacred river ran . . ."

____ 13. The final image of "Kubla Khan" is that of the
   a. fountain bursting with foam.
   b. damsel absorbed in her music.
   c. poet feverish with inspiration.
   d. emperor flushed with pride.

____ 14. Which sound device helps to emphasize the largeness of the area of the grounds of the pleasure dome in these lines?

   So twice five miles of fertile ground
   With walls and towers were girdled round . . .

   a. alliteration—repetition of the *w* sound
   b. assonance—repetition of the long *i* sound
   c. consonance—repetition of the *s* sound
   d. consonance—repetition of the *d* sound

Vocabulary and Grammar

On the line, write the letter of the one best answer.

____ 15. Which word or phrase is closest in meaning to *adjourn*?
   a. end for the day
   b. cancel
   c. begin
   d. destroy

_____ 16. Which phrase is most nearly the opposite of *sojourn*?
   a. pass through
   b. end forever
   c. long stay
   d. end for the day

_____ 17. The word *reverence* means _____.
   a. ministers
   b. hatred
   c. prayer
   d. respect

_____ 18. Which sentence most correctly rearranges the order of the inverted words from "The Rime of the Ancient Mariner"?

> Ah wretch! said they, the bird to slay,
> That made the breeze to blow!

   a. Ah wretch! they said, the bird to slay is the one that made the breeze to blow!
   b. Ah wretch! they said, to slay the bird that made the breeze to blow!
   c. Ah wretch! they said, slay the bird that will make the breeze to blow!
   d. Ah! they said, to slay the wretched bird that made the breeze to blow!

_____ 19. Which sentence most correctly rearranges the order of the inverted words from "The Rime of the Ancient Mariner"?

> O happy living things! no tongue
> Their beauty might declare . . .

   a. O happy living things! your tongues might declare their beauty.
   b. O happy living things! their beauty might declare no tongue.
   c. O happy things living! no tongue their beauty might declare.
   d. O happy living things! no tongue might declare their beauty.

_____ 20. Which sentence most correctly rearranges the order of the inverted words from "The Rime of the Ancient Mariner"?

> How long in that same fit I lay,
> I have not to declare . . .

   a. I do not have to declare how long I lay in that same fit.
   b. I have to declare how long I lay, not in that same fit.
   c. I have not to declare how long I lay in that same fit.
   d. I have to not declare how long I lay in that same fit.

Essay Questions

21. Nature plays an important role in both "The Rime of the Ancient Mariner" and "Kubla Khan." Write an essay comparing and contrasting Coleridge's characterization of nature in both poems. What powers does nature possess in each poem, and what effect does it have on human beings?

22. In "Kubla Khan," Coleridge explores a fascination with exotic places and things. Write an essay analyzing his view and portrayal of Xanadu as an exotic place. Why do you think Coleridge is attracted to the exotic?

23. In "The Rime of the Ancient Mariner," the Polar Spirit's fellow demons describe him as follows: "The spirit who bideth by himself / In the land of mist and snow, / He loved the bird that loved the man / Who shot him with his bow." Write an essay analyzing the role that these lines play in "The Rime of the Ancient Mariner." Why are these lines important to the plot of the poem? What poetic effects does Coleridge use in these lines? What tone is created by the poetic effects in these lines?

"She Walks in Beauty," from ***Childe Harold's Pilgrimage*** and **from *Don Juan***
by George Gordon, Lord Byron

Selection Test

Critical Reading

On the line, write the letter of the one best answer.

_____ 1. A central theme of "She Walks in Beauty" is the woman's _____.
    a. joy   c. love
    b. virtue   d. sorrow

_____ 2. Which line from "She Walks in Beauty" best answers the question "To what does the speaker compare the woman in the poem?"
    a. "She walks in beauty, like the night . . ."
    b. "Thus mellowed to that tender light . . ."
    c. "How pure, how dear their dwelling place. . . ."
    d. "But tell of days in goodness spent . . ."

_____ 3. Which pair of lines from "She Walks in Beauty" contains an example of personification?
    a. "She walks in beauty, like the night / Of cloudless climes and starry skies . . ."
    b. "And all that's best of dark and bright / Meet in her aspect and her eyes . . ."
    c. "Where thoughts serenely sweet express / How pure, how dear their dwelling place."
    d. "A mind at peace with all below, / A heart whose love is innocent!"

_____ 4. Why does the speaker of *Childe Harold's Pilgrimage* admire the ocean?
    a. Many people depend on fish from the ocean for food.
    b. The ocean is beautiful and its sounds are soothing.
    c. The ocean provides a way to travel to faraway places.
    d. The ocean is unchanged by human activities.

_____ 5. Which question is answered by the line from *Childe Harold's Pilgrimage*?

    I love not man the less, but nature more

    a. What is the theme of the poem?
    b. Whom does the narrator love?
    c. How does the narrator feel about nature?
    d. Why do people rely on nature for sustenance?

_____ 6. Which of the lines from *Childe Harold's Pilgrimage* is an example of personification?
    a. "And monarchs tremble in their capitals . . ."
    b. ". . . thou dost arise / And shake him from thee . . ."
    c. "And howling, to his gods, where haply lies / His petty hope . . ."
    d. "Calm or convulsed—in breeze, or gale, or storm . . ."

_____ 7. What does the line from *Childe Harold's Pilgrimage* suggest?

    There is society, where none intrudes

    a. Nature itself is sufficient society for an individual.
    b. The people who live near the ocean are afraid to go into it.
    c. People should live alone in nature and not with other people.
    d. It is impossible to escape society, even in nature.

_____ 8. A central theme of *Childe Harold's Pilgrimage* is the ocean's ____.
   a. malice
   b. permanence
   c. rhythm
   d. generosity

_____ 9. A central idea of this excerpt from *Don Juan* is that the speaker's
   a. mind has increased its perception.
   b. heart has lost its power to feel.
   c. fame has dulled the dread of death.
   d. emotions have kept their intensity.

_____ 10. To what is the speaker comparing his life in this line?

   I / Have spent my life, both interest and principal . . .

   a. travel
   b. learning
   c. money
   d. illness

_____ 11. To which question do these lines from *Don Juan* best provide an answer?

   My days of love are over; me no more
   The charms of maid, wife, and still less of widow
   Can make the fool of which they made before . . .

   a. When did the speaker pursue women?
   b. Why does the speaker avoid women?
   c. What was the speaker like when he was younger?
   d. What is the speaker like now?

_____ 12. Which excerpt from *Don Juan* contains a metaphor?
   a. "Some liken it to climbing up a hill . . ."
   b. ". . . a chymic treasure / Is glittering youth . . ."
   c. "The freshness of the heart can fall like dew . . ."
   d. "Hived in our bosoms like the bag o' the bee . . ."

_____ 13. At the end of the excerpt, the speaker appears to be trying to
   a. attack his critics.
   b. dismiss his peers.
   c. confess his sins.
   d. justify his book.

_____ 14. The speaker's words reveal him to be
   a. vain and cynical.
   b. fulfilled and satisfied.
   c. passionate and undaunted.
   d. wise and pious.

Vocabulary and Grammar

On the line, write the letter of the word or phrase that best completes the sentence.

_____ 15. Where thoughts serenely sweet ____ / How pure, how dear their dwelling place.
   a. has expressed
   b. was expressing
   c. express
   d. expresses

____ 16. There ____ a rapture on the lonely shore. . . .
   a. is
   b. are
   c. were
   d. be

____ 17. I / ____ squandered my whole summer while 'twas May. . . .
   a. Has
   b. Have
   c. Having
   d. To have

On the line, write the letter of the one best answer.

____ 18. The *arbiter* of war referred to by the speaker of *Childe Harold's Pilgrimage* could also be called
   a. the wager of war.
   b. the judge of war.
   c. the outcome of war.
   d. the winner of war.

____ 19. What does the speaker of *Don Juan* mean when he states that he no longer feels "the spirit to *retort*"?
   a. He thinks that he is not as spiritual as he used to be.
   b. He no longer feels driven to try to become famous.
   c. He does not feel the need to live his youth over again.
   d. He no longer feels able to respond with a wisecrack.

____ 20. The speaker of *Don Juan* says that the only vice left to him is *avarice*. If he behaved avariciously, what might he do?
   a. He might stay up too late at night.
   b. He might stop bathing regularly.
   c. He might amass money and possessions.
   d. He might brag about himself endlessly.

Essay Questions

21. The speaker of the excerpt from *Don Juan* reflects on how he spent his youth and what he can look forward to in the years to come. Write an essay giving your interpretation of the speaker's approach to life. What do you think that he has learned from his life thus far? How do you think that he will live his life in the future? Support your argument with evidence from the poem.

22. The word *apostrophe* can refer to words that are spoken to an object that is being personified. Write an essay explaining how the excerpt from *Childe Harold's Pilgrimage* is an "Apostrophe to the Ocean." How does the speaker compare the ocean to a person? According to the speaker, if the ocean were a person, what kind of person would the ocean be?

23. The speakers of "She Walks in Beauty" and "Apostrophe to the Ocean" express admiration for their subjects. But the speaker of *Don Juan* mocks his subject, which in this excerpt is himself. Write an essay contrasting the narrative styles of the three poems. How do the speakers of the first two poems use metaphors, similes, and personification to elevate their subjects? How does the speaker of *Don Juan* use these techniques to make fun of himself?

"Ozymandias," "Ode to the West Wind," and **"To a Skylark"**
by Percy Bysshe Shelley

Selection Test

Critical Reading

On the line, write the letter of the one best answer.

_____ 1. One of the most important ideas of "Ozymandias" is the
   a. permanence of sculpted monuments.
   b. insignificance of physical death.
   c. meaninglessness of earthly power.
   d. poetry of glorious inscriptions.

_____ 2. Which sentence best explains who Ozymandias was?
   a. He was a king of Egypt during Shelley's time.
   b. He was a king of Egypt thousands of years before Shelley wrote.
   c. He was a traveler who discovered the king's statue.
   d. He was the speaker of the poem "Ozymandias."

_____ 3. What is suggested by the following image from "Ozymandias"?

   Round the decay / Of that colossal wreck, boundless and bare, / The lone and level
   sands stretch far away.

   a. No statue could survive exposure to desert conditions.
   b. Ozymandias actually accomplished little in his reign.
   c. There was no limit to the extent of Ozymandias's kingdom.
   d. Nature is more powerful than any human king.

_____ 4. In "Ozymandias," Shelley describes only what the traveler saw. What else might the
   traveler have experienced while looking at the statue?
   a. the singing of birds
   b. the heat of the sun
   c. the taste of fresh water
   d. the smell of cooking food

_____ 5. What do you think is the political message of "Ozymandias"?
   a. No dictator can ever truly rule absolutely.
   b. It is better to live without any kind of government.
   c. People should rule their country democratically.
   d. Those who rule should do so with kindness and compassion.

_____ 6. The descriptions of the West Wind in the first two sections of "Ode to the West Wind"
   are dominated by images of
   a. violence, death, decay, and burial.
   b. sleep, dreams, fantasy, and reverie.
   c. peace, birth, growth, and blossoming.
   d. translucence, light, color, and radiance.

_____ 7. Which statement best summarizes Shelley's depiction of the West Wind?
   a. The West Wind represents the goodness of nature.
   b. The West Wind represents the destructive power of nature.
   c. The West Wind's destructiveness makes new life possible.
   d. The West Wind brings the spring.

Unit 4: Rebels and Dreamers (1790–1832)

____ 8. Which image best expresses the speaker's hopes for the West Wind?
   a. "Scatter, as from an extinguished hearth / Ashes and sparks . . ."
   b. "Make me thy lyre, even as the forest is . . ."
   c. ". . . he lay, / Lulled by the coil of his crystalline streams . . ."
   d. "If I were a dead leaf thou mightest bear . . ."

____ 9. What images do the lines from "Ode to the West Wind" suggest?

   Loose clouds like earth's decaying leaves are shed, / Shook from the tangled boughs of Heaven and Ocean . . .

   a. Heaven and Ocean are like large trees.
   b. Clouds ascend to Heaven from earth.
   c. Clouds fall to earth after they decay.
   d. Heaven and Ocean are connected by trees.

____ 10. In "To a Skylark," what quality does Shelley perceive and praise above all in the skylark's existence?
   a. the poignancy and melancholy of its song
   b. the clarity and wisdom of its understanding
   c. the purity and simplicity of its joy
   d. the variety and intensity of its emotions

____ 11. Which image from "To a Skylark" suggests that the skylark's music is everywhere at once?
   a. "The pale purple even / Melts around thy flight . . ."
   b. "As from thy presence showers a rain of melody."
   c. "Like a glowworm golden / In a dell of dew . . ."
   d. "Like a rose embowered / In its own green leaves . . ."

____ 12. According to the speaker of "To a Skylark," how is human happiness different from the skylark's happiness?
   a. The skylark does not know that it will die one day.
   b. Humans know too much to experience the skylark's simple joy.
   c. Humans cannot know the joy of flying.
   d. Human happiness is always tinged with sorrow.

____ 13. Which statement best describes the overall image of the skylark presented in "To a Skylark"?
   a. The skylark is often invisible.
   b. The skylark appears everywhere.
   c. The skylark is bright and colorful.
   d. The skylark is gray and drab.

____ 14. Which statement best describes Shelley's depiction of nature in "Ozymandias," "Ode to the West Wind," and "To a Skylark"?
   a. Nature has much to teach us.
   b. Nature is destructive but beautiful.
   c. Nature should be protected and preserved.
   d. Nature should be admired for its delicate beauty.

____ 15. How is the image Shelley draws of the wind in "Ode to the West Wind" similar to the image he creates of the skylark in "To a Skylark"?
   a. Both are bright and cheerful.
   b. Both are visible only at certain times of the year.
   c. Both are constantly in motion.
   d. Both are startling and fearsome.

Vocabulary and Grammar

On the line, write the letter of the one best answer.

____ 16. What does Shelley mean by these words in "Ode to the West Wind"?

> this closing night / Will be the dome of a vast *sepulcher*

    a. The night is like a womb.   c. The night is like a church.
    b. The night is like a tomb.   d. The night is like a storm.

____ 17. Which phrase from "Ode to the West Wind" is written in the subjunctive mood?
    a. "Angels of rain and lightning: there are spread . . ."
    b. "Black rain, and fire, and hail will burst: oh, hear!"
    c. "If I were a swift cloud to fly with thee . . ."
    d. "Oh, lift me as a wave, a leaf, a cloud!"

____ 18. Which sentence best paraphrases this passage from "Ode to the West Wind"?

> . . . share / The impulse of thy strength . . . O uncontrollable!

    a. Share the spontaneity of your strength!
    b. Share the ferocity of your strength!
    c. Share the passion of your strength!
    d. Share the driving force of your strength!

____ 19. Which word could replace *blithe* in this line from "To a Skylark"?

> Hail to thee, blithe spirit!

    a. cheerful   c. goofy
    b. depressed   d. angry

____ 20. Which passage contains a verb in the subjunctive mood?
    a. "What thou art we know not; / What is most like thee?"
    b. "With thy clear keen joyance / Languor cannot be. . . ."
    c. "Or how could thy notes flow in such a crystal stream?"
    d. "If I were a swift cloud to fly with thee."

Essay Questions

21. The Romantic poets admired nature for its beauty and power. Write an essay describing the approach to nature that Shelley develops in "Ozymandias," "Ode to the West Wind," and "To a Skylark." Why does Shelley admire nature? How does Shelley compare nature to humans? What does Shelley seem to think the relationship between nature and humanity should be like? Use examples from the poems to support your answer.

22. At the end of "Ode to the West Wind," the speaker asks the wind, "If Winter comes, can Spring be far behind?" Write an essay in which you interpret the meaning of this question. How does this question help to explain why the speaker admires the West Wind so much? Read in the light of this passage, what does "Ode to the West Wind" suggest about Shelley's attitude toward death? Use examples from the poem to support your answer.

23. The speaker of "Ode to the West Wind" speaks not only of the wind, but of himself. Write an essay explaining what the speaker hopes to gain from his relationship with the West Wind. Why does he address the wind? What problem is disturbing the speaker? Use examples from the poem to support your answer.

Poetry of John Keats

Selection Test

Critical Reading

On the line, write the letter of the one best answer.

_____ 1. In "On First Looking Into Chapman's Homer," what does Keats mean by "the realms of gold"?
    a. tropical oceans
    c. literary classics
    b. foreign countries
    d. ancient civilizations

_____ 2. In "On First Looking Into Chapman's Homer," Keats likens Homer to a
    a. conqueror.
    c. discoverer.
    b. scientist.
    d. monarch.

_____ 3. Which is the best paraphrase of this excerpt from "On First Looking Into Chapman's Homer"?

> . . . all his men / Looked at each other with a wild surmise— / Silent . . .

    a. All his men looked at one another in silent surprise.
    b. All his men looked at one another, guessing wildly and struck silent.
    c. All his men looked at one another wildly, trying to guess why they were so silent.
    d. All his men looked at one another silently, quietly, and wildly.

_____ 4. Which line best paraphrases this excerpt from "When I Have Fears That I May Cease to Be"?

> And when I feel, fair creature of an hour,
> That I shall never look upon thee more . . .

    a. And when I think that I'll never see you again, beautiful creature . . .
    b. And when I feel like a fair creature, I'll never see you again . . .
    c. Oh beautiful creature, I fear I will never see you again . . .
    d. It's not fair that I will never see you again . . .

_____ 5. What do you think Keats means in these lines from "When I Have Fears That I May Cease to Be"?

> I may never live to trace / Their shadows, with the magic hand of chance . . .

    a. I may never live to paint pictures of them.
    b. I may never have a chance to look at them again.
    c. I may never leave the shadows as long as I live.
    d. I may never live to write about them.

_____ 6. In "When I Have Fears That I May Cease to Be," what is Keats symbolizing in the image of "high-piled books" that "Hold like rich garners the full ripened grain"?
    a. his completed poems
    c. his untapped ideas
    b. places he wants to visit
    d. volumes he wants to read

_____ 7. For the speaker of "Ode to a Nightingale," the nightingale itself symbolizes all that is
    a. rational.
    c. timeless.
    b. painful.
    d. changeable.

8. Which image from "Ode to a Nightingale" appeals most directly to the sense of smell?
   a. "Nor what soft incense hangs upon the boughs / But, in embalmed darkness, guess each sweet . . ."
   b. "O for a beaker full of the warm South, / Full of the true, the blushful Hippocrene . . ."
   c. "Adieu! adieu! thy plaintive anthem fades / Past the near meadows, over the still stream . . ."
   d. "Save what from heaven is with the breezes blown / Through verdurous glooms and winding mossy ways."

9. For the speaker in "Ode to a Nightingale," the idea of death is full of
   a. excitement and intrigue.
   b. horror and dread.
   c. pleasure and delight.
   d. relief and ease.

10. Which describes the stanza structure of "Ode to a Nightingale"?
    a. homostrophic
    b. antistrophic
    c. strophe, antistrophe, epode
    d. no structure

11. How is a Pindaric ode structured?
    a. strophe, strophe, antistrophe
    b. strophe, homostrophe, antistrophe
    c. strophe, antistrophe, epode
    d. homostrophic

12. Which kind of ode is "Ode on a Grecian Urn"?
    a. Pindaric
    b. Horatian
    c. irregular
    d. devotional

13. Which line best paraphrases the excerpt from "Ode to a Nightingale"?

    Away! away! for I will fly to thee,
    Not charioted by Bacchus and his pards,
    But on the viewless wings of Poesy . . .

    a. I will not visit you in your chariot but will read poems to you.
    b. I will fly to you, not on Bacchus's wings but with my own wings.
    c. I will fly to you, not drunk with wine but on the wings of fantasy.
    d. I will fly with you and Bacchus, reading poems.

14. Which line best paraphrases the excerpt from "Ode on a Grecian Urn"?

    Ah, happy, happy boughs! that cannot shed
    Your leaves, nor ever bid the Spring adieu . . .

    a. Happy branches, that will never see the spring again . . .
    b. Happy branches, you will never weep at the end of spring . . .
    c. Happy branches, that will never lose your leaves or speak a single word . . .
    d. Happy branches, that will never lose your leaves or leave the springtime . . .

15. For Keats in "Ode on a Grecian Urn," the lovers pictured on the urn symbolize his theme of
    a. eternal youth and hope.
    b. maturation and full fruition.
    c. despair and frustrated desire.
    d. deep satisfaction and fulfillment.

Vocabulary and Grammar

On the line, write the letter of the one best answer.

____ 16. What does the word *ken* mean?
   a. large body of water
   b. range of sight or knowledge
   c. galaxy
   d. way of thinking

____ 17. Which word means the opposite of *teeming*?
   a. tired
   b. stupid
   c. empty
   d. old

____ 18. The word *gleaned* means
   a. examined.
   b. picked or gathered.
   c. worn out.
   d. emptied.

____ 19. Which line from "Ode to a Nightingale" contains an example of direct address?
   a. "O, for a draft of vintage!"
   b. "Thou wast not born for death, immortal Bird!"
   c. "Forlorn! The very word is like a bell . . ."
   d. "Was it a vision, or a waking dream?"

____ 20. Which quotation from "Ode on a Grecian Urn" contains an example of direct address?
   a. "Heard melodies are sweet, but those unheard / Are sweeter . . ."
   b. "Who are these coming to the sacrifice?"
   c. "What little town by river or seashore . . ."
   d. "And, little town, thy streets forevermore / Will silent be . . ."

Essay Questions

21. As is typical of the Romantic poets, Keats evokes powerful emotions in his works. Choose an emotion that you find prevalent in at least two of these poems, and write an essay explaining why you find it so significant. How does Keats's use of content and style or language create this feeling?

22. In "Ode to a Nightingale" and "Ode on a Grecian Urn," Keats addresses different objects. Write an essay comparing and contrasting the objects of these two poems. Include details from the text to support your interpretation. What does he admire in the different subjects?

23. Keats deals with the concepts of mortality and immortality throughout the four poems. Write an essay about the significance of mortality and/or immortality in each of the poems, using examples from the texts. Judging by these poems and what you know about his life, why do you think he might have considered these ideas important?

"The Lorelei" by Heinrich Heine
Haiku by Bashō, Yosa Buson, and Kobayashi Issa

Selection Test

Critical Reading

On the line, write the letter of the one best answer.

_____ 1. Read the two haiku by Basho; then choose the idea below that underlies both poems.

> Poverty's child—
> He starts to grind the rice,
> And gazes at the moon.

> Clouds come from time to time—
> And bring to men a chance to rest
> From looking at the moon.

    a. Poverty and unhappiness come from avoiding responsibility.
    b. The moon will fade, but the troubles of life will not.
    c. Everyday life and spiritual life are complementary.
    d. Gazing at the moon is essentially a frivolous pastime.

_____ 2. What can you deduce from the imagery alone in this haiku by Buson?

> Fuji alone
> Left unburied
> By young green leaves.

    a. The time of year is summer.
    b. The speaker feels burdened and sad.
    c. The mountain is very high.
    d. The leaves are falling from the trees.

_____ 3. Which idea is the focus of the imagery in this haiku by Issa?

> A world of dew:
> Yet within the dewdrops—
> Quarrels.

    a. the futility of human emotions
    b. the changeability of natural forms
    c. the harmony that exists in nature
    d. the insignificance of the natural world

_____ 4. Read these two haiku by Issa; then choose the central idea that underlies both poems.

> Far-off mountain peaks
> Reflected in its eyes:
> The dragonfly.

> With bland serenity
> Gazing at the far hills:
> A tiny frog.

    a. Fragile things lose their beauty quickly.
    b. It is important to leave home for distant vistas.
    c. Nature neglects its smallest creatures.
    d. Nature contains both vast and tiny marvels of creation.

_____ 5. Which is a central idea in "The Lorelei"?
   a. Passion can make a person blind to danger.
   b. The music of the Lorelei is the music of heaven.
   c. Singing can numb the sorrow of unfulfilled longing.
   d. Dreams are better than reality.

_____ 6. What do the rocks in the river symbolize?
   a. stepping stones to a new land   c. the perils of longing
   b. the faces of the drowned   d. the heart of his beloved

_____ 7. What is the dominant emotion that Heine is expressing in "The Lorelei"?
   a. regret that the Lorelei did not sing for him
   b. concern that he will be shipwrecked on the rocks
   c. pity that the boatman drowned in the river
   d. fear that love will cause him to suffer

_____ 8. By describing the boatman the way he does, Heine seems to suggest that love can
   make a person
   a. fulfilled and content.   c. courageous and heroic.
   b. joyful and carefree.   d. crazed and reckless.

_____ 9. What tone, or emotional quality, is evident in the reference to the Lorelei at the end
   of the poem?

       And this she did with her singing,
       The golden Lorelei.

   a. bitter and accusatory   c. awestruck and enthralled
   b. horrified and sorrowful   d. intrigued and curious

_____ 10. Heine's choice of a subject and unifying image for his poem reflects the Romantic
   emphasis on
   a. folklore and legends.   c. observation and logic.
   b. nature and imagination.   d. optimism and adventure.

Essay Questions

11. The most repeated image in Heine's lyric is "gold" and "golden." Write an essay that explores how the other images in the poem work with or against this one to create a sense of hopelessness and sadness. Consider all the details of the setting: How do they build up a fatal atmosphere around the attractions of the Lorelei?

12. A haiku is a good example of the adage "less is more." In an essay, explain what you find "less of" and what you find "more of" in a haiku. In your explanation, describe the basic characteristics of a haiku. Consider the purpose and central ideas of the haiku you have read as well as their formal elements, such as imagery, use of language, and structure. Use examples from all three poets you have read to support your ideas.

13. Consider the way in which Heine's "The Lorelei" and the following haiku by Basho share a central idea about human aspirations toward an ideal:

Summer grasses—
All that remains
Of soldiers' visions.

Both poems suggest that a force beyond human power crushes these aspirations. Write a detailed essay analyzing how the poems are similar in suggesting rather than saying what both the aspirations and the force are. Be sure to explain the similar use of nature in the two poems. Would you say that one poem shows greater ambivalence about impossible aspirations than the other does?

Part Test, Unit 4, Part 2: Focus on Literary Forms—Lyric Poetry

Critical Reading

The questions below are based on the following selections.

In "My Heart Leaps Up When I Behold" by William Wordsworth, the speaker expresses the desire to continue to view nature with a childlike sense of wonder. In "A Dirge," Percy Bysshe Shelley asks that the world be mourned.

My Heart Leaps Up When I Behold

My heart leaps up when I behold

    A rainbow in the sky:

So was it when my life began;

So is it now I am a man;

[5] So be it when I shall grow old,

    Or let me die!

The child is father of the man;

And I could wish my days to be

Bound each to each by natural piety.[1]

A Dirge

Rough wind, that moanest loud

    Grief too sad for song;

Wild wind, when sullen cloud

    Knells all the night long;

[5] Sad storm, whose tears are vain,

Bare woods, whose branches strain,

Deep caves and dreary main,—

    Wail, for the world's wrong!

[1]**natural piety:** Devotion to nature

On the line, write the letter of the one best answer.

_____ 1. Which is the best paraphrase for lines 3–5 of "My Heart Leaps Up When I Behold"?
   a. It was this way from the beginning of time, and it will be this way to the end of time.
   b. A person is born, matures, and dies.
   c. It was this way when I was born; it is this way now that I'm mature; and it will be this way when I am old.
   d. Because it was this way when I was born does not mean it will be the same when I am old.

_____ 2. How does the speaker feel when he sees a rainbow?
    a. angry   c. indifferent
    b. happy   d. depressed

_____ 3. In a metaphor, to what does the speaker compare a child?
    a. a man   c. a wish
    b. a rainbow   d. a father

_____ 4. The poem is an example of Romanticism because it
    a. expresses personal feelings.
    b. contains wit.
    c. is an example of logical reasoning.
    d. speaks against nature.

_____ 5. Which excerpt from "A Dirge" contains alliteration?
    a. "Bare woods, whose . . ."
    b. "Wild wind, when sullen cloud"
    c. "Rough wind, that moanest loud"
    d. ". . . whose tears are vain"

_____ 6. In "Dirge," what moans in grief?
    a. the sad storm   c. the wild wind
    b. the bare woods   d. the deep caves

_____ 7. Which excerpt from "Dirge" is an example of personification?
    a. "Grief too sad for song"
    b. "Sad storm, whose tears are vain"
    c. "Bare woods, whose branches . . ."
    d. "Knells all the night long"

_____ 8. What should mourn the world's misery?
    a. nature   c. tears
    b. grief   d. sorrow

_____ 9. Which line from "The Dirge" appeals to the sense of hearing?
    a. "Wild wind, with sullen cloud"
    b. "Deep caves and dreary main"
    c. "Rough wind, that moanest loud"
    d. "Sad storm, whose tears are vain"

_____ 10. What do you think the speaker might mean by "the world's wrong"?
    a. The world is worth saving.
    b. The world has enough good people to help the desperate.
    c. The world has an ample supply of wise political leaders.
    d. The world is full of hypocrisy and injustice.

Vocabulary and Grammar

The questions below consist of a related pair of words in CAPITAL LETTERS followed by four lettered pairs of words. Choose the pair that best expresses a relationship similar to that of the pair in capital letters.

_____ 11. REVERENCE : RESPECT ::
    a. helpful : useful
    b. admiration : dislike
    c. forgiveness : mercy
    d. patient : calm

____ 12. ARBITER : JUDGE ::
   a. healer : doctor
   b. sing : performer
   c. friendship : friend
   d. office : employee

On the line, write the letter of the one best answer.

____ 13. What is the complete present participle phrase in the sentence?

   Can you hear the waters rolling from mountain springs?

   a. Can you hear the waters
   b. hear the waters
   c. from mountain springs
   d. rolling from mountain springs

____ 14. Which sentence contains an example of inverted word order?
   a. The ancient Mariner returned to his home.
   b. Out of the sea came he.
   c. The sun rose upon the right.
   d. I stood on land.

____ 15. Choose the best definition of the word *blithe* as it is used in this sentence: The bird's blithe spirit is inspiring to the poet.
   a. angry
   b. depressed
   c. cheerful
   d. complicated

____ 16. Which line from Keats's "Ode to a Nightingale" contains a word of direct address?
   a. "Thou wast not born for death, immortal bird!"
   b. "Was it a vision, or a waking dream?"
   c. "She stood in tears amid the alien corn . . ."
   d. "Forlorn! the very word is like a bell . . ."

On the line, write the letter of the word or words that best complete the sentence.

____ 17. He ____ sure that his life would be better if only he ____ like a skylark.
   a. was, was
   b. were, was
   c. were, were
   d. was, were

____ 18. In the sentence, the word *credulous* means ____.

   As he examines his life, Don Juan feels that he no longer has a credulous hope.

   a. without belief
   b. willing to believe
   c. with understanding
   d. less capable of comprehending

____ 19. The sounds of the ocean ____ his attention, and the beauty of the pathless woods ____ him pleasure.
   a. captures, gives
   b. captures, give
   c. capture, gives
   d. capture, give

© Prentice-Hall, Inc.

____ 20. Boats barely moved as they sat in the quiet, ____ waters surrounding the city.
   a. sinuous
   b. stagnant
   c. confounded
   d. teeming

Essay Questions

21. In poems, writers use imagery, or descriptive language, to re-create sensory experiences and lead readers to meaning. Choose a poem from the section that you feel uses imagery effectively. Write an essay in which you describe the poem's imagery and how it relates to the poem's meaning.

22. Many lyric poems of the Romantic period reveal a poet's admiration and respect for nature. Poets often turned to aspects of the natural world in search of spirituality and creativity. In an essay, describe two poems from this section that focus on the beauty of nature. How do these images relate to theme in each poem?

23. Poems are often meant to be heard, and poets often use sound devices such as alliteration, consonance, assonance, and internal rhyme to create interesting effects. Write an essay about a poem from this section that uses sound devices to create poetic effect. What devices are used in the poem you chose? What effect do these devices create.

24. Writers are often inspired to write poems that reflect societal problems. In an essay, describe a poem from this section that reveals social ills or difficulties faced by people in a particular place or time period, or that encourages human change.

25. Romanticism was an important literary movement of the late eighteenth century that reacted against the rationalism and wit of Neoclassicism. In an essay, describe the most important aspects of Romanticism. Then choose and describe two selections from the section that reflect the ideals of Romanticism. Give concrete details from the selections you choose.

"Speech to Parliament: In Defense of the Lower Classes"
by George Gordon, Lord Byron
"A Song: 'Men of England' " by Percy Bysshe Shelley
"On the Passing of the Reform Bill" by Thomas Babington Macaulay

Selection Test

Critical Reading

On the line, write the letter of the one best answer.

_____ 1. In "A Song: 'Men of England,'" whom does Shelley characterize as *drones*?
    a. England's unemployed citizens
    b. political protesters
    c. society's richest and most powerful people
    d. farmers, weavers, and smiths

_____ 2. What irony does Shelley suggest by asking why English workers forge "Many a weapon, chain, and scourge"?
    a. Chains, whips, and weapons should not be used against bees.
    b. Implements that the workers make are later used against them.
    c. Punishment can be meted out in various cruel ways.
    d. English tradespeople are among the most skillful in the world.

_____ 3. What change in attitude does Shelley's speaker show in these lines?

       Why shake the chains ye wrought? Ye see
       The steel ye tempered glance on ye.

    a. The speaker has lost his composure and grown angry.
    d. For the first time, the speaker truly believes that workers can overcome their tyrannical employers.
    c. The speaker's optimism about workers' improving their own fortunes has been replaced with fatalism.
    d. The speaker no longer believes that workers have an obligation to revolt.

_____ 4. In "A Song: 'Men of England'" Shelley's attitude toward his subject might best be described as _____.
    a. dignified   c. dispassionate
    b. optimistic   d. embittered

_____ 5. Which would be the *least* appropriate purpose for reading "A Song: 'Men of England'"?
    a. to increase your knowledge about Percy Bysshe Shelley
    b. to learn facts about production methods of textiles, agricultural products, and iron in early nineteenth-century England
    c. to appreciate poetic devices
    d. to compare the situations of early nineteenth-century English workers and contemporary American workers

_____ 6. What is the primary focus of Lord Byron's protest in his "Speech to Parliament: In Defense of the Lower Classes"?
    a. the punishment of men who destroyed factory looms
    b. needlessly slow trials for men who vandalized factory looms
    c. legislators' lack of evidence against the accused men
    d. the extreme level of violence displayed by the vandals

_____ 7. Why might Byron have devoted the early part of his speech to a direct comparison of destructive weavers and distinguished members of the House of Lords?
   a. He wished to surprise and alienate his audience.
   b. He hoped to gain the trust and sympathy of audience members with working-class origins.
   c. He hoped to stir in his audience feelings of guilt and personal responsibility for the difficulties of the unemployed weavers.
   d. He wanted to emphasize the impressive power of the House of Lords.

_____ 8. Which word best describes Byron's tone in this sentence?

   That most favorite state measure, so marvelously efficacious in many and recent instances, temporizing, would not be without its advantages in this.

   a. indignant
   b. offhand
   c. comic
   d. sarcastic

_____ 9. Given the title "Speech to Parliament: In Defense of the Lower Classes," which of the following purposes would have been ineffective for reading Lord Byron's commentary?
   a. analyzing Byron's poetic style
   b. deepening understanding of British class divisions
   c. determining if Byron appeals to the hearts or the heads of his audience
   d. analyzing Byron's use of rhetorical devices

_____ 10. The author of "On the Passing of the Reform Bill" asserts that even a "majority of one" in Parliamentary voting promises a good outcome. Which is the best explanation of this idea?
   a. One person's affirmative vote will assure the bill's passage.
   b. Passage of the bill is possible by a margin of a single vote, and its passage is vital to avoid public outrage.
   c. The bill's passage will remind legislators of the necessity of compromise in ratifying social legislation.
   d. The bill will provide aid to more working-class citizens than has any other British law in history.

_____ 11. By comparing his view of a Parliamentary vote to "seeing Caesar stabbed in the Senate House" and "seeing Oliver [Cromwell] taking the mace from the table," Thomas Babington Macaulay emphasizes
   a. that supporting the Reform Bill is akin to committing a criminal act.
   b. his own long, distinguished political career.
   c. the historical significance of the passage of the Reform Bill.
   d. that the Reform Bill will benefit politicians as well as ordinary citizens.

_____ 12. What is the purpose of a political commentary?
   a. to persuade readers to take some particular action
   b. to support an original political argument with examples and explanations from literature
   c. to express opinions on political issues
   d. to use rhetorical devices to clarify the need for social change

_____ 13. One reason for setting a purpose for reading is to
   a. improve your reading rate.
   b. make a piece of literature easier to summarize.
   c. make literary works seem more vivid and accessible.
   d. focus and deepen your experience of a piece of literature.

_____ 14. What is the most important way in which Lord Byron's audience differs from that of Thomas Babington Macaulay?
   a. Byron's audience is better educated than Macaulay's.
   b. Byron's audience is a group of people, whereas Macaulay's is an individual.
   c. Macaulay's audience knows him personally, whereas part of Byron's audience does not know him at all.
   d. Unlike Macaulay's audience, Byron's is composed of experienced public speakers.

Vocabulary and Grammar

On the line, write the letter of the one best answer.

_____ 15. Which word means the opposite of _efficacious_?
   a. fruitful   b. ineffective   c. barren   d. obliging

_____ 16. Which phrase is most nearly the same in meaning to _inauspicious_?
   a. giving hope   c. suspecting guilt
   b. not promising a good outcome   d. not wavering

_____ 17. The word _impediments_ means
   a. obstructions.   b. tools.   c. hourly wages.   d. arguments.

_____ 18. Which line from the three political commentaries contains correlative conjunctions?
   a. "I have little news for you, except what you will learn from the papers as well as from me."
   b. "If you proceed by the forms of laws, where is your evidence?"
   c. "It is clear that the Reform Bill must pass, either in this or in another Parliament."
   d. "Sow seed—but let no tyrant reap. . . ."

_____ 19. Correlative conjunctions are used to
   a. introduce subordinate clauses.
   b. link grammatically equal words or groups of words.
   c. separate nonessential phrases from other words in a sentence.
   d. connect subjects and verbs.

_____ 20. Which pair of words can function as correlative conjunctions?
   a. yet, still   b. only, also   c. if, or   d. neither, nor

Essay Questions

21. In "A Song: 'Men of England,'" Shelley characterizes "the lords who lay ye [men of England] low" as _tyrants_ and as _impostors_. Explain what keeps the "tyrants" in power and the men of England "low." In what way are these lords "impostors"? In what sense are English laborers "low"?

22. In his argument against a sentence of execution for condemned British weavers, Lord Byron repeatedly uses words related to food (_famished, starving, daily bread_) and war (_destructive warfare, lancets of your military, martial law, dragooned, grenadiers_). Write an essay in which you evaluate the effectiveness of these images in Byron's political commentary. How direct is the connection between the weavers' hunger and their crimes? Is there any relationship between hunger and war? To which of the audience's emotions or human attributes do such images appeal?

23. Shelley and Byron considered themselves to be artists, yet both were also passionately political men. Using references to two or three of the selections you've just read, write an essay in which you discuss the relationship between politics and art. Is an art form such as poetry suitable for delivering political messages? Do you think politics and art are best kept separate? Is it possible to create a work of art without political content? Do the goals of the artist and the political commentator conflict with one another?

Name _____ Date _____

"On Making an Agreeable Marriage" by Jane Austen
from *A Vindication of the Rights of Woman* by Mary Wollstonecraft

Selection Test

Critical Reading

On the line, write the letter of the one best answer.

_____ 1. Above all other considerations, Jane Austen felt that her niece should marry
    a. the eldest son of a wealthy man.
    b. a smart man.
    c. a man she respected.
    d. a man she liked.

_____ 2. "On Making an Agreeable Marriage" makes it clear that Austen believes her niece is probably
    a. still in love.   c. too immature to marry.
    b. not in love.   d. nervous about marriage.

_____ 3. "On Making an Agreeable Marriage" might be read as a form of social commentary that
    a. criticizes society.
    b. criticizes a certain person.
    c. purposefully records society's foibles.
    d. unconsciously reflects social attitudes.

_____ 4. Jane Austen's letter to her niece suggests that she hopes Fanny will
    a. never marry.   c. go on as before.
    b. marry well.   d. be cold to Mr. J. P.

_____ 5. Mary Wollstonecraft wrote *A Vindication of the Rights of Woman* to
    a. complain about her lack of education.
    b. record the customs of the day.
    c. criticize society's view of women.
    d. criticize men.

_____ 6. Mary Wollstonecraft felt that women's weakness was
    a. artificial.   c. a libertine notion.
    b. caused by men.   d. natural.

_____ 7. Mary Wollstonecraft's *A Vindication of the Rights of Woman* might be subtitled
    a. *A Demand for Understanding.*
    b. *A Plea for Better Education for Women.*
    c. *A Request for Equal Employment Opportunity for All.*
    d. *A Lament for the Sorrows of Women.*

_____ 8. Mary Wollstonecraft compares women's minds to
    a. the minds of children.   c. flowers planted in soil that is too rich.
    b. a mistake of nature.   d. infertile soil.

_____ 9. According to Wollstonecraft, mistaken notions of female excellence lead women to
    a. behave like children.
    b. scheme about the best way to get a husband.
    c. lose interest in intellectual pursuits entirely.
    d. behave in a masculine manner.

____ 10. Which line from *A Vindication of the Rights of Woman* conveys the essay's main theme?
   a. "I have turned over various books written on the subject of education . . ."
   b. "this artificial weakness produces a propensity to tyrannize, and gives birth to cunning . . ."
   c. "there is little reason to fear that women will acquire too much courage or fortitude . . ."
   d. "women . . . ought to cherish a nobler ambition, and by their abilities and virtues exact respect. . . ."

____ 11. Wollstonecraft's purpose in writing *A Vindication of the Rights of Woman* was to
   a. persuade readers to accept her point of view.
   b. explain a social problem to readers.
   c. rally female readers to her cause.
   d. publish her thoughts on feminist philosophy.

____ 12. Which describes how the word *vindication* in the title of Mary Wollstonecraft's essay reflects her purpose for writing?
   a. *Vindication* means "placing blame"; Wollstonecraft wishes to criticize men for holding women back.
   b. *Vindication* means "justification"; Wollstonecraft is justifying why women should have equal rights.
   c. *Vindication* means "the state of being spiteful or critical"; Wollstonecraft is venting her frustration over the state of women's education.
   d. *Vindication* means "reasoned and well thought out"; Wollstonecraft wishes to explain a long history of poor treatment of women.

____ 13. One of the main points in *A Vindication of the Rights of Woman* is that women should be
   a. loved for themselves.
   b. respected, not simply admired.
   c. given physical training to improve their strength.
   d. encouraged to be ambitious.

____ 14. At the time Jane Austen and Mary Wollstonecraft were writing, women's education tended to focus mainly on
   a. instruction in how to run a household.
   b. lessons taught by a governess.
   c. ladylike accomplishments.
   d. indoor pursuits.

Vocabulary and Grammar

On the line, write the letter of the word that best completes the sentence.

____ 15. A person who behaves with *solicitude* is being ____ .
   a. careful   c. faithful
   b. proper   d. thoughtful

____ 16. An *amiable* person is ____ .
   a. antisocial   c. trusting
   b. friendly   d. happy

____ 17. If a seller makes a *specious* claim, that person is being ____ .
   a. disloyal   c. inappropriate
   b. deceptive   d. unctuous

On the line, write the letter of the one best answer.

____ 18. Which sentence uses serial commas correctly?
   a. Women have long been expected to balance a full-time job, and a household, with children.
   b. In the past, women's education focused mainly on accomplishments such as embroidery singing, and playing a musical instrument.
   c. Women were looked at as physically, mentally, and socially, unequal to men.
   d. Most women had only a few options, such as living on the charity of relatives, finding posts as governesses, or teaching at girls' schools.

____ 19. In a series of three items, a final series comma comes
   a. immediately before the final noun.
   b. immediately after the final noun.
   c. immediately before the conjunction.
   d. immediately after the conjunction.

____ 20. Which sentence uses serial commas correctly?
   a. Mary Wollstonecraft, Jane Austen, and, others wrote perceptively about the society of their time.
   b. Trust, and respect, and mutual affection were the qualities Jane Austen felt were necessary for an agreeable marriage.
   c. Mary Wollstonecraft thought that most women of her day were undereducated underchallenged, and underachieving.
   d. Austen wrote *Pride and Prejudice, Emma,* and *Sense and Sensibility.*

Essay Questions

21. Jane Austen's letter to her niece Fanny provides many clues to Austen's great popularity as a novelist. Write an essay in which you cite examples from the selection that point up Austen's perception about human nature and the society in which she lived.

22. Jane Austen and Mary Wollstonecraft lived around the same time and shared many of the same ideas, although their writing styles differed radically. Write an essay that compares and contrasts the ideas in Austen's "On Making an Agreeable Marriage" with those in Wollstonecraft's *A Vindication of the Rights of Woman.*

23. When *A Vindication of the Rights of Woman* was first published, it caused great public out-cry, not only because of its content but also because of its straightforward, blunt style. In those days people were not accustomed to women's speaking their minds. Write an essay that defines Wollstonecraft's style. Do you think her style would be considered blunt by today's standards?

from the Screenplay of *Sense and Sensibility* and Diaries
by Emma Thompson

Selection Test

Critical Reading

On the line, write the letter of the one best answer.

____ 1. Edward hopes to find fulfillment in life by
  a. owning his own barouche.
  b. becoming a barrister or soldier.
  c. heading an expedition to China.
  d. living quietly in the country.

____ 2. The direction "His tone is light but there is an underlying bitterness to it" suggests that Edward
  a. envies the Dashwoods their barouche.
  b. looks down on Elinor's family for not being in "the first circles."
  c. resents Margaret's casual treatment of him.
  d. scorns his mother's values.

____ 3. This entire dialogue helps to characterize Edward as
  a. stubborn and ungrateful.
  b. affected and patronizing.
  c. caring and good-natured.
  d. superficial.

____ 4. The screenplay hints at inequity among classes in Edward's remark:
  a. " 'I am to go as her servant but only on the understanding that I will be very badly treated.' "
  b. " 'Piracy is our only option.' "
  c. " 'A country living is my ideal.' "
  d. " 'Our circumstances are therefore precisely the same.' "

____ 5. Overall the screenplay suggests that if Edward ignores his mother's preferences, he might
  a. lose Elinor's respect.
  b. be disinherited by his mother.
  c. turn criminal.
  d. feel stuck in a small parish.

____ 6. London does not suit Edward because
  a. it is his mother's home.
  b. he finds it too busy and noisy.
  c. he feels useless there.
  d. it is too far from Norland.

____ 7. By what means does society expect women of Elinor's class to find financial security if they cannot earn or inherit a fortune?
  a. marriage
  b. piracy
  c. travel
  d. savings

© Prentice-Hall, Inc.

8. The difference between Edward and his mother over his career
   a. has arisen because of Mr. Dashwood's death.
   b. has spoilt his sense of humor.
   c. has existed for a long time.
   d. has made him uncertain about his real desires.

9. Elinor's protest against the restrictions on females of her class is comically echoed in
   a. Mrs. Dashwood's smile.
   b. the snobbery of Edward's mother.
   c. Edward's own complaints.
   d. her youngest sister's impossible plans.

10. Edward and Elinor's relationship develops in a setting full of
    a. expensive property.
    b. natural beauty.
    c. reminders of London.
    d. funereal gloom.

Essay Questions

11. Evidently Edward and his mother disagree radically about his future. Using details from the selection, write an essay demonstrating that their conflict is essentially between substance and surface, between individual fulfillment and social image. Comment on how the screenplay makes Edward's preference seem right.

12. These three short scenes trace Elinor and Edward's progression from warm friendliness to intimacy. Write a detailed essay explaining how the screenplay builds up a sense not just of their compatibility, but also of the obstacles to their possible courtship.

13. Elinor explicitly tells Edward that their society restricts women even more than men. Write an essay analyzing how the screenplay uses Margaret's carefree indifference to gender roles to make the same point as Elinor's open criticism. What are the clues that Margaret has not yet been socialized into "appropriate" or ladylike female behavior and expectations?

Name _____ Date _____

Part Test, Unit 4, Part 3: The Reaction to Society's Ills

Critical Reading

The questions below are based on the following selection.

George Gordon, Lord Byron, included the poem, "So We'll Go No More A-Roving," as part of a letter to Thomas Moore on February 28, 1817. In self-imposed exile from England since 1816, Byron wrote to Moore from Venice, where he had just spent carnival season, and at age twenty-nine found himself in a period of deep personal reflection.

So We'll Go No More A-Roving

So we'll go no more a-roving

    So late into the night,

Though the heart be still as loving,

    And the moon be still as bright.

[5] For the sword outwears its sheath,

    And the soul wears out the breast,

And the heart must pause to breathe,

    And Love itself have rest.

Though the night was made for loving,

[10]   And the day returns too soon,

Yet we'll go no more a-roving

    By the light of the moon.

On the line, write the letter of the one best answer.

____ 1. What change is revealed in "So We'll Go No More A-Roving"?
  a. The speaker resolves to live a quieter life.
  b. The speaker's beloved no longer loves him.
  c. The speaker's friends forsake him.
  d. The speaker begins an exciting journey of self-discovery.

____ 2. According to the speaker, what has *not* changed?
  a. his feelings about himself
  b. the moon's brightness
  c. the sheath's strength
  d. his understanding of love

____ 3. Which is the best interpretation of these lines?

    For the sword outwears its sheath / And the soul wears out the breast?

  a. Love and hatred cannot coexist.
  b. We often love without understanding love's source.
  c. Eventually, we tire of pleasure and become jaded.
  d. Old age brings bitterness.

Unit 4: Rebels and Dreamers (1790–1832)

____ 4. In "So We'll Go No More A-Roving," what social commentary might Byron have implied?
    a. A life based on pleasure can be unfulfilling.
    b. The upper classes waste their time in idle pursuits.
    c. Friendships that center on having a good time cannot withstand the pressures of real-life problems.
    d. Women in Byron's day were treated as second-class citizens.

____ 5. If your purpose in reading "So We'll Go No More A-Roving" is to discover the poem's meaning, you would most likely
    a. pay attention to word choice.
    b. identify the rhythm.
    c. map out the rhyme scheme.
    d. examine the main ideas and details.

____ 6. What is Byron's purpose in writing "So We'll Go No More A-Roving"?
    a. to address personal issues
    b. to incite social reform
    c. to create a distinct literary character
    d. to condemn certain social activities

____ 7. Paying particular attention to the poem's stanza structure and rhyme scheme shows the reader's purpose is to
    a. discover the poet's purpose.
    b. analyze the poet's style.
    c. compare and contrast this poem with others.
    d. interpret the poem's imagery.

____ 8. If the speaker and his friends will "go no more a-roving," what will they do instead?
    a. They will try to reform those who continue roving at night.
    b. They will go a-roving at some point in the future.
    c. They will reflect on their days of roving.
    d. They will go a-roving during the daytime.

____ 9. Which word best describes the mood of Byron's poem?
    a. galloping
    b. morose
    c. resigned
    d. resentful

____ 10. Why might "So We'll Go No More A-Roving" be seen as a commentary on society's ills in Byron's day?
    a. The speaker believes love no longer remains.
    b. The poem was written while Byron was away from England, in Venice.
    c. People worked hard and could not afford to go "a-roving."
    d. The poem conveys a sense of disillusionment with the way things are.

Vocabulary and Grammar

On the line, write the letter of the one best answer.

____ 11. What word means the opposite of *efficacious*?
    a. disastrous   c. ineffective
    b. inconclusive   d. desirable

____ 12. What word means the opposite of *amiable*?
    a. disagreeable   c. social
    b. isolated   d. inconsequential

On the line, write the letter of the one best answer.

____ 13. Mary Wollstonecraft saw unequal education and male prejudice as ____ to the advancement of women's rights.
   a. decimation
   b. impediments
   c. fortitude
   d. preponderates

____ 14. ____ Byron ____ Shelley spoke out in support of the working class.
   a. Either, or
   b. Neither, nor
   c. Both, and
   d. Whether, or

____ 15. Macaulay ____ wrote about politics ____ served in the House of Commons.
   a. neither, nor
   b. not only, but also
   c. either, or
   d. just as, so too

Essay Questions

16. The writers of the selections in this section voice definite opinions about political and social ills in Britain resulting partly from the Industrial Revolution. Choose the selection whose message you found most compelling, and write an essay explaining the selection's effectiveness. You might focus on the writer's argument, writing style, or choice of topic.

17. The political and social issues addressed in this section's selections reveal a nation divided along many lines. How might political and social issues have crossed lines? Examine the issues addressed in two of the selections, one pertaining to politics and the other to social ills. Write an essay explaining connections that can be made between the two problems.

18. The writers in this section aim to expose or explain particular ills in society. However, their attacks are not always direct; some are implied through the writers' use of language, imagery, or tone. Choose a selection in which a writer addresses a political or social situation through a combination of direct and indirect criticism. Write an essay analyzing these criticisms and comparing and contrasting the use of direct and indirect commentary.

from "In Memoriam, A.H.H.," "The Lady of Shalott," "Ulysses," and from _The Princess_: "Tears, Idle Tears" by Alfred, Lord Tennyson

Selection Test

Critical Reading

On the line, write the letter of the one best answer.

_____ 1. "In Memoriam, A.H.H." was written by Tennyson to commemorate
    a. a dead close friend.
    b. the end of a love affair.
    c. sailors who died in a critical naval battle.
    d. the lives of common people.

_____ 2. To evaluate the validity of the poet's logic, imagery, and purpose is called
    a. judging the author's message
    b. identifying with a character
    c. predicting the outcome
    d. responding to the story

_____ 3. The speaker of "In Memoriam, A.H.H." seems to be
    a. a casual acquaintance of A.H.H.
    b. someone who never knew A.H.H.
    c. one who contemplates death impersonally.
    d. Tennyson himself.

_____ 4. Gradually, the speaker of "In Memoriam, A.H.H."
    a. adjusts to pain by letting go of his friend's memory.
    b. merges acceptance of death with love of his friend.
    c. begins to long for his own death.
    d. grows to understand the meaning of death.

_____ 5. What is the meaning of the line in "In Memoriam, A.H.H."?

      Far off thou art, but ever nigh

    a. The speaker regrets that A.H.H. ever left the country.
    b. No matter how much he remembers, death still removes his friend forever.
    c. Although A.H.H. is dead, the speaker holds his memory close.
    d. Death and life are closer than it may seem.

_____ 6. What is the theme of "In Memoriam, A.H.H."?
    a. the endurance of love beyond death
    b. the tragic termination of friendship
    c. the awful injustice of dying young
    d. the gradual fading of painful memories

_____ 7. In form and content, "The Lady of Shalott" recalls
    a. Christian allegories.   c. medieval romances.
    b. national epics.   d. classical drama.

_____ 8. Why may the Lady in "The Lady of Shalott" _not_ leave her island?
    a. She has no means of transport at the poem's beginning.
    b. A curse is on her that forbids her doing so.
    c. The king in Camelot has forbidden her to do so.
    d. She is too overburdened with her weaving to do so.

_____ 9. One part of Tennyson's message in "The Lady of Shalott" is the
      a. beauty of romantic love.
      b. social isolation of artists.
      c. danger of romantic love.
      d. sinister aspects of art.

_____ 10. In what ways is the Lady in "The Lady of Shalott" like an artist?
      a. She suffers from a curse.
      b. She lives on a silent isle.
      c. She is robed in snowy white.
      d. She weaves a magic web.

_____ 11. Which of the following lines from "The Lady of Shalott" is the best evidence to support the poet's message that the Lady is doomed?
      a. "She knows not what the curse may be,"
      b. "She hath no loyal knight and true,"
      c. "She left the web, she left the loom"
      d. "There she weaves by night and day"

_____ 12. What is "Tears, Idle Tears" mostly about?
      a. the death of friends
      b. the futility of crying
      c. the pain of remembrance
      d. the horror of death

_____ 13. In "Tears, Idle Tears," when the speaker describes kisses that are "by hopeless fancy feigned," he means kisses that are
      a. secret.   c. regretted.
      b. insincere.   d. imagined.

_____ 14. In "Tears, Idle Tears," why does the poet describe the past as "Death in Life"?
      a. Events end and "die," and we experience that in life.
      b. The speaker's life no longer has meaning to him.
      c. Thoughts of death dominate the speaker's life.
      d. The past seems more alive than the present.

_____ 15. In Tennyson's "Ulysses," which passage best summarizes the speaker's feelings about growing old?
      a. "Though much is taken, much abides . . ."
      b. ". . . Life piled on life / Were all too little . . ."
      c. ". . . heroic hearts, / Made weak by time and fate . . ."
      d. ". . . I mete and dole / Unequal laws unto a savage race . . ."

Vocabulary and Grammar

On the line, write the letter of the one best answer.

_____ 16. Parallel structure is the
      a. use of lines that are all more or less the same length.
      b. dispersal of thematic elements evenly throughout a work.
      c. balanced arrangement of stanzas in the sections of a narrative poem.
      d. use of repeated words, phrases, or grammatical forms.

____ 17. In "The Lady of Shalott," what are these lines an example of?

> She left the web, she left the loom, / She made three paces through the room

    a. emotive language   c. foreshadowing
    b. parallel structure   d. onomatopoeia

____ 18. A *furrow* is a _____.
    a. forehead
    b. ridge
    c. groove
    d. longboat

____ 19. Things that are *waning* are _____.
    a. growing
    b. diminishing
    c. drenched
    d. enduring

____ 20. Something that is *diffusive* is _____.
    a. laborious
    b. flammable
    c. vanished
    d. spread out

Essay Questions

21. Some critics have seen "The Lady of Shalott" as Tennyson's comment on the loneliness of being an artist. Why might this be a reasonable interpretation? Write an essay in which you identify things in the Lady's isolated life on her island that might be like the life of an artist. Use specific examples from the poem for your comparison.

22. In "Ulysses," an old man longs for one more chance to relive the glory of his youth. Write an essay in which you describe the nature of heroism the speaker of "Ulysses" hopes to display. Use specific examples from the poem to support your ideas.

23. Psychologists tell us that grieving for a loved one is a process in which a person goes through stages. In what sense does "In Memoriam, A.H.H." reflect such a process? Write an essay in which you explain how the poem progresses from one kind of feeling about death to others. Use examples from the poem to support your ideas.

Name _____ Date _____

"My Last Duchess," "Life in a Love," and **"Love Among the Ruins"**
by Robert Browning
Sonnet 43 by Elizabeth Barrett Browning

Selection Test

Critical Reading

On the line, write the letter of the one best answer.

_____ 1. The speaker in "My Last Duchess" addresses
   a. no one.
   b. an artist painting a portrait.
   c. an agent representing a woman he wishes to marry.
   d. a sculptor he has hired to make a sculpture.

_____ 2. Judging by these following lines, what inference can the reader draw about the speaker in "My Last Duchess"?

   The bough of cherries some officious fool / Broke in the orchard for her . . .

   a. The speaker is cruel and murderous.
   b. The speaker is protective and fatherly.
   c. The speaker is passionate about gardening.
   d. The speaker is arrogant and patronizing.

_____ 3. Which lines from "My Last Duchess" reveal the speaker's jealous personality?
   a. "Oh, sir, she smiled . . . / . . . but who passed without / Much the same smile?" . . .
   b. "Though his fair daughter's self, as I avowed / At starting, is my object." . . .
   c. "That's my last Duchess painted on the wall, / Looking as if she were alive. . . ."
   d. ". . . that pictured countenance, / The depth and passion of its earnest glance . . ."

_____ 4. "My Last Duchess" by Robert Browning is considered a dramatic monologue because the speaker
   a. reveals himself through his own words.
   b. addresses his remarks to an absent person.
   c. discusses highly emotional issues.
   d. acts like a character in a play.

_____ 5. What is the conflict in the dramatic monologue "Life in a Love"?
   a. The speaker must confess his lack of feeling for his beloved.
   b. The speaker suffers repeated rejections from his beloved.
   c. The speaker realizes he must find another love.
   d. The speaker is unable to tell his beloved of his feelings.

_____ 6. What inference can we make about the speaker's personality in "Life in a Love"?
   a. The speaker is shy.   c. The speaker is insecure.
   b. The speaker is judgmental.   d. The speaker is confident.

_____ 7. In "Love Among the Ruins," for whom does the speaker wait?
   a. a shepherd
   b. a tour guide
   c. a girl
   d. a soldier

_____ 8. Which statement describes the theme, or central idea, of "Love Among the Ruins"?
   a. Past civilizations live on through present ones.
   b. Simple love surpasses all other human values.
   c. Patience is the greatest human virtue.
   d. Even love is subject to destruction.

_____ 9. The alternating long and short lines in "Love Among the Ruins" suggest a contrast between
   a. sun and shadows.   c. truth and beauty.
   b. past and present.   d. poetry and prose.

_____ 10. Through his dramatic monologue, the speaker of "Love Among the Ruins" reveals that he
   a. is a pacifist.
   b. values love above fame or power.
   c. is impatient.
   d. cares only about himself.

_____ 11. Sonnet 43 is mainly about
   a. the death of the speaker's beloved.
   b. the appearance of the speaker's beloved.
   c. the ways in which the speaker loves her beloved.
   d. the speaker's religious beliefs.

_____ 12. What can you infer about the speaker of Sonnet 43 from these lines?

   I love thee with a love I seemed to lose
   With my lost saints . . .

   a. She values religion more than love.
   b. She cannot sustain her love.
   c. She is extremely religious.
   d. She values love more than religion.

_____ 13. The theme of Sonnet 43 concerns the
   a. promise of life after death.
   b. obsessive quality of romantic love.
   c. difficulty of describing romantic love.
   d. transcendent value of romantic love.

_____ 14. In Sonnet 43, the speaker's references to "old griefs," "childhood's faith," and "lost saints" suggest that love
   a. reinterprets the emotions of the past.
   b. reactivates the problems of the past.
   c. buries the concerns of the past.
   d. mourns the losses of the past.

Vocabulary and Grammar

On the line, write the letter of the word that best completes the sentence.

_____ 15. The source of his wife's happiness _____ the Duke.
   a. countenances   c. minions
   b. officious   d. eludes

_____ 16. Despite his power and position, the Duke became jealous even when _____ paid attention to his wife.
   a. munificence   c. minions
   b. dowry   d. vestige

_____ 17. Hoping to win the woman's affection, the suitor demonstrated his _____ by sending her expensive gifts.

a. countenance   c. dowry
b. munificence   d. minions

On the line, write the letter of the one best answer.

_____ 18. Which sentence demonstrates the correct use of _like_?

a. No one wrote dramatic monologues as well like Robert Browning.
b. Sonnet 43 has fourteen lines like a sonnet should.
c. I thought romances like theirs happened only in the movies.
d. The ruins looked like they did in the photograph.

_____ 19. Which sentence demonstrates the correct use of _as_?

a. My beloved replied as I hoped she would.
b. The moon shone as a penny above the hillside.
c. The Duke treated his wife as an object.
d. Readers as you must make inferences about the Duke's behavior.

_____ 20. Poets _____ the Brownings were as well-known in their time _____ today's entertainers.

a. like; like
b. as; as
c. like; as
d. as; like

Essay Questions

21. Robert Browning is considered the master of the dramatic monologue. In an essay, analyze two of Browning's poems, explaining how they are examples of dramatic monologue and what they reveal about the speaker. Support your analysis with examples from the poems you choose.

22. The speakers in these poems profess their feelings openly. However, they may not be aware of just how much they actually reveal about themselves. In your opinion, which speaker reveals the most without realizing it? Write an essay in which you state and defend your opinion. Use examples from the poems to support your answer.

23. The speakers of "Love Among the Ruins" and Sonnet 43 both profess strong views of romantic love. How do the speakers convey their ideas? Which opinions are conveyed directly? Which do you have to infer? Write an essay in which you compare and contrast the speakers' ideas about love and their means of expressing them.

Name _____ Date _____

"You Know the Place: Then" by Sappho
"Invitation to the Voyage" by Charles Baudelaire

Selection Test

Critical Reading

On the line, write the letter of the one best answer.

_____ 1. Which best summarizes the theme of "Invitation to the Voyage"?
   a. the conflict between the good and evil selves
   b. the search for beauty in the midst of ugliness
   c. the emotional aspects of human relationships
   d. the desire to share love and bliss with another

_____ 2. What type of place does the poet's ideal destination most resemble?
   a. a hidden desert oasis
   b. a bustling port city
   c. a peaceful country village
   d. an exotic tropical island

_____ 3. The tone, or emotional quality, that pervades "Invitation to the Voyage" is best described as
   a. bitter and tormented.
   b. wild and passionate.
   c. rapturous and dreamy.
   d. joyful and content.

_____ 4. What is the poet really searching for when he repeats the word *there* in the verses and refrains of "Invitation to the Voyage"?
   a. a place where he can find his true self
   b. a state of permanent unity with another
   c. a place where he can escape from the city
   d. a state of artistic freedom and respect

_____ 5. What scene do these lines from the second stanza of "Invitation to the Voyage" describe?

> Furniture that wears
> The luster of the years

   a. wild adventure
   b. quiet domesticity
   c. pensive loneliness
   d. bitter regret

_____ 6. Which motif is present in both Sappho's "You Know the Place: Then" and Baudelaire's "Invitation to the Voyage"?
   a. sleep   c. springtime
   b. sailing   d. gold cups

_____ 7. In "You Know the Place: Then," the speaker addresses
   a. her long-lost lover.
   b. a secret admirer.
   c. the goddess of love.
   d. her ideal partner.

190 Formal Assessment   © Prentice-Hall, Inc.

8. The line "rose thicket shades the ground" in "You Know the Place: Then" most appeals to the sense of _____.
    a. sight
    b. smell
    c. sound
    d. touch

9. Which animals are mentioned in "You Know the Place: Then"?
    a. doves
    b. horses
    c. unicorns
    d. tigers

10. In "You Know the Place: Then," the speaker describes a place appropriate for
    a. sleep
    b. gardening
    c. pleasant conversation
    d. love

Essay Questions

11. Much of "Invitation to the Voyage" describes the speaker's own dreams and desires. In an essay, explain to whom this poem is addressed. Cite examples of lines where Baudelaire actually addresses another person. Compare Baudelaire's treatment of the addressee with Sappho's in "You Know the Place: Then."

12. Sappho's "You Know the Place: Then" is filled with imagery that appeals to the senses. Write an essay demonstrating which senses are invoked by which images in the poem. Analyze the overall effect of such images, describing what mood they help to create. Compare Sappho's use of sensual imagery, and the resulting mood, with Baudelaire's in "Invitation to a Voyage."

13. Both Sappho and Baudelaire describe distinct places where love can flourish. Write an essay discussing the settings of the two poems. Make a judgment about which place is better suited to a love story.

Part Test, Unit 5, Part 1: Relationships

Critical Reading

The questions below are based on the following selection.

In these final two stanzas from "Love Among the Ruins," a poem by Robert Browning, a shepherd meets his wife or girlfriend at the end of the day. In the first five stanzas, the speaker describes the countryside and imagines the splendor that once surrounded a now-ruined city. All that remains is a single turret, where the woman now awaits the shepherd. The "he" in line 61 is the king who once ruled the city.

from Love Among the Ruins

But he looked upon the city, every side,

   Far and wide,

All the mountains topped with temples, all the glades'

   Colonnades,[1]

[65] All the causeys,[2] bridges, aqueducts—and then,

   All the men!

When I do come, she will speak not, she will stand,

   Either hand

On my shoulder, give her eyes the first embrace

[70]   Of my face,

Ere we rush, ere we extinguish sight and speech

   Each on each.

In one year they sent a million fighters forth

   South and North,

[75] And they built their gods a brazen pillar[3] high

   As the sky,

Yet reserved a thousand chariots in full force—

   Gold, of course.

Oh heart! oh blood that freezes, blood that burns!

[80]   Earth's returns

For whole centuries of folly, noise and sin!

   Shut them in,

With their triumphs and their glories and the rest!

   Love is best.

---

[1] **Colonnades:** Here, groups of trees surrounding an open area.

[2] **causeys:** Causeways or raised roads.

[3] **brazen pillar:** Built from the brass of captured chariots.

On the line, write the letter of the one best answer.

_____ 1. Which line from the selection uses emotive language?
   a. "All the mountains topped with temples"
   b. "When I do come, she will speak not"
   c. "In one year they sent a million fighters forth"
   d. "Oh heart! oh blood that freezes, blood that burns!"

_____ 2. Why does the speaker say "Shut them in" in line 82?
   a. He wants to stop imagining the chariots and men of the past.
   b. He has no desire for the riches or spoils of the past.
   c. He feels that the excesses of the past were shameful and should be forgotten.
   d. He has reached the fold and is ready to shut his sheep in for the night.

_____ 3. What did "he" [the king] look out upon?
   a. his great city and the many buildings and people
   b. the mountaintops
   c. the woman waiting in the turret
   d. a thousand gold chariots

_____ 4. What can you infer about the speaker's attitude toward the ruined city?
   a. He wishes he could have seen its splendor.
   b. He can imagine and appreciate its past glory but wants nothing further to do with it.
   c. He admires the courage and boldness of the fighters in their chariots.
   d. He believes that the buildings and temples must have been great achievements.

_____ 5. How might the speaker's experience in "Love Among the Ruins" relate to Browning's own attitudes?
   a. Perhaps Browning once met a girl among the ruins of an ancient city.
   b. Perhaps Browning once visited the ruins of an ancient city and imagined its past magnificence.
   c. Perhaps Browning feels, too, that "Love is best."
   d. Perhaps Browning once saw a painting of a ruins and imagined a romantic scene.

_____ 6. How do the shepherd and the woman greet each other?
   a. First she looks at his face and then they embrace.
   b. They embrace immediately.
   c. They speak upon seeing each other.
   d. They say nothing, merely standing, looking at each other.

_____ 7. In line 81, to what does the following phrase refer?

   whole centuries of folly, noise and sin!

   a. a long period of warfare
   b. time past when men desired and valued material goods more than anything else
   c. the centuries during which this ruined city flourished
   d. the period of time before he met and fell in love with the woman who now awaits him

_____ 8. What contrast does the speaker in this poem express?
   a. a contrast between the residents of the ruined city and their enemies
   b. a contrast between himself and the woman he meets in the ruins
   c. a contrast between material wealth and power and love
   d. a contrast between the ruins and the glories of the past

_____ 9. Which words in "Love Among the Ruins" express a bias against the ancient past?
   a. causeys, bridges, aqueducts   c. a million fighters
   b. thousand chariots   d. lust of glory

____ 10. Which is a logical inference made about the speaker in this poem?
a. He puts little value in material wealth.
b. He has no occupation and spends his time dreaming of what could be.
c. He admires the men who once lived in this ancient city.
d. He is dazzled by the stories of ancient wealth that are told about the ruined city.

Vocabulary and Grammar

On the line, write the letter of the word that is closest in meaning to the word in CAPITAL LETTERS.

____ 11. WANING
a. ashen
b. sunken
c. declining
d. flowing

____ 12. ELUDES
a. avoids
b. frustrates
c. pursues
d. oversees

On the line, write the letter of the one best answer.

____ 13. Which poetic line contains an example of *parallelism*?
a. "Behold the man that loved and lost . . ."
b. To dance with death, to beat the ground,
c. He is not here; but far away
d. My love involves the love before

____ 14. In which sentence is the word *like* or *as* used correctly?
a. Tennyson was appointed Poet Laureate of England, as Wordsworth had been.
b. Tennyson depicted Odysseus like he chose.
c. As many readers, you may be captivated by the Brownings' devotion to each other.
d. Like you might expect, the sickly Elizabeth died much earlier than her husband did.

____ 15. Which passage contains prepositional phrases that form a parallel structure?
a. "Or at the casement seen her stand? / Or is she known in all the land,"
b. "There the river eddy whirls, / And there the surly village churls,"
c. "I have thee still, and I rejoice; / I prosper, circled with thy voice; "
d. "Ah, sweeter to be drunk with loss, / To dance with death, to beat the ground."

Essay Questions

16. What views of romantic love are expressed or represented in Tennyson's "The Lady of Shalott," Robert Browning's "My Last Duchess" and "Life in a Love," and Elizabeth Barrett Browning's Sonnet 43? Choose two poems and compare and contrast the views. Support your comparison with details from the poems.

17. The story of Robert Browning and Elizabeth Barrett Browning's courtship and marriage has become famous. Choose one poem from Part 1 written by either of the Brownings. Is the poem "predictable," given the poets' romantic courtship and marriage? Alternatively, does it surprise you somehow in the attitudes expressed in the poem? In an essay, explain how your knowledge of the poets' background affects your reading of the poem.

18. Several of the speakers in the poems in Part 1 take journeys or travel through some physical or emotional process. Choose one of the speakers and explain what his or her journey is, what the speaker accomplishes, and how the speaker is changed by the journey.

from *Hard Times* by Charles Dickens
from *Jane Eyre* by Charlotte Brontë

Selection Test

Critical Reading

On the line, write the letter of the one best answer.

_____ 1. In *Hard Times*, on what principle is Thomas Gradgrind's teaching style based?
   a. Teach gently but firmly.
   b. Teach boys and girls to distinguish between facts and fancy.
   c. Teach boys and girls nothing but facts.
   d. Teach boys and girls to respect education and their elders.

_____ 2. What is Dickens's purpose in describing Thomas Gradgrind as a "cannon loaded to the muzzle with facts" who will blow his students "clean out of the regions of childhood at one discharge"?
   a. to reveal hatred of Gradgrind's inflexible and close-minded teaching style
   b. to show Gradgrind's grasp of mathematics and basic facts
   c. to encourage readers to admire Gradgrind's firm command of his classroom
   d. to show Gradgrind's interest in the children he is teaching

_____ 3. In *Hard Times*, who are the "little pitchers" waiting to be filled with facts?
   a. imaginative students   c. all students
   b. teachers   d. students interested in facts

_____ 4. Why does Dickens have Gradgrind refer to Sissy Jupe as "girl number twenty"?
   a. to criticize Gradgrind's inability to remember names and faces
   b. to criticize the fact that students in the overpopulated school are treated as numbers, not individuals
   c. to show readers the school's emphasis on mathematics
   d. to take readers' attention away from individual students

_____ 5. Why does Gradgrind insist that Sissy Jupe's father is a veterinary surgeon and not just a rider of horses?
   a. He wants to introduce a lesson on horses.
   b. The surgeon's job is technical and practical, something Gradgrind values.
   c. He wants Sissy to appreciate the value of her father's work with horses.
   d. The surgeon's job is something he believes might interest his students.

_____ 6. What is Dickens's purpose in describing the schoolmasters as being "turned out at the same time, in the same factory, on the same principles, like so many pianoforte legs"?
   a. to show society's renewed interest in education and the proper instruction of teachers
   b. to reveal his respect for educational institutions
   c. to describe the training the teachers had to receive before teaching class
   d. to attack the cold, mechanical nature of the teachers' approach to education

_____ 7. What does Thomas Gradgrind's name suggest?
   a. his dedication to his job as educator
   b. his enjoyment of his students
   c. the way he forces his ideas into the heads of his students
   d. the way he molds children to be productive

_____ 8. In this selection from *Hard Times*, Charles Dickens is mainly criticizing
   a. the lack of respect young people have for education
   b. schools that smother imagination and treat children like machines
   c. schools that hire too many teachers
   d. schools that focus too much on discussion and not enough on reading and writing

_____ 9. In *Jane Eyre*, what is Lowood?
   a. a summer camp
   b. a strict boarding school for girls and young women without title or money
   c. a program for privileged girls and young woman
   d. a school that both wealthy and poor girls and young women attend

_____ 10. What is the best way to describe Miss Scatcherd, as she is portrayed in *Jane Eyre*?
   a. understanding
   b. knowledgeable
   c. strict but supportive
   d. overly critical and cruel

_____ 11. What is Brontë's main purpose in describing Jane's meals and activities at Lowood?
   a. to show how all schools operate
   b. to show the discomforts she endures at Lowood
   c. to show the interesting aspects of Jane's life at Lowood
   d. to show how students interact with one another

_____ 12. How might you best describe the character of Helen Burns in *Jane Eyre*?
   a. humble and dutiful
   b. unintelligent
   c. bitter and angry
   d. miserable

_____ 13. According to Helen in *Jane Eyre*, why is Miss Scatcherd severe with her?
   a. She is unhappy with her life.
   b. She is a wicked person.
   c. She dislikes Helen's faults.
   d. She enjoys using her authority.

_____ 14. In *Jane Eyre*, what is the main difference between Helen and Jane?
   a. Jane enjoys quiet reflection, whereas Helen enjoys conversing.
   b. Jane is young and inexperienced, whereas Helen is older and wiser.
   c. Jane dislikes learning, whereas Helen loves learning.
   d. Jane wants to fight back at injustices, whereas Helen quietly accepts them.

_____ 15. In *Jane Eyre*, what do Helen's words mean?

   "degradation never too deeply disgusts me, injustice never crushes me too low:
   I live in calm, looking to the end."

   a. She looks forward to leaving Lowood.
   b. She gets through every day by thinking of night, when she can be alone.
   c. She can calmly tolerate the sadness and injustices of her life because she knows she will be rewarded after death.
   d. She struggles every day to understand the injustices of life.

_____ 16. In *Jane Eyre*, what does Helen's conversation with Jane reveal about the institution in which they live?
   a. It encourages meditation and introspection.
   b. It places the most value on learning
   c. It denies people self-respect and individuality.
   d. It is a place where people must work hard to better themselves.

Vocabulary and Grammar

On the line, write the letter of the one best answer.

_____ 17. Which is punctuated correctly?
   a. Mr. Gradgrind shouted "Do not call yourself Sissy"!
   b. Mr. Gradgrind shouted, "Do not call yourself Sissy"!
   c. Mr. Gradgrind shouted "Do not call yourself Sissy!"
   d. Mr. Gradgrind shouted, "Do not call yourself Sissy!"

_____ 18. Which is the best meaning of the word *indignant* as it is used in the sentence?

   Students shouted the wrong answers and Thomas Gradgrind gave them an indignant look.

   a. confused
   b. amazed
   c. displeased
   d. helpless

_____ 19. Which contains a punctuation error?
   a. Did you hear him say, "Do not paper a room with pictures of flowers?"
   b. "You are not, Cecilia Jupe," Mr. Gradgrind repeated, "to do such a thing."
   c. "This is a new principle," said the teacher.
   d. The class cried out, "Yes, Sir!"

_____ 20. Which is the best meaning of the word *truculent* as it is used in the sentence?

   Jane spoke in a bitter and truculent manner when she was angry or excited.

   a. harsh
   b. polite
   c. honest
   d. loud

Essay Questions

21. In *Jane Eyre*, what do Helen Burns and Jane discuss? Write an essay describing the conversation. Explain what their conversation reveals about their characters and their philosophies of life.

22. The selection from *Hard Times* calls attention to two different students in Thomas Gradgrind's classroom: Sissy Jupe and Bitzer. How are these students different from each other? What specific details in the selection reveal these differences? What ideas does each character represent? What is the author's purpose in drawing attention to them in the selection? Answer these questions in an essay.

23. Many nineteenth-century English novels call attention to social injustices that existed at the time the works were written. In an essay, explain why *Hard Times* and *Jane Eyre* can be considered novels of social criticism. What societal attitudes and institutions does each selection examine? What specific details reveal the authors' opinions about these attitudes and institutions?

from *War and Peace* by Leo Tolstoy

Selection Test

Critical Reading

On the line, write the letter of the one best answer.

_____ 1. What city did Kutuzov's army abandon?
    a. St. Petersburg   c. Moscow
    b. Paris   d. Warsaw

_____ 2. Which word best describes the tone of this selection from *War and Peace*?
    a. timid   c. indignant
    b. honest   d. magnanimous

_____ 3. According to Tolstoy, Napoleon was
    a. responsible for the burning of Moscow.
    b. a person of great importance.
    c. a superior leader and general.
    d. an insignificant tool of history.

_____ 4. Which details does Tolstoy use to emphasize Kutuzov's human dignity and common decency?
    a. He groomed his own horse and cooked his own meals.
    b. He often wept at the suffering caused by the war.
    c. He wrote letters home and made jokes with soldiers.
    d. He sacrificed himself for Russia.

_____ 5. According to Tolstoy, the majority of Russian historians considered Kutuzov to be
    a. the Tsar's worst enemy.
    b. a pitiful, shameful person.
    c. second in genius only to Napoleon.
    d. the savior of Russia.

_____ 6. What does Kutuzov's reaction to the appointment of a new artillery commander signify for Tolstoy?
    a. Kutuzov's mastery of army politics
    b. Kutuzov's grasp of the relative importance of events
    c. Kutuzov's bad relations with the Tsar
    d. Kutuzov's inability to control his troops

_____ 7. Kutuzov's aim during the war was
    a. to chase Napoleon all the way back to Paris at any cost.
    b. to make a name for himself as the best general in all of Russia.
    c. to defeat the French with minimal suffering and loss of life.
    d. to abandon Moscow without a battle.

_____ 8. What does the fact that "Kutuzov never talked of 'forty centuries looking down from the Pyramids'" signify for Tolstoy?
    a. Kutuzov was secretly jealous of the fame accorded to Napoleon.
    b. Kutuzov was certain he would be rewarded for his sacrifices in defense of Russia.
    c. Kutuzov was unconcerned with how he would be judged by history.
    d. Kutuzov patterned his humility and modesty after Egyptian kings.

_____ 9. Unlike most of his contemporaries and historians, Kutuzov considered the Battle of Borodino to be
   a. the Tsar's finest moment.
   b. the end of Napoleon.
   c. a victory for Russia.
   d. the worst defeat of the war.

_____ 10. What does Tolstoy suggest by writing "the thoughts and words that serve as its [life's] expression are never the motive force of men"?
   a. Great men lie to get what they want.
   b. Historians in general are mistaken about the causes of historic events.
   c. A true hero seldom reveals his innermost thoughts.
   d. Men are unfailingly hypocritical.

Essay Questions

11. Write an essay describing the theory of the *grand homme* (great person) against which Tolstoy is writing in this passage. Contrast the prevailing notions of a great person with Tolstoy's own views on the subject. Identify someone from another novel or film, or in your own life or experience, and describe why the individual does or does not fit Tolstoy's version of a great person.

12. Elsewhere in *War and Peace* Tolstoy writes that ascribing the course of history to the actions of a few "great" men is like looking at a forest from a distance and determining that only trees exist there. History, in other words, is not made by a few exceptional people but results from the accumulation and interaction of a vast number of small, seemingly insignificant actions. Write an essay in which you agree or disagree with this point of view. How is Tolstoy's theory of history reflected in the passage about Kutuzov? In your answer, contrast Tolstoy's treatment of Russia's war against France with an example of your own choosing.

13. Tolstoy has one of the strongest and most recognizable authorial voices in all of world literature. In an essay, discuss the tone and emotional qualities of this passage about Kutuzov. What details make absolutely clear the author's opinion of the people he discusses? What picture of the author results from the way Kutuzov and those around him are described?

Part Test, Unit 5, Part 2: Focus on Literary Forms—The Novel

Critical Reading

The questions below are based on the following selection.

This passage from A Christmas Carol *by Charles Dickens introduces wealthy Ebenezer Scrooge, the novel's central character. Set in nineteenth-century London, the story tells of Scrooge's encounters with three ghosts on Christmas Eve. These experiences lead him to evaluate his past, his present, and his future.*

from A Christmas Carol
by Charles Dickens

External heat and cold had little influence on Scrooge. No warmth could warm, nor wintry weather chill him. No wind that blew was bitterer than he, no falling snow was more intent upon its purpose, no pelting rain less open to entreaty. Foul weather didn't know where to have him. The heaviest rain, and snow, and hail, and sleet could boast of the advantage over him in only one respect. They often "came down" handsomely, and Scrooge never did.

Nobody ever stopped him in the street to say, with gladsome looks, "My dear Scrooge, how are you? when will you come to see me?" No beggars implored him to bestow a trifle, no children asked him what it was o'clock, no man or woman ever once in all his life inquired the way to such and such a place, of Scrooge. Even the blindmen's dogs appeared to know him; and when they saw him coming on, would tug their owners into doorways and up courts; and then would wag their tails as though they said "no eye at all is better than an evil eye, dark master!"

_____ 1. This passage describes
   a. the difficulties of London in winter.
   b. Scrooge's ability to withstand cold.
   c. the difficult social conditions of London streets.
   d. the personality of Ebenezer Scrooge.

_____ 2. This passage shows that Ebenezer Scrooge
   a. is physically vigorous.   c. is a cold-hearted person.
   b. is respected in the community.   d. is dissatisfied with his life.

_____ 3. Which of the following shows evidence of social conditions in London?
   a. people in need of directions
   b. the effect of rain, snow, hail, and sleet
   c. Scrooge's isolation from society
   d. beggars and blindmen on the streets

_____ 4. Which of the following might be one of Dickens's purposes in the passage?
   a. to show Scrooge as isolated from normal people
   b. to show Scrooge as a man of purpose
   c. to show the difficult circumstances of the blind.
   d. to show Scrooge's wealth

_____ 5. What does the sentence mean?

   Foul weather didn't know where to have him.

   a. Scrooge was able to avoid extremes in weather conditions.
   b. Poor weather could never defeat his purposes.
   c. Scrooge prepared carefully for any type of weather.
   d. It was impossible to predict Scrooge's movements.

_____ 6. When Dickens writes that snow, rain, and sleet came down "handsomely, and Scrooge never did," he is saying that
   a. Scrooge was physically unattractive.
   b. Scrooge's moods varied with the weather.
   c. Scrooge didn't bother to present himself well to people.
   d. Scrooge had no appreciation for the beauty of nature.

_____ 7. What evidence of Dickens's attitude toward poverty appears in this passage?
   a. Dickens shows how miserable people are who aren't as strong as Scrooge.
   b. Neither weather nor social conditions affect Scrooge.
   c. Poverty can be overcome if people act with as much determination as Scrooge.
   d. Less fortunate people are portrayed more sympathetically than Scrooge.

_____ 8. What purpose does it serve to show how people stay away from Scrooge?
   a. It shows how thoroughly unlikable Scrooge is.
   b. It shows the degree to which Scrooge is respected.
   c. It provides an out-of-door setting for the story.
   d. It shows the poverty in which most Londoners live.

_____ 9. The overall purpose of these two paragraphs is probably to
   a. describe Scrooge and his effect on people.
   b. provide some action to keep the story moving.
   c. contrast rich people and poor people.
   d. develop sympathy for the central character.

_____ 10. How does the characterization of wealthy Scrooge imply social comment?
   a. It is a graphic depiction of terrible conditions.
   b. Self-centered Scrooge has misplaced priorities.
   c. Scrooge's success can be seen as a model.
   d. Personal isolation leads to loneliness.

Vocabulary and Grammar

On the line, write the letter of the one best answer.

_____ 11. Someone who is _obstinate_ is _____.
   a. confused
   b. mysterious
   c. intense
   d. stubborn

_____ 12. An _indignant_ remark would indicate _____.
   a. apathy
   b. outrage
   c. surprise
   d. depression

_____ 13. If one thing _comprises_ other things, it _____.
   a. explains them
   b. excludes them
   c. includes them
   d. refutes them

_____ 14. Which sentence shows _correct_ punctuation of a quotation?
   a. She said "It would be all right."
   b. She said, "It would be all right".
   c. She said, "It would be all right."
   d. She said, it would be all right.

____ 15. Which sentence shows *correct* punctuation of a quotation?
   a. Can you believe he just taught "Facts"?
   b. Can you believe he just taught "Facts!"
   c. Can you believe he just taught Facts.
   d. Can you believe he just taught "Facts?"

Essay Questions

16. The selections in this part were written for readers of their time as if the characters really existed. Readers then as now responded to the social criticism contained in the works. Choose one of the selections in this part and explain how it makes a social comment. Use examples from the selection you choose to support your ideas.

17. The selections in this part frequently criticize society's institutions. What strategies do these authors use to achieve this purpose? Choose one of the selections and write an essay that explains what purpose the author has and the means by which he or she achieves it. Use examples from the selection to support your ideas.

18. In all of the selections in this part, the authors show their views of competing attitudes on social issues. What are some of the attitudes in competition in these selections? Choose one of the selections and write an essay that identifies competing attitudes about a social issue, how the author represents those attitudes, and how he or she reveals his or her opinion.

"Dover Beach" by Matthew Arnold
"Recessional" and **"The Widow at Windsor"** by Rudyard Kipling

Selection Test

Critical Reading

On the line, write the letter of the one best answer.

_____ 1. What view of the world does the speaker of "Dover Beach" express?
   a. The world is a calm place, much like the feeling one has when watching ocean waves roll in.
   b. The world is only a struggle of constant violence.
   c. The world does not contain joy or love or peace for those who dwell in it.
   d. The world is and always has been a place of sadness, with no hope of any change.

_____ 2. What can a reader logically infer about the poet's beliefs from this passage?

> The Sea of Faith
>
> Was once, too, at the full, and round earth's shore / Lay like the folds of a bright girdle furled. / But now I only hear / Its melancholy, long, withdrawing roar, / Retreating, to the breath / Of the night wind, down the vast edges drear / And naked shingles of the world.

   a. The poet probably believes in God.
   b. The poet finds religion ridiculous.
   c. The poet does not respect people who believe in God.
   d. The poet believes that there is a strong connection between nature and God.

_____ 3. From the details in "Dover Beach," what conclusion can you draw about the speaker's attitude about the "Sea of Faith"?
   a. He believes that people's faith in God ebbs and flows like the ocean.
   b. The speaker believes faith will return daily, as if with the tide.
   c. The speaker believes that faith is like a mighty ocean.
   d. The speaker believes that people no longer have faith.

_____ 4. What emotional words does Arnold use in the passage about the "Sea of Faith" to create mood?
   a. Sea of Faith, full, night
   b. melancholy, withdrawing, retreating
   c. earth's shore, night wind, naked shingles
   d. Lay, hear, down

_____ 5. Which best paraphrases the final three lines of "Dover Beach"?
   a. We are out on a field in the dark night, walking unawares into the middle of a battle.
   b. We live in a confusing world, guided only by ourselves.
   c. We are alone in the universe, with no one to watch out for us.
   d. The ocean sounds like armies fighting.

_____ 6. How do the sensory images in the first two stanzas create mood?
   a. The waves smashing against the cliffs creates an angry, violent mood.
   b. The unseen reaches of the sea at night create an ominous mood.
   c. The rhythmic flow of the ocean's waves creates a peaceful mood.
   d. The moonlight and the isolation of the beach create a mysterious mood.

_____ 7. To whom is "Recessional" addressed?
    a. to Queen Victoria   c. to the poet
    b. to the British Empire   d. to God

_____ 8. What is the "recessional" to which the title refers?

    I.   part of the parade connected with Queen Victoria's Diamond Jubilee
    II. the possible decline of the British Empire
    III. the way the British Army presents itself in British colonies
    IV. the withdrawal from daily life of trusting in God

    a. I and II   b. I and III   c. II and III   d. II and IV

_____ 9. What do Kipling's words "we hold / Dominion over palm and pine—" refer?
    a. human control over nature
    b. the variety of God's creation
    c. the extent of the British Empire
    d. the speaker's view as he addresses the poem's subject

_____ 10. How do the last two lines of this passage affect the mood of the stanza?

    God of our fathers, known of old— / Lord of our far-flung battle-line— /
    Beneath whose awful Hand we hold / Dominion over palm and pine— /
    Lord God of Hosts, be with us yet / Lest we forget—lest we forget!

    a. They create a sense of sincere desperation.
    b. They create an old-fashioned feeling with the use of the word _lest_.
    c. They reveal the speaker's sense of abandonment, creating an angry mood.
    d. They create a prayer-like mood that brings out religious feelings in the reader.

_____ 11. What conclusion can you draw about the speaker's attitude from these lines?

    Lo, all our pomp of yesterday / Is one with Nineveh and Tyre!

    a. The speaker feels Britain's greatness is similar to that of ancient cities.
    b. The speaker believes the greatness of Britain could all disappear, just as did that
        of Nineveh and Tyre.
    c. The speaker feels that the greatness of Britain will be everlasting, like that of Nin-
        eveh and Tyre.
    d. The speaker believes that great cities or nations all hold the same attitudes toward
        power and success, which contribute to their greatness.

_____ 12. To whom does the title of "The Widow at Windsor" refer?
    a. the speaker's mother   c. an old woman in an old house
    b. the poet's mother   d. Queen Victoria

_____ 13. What conclusion can you draw about the speaker from this passage?

    Walk wide o' the Widow at Windsor,
         For 'alf o' Creation she owns:
    We 'ave bought 'er the same with the sword an' the flame,
         An' we've salted it down with our bones.

    a. The speaker is afraid of the Widow and wishes to avoid her.
    b. The speaker uses sword and flame to get what he wants.
    c. The speaker is a soldier who serves in the Widow's army.
    d. The speaker views the Widow as a ruthless materialist who owns everything she
        can get her hands on.

____ 14. Which aspect of "The Widow at Windsor" reveals the common nature of the speaker?
     a. the dialect
     b. the use of the sentences in parentheses
     c. the attitude expressed about the Widow
     d. the use of the phrase "Widow at Windsor"

____ 15. Which best expresses the attitude of the speaker in "The Widow at Windsor"?
     a. He is resentful and bitter toward the Widow and her power.
     b. He is respectful of her but realistic about his own role in the Widow's world.
     c. He is in awe of her and has only positive things to say about her and how she uses her power.
     d. He is protective of her and sees her as something fragile to be guarded and taken care of.

____ 16. The informal, slightly disrespectful mood of "The Widow at Windsor" helps lead readers to the poem's theme, which is that
     a. soldiers always rebel against their leaders.
     b. rulers always think of their soldiers as inferior or "underlings."
     c. rulers are far removed from the realities of empire building.
     d. the Empire is great, but greatness comes with a price.

Vocabulary and Grammar

On the line, write the letter of the one best answer.

____ 17. Arnold describes an ocean bay that is *tranquil*, or
     a. calm and smooth.
     c. deep and dark.
     b. frothy with white-capped waves.
     d. a very pleasant place.

____ 18. Kipling's poems both have to do with *dominion*, which means
     a. a kind of residence.
     c. a place of rule.
     b. a type of influence.
     d. a kind of service.

____ 19. Choose the sentence that contains a present-tense verb.
     a. The cliffs of England stand, glimmering and vast, out in the Straits of Dover.
     b. Sophocles heard it long ago on the Aegaean Sea.
     c. The Sea of Faith was once, too, at the full and lay around the shore.
     d. The world would have no comfort for those who sought it.

____ 20. Which are functions of present-tense verbs?
     a. expressing actions recently completed and to be completed
     b. expressing current action and general truths
     c. expressing intended action and characters' actions in a story or poem
     d. expressing past action and ongoing consequences

Essay Questions

21. Kipling wrote "Recessional" more than a hundred years ago at the height of England's power. What is the message of the poem, and what does it say about power and people? Write an essay in which you explain how Kipling's commentary on vanished ancient cities applies to us today. Use examples from the poem to illustrate your points.

22. Kipling was considered an imperialist. That means he favored the influence and power that Great Britain held over far-flung corners of the world. In an essay, discuss whether Kipling's belief in imperialism emerges in these poems. Cite passages that lead to your conclusion.

23. In "Dover Beach," Arnold moves from a Romantic view to a more modern one. In an essay, discuss Arnold's view of nature. Use examples from the poem to support your idea.

____ 8. As a journalistic essay, what does the *London News* article attempt to do?
   a. describe the beauties of Ireland
   b. judge the events surrounding the Famine and introduce possible solutions
   c. share one individual's experience of living through a famine
   d. defend laws designed to end the Famine

____ 9. What is the main purpose of the essay "Progress in Personal Comfort"?
   a. to describe improvements in transportation
   b. to describe government reforms
   c. to describe one man's view of changes that people take for granted
   d. to describe one man's view of the negative effects of progress

____ 10. In "Progress in Personal Comfort," Smith describes symbols of progress without giving much detail about the actual design and implementation of these changes. What impression does this give?
   a. that progress is not easily understood by everyone
   b. that the narrator does not understand change
   c. that changes do not occur easily
   d. that progress emerges out of nowhere, almost magically

____ 11. Which sentence or phrase from "Progress in Personal Comfort" creates emotional effect?
   a. "Gas was unknown . . ."
   b. "It is of some importance at what period a man is born."
   c. ". . .in all but the utter darkness of a twinkling oil lamp . . ."
   d. "I can walk, by the assistance of the police, from one end of London to the other . . ."

____ 12. How might you describe Mr. Smith's feelings toward the time in which he lives?
   a. proud   c. uncomfortable
   b. bitter   d. bored

____ 13. About what does Mr. Smith feel ashamed?
   a. that he was not responsible for creating change
   b. that more important changes have not been made
   c. that he was not more discontented before the changes took place
   d. that he depends too much on conveniences

____ 14. In what way is Mr. Smith's fascination with his own era innocent?
   a. He seems to feel that only roads and umbrellas matter.
   b. He seems to feel that progress will stop with his era.
   c. He seems to feel that he will never be uncomfortable again.
   d. He seems to feel that progress affects the way in which government is run.

____ 15. What does "Progress in Personal Comfort" reveal about the effect of progress on people?
   a. Progress helps people to be more safe.
   b. Progress brings shame to people.
   c. Progress encourages unrealistic expectations.
   d. What at first seems new and luxurious quickly becomes indispensable to people.

Vocabulary and Grammar

On the line, write the letter of the one best answer.

____ 16. Which is the best meaning of the word *melancholy* as it is used in this sentence?

   We witnessed the melancholy farmer offering to work the field.

   a. energetic   c. sad
   b. aggressive   d. stubborn

_____ 17. Which sentence contains a coordinating conjunction?
   a. Allow farmers to grow their crops.
   b. The roads were now paved.
   c. He could not keep his clothes in their proper place.
   d. Laws were passed calmly, quietly, but very ignorantly.

_____ 18. Which is the best meaning of the word *depredation* as it is used in this sentence?

   The man walked the dark streets, fearing depredation.

   a. attack
   b. discovery
   c. illness
   d. helplessness

_____ 19. Which sentence contains a coordinating conjunction?
   a. Why can't people plant their potato gardens?
   b. The country suffered from disease and homelessness.
   c. The streets always seemed much darker before gaslights.
   d. Do you have an umbrella?

_____ 20. Which is the best meaning of the word *sanction* as it is used in the sentence?

   We waited for the sanction of legislators.

   a. group
   b. speeches
   c. disgust
   d. approval

Essay Questions

21. In "Condition of Ireland," the writer conveys ideas about the problems in Ireland, using informative and emotive language. In an essay, describe the use of these two types of language and their effectiveness in "Condition of Ireland." Support your analysis with examples from the text.

22. In an essay, compare and contrast the different styles and topics of "Condition of Ireland" and "Progress in Personal Comfort." What distinctive voice does each piece have? How does voice affect the presentation of facts in each piece?

23. The selections you have read present different views of progress. In an essay, compare and contrast the ways in which progress is measured by the article "Condition of Ireland," the British government during the Irish famine, and Mr. Smith in "Progress in Personal Comfort."

"Opening Statement for the Inaugural Session of the Forum for Peace and Reconciliation" by Judge Catherine McGuinness

Selection Test

Critical Reading

On the line, write the letter of the one best answer.

____ 1. McGuinness grew up a _____.
   a. republican
   b. Protestant
   c. Dubliner
   d. Catholic

____ 2. McGuinness mentions "traditions" several times because she believes that
   a. those who came to Ireland more than 400 years ago are the most valuable citizens.
   b. Ireland's strength lies in the diverse contributions of all its citizens.
   c. Ireland needs to turn its back on a painful past.
   d. the North has a richer tradition than the South.

____ 3. The potato famine marked a period of
   a. particular severity by the English toward Ireland.
   b. denunciation of mindless patriotism.
   c. poverty for McGuinness's family.
   d. trust and cooperation between Ireland and England.

____ 4. What does McGuinness intend by calling herself "a citizen of Ireland"?
   a. She implies that Belfast is the most patriotic area to come from.
   b. She rejects her great grandfather's English heritage.
   c. She stresses that no one city, party, or county of her nation is the "most Irish."
   d. She suggests that North and South are already unified.

____ 5. Which sentence most dramatically expresses the everyday loss and pain still caused for families by the armed conflict?
   a. "We cannot pretend that the armed conflict of the past twenty-five years did not happen."
   b. "We are conscious of homes where there are empty chairs."
   c. "We must be able to express regret for past wrongs."
   d. "We know that all wars are cruel, bloody, harsh and merciless."

____ 6. To participate in the Forum, groups and parties must pledge themselves to
   a. support Presbyterian values.
   b. follow peaceful and democratic means.
   c. put aside economic issues.
   d. give up the desire for Irish self-determination.

____ 7. According to McGuinness, Ireland's legacy of twenty-five years of armed violence includes
   a. reconciliation between Protestants and Catholics.
   b. immigration to America.
   c. grief over lost family members.
   d. the execution of James Connolly.

_____ 8. What does McGuinness emphasize by quoting James Connolly's statement, "Ireland, as distinct from her people, is nothing to me"?
   a. The Forum excludes socialists.
   b. Some patriots are determined to expand the Irish territories.
   c. Republicans are not true patriots.
   d. The Forum's top priority is rights and freedoms for all Irish citizens.

_____ 9. McGuinness describes her own personal background in order to illustrate
   a. feminist values.
   b. national diversity.
   c. English loyalties.
   d. atheist pride.

_____ 10. McGuiness emphasizes the problems of poverty and unemployment because
   a. she wants to show that there are matters that everyone can agree on.
   b. religious conflict between Catholics and Protestants is no longer a problem.
   c. she does not realize that the conflict between North and South is a bigger issue.
   d. she is the Minister of Labor and is promoting her own agenda.

Essay Questions

11. McGuinness concludes her statement with the claim "No party or group or tradition has a monopoly of wisdom." Write an essay analyzing this statement. What specifics has she used to show that wisdom has diverse sources?

12. A strong sense of the past often fuels conflicts like that in Ireland. Write an essay explaining how McGuinness thinks Ireland should relate to its past, especially when it comes to pride. What balance of attitudes does she encourage about the past, and why?

13. Using McGuinness's quotation of James Connolly as your starting point, write an essay speculating on what McGuinness means by "mindless so-called patriotism." How does she establish this definition indirectly? Go on to describe what she considers true or thoughtful patriotism. Make a judgment about her position.

Part Test, Unit 5, Part 3: The Story of Britain— The Empire and Its Discontents

Critical Reading

The questions below are based on the following selection.

In his poem "To Marguerite—Continued," Matthew Arnold expresses feelings of isolation from other human beings. He uses the analogy of an island to convey his ideas.

To Marguerite—Continued

Yes! in the sea of life enisled,[1]

With echoing straits between us thrown,

Dotting the shoreless watery wild,

We mortal millions live *alone*.

[5]   The islands feel the enclasping flow,

And then their endless bounds they know.

But when the moon their hollows lights,

And they are swept by balms of spring,

And in their glens, on starry nights,

[10] The nightingales divinely sing;

And lovely notes, from shore to shore,

Across the sounds and channels pour—

Oh! then a longing like despair

Is to their farthest caverns sent;

[15] For surely once, they feel, we were

Parts of a single continent!

Now round us spreads the watery plain—

Oh might our marges meet again!

Who ordered, that their longing's fire

[20] Should be, as soon as kindled, cooled?

Who renders vain their deep desire?

A God, a God their severance ruled!

And bade betwixt their shores to be

The unplumbed, salt, enstranging sea.

[1] **enisled:** Isolated, as if placed on an island.

On the line, write the letter of the one best answer.

_____ 1. What makes the "islands" want to meet the other islands again?
      a. the feeling of the flow of the sea around them
      b. the presence of humans
      c. the loveliness of moonlight, springtime, and nightingales' songs
      d. the sight of continents in the distance

_____ 2. What is the best restatement of the following excerpt?

        that their longing's fire / Should be, as soon as kindled, cooled?

      a. that the fire should be quenched as soon as it is kindled
      b. that their longing should cease as soon as it begins
      c. that the longing should be restarted as soon as it starts to fade
      d. that the kindling of their longing should serve to cool them

_____ 3. What words in the first stanza express the mood of that stanza?
      a. sea of life, straits, shoreless
      b. wild, mortal, bounds
      c. echoing, water, flow
      d. enisled, *alone*, islands

_____ 4. Which line uses emotive language?
      a. "With echoing straits between us thrown,"
      b. "The islands feel the enclasping flow,"
      c. "Oh! then a longing like despair"
      d. "Who renders vain their deep desire?"

_____ 5. What logical conclusion can you draw from lines 13–16?
      a. The speaker feels isolated but longs to be connected to other people again.
      b. The poet believes in the theory that all existing land masses were once connected.
      c. The speaker despairs of ever seeing anyone again.
      d. The people would live in caverns on these islands.

_____ 6. Who or what are the islands referred to in line 5?
      a. The islands in the "shoreless watery wild"
      b. each of the "mortal millions"
      c. the islands that exist all over the earth
      d. any person who feels isolated from other people

_____ 7. What is the speaker's answer to his own question about who "renders vain their deep desire"?
      a. the islands themselves
      b. isolated people
      c. the seas
      d. a God

_____ 8. The mood in lines 22–24 is the main key to the poem's theme. What is that theme?
      a. We are destined to be isolated from each other and cannot change that condition.
      b. All things are decided upon by a god.
      c. People who are attached to each other are bound to drift apart.
      d. Someone who becomes isolated will always be isolated.

_____ 9. Which best describes the mood of the second stanza?
      a. hopeless and despairing
      b. sentimental and reminiscent
      c. bitter and angry
      d. sad and mourning

_____ 10. Given the ideas expressed in this poem, what logical conclusion can readers draw about the poet, Matthew Arnold?
   a. Arnold was a sailor but disliked the sea.
   b. Arnold was sensitive to the beauties of nature.
   c. Arnold felt a sense of isolation or alienation from the world.
   d. Arnold believed in God.

Vocabulary and Grammar

On the line, write the letter of the one best answer.

_____ 11. Loyalty and unquestioning obedience were the _____ for good soldiers in Queen Victoria's army.
   a. interests
   b. ingredients
   c. options
   d. requisites

_____ 12. Though the sea was _____, the ships still had difficulty docking safely.
   a. tranquil
   b. perilous
   c. shallow
   d. indolent

_____ 13. Which word is a coordinating conjunction in the sentence?

   Essayist Smith writes of personal comforts, but they may sound like hardships to us.

   a. of
   b. may
   c. but
   d. to

_____ 14. Which sentence contains a present-tense verb?
   a. The destruction of the potato for one season would not have doomed them.
   b. Yet the land lies idle and unfruitful.
   c. I groped about the streets of London in all but the utter darkness of an oil lamp.
   d. There were no banks to receive the savings of the poor.

_____ 15. In which line does the poet use the present tense to express a general truth?
   a. "The sea is calm tonight."
   b. "Come to the window, sweet is the night air!"
   c. "Listen! you hear the grating roar"
   d. "Where ignorant armies clash by night."

Essay Questions

16. Several selections in Part 2 reflect or comment on the state of the British Empire. Identify the viewpoint of one selection, whether it is Arnold's in "Dover Beach," Kipling's in "The Widow at Windsor," or that of the author of "Condition of Ireland." Explain just what the poet or essayist is saying about the Empire. Support your explanation with details from your chosen selection.

17. The articles "Condition of Ireland" and "Progress in Personal Comfort" are called journalistic essays. What is their purpose? What characteristics distinguish them from other essays? Use examples from either or both journalistic essays to support your points.

18. As poets and essayists express ideas, they may use emotive language. Why would someone expressing an idea about a political issue use emotive language? What effect does this have on readers? How did Arnold, Kipling, and the journalistic essayists use emotive language in the selections in Part 2? In your essay, use examples from at least two selections to support your points.

"Remembrance" by Emily Brontë
"The Darkling Thrush" and **"Ah, Are You Digging on My Grave?"** by Thomas Hardy

Selection Test

Critical Reading

On the line, write the letter of the one best answer.

_____ 1. Which best summarizes the theme of "Remembrance"?
   a. There are some losses from which one cannot recover.
   b. The living should not forget the dead.
   c. Pondering death is dangerous.
   d. Life goes on, even in the face of extreme grief.

_____ 2. What does the speaker of "Remembrance" plan to do?
   a. build a monument to her love
   b. find a new love
   c. forget her love
   d. mourn her love until her own death

_____ 3. What is the meaning of this stanza from "Remembrance"?

> Sweet Love of youth, forgive if I forget thee
> While the World's tide is bearing me along:
> Other desires and other hopes beset me,
> Hopes which obscure but cannot do thee wrong.

   a. The living must find a way to survive after a loss.
   b. After the death of a loved one, all hope is gone.
   c. We become disillusioned with age.
   d. Our hopes do injustice to the memory of the dead.

_____ 4. What is ironic about the speaker's words by the end of "Remembrance"?
   a. The speaker feels joyful.
   b. The speaker has found a way to cherish life.
   c. The speaker is bitter and resentful.
   d. The speaker is also dead.

_____ 5. Which words best describe the speaker of "Remembrance"?
   a. young and carefree   c. resigned and reflective
   b. angry and frightened   d. disillusioned and confused

_____ 6. What is significant about the setting of "The Darkling Thrush"?
   a. It is the last night of the century.
   b. The speaker is lost.
   c. The speaker describes a bird sanctuary.
   d. It is almost dawn.

_____ 7. What is the speaker's tone in these lines from "The Darkling Thrush"?

> . . . And every spirit upon earth / Seemed fervorless as I.

   a. resentful   c. passionate
   b. discouraged   d. skeptical

_____ 8. "The Darkling Thrush" is ironic because

a. the ending is humorous.

b. the bird cannot be seen in the dark.

c. the speaker feels hopeful.

d. the mood changes unexpectedly.

____ 9. What is the central idea of "The Darkling Thrush"?

a. the estrangement of humans from nature

b. the mysterious renewal of nature

c. human conflict with himself

d. the inevitable defeat of hope

____ 10. What is the mood in the final lines of "The Darkling Thrush"?

a. grateful celebration

b. bitter pessimism

c. cautious optimism

d. curiosity

____ 11. In "Ah, Are You Digging on My Grave?" who is digging on the speaker's grave?

a. her husband

b. a relative

c. an enemy

d. her dog

____ 12. By connecting the main ideas in the stanzas of "Ah, Are You Digging on My Grave?" the reader

a. discovers how the speaker died.

b. realizes the poem's dark humor.

c. discovers the poem's mood is sentimental.

d. eliminates the poem's irony.

____ 13. "Ah, Are You Digging on My Grave?" is ironic because

a. the reader expects someone to grieve.

b. dogs are incapable of grief.

c. the speaker is a dead person.

d. the reader expects a surprise ending.

____ 14. The author's principal purpose in "Ah, Are You Digging on My Grave?" is to

a. explore human grief.

b. emphasize death's horror.

c. undercut sentimental assumptions.

d. develop comic situations.

Vocabulary and Grammar

On the line, write the letter of the word that best completes the sentence.

____ 15. Like the barren twigs, the darkling thrush is _____.

a. languish

b. rapturous

c. gaunt

d. terrestrial

____ 16. Rather than _____ for his deceased wife, the woman's husband soon remarries.

a. languish

b. rapturous

c. gaunt

d. terrestrial

Remembrance/Darkling Thrush/Digging on My Grave **215**

_____ 17. In a _____ voice, the young woman excitedly described her feelings for her love.
  a. languish
  b. rapturous
  c. gaunt
  d. terrestrial

_____ 18. The woman's relatives showed as much respect as _____.
  a. me
  b. him
  c. them
  d. we

_____ 19. The frail bird sings better than _____.
  a. I
  b. me
  c. him
  d. her

On the line, write the letter of the one best answer.

_____ 20. In which sentence does the correct pronoun follow *than* or *as*?
  a. No one grieved more than she.
  b. Everyone was as surprised by his death as us.
  c. Few people were closer to him than me.
  d. We were as heartbroken as them.

Essay Questions

21. Although each stanza in a poem is a unit of meaning, the stanzas work together to convey the poem's overall idea. In an essay, explain how reading stanzas as units of meaning helps you arrive at a deeper meaning for the whole poem. Use examples from Brontë's and Hardy's poems to support your points.

22. All of these poems have a regular stanza structure. Through their stanza forms, Brontë and Hardy create expectations, which they eventually shatter. In an essay, discuss how one of these poets uses stanza structure to create irony. Support your main points with evidence from the poem.

23. Brontë has been classified as a Romantic and Hardy as a Naturalist. Romanticism celebrates nature's wildness and the human soul and imagination, while Naturalism views individuals as governed by social and natural forces often beyond their control. In an essay, decide whether these poems represent the literary movements to which the poets are linked. Give evidence from the poems to support your opinion.

"God's Grandeur" and **"Spring and Fall: To a Young Child"**
by Gerard Manley Hopkins
"To an Athlete Dying Young" and **"When I Was One-and-Twenty"**
by A. E. Housman

Selection Test

Critical Reading

On the line, write the letter of the one best answer.

____ 1. Gerard Manley Hopkins's "God's Grandeur" contrasts
  a. the flame of poetry with the oil of commerce.
  b. the splendor of creation with the dullness of mankind.
  c. western darkness with eastern light.
  d. the sad wisdom of age with the fresh inexperience of youth.

____ 2. What type of rhythm is used in this line from "Spring and Fall: To a Young Child"?

  Áh! ás the heart grows older

  a. trochaic rhythm   c. blank rhythm
  b. sprung rhythm   d. iambic pentameter

____ 3. What characteristic of counterpoint rhythm does this line from "God's Grandeur" illustrate?

  World broods with warm breast and with ah! bright wings

  a. a regular pattern of stressed syllables
  b. the omission of prepositions as connectors
  c. two opposing rhythms appearing together
  d. the use of iambic tetrameter

____ 4. Which of the lines from "God's Grandeur" is most indicative of Hopkins's religious faith?
  a. "Because the Holy Ghost over the bent / World broods with warm breast and with ah! bright wings."
  b. "Generations have trod, have trod, have trod; / And all is seared with trade . . ."
  c. ". . . the soil / Is bare now, nor can foot feel, being shod."
  d. "And for all this, nature is never spent; / There lives the dearest freshness deep down things;"

____ 5. Which passage summarizes the theme, or central idea, of "God's Grandeur"?
  a. "Generations have trod, have trod, have trod; / And all is seared with trade . . ."
  b. "It will flame out, like shining from shook foil; / It gathers to a greatness, like the ooze of oil . . ."
  c. "And though the last lights off the black West went / Oh, morning, at the brown brink eastward, springs—"
  d. "The world is charged with grandeur of God / . . . Why do men then now not reck his rod?"

____ 6. What event occasions Gerard Manley Hopkins's "Spring and Fall: To a Young Child"?
  a. the destruction of a forest
  b. the death of a child of a family friend
  c. a child's sadness at fallen leaves
  d. the death of a child's parents

God's Grandeur/Spring and Fall/Dying Young/One-and-Twenty **217**

_____ 7. In "Spring and Fall: To a Young Child," the image of "wanwood leafmeal" suggests the
     a. bounty of harvest.
     b. process of decay.
     c. mystery of the forest.
     d. innocence of childhood.

_____ 8. In "Spring and Fall: To a Young Child," the "blight man was born for" refers to
     a. man's destruction of nature.
     b. understanding of forest ecology.
     c. inevitable death.
     d. the loss of innocence.

_____ 9. Hopkins's profession as a priest may suggest an interpretation of "Spring and Fall: To a Young Child" that includes
     a. death as an inevitable, but not an evil, force.
     b. considering the child's feelings to be mistaken.
     c. the idea of "Fall" as original sin.
     d. regarding nature as a lesser power than God.

_____ 10. "Spring and Fall: To a Young Child" is mostly about
     a. recognizing that all things die.
     b. the glory of divine grace.
     c. accepting a child's death.
     d. appreciating the four seasons.

_____ 11. The theme of "To An Athlete Dying Young" may be described as
     a. the tragedy of early death.
     b. the futility of athletic achievement.
     c. the corruption of character through time.
     d. the horror of physical decay.

_____ 12. Which lines from "To an Athlete Dying Young" suggest that glory does not last?
     a. "The time you won your town the race / We chaired you through the market place;"
     b. "And early though the laurel grows / It withers quicker than the rose."
     c. "And silence sounds no worse than cheers / After earth has stopped the ears."
     d. "Eyes the shady night has shut / Cannot see the record cut."

_____ 13. What do these lines from "To an Athlete Dying Young" describe?

     Today, the road all runners come, / Shoulder-high we bring you home, / And set you at your threshold down / Townsman of a stiller town

     a. the athlete's victory
     b. the celebration after the race
     c. the hollowness of victory
     d. the athlete's funeral

_____ 14. The tone of "When I Was One-and-Twenty" is _____.
     a. regretful
     b. sarcastic
     c. respectful
     d. angry

_____ 15. In A. E. Housman's "When I Was One-and-Twenty," the line "I heard a wise man say" contains which kind of metrical foot?
     a. dactyl
     b. trochee
     c. iamb
     d. anapest

Vocabulary and Grammar

On the line, write the letter of the one best answer.

____ 16. Which words referring to compass points should be capitalized?
   a. all
   b. those referring to specific regions
   c. those referring to a direction of travel
   d. those referring to longitudes only

____ 17. Which sentence displays *correct* capitalization of compass points?
   a. One goes due North from London to get to Oxford.
   b. Hopkins studied in North Wales.
   c. Shropshire is in Western England.
   d. To a Londoner, the west coast means Devon.

____ 18. The word *rue* means
   a. contempt.   c. shade.
   b. joy.   d. regret.

____ 19. In "To An Athlete Dying Young," Housman refers to "the rout / of lads that wore their honors out." A *rout* is
   a. a failed plan.   c. a traveled path.
   b. a loud clamor.   d. a disorderly mob.

____ 20. A *blight* is a
   a. withering.   c. effort.
   b. fate.   d. radiance.

Essay Questions

21. To make his point about early death, A. E. Housman might have chosen any young person as a symbol, before disappointment or corruption could mar life. Instead, he chose an athlete in "To an Athlete Dying Young." Why does an athlete emphasize Housman's theme especially well? Write an essay in which you explain what it is about an athlete that symbolizes Housman's points about time and life effectively. Use examples from the poem to illustrate your ideas.

22. The beauty of nature is keenly on Gerard Manley Hopkins's mind as he writes. In both "God's Grandeur" and "Spring and Fall: To a Young Child," scenes of natural beauty illustrate Hopkins's love of the world. Where, to Hopkins, do humans fit into the scene? Write an essay in which you discuss Hopkins's concept of humanity's relationship to nature, as revealed in the two poems of this section. Use examples from the poems to support your ideas.

23. In the poetry of A. E. Housman, time and experience play an important role. The role of experience, however, is not the same in every poem. Compare and contrast the representations of the value of experience in "To an Athlete Dying Young" and "When I Was One-and-Twenty." What do these poems suggest about life as Housman sees it? Write an essay in which you discuss the nature of experience as represented in the two poems, giving examples from the poems to support your points.

"**Eternity**" by Arthur Rimbaud

Selection Test

Critical Reading

On the line, write the letter of the one best answer.

____ 1. The speaker describes his soul as liberating itself from
   a. humdrum daily concerns.
   b. its ardor.
   c. a solemn vow.
   d. eternity.

____ 2. "Sentinel soul" in line 5 suggests that the speaker has
   a. kept careful watch for moments of eternity.
   b. been a soldier.
   c. stayed alert to society's pleasures.
   d. limited his yearnings.

____ 3. With which word does Rimbaud create a traditional Romantic image of the soul as a bird?
   a. ardor
   b. embers
   c. exhales
   d. soar

____ 4. Which words encourage the reader to identify the speaker as a poet or as Rimbaud himself?
   a. night so void
   b. skill with patience
   c. ardor alone
   d. never a hope

____ 5. What is the poetic technique used in these lines called?

   It is the sea / Matched with the sun

   a. alliteration
   b. simile
   c. rhyme
   d. personification

____ 6. In line 20, "Anguish is certain" because
   a. the speaker finds himself in ordinary reality again.
   b. the embers are still hot enough to burn.
   c. the speaker feels too solitary.
   d. someday the sun may not meet the sea.

____ 7. Rimbaud uses the words "embers of satin" (line 14) because satin recalls the sun's _____.
   a. color
   b. shiny aspect
   c. texture
   d. rays

_____ 8. A central idea of the poem is that
   a. it is crucial to keep one's promises.
   b. a sea vacation is refreshing.
   c. it is the speaker's duty to leave at dawn.
   d. everyday life constrains the spirit.

_____ 9. By using "common transports" (line 10) as a contrast to the "recovery of eternity," the poem suggests that eternity involves
   a. an exceptionally spiritual rapture.
   b. a rare overseas voyage.
   c. aristocratic values.
   d. impatience.

_____ 10. The speaker links a lack of genesis with a similar lack of _____.
   a. sanctions
   b. vows
   c. hope
   d. patience

Essay Questions

11. Write an essay analyzing how Rimbaud uses the structure and the wording of "Eternity" to suggest that the speaker goes through cycles of losing and reaching his desired goal.

12. "Eternity" relies heavily on images of light and heat to evoke the soul in eternity. Write an essay describing these images and their usage. Speculate on _why_ Rimbaud specifically chose such imagery to illustrate the ideas in this poem.

13. Write an essay arguing whether Rimbaud is describing a sunrise, a sunset, or both. How can you tell? Make a judgment as to whether the image is clear, or if the poem is too ambiguous to tell. Explain why he made the choice he did in favor of clarity or ambiguity.

Name _____ Date _____

Part Test, Unit 5, Part 4: Gloom and Glory

Critical Reading

The questions below are based on the following selection.

The poem "Loveliest of Trees" is one of the most famous by A. E. Housman (1859–1963).

Loveliest of Trees

Loveliest of Trees, the cherry now

Is hung with bloom along the bough,

And stands about the woodland ride

Wearing white for Eastertide.

[5] Now, of my threescore years and ten,

Twenty will not come again,

And take from seventy springs a score,

It only leaves me fifty more.

And since to look at things in bloom

[10] Fifty springs are little room,

About the woodland I will go

To see the cherry hung with snow.

On the line, write the letter of the one best answer.

_____ 1. In what season is "Loveliest of Trees" set?
   a. spring
   b. summer
   c. fall
   d. winter

_____ 2. What do these lines mean?

   Now, of my threescore years and ten, / Twenty will not come again

   a. The speaker regrets the last twenty years.
   b. The speaker does not expect to live another twenty years.
   c. The speaker has been visiting this wood for twenty years.
   d. The speaker is twenty years old.

_____ 3. The underlined segment of this line of poetry is an example of what metrical unit?

   Is hung with bloom along the bough

   a. sentence
   b. line
   c. foot
   d. stanza

Name _____ Date _____

"Condition of Ireland," *The Illustrated London News*
"Progress in Personal Comfort" by Sydney Smith

Selection Test

Critical Reading

On the line, write the letter of the one best answer.

_____ 1. What is the "present condition of the Irish" described by the *London News* article?
    a. They are experiencing a terrible drought.
    b. The country is overpopulated.
    c. They suffer from famine and economic hardship.
    d. They are unable to control political uprisings.

_____ 2. According to the *London News* article, what is the cause of the destruction of Ireland?
    a. Poor-Laws
    b. lack of rainfall
    c. ignorance of farming techniques
    d. disease

_____ 3. Which sentence contains emotive language?
    a. "The low grounds or *Corcasses* of Clare are celebrated for their productiveness."
    b. "We shall fully consider that question before we quit the subject."
    c. "It has an area of 827,994 acres, 372,237 of which are uncultivated."
    d. "The sparkling Shannon, teeming with fish, still flows by their doors."

_____ 4. How does the *London News* article characterize British legislators' attempts to solve problems in Ireland?
    a. as not aggressive enough
    b. as ignorant and insensitive
    c. as sound attempts at solving a complicated problem
    d. as malevolent

_____ 5. According to the *London News* article, what would have kept the Great Famine from evolving into a crisis?
    a. establishing workhouses
    b. introducing new crops
    c. continued support from taxes and charities
    d. allowing fewer farmers

_____ 6. According to the *London News* article, why did Britain respond so dramatically to the Great Famine?
    a. to show ill-will toward the Irish
    b. to stop unemployment and increase productivity
    c. to introduce variety into the lives of the Irish
    d. to stop suffering

_____ 7. What does the *London News* article introduce as an obvious solution to the problems in Ireland?
    a. move people out of Ireland
    b. enact more laws
    c. allow Irish farmers to cultivate the land
    d. end farming in Ireland

_____ 4. Each of the three sentences in "Loveliest of Trees" makes up a
    a. stanza.   c. sprung rhythm.
    b. trimeter.   d. trochee.

_____ 5. What does Housman mean by these words?

> to look at things in bloom/Fifty springs are little room

    a. The forest is no longer extensive.
    b. There is not enough time in fifty years.
    c. He is fifty years old.
    d. He would prefer to see a larger wood.

_____ 6. Which detail of Housman's life is most applicable to understanding "Loveliest of Trees"?
    a. Housman's mother died when he was twelve.
    b. Though a brilliant student, he failed his final examinations.
    c. His early childhood was spent in a rural area.
    d. Housman eventually became a professor of Latin.

_____ 7. The most prevalent metric unit in "Loveliest of Trees" is the
    a. trochee.   c. pentameter.
    b. stanza.   d. iamb.

_____ 8. The three stanzas of "Loveliest of Trees" divide the poem into
    a. perfectly regular iambic pentameter.
    b. a setting, a realization, and a resolution.
    c. paragraphs.
    d. three distinct scenes.

_____ 9. Housman was known personally as a restrained and quiet man. Which feature of "Loveliest of Trees" seems to support that idea most?
    a. The poem is about nature.
    b. The poem expresses a private resolution.
    c. There are no people in the poem.
    d. The beauty of the woods is indescribable.

_____ 10. The best interpretation of "Loveliest of Trees" is that
    a. nature is eternally beautiful.
    b. time and nature roll on forever.
    c. life is short, so one should value what's valuable.
    d. one should live quietly and alone.

Vocabulary and Grammar

On the line, write the letter of the one best answer.

_____ 11. *Terrestrial* things, such as mountains and trees, are items
    a. that are frightening.
    b. arranged in lines.
    c. that are immovable.
    d. of the earth.

_____ 12. A broken heart fills one with *rue*, or ____.
    a. color   c. revenge
    b. regret   d. restraint

_____ 13. To *languish* from unhappiness is to see one's strength ____.
    a. weaken   c. remain unchanged
    b. increase   d. become more focused

_____ 14. Which sentence capitalizes directions *correctly?*
   a. Housman grew up West of London.
   b. We drove Northeast for two hours.
   c. In the Southwest, Native American culture reamins.
   d. Business is done differently in the far east.

_____ 15. Which sentence uses the pronoun at the end *correctly?*
   a. No poet expressed faith better than he.
   b. Few in her century wrote more books than her.
   c. None could love them more than me.
   d. We read as many as them.

Essay Questions

16. Almost all of the poems in this part express a dark or painful view of life. Choose one of the selections that you found to express a particularly gloomy outlook. Write an essay explaining the features of this poem that make the selection seem especially bleak. You might consider the setting of the poem, the story it tells, or the expressions the author uses. Cite specific examples from the poem you choose.

17. Poets vary considerably in their use of irony, from gentle to harsh, even to humorous. Choose one of the poems in this part that you consider to employ irony for its effect, and write an essay that explains the ironic elements of the poem and how the poet uses them for effect. Be specific as you explain the irony.

18. Most of the poems in this part are about memory in one form or another and how human beings deal with it. Choose one of the poems and write an essay that analyzes the poem's treatment of human memory and how the poet creates that particular message about memory. Use examples from the poem to support your ideas.

Poetry of William Butler Yeats

Selection Test

Critical Reading

On the line, write the letter of the one best answer.

____ 1. "When You Are Old" is addressed to
   a. the speaker considering his advancing years.
   b. a woman once loved by the speaker.
   c. the speaker's mother.
   d. all readers as they consider the future.

____ 2. Which is possible to infer about the speaker of "When You Are Old"?
   a. He is saddened by rejection.
   b. He conceals his love out of pride.
   c. He remembers with great pleasure.
   d. He enjoys the peace and solitude of old age.

____ 3. In "When You Are Old," what do the lines imply?

   How many loved your moments of glad grace / And loved your beauty with love
   false or true

   a. One cannot tell if love of beauty is genuine.
   b. The old woman will have had many admirers.
   c. The speaker's jealousy is justified.
   d. Many were deceived by her joy and beauty.

____ 4. In "When You Are Old," the speaker's love of "the pilgrim soul" and "the sorrows of
   your changing face" means that he loved the
   a. woman for who she really was.
   b. way the world changed her.
   c. causes she believed in, whether they succeeded or failed.
   d. way the time took its toll on her.

____ 5. Knowing Yeats's relationship with actress Maud Gonne helps explain why "When
   You Are Old" is about
   a. the shallowness of public affection.
   b. the sacrifices of political life.
   c. the fleeting nature of beauty.
   d. deep love not returned.

____ 6. What is the main idea expressed in Yeats's "The Lake Isle of Innisfree"?
   a. a love of cities
   b. a feeling of longing
   c. contempt for urban life
   d. nostalgia for youth

____ 7. The island in "The Lake Isle of Innisfree" is a symbol for
   a. isolation.
   b. mystery.
   c. contentment.
   d. effort.

____ 8. Which statement best summarizes the central idea of "The Wild Swans at Coole"?
   a. Nature cares nothing for human feelings.
   b. People need to feel powerful emotions.
   c. The beauty of nature is temporary.
   d. Human passions cannot remain the same.

____ 9. What do these lines from "The Wild Swans at Coole" reveal about the speaker?

> Among what rushes will they build,
> By what lake's edge or pool
> Delight men's eyes when I awake some day
> To find they have flown away.

   a. The speaker is realistic, tempering his musings with scientific knowledge of animal behavior.
   b. The speaker is restless and wants to fly away with the birds to new and exotic lands.
   c. The speaker is resigned, recognizing that all things change.
   d. The speaker is deceived, believing that he will live forever.

____ 10. Which best reflects the central message of "The Second Coming"?
   a. In world history, a cycle of order follows a cycle of chaos.
   b. Society is doomed to revert to its barbaric origins.
   c. Humanity is powerless to do anything against the forces of time and nature.
   d. A dark future is foreshadowed by the violence of the present.

____ 11. Yeats's belief in a cyclic theory of world history reveals itself in "The Second Coming" through
   a. images of circling and completion.
   b. symbols of birds and the Sphinx.
   c. references to stone and violence.
   d. allusions to religious prophecies.

____ 12. The "lion body and the head of a man" and "the rocking cradle" in "The Second Coming" symbolize
   a. Yeats's ideas of communism and capitalism.
   b. systems of philosophy alternating in power.
   c. adult knowledge and childhood innocence.
   d. England and Ireland's political relationship.

____ 13. In "Sailing to Byzantium," Yeats implies that the natural world is
   a. cold in its destruction of life.
   b. adverse to the life of the mind.
   c. chaotic in its proliferation of species.
   d. blind to the horrors of death and disease.

____ 14. For Yeats, Byzantium symbolizes
   a. the mind's eternal life.
   b. the perfect social order.
   c. the distant quality of hope.
   d. divine revelation.

____ 15. When he wrote "Sailing to Byzantium," Yeats believed that the world of art and thought is superior to the life of body and feeling. This idea exhibits itself in the poem in
   a. a sea voyage as a means to escape old age.
   b. the admiration of Eastern "singing-masters."
   c. a movement from natural "birds in the trees" to mechanical ones "upon a golden bough."
   d. the image of a "drowsy Emperor."

Vocabulary and Grammar

On the line, write the letter of the one best answer.

_____ 16. A *clamorous* gathering of people is one that is
        a. joyful.
        b. angry.
        c. noisy.
        d. religious.

_____ 17. A country in *anarchy* is a nation in
        a. rebellion.
        b. chaos.
        c. sovereignty.
        d. theocracy.

_____ 18. A person without *conviction* has no
        a. strategies.
        b. offenses.
        c. procedures.
        d. beliefs.

_____ 19. What is the *noun clause* in the sentence?

      Whoever is interested in history will like "The Second Coming."

        a. Whoever is interested in history   c. will like
        b. in history   d. will like "The Second Coming"

_____ 20. A noun clause acts in a sentence
        a. anywhere in the subject.
        b. as a direct or indirect object, but not a subject.
        c. in any way that a noun can.
        d. as an independent clause.

Essay Questions

21. All five poems in this section reveal a sense of longing, of wanting something not available. What Yeats yearns for may vary from poem to poem, and he may express his wishes with images, symbols, or direct statement. What is Yeats seeking in each of these poems, and how does he disclose that longing? Write an essay in which you identify what Yeats longs for in any three of the poems in this selection, and discuss the way he conveys that sense of longing in each poem. Use specific examples from the poetry to support your ideas.

22. A symbol is a word, character, object, or action that stands for something beyond itself. Yeats employed and invented symbols throughout his poetry. What symbols appear in this selection of Yeats's work? Write an essay in which you discuss the symbols and what they may symbolize in any three of the poems in this selection. Explain how they fit with both the poem and the world beyond it, using specific examples from the poetry.

23. The world of nature is often a subject for poets. In Yeats's work, the world of nature is almost always present in some way. How does Yeats use natural imagery in his poetry? What conclusions might one draw about Yeats's attitude toward humanity and nature? Write an essay in which you discuss Yeats's use of the idea of nature in any three of the poems in this section. Explain how his use of nature in a poem relates to the thought or central idea of each. Use specific examples from the poems you choose.

                     Poetry of William Butler Yeats   **227**

"Preludes," "Journey of the Magi," and "The Hollow Men"
by T. S. Eliot

Selection Test

Critical Reading

On the line, write the letter of the one best answer.

_____ 1. In the first stanza of "Preludes," what setting is described?
a. a rural area in the stifling heat of summer
b. a rural setting on a rainy winter evening
c. a city on a rainy, winter evening
d. a city on a foggy morning

_____ 2. According to the speaker in "Preludes," what happens in the morning?
a. People carry on with their various masquerades.
b. People greet each other warmly at early morning coffee stands.
c. People watch a thousand sordid images.
d. People gather fuel.

_____ 3. What does Eliot suggest about modern urban life with the images in the passage from "Preludes"?

> And now a gusty shower wraps / The grimy scraps / of withered leaves about your feet . . . The showers beat / On broken blinds and chimney-pots, and at the corner of the street / A lonely cab-horse steams and stamps.

a. It is filled with hidden, natural beauty.
b. It is lonely and sad until rain cleanses it.
c. It is lonely, ugly, and filled with despair.
d. It is filled with energy and life.

_____ 4. In "Preludes," what is the "infinitely gentle/Infinitely suffering thing" described by Eliot?
a. a lonely cab-horse
b. human spirituality, and the human will to live
c. stormy weather
d. the smells and masquerades of morning

_____ 5. What feeling or idea does Eliot express in the final lines of "Preludes"?
a. that human beings are hopeless and doomed to suffer
b. hope that the human spirit might move beyond its dreary circumstances
c. that there is much laughter in the world
d. that people are unable to recognize what is gentle and humorous

_____ 6. What do repeated details in the poem "Journey of the Magi" reveal about the journey?
a. The journey helps the Magi to appreciate humanity and nature.
b. The journey brings the Magi into contact with interesting and friendly people.
c. The journey is filled with excitement and adventure.
d. The journey is long and difficult.

_____ 7. What do the lines reveal about the Magi?

> At the end we preferred to travel all night, / Sleeping in snatches, / With the voices singing in our ears, saying / That this was all folly.

    a. They remained faithful, even when they had doubts and their journey became difficult.
    b. They were tired and resentful throughout their journey.
    c. They were continually in search of fun and folly.
    d. They did not want people to discover them, so they were forced to hide at night.

_____ 8. Considering the religious beliefs of the Magi, why was the important birth like death?
    a. The birth meant the death of the Magi's journey.
    b. The child was born to die in order to save human souls.
    c. The birth would undoubtedly lead to human death.
    d. The birth meant the death of dreams for a better world.

_____ 9. Why are the Magi no longer at ease when they return to their kingdoms?
    a. They wanted more journeys and adventure.
    b. After the unfriendly journey, they no longer had respect for people.
    c. The birth of the baby changed their lives and their faith.
    d. They no longer believed in any form of religion.

_____ 10. The allusion to Mistah Kurtz in "The Hollow Men" implies that
    a. the hollow men were corrupted by outside influences.
    b. one may become hollow by living among hollow men.
    c. the hollow men will cause the end of the world.
    d. self-delusion is the hollow men's greatest folly.

_____ 11. Which image from "The Hollow Men" suggests the corruption of modern life?
    a. ". . . wind in dry grass"
    b. ". . . crossed staves / In a field"
    c. ". . . the eyes are / Sunlight on a broken column"
    d. "This broken jaw of our lost kingdoms"

_____ 12. In "The Hollow Men," how might you interpret Eliot's use of the words _hollow_, _dried_, and _broken_ to describe the hollow men?
    a. The hollow men spend their lives making repairs and gathering supplies.
    b. The lives of the hollow men are empty—void of spirituality or meaning.
    c. The hollow men suffer from the damaging effects of heat and wind.
    d. The hollow men are without money that would allow them to repair their homes.

_____ 13. The passage that begins "Here we go round the prickly pear" from "The Hollow Men" conveys the idea of
    a. people's adaptability to progress and new developments.
    b. the perpetuation of childhood innocence in adulthood.
    c. people's ability to amuse themselves.
    d. the meaningless and repetitive behavior of modern life.

_____ 14. One of the main ideas of "The Hollow Men" is that
    a. religious writings are irrelevant to modern life.
    b. salvation requires an act of will.
    c. life is too brief to be wasted.
    d. adults must avoid childish behavior.

Vocabulary and Grammar

On the line, write the letter of the one best answer.

____ 15. The camels used by the Magi are called *refractory* because they are
a. tall and lean.
b. exhausted.
c. difficult to manage.
d. calm and gentle.

____ 16. Which is the best meaning of the word *dispensation* as it is used in the line from "Journey of the Magi"?

> We returned to our places, these Kingdoms, / But no longer at ease here, in the old *dispensation*, / With an alien people clutching their gods.

a. environment
b. religious system
c. organization
d. business

____ 17. In "The Hollow Men," people are gathered on the beach of a *tumid* river, which is a river that is
a. swollen with excess water.
b. icy and cold.
c. shallow and muddy.
d. cluttered with leaves and trash.

____ 18. Identify the adjectival modifier in "You clasped the yellow soles of feet."
a. You clasped the yellow soles
b. You clasped
c. the yellow soles
d. of feet

____ 19. Which sentence contains a prepositional phrase used as an adjectival modifier?
a. The worlds revolve like ancient women.
b. The smell of steaks fills the winter evening.
c. You tossed a blanket.
d. I am moved by fancies.

____ 20. Which sentence contains an adjective clause used as an adjectival modifier?
a. We preferred to travel at night.
b. Then at dawn we came to a temperate valley.
c. This was birth, certainly.
d. We are people who are no longer at ease.

Essay Questions

21. In an essay, describe the journey that is the focus of "Journey of the Magi." How do the Magi feel while on this journey? How do you know the journey is important to them? In what way does it change their lives? What specific images add to the meaning of the poem?

22. In "Preludes," Eliot describes a world in which a "gusty shower wraps / The grimy scraps / Of withered leaves about your feet" and a world of "muddy feet that press / To early coffee-stands. / With the other masquerades / That time resumes." In "The Hollow Men," Eliot writes of hollow men "Leaning together / Headpiece filled with straw. . ." and "dried voices, when / We whisper together / Are quiet and meaningless / As wind in dry grass / Or rats' feet over broken glass." In an essay, consider what images such as these in the two poems have in common. What ideas and attitudes do they express toward humanity and the world?

23. In an essay, describe why the poems "Preludes" and "The Hollow Men" are expressions of Modernism. In your essay, answer the following questions: What attitude toward humanity in the modern world is expressed in both poems? What style does the poet use to express this attitude? What specific images in both pieces convey the poet's meaning?

"In Memory of W. B. Yeats" and **"Musée des Beaux Arts"**
by W. H. Auden
"Carrick Revisited" by Louis MacNeice
"Not Palaces" by Stephen Spender

Selection Test

Critical Reading

On the line, write the letter of the one best answer.

____ 1. "In Memory of W. B. Yeats" is an unusual elegy because the speaker claims that
    a. Yeats was foolish in some ways.
    b. Yeats's death was mourned by nature.
    c. Yeats will eventually be forgotten.
    d. Yeats's poetry is vitally important.

____ 2. According to the speaker in the poem "In Memory of W. B. Yeats," Yeats's poetic legacy is his
    a. readers' individual reactions to his verse.
    b. rejuvenation of Irish poetry in the modern world.
    c. radicalization of Irish politics.
    d. influence on Modernist poets.

____ 3. Which is the best paraphrase of the following lines from "In Memory of W. B. Yeats"?

> The words of a dead man
> Are modified in the guts of the living.

    a. The living don't understand Yeats's poetry.
    b. After his death, Yeats became a more important poet.
    c. The speaker does not agree with some interpretations of Yeats's poetry.
    d. Yeats's poetry inspires his readers in different ways.

____ 4. What is the theme of "In Memory of W. B. Yeats"?
    a. Yeats's personal life was painful and tragic.
    b. Yeats changed the course of Irish politics through poetry.
    c. Yeats's poetry continues to inspire his readers.
    d. Many people failed to appreciate Yeats's gifts.

____ 5. In "Musée des Beaux Arts," Auden suggests in the statement "the sun shone / As it had to" that
    a. nature is indifferent to human suffering.
    b. tragedies are inevitable.
    c. the sun is independent of the earth.
    d. God preordains everything that happens.

____ 6. In which passage from "Musée des Beaux Arts" does Auden use a description of a painting as a metaphor for people's indifference to the suffering of others?
    a. "Children who did not specially want it to happen . . ."
    b. ". . . skating / On a pond at the edge of the wood:"
    c. ". . . the dogs go on with their doggy life . . ."
    d. ". . . the white legs disappearing into the green / Water . . ."

____ 7. What does Auden imply about art in "Musée des Beaux Arts"?
   a. People should venerate the work of great artists.
   b. Art can be relevant to everyday life.
   c. Art speaks only to its own generation.
   d. Only the well educated fully appreciate art.

____ 8. What is the theme of "Musée des Beaux Arts"?
   a. Society should do more to help the unfortunate.
   b. There are as many interpretations of a painting as there are viewers.
   c. Tragedy means nothing to those who are unaffected by it.
   d. The Old Masters were obsessed with human suffering.

____ 9. What does the speaker of "Carrick Revisited" mean when he says he was "schooled from the age of ten to a foreign voice"?
   a. The speaker did not attend school until age ten.
   b. Born in Ireland, the speaker was educated in England.
   c. The speaker forgot the language of his birth.
   d. The speaker now refuses to speak English.

____ 10. Which is the best paraphrase of the following lines from "Carrick Revisited"?

> . . . Our past we know
> But not its meaning—whether it meant well.

   a. Memories of childhood are painful.
   b. The speaker understands his past by returning to his childhood home.
   c. We can never truly understand how past experiences have shaped us.
   d. One should live in the present, not the past.

____ 11. Which statement best summarizes the theme of "Carrick Revisited"?
   a. Artists are more sensitive to their surroundings than are other people.
   b. A conflict of national identity can result in a personal identity crisis.
   c. Artists draw their inspiration from childhood memories.
   d. An artist yearns to understand the influences that have shaped his identity.

____ 12. What does the speaker of "Not Palaces" urge the audience to do?
   a. build palaces
   b. change ideas about art
   c. become poets
   d. feed the hungry

____ 13. Which is the best paraphrase of the lines from "Not Palaces"?

> Touch, love, all senses;
> Leave your gardens, your singing feasts,
> Your dreams of suns circling before our sun,
> Of heaven after our world.

   a. Abandon simple pastimes.
   b. Open yourselves up to new interpretations of art.
   c. Consider new scientific theories.
   d. Focus on sensory details.

____ 14. In "Not Palaces," the speaker's tone is best described as
   a. angry.
   b. disillusioned.
   c. sarcastic.
   d. insistent.

Vocabulary and Grammar

On the line, write the letter of the one best answer.

____ 15. Which poet's interpretation of poetry most _____ you?
   a. sequestered
   b. affinities
   c. topographical
   d. intrigues

____ 16. This atlas indicates _____ details, such as mountains and rivers.
   a. sequestered
   b. topographical
   c. affinities
   d. prenatal

____ 17. _____, such as a love of poetry, drew Auden to Yeats and his poetry.
   a. Intrigues
   b. Sequestered
   c. Prenatal
   d. Affinities

____ 18. Which set of lines best demonstrates parallel structure?
   a. "It is too late for rare accumulation, / For family pride, for beauty's filtered dusts;"
   b. "Earth, receive an honored guest; / William Yeats is laid to rest:"
   c. "They never forgot / That even the dreadful martyrdom must run its course"
   d. "Back to Carrick, the castle as plumb assured / As thirty years ago—Which war was which?"

____ 19. Which italicized part indicates parallel structure?
   a. *Yeats*, who was Irish, and MacNeice, who was British, both wrote about Ireland.
   b. Yeats, who was Irish, *and* MacNeice, who was British, both wrote about Ireland.
   c. Yeats, who was Irish, and *MacNeice, who was British,* both wrote about Ireland.
   d. Yeats, who was Irish, and MacNeice, who was British, *both wrote about Ireland.*

____ 20. Which sentence best demonstrates parallel structure?
   a. The Old Masters include artists such as Bruegel, Rembrandt, and Michelangelo.
   b. The Old Masters include artists such as Bruegel, Rembrandt, and Michelangelo, who was Italian.
   d. The Old Masters include artists such as Bruegel, who painted *The Fall of Icarus*, Rembrandt, and Michelangelo.
   d. The Old Masters include artists such as Bruegel, the Dutchman Rembrandt, and the Italian Michelangelo.

Essay Questions

21. Poetry often expresses ideas in complex language that can be more easily understood through paraphrasing. Study the imagery or figurative language in "Carrick Revisited" or "Not Palaces." In an essay, explain how paraphrasing helps you understand the poem's deeper meaning. Include your paraphrases in your essay.

22. As in all literary works, theme in poetry can be either stated directly or implied. In an essay, identify the theme of two of the poems, and explain whether the poets state the theme directly or imply it. Support your conclusions about theme with evidence from the poems.

23. Of these three poets, whose interpretation of poetry and art resonates most with your own? Why? In an essay, explain the poet's views and why you agree with them. Contrast this poet and his views with the poet whose views are most in conflict with your own.

W. B. Yeats/Musée/Carrick/Not Palaces

"Shooting an Elephant" by George Orwell

Selection Test

Critical Reading

On the line, write the letter of the one best answer.

_____ 1. What is Orwell's purpose in writing "Shooting an Elephant"?
   a. to describe life in Burma
   b. to expose the evils of imperialism
   c. to argue for wildlife conservation
   d. to promote Burmese independence

_____ 2. What attitude does Orwell's description express?

   > wretched prisoners huddling in the stinking cages of the lockups, the gray, cowed faces of the long-term convicts . . .

   a. curiosity
   b. embarrassment
   c. indifference
   d. rage

_____ 3. Why does Orwell object to the Burmese's prejudice against him?
   a. He isn't important enough to worry about.
   b. The Burmese injure him whenever they can.
   c. He opposes British imperialism.
   d. He thinks the British behave impeccably.

_____ 4. Orwell's resentful feelings toward the Burmese are ironic because
   a. the Burmese do nothing to hurt him.
   b. the British are naturally superior.
   c. he professes to be a pacifist.
   d. he believes the Burmese are oppressed by the British.

_____ 5. What effect do the words have?

   > That is invariably the case in the East: a story always sounds clear enough at a distance, but the nearer you get to the scene of events the vaguer it becomes . . .

   a. They underscore the tension between imperialist forces and native population.
   b. They create suspense.
   c. They reveal the author's purpose.
   d. They give a voice to the Burmese population.

_____ 6. What can be inferred from the statement?

   > Feelings like these are the normal byproducts of imperialism; ask any Anglo-Indian official, if you can catch him off duty . . .

   a. Police officers are very busy.
   b. The officials had no problems with imperialism.
   c. Officials only admit their misgivings about imperialism privately.
   d. The imperialist officers are planning a revolution.

____ 7. Why is Orwell asked to do something about the elephant?
   a. The Burmese refuse to control the elephant.
   b. He has experience handling elephants.
   c. Only the British police force has weapons.
   d. The mahout has requested his assistance.

____ 8. Which detail discredits the stereotype that Burmese are unable to give precise information?
   a. The people describe how the elephant has killed the coolie.
   b. Some people have never heard of the elephant.
   c. The Burmese bring knives and baskets to the elephant's side.
   d. No one is certain where the mahout is.

____ 9. What irony is expressed in the statement?

   > A sahib has got to act like a sahib; he has got to appear resolute, to know his own mind and do definite things . . .

   a. Orwell objects to the term *sahib*.
   b. Although he knows his own mind, Orwell cannot do what he thinks he should.
   c. Orwell does not appear resolute in front of the crowd.
   d. Orwell cannot make a decision about the elephant, even though he knows he should.

____ 10. When he states that it "would never do" to have the Burmese laugh at him, Orwell reveals his
   a. anger.
   b. embarrassment.
   c. pride.
   d. frustration.

____ 11. What is ironic about the description?

   > thick blood welled out of him like red velvet . . .

   a. The elephant's thick, rough skin contrasts with the smoothness of velvet.
   b. The luxurious image contrasts with the brutal reality of the elephant's dying.
   c. The mahout would be too poor to afford an expensive material like velvet.
   d. Orwell did not want to kill the elephant.

____ 12. In his description of the dying elephant, what tone does Orwell create by repeating the word *tortured*?
   a. detached
   b. anguished
   c. hostile
   d. respectful

____ 13. In the years since he worked in Burma, Orwell believes he has become
   a. sophisticated.
   b. ineffective.
   c. prejudiced.
   d. contented.

____ 14. What is the theme of "Shooting an Elephant"?
   a. The British civil service is a model of efficiency.
   b. An individual's livelihood is as important as public safety.
   c. Rarely can anyone fully understand another culture.
   d. Anyone working for an imperialist power is morally compromised.

Vocabulary and Grammar

On the line, write the letter of the one best answer.

_____ 15. The British had _____ over the Burmese for more than fifty years.
   a. despotic
   b. squalid
   c. dominion
   d. senility

_____ 16. The _____ conditions of the holding cells were a testament to the _____ regime.
   a. prostrate, imperialism
   b. despotic, dominion
   c. senility, squalid
   d. squalid, despotic

_____ 17. Orwell was able to take better aim at the elephant from a _____ position.
   a. prostrate
   b. despotic
   c. squalid
   d. senility

_____ 18. Which sentence contains a restrictive participial phrase?
   a. The crowd gathered to watch Orwell as if he were performing.
   b. The mahout, heading in the opposite direction, lost the elephant.
   c. Orwell, pressured by the crowd, changes his mind about shooting the elephant.
   d. The man trampled by the elephant was a poor laborer.

_____ 19. Which sentence contains a nonrestrictive participial phrase?
   a. The Burmese, crowding around Orwell, want some fun.
   b. The rifle that Orwell brings is too small for the job.
   c. After the killing, people run to get knives and baskets.
   d. The elephant gasped and slowly collapsed to the ground.

_____ 20. Which underlined item is a restrictive participial phrase?
   a. <u>Blood</u> streaming from the wound looked like red velvet.
   b. Blood <u>streaming from the wound</u> looked like red velvet.
   c. Blood streaming from the wound <u>looked like red velvet</u>.
   d. Blood <u>streaming from the wound looked like red velvet</u>.

Essay Questions

21. Orwell states that the incident with the elephant "gave me a better glimpse than I had had before of the real nature of imperialism—the real motives for which despotic governments act." In an essay, explain Orwell's statement. Use examples from his essay to support your main points.

22. In "Shooting an Elephant," Orwell uses the phrase "stuck between" to describe his situation in Burma. Write an essay in which you show how this phrase applies to much of what Orwell reveals about himself in his essay.

23. Orwell writes that "when the white man turns tyrant it is his own freedom that he destroys." Using this statement as a starting point, analyze Orwell's use of irony in "Shooting an Elephant." Include specific examples of irony in your essay.

"**The Demon Lover**" by Elizabeth Bowen

Selection Test

Critical Reading

On the line, write the letter of the one best answer.

_____ 1. Why is Mrs. Drover in London?
  a. to check on the house and make sure the caretaker is doing his job
  b. to meet her husband and sister
  c. to fulfill a promise she had made twenty-five years ago
  d. to do some shopping and get some things from the house

_____ 2. Which line best expresses Mrs. Drover's sense of isolation on this particular day?
  a. "Though not much dust had seeped in, each object wore a film of another kind . . ."
  b. "Indeed, the silence was so intense . . . that no tread could have gained on hers unheard."
  c. "No other way of having given herself could have made her feel so apart, lost and foresworn."
  d. "She remembered . . . the complete suspension of *her* existence during that August week."

_____ 3. What significance do the stained mantelpiece and bruised wallpaper have?
  a. They are familiar details that seem somehow strange.
  b. They tell of further damage from bombings.
  c. They put further burden on Mrs. Drover's need for repairs.
  d. They indicate the destructiveness of the Drover children.

_____ 4. Which detail from the story helps emphasize the abnormality of the city?
  a. Mrs. Drover's use—and mistrust—of a caretaker
  b. the shortness of the taxi line
  c. the fact that "no human eye" watched Mrs. Drover
  d. the lack of telephone service

_____ 5. Why does a war setting make a ghost story believable?
  a. Amid violent fighting, innocent people often get hurt.
  b. So many people die that having ghosts as characters seems reasonable.
  c. Once the expectation of normality is gone, anything can happen.
  d. Deserted houses are appropriate settings for ghosts.

_____ 6. Why might the author of "The Demon Lover" want you to think about times when you have been lonely or vulnerable?
  a. By remembering your own experiences, you identify with the situations in the story and understand the author's purpose.
  b. The author wants you to pay attention to your own memory rather than the story.
  c. The author wants you to see how bizarre Mrs. Drover is.
  d. You are more likely to read more of the author's books if you remember your own experiences.

_____ 7. In what way does Mrs. Drover's response to her reflection in the mirror provide a typical ghost story element?

    a. The whiteness of her lips hints at a ghostly element.

    b. Her response is very normal, and ghost stories contain "normal" elements.

    c. The fact that she has to clear a patch in the mirror suggests mystery.

    d. Mrs. Drover reveals uncertainty about herself, which can hint at supernatural occurrences.

_____ 8. How does Mrs. Drover control her fear?

    a. She refuses to acknowledge it.   c. She focuses on practical activities.

    b. She turns it into anger.   d. She gives herself a pep talk.

_____ 9. What hint of strangeness is there in the farewell scene between Kathleen and her fiancé?

    a. Kathleen knows she doesn't really love him.

    b. The scene takes place in secret because Kathleen's family disapproves.

    c. The only thing she can recall are the buttons on his uniform.

    d. The fiancé's face is not visible and makes her feel as if she has _never_ seen his face.

_____ 10. In the flashback, the image of "spectral glitters in the place of his eyes" indicates that Kathleen was

    a. fearless.   c. literary.

    b. imaginative.   d. romantic.

_____ 11. If you responded to the beginning of the story with apprehension or dread, what excerpt best shows how the author has evoked that response?

    a. "Toward the end of her day in London Mrs. Drover went round to her shut-up house to look for several things she wanted to take away."

    b. "Mrs. Drover put down her parcels on the escritoire and left the room to proceed upstairs . . ."

    c. "She stopped dead and stared at the hall table—on this lay a letter addressed to her."

    d. "She thought first—then the caretaker _must_ be back."

_____ 12. Why does Mrs. Drover become comforted at the thought of the taxi?

    a. The idea of not being all alone appealed to her.

    b. She knew the taxi driver.

    c. The presence of taxis meant that normal activities were once again operating in London.

    d. It gave her something else to think about.

_____ 13. Which is an example of a reader's identifying with Mrs. Drover in this passage?

> As a woman whose utter dependability was the keystone of her family life she was not willing to return to the country, to her husband, her little boys and her sister, without the objects she had come up to fetch. Resuming work at the chest she set about making up a number of parcels in a rapid, fumbling-decisive way. These, with her shopping parcels, would be too much to carry: these meant a taxi—at the thought of the taxi her heart went up and her normal breathing resumed.

    a. I remember I had to call a taxi once.

    b. I understand "fumbling-decisive"; I think that's how I act when I'm nervous or upset.

    c. I don't think I'm very dependable.

    d. I have a sister, but not a husband or little boys.

_____ 14. What is the theme of this story?

    a. the disorientation caused by war   c. the inevitability of destiny

    b. the effect of fatigue   d. the tragedy of not knowing oneself

____ 15. Which lines make a connection between wartime London and the supernatural?
   a. ". . . at the moment the trees down the pavement glittered in an escape of humid yellow afternoon sun."
   b. "In her once familiar street, as in any unused channel, an unfamiliar queerness had silted up . . ."
   c. "Across the open end of the square two buses impassively passed each other . . ."
   d. ". . . as the clouds sharpened and lowered, the trees and rank lawns seemed already to smoke with dark."

Vocabulary and Grammar

On the line, write the letter of the one best answer.

____ 16. Mrs. Drover is able to see the taxi driver because of the *aperture*, or
   a. mirror.
   b. opening.
   c. picture.
   d. inner sight.

____ 17. As a wife and mother, Mrs. Drover's life was *circumscribed*, which means
   a. oppressed.
   b. limited.
   c. contented.
   d. ideal.

____ 18. A sense of *dislocation* exists in the story because
   a. the bombings are creating chaos.
   b. Mrs. Drover feels isolated from her family.
   c. Mrs. Drover has been expecting her former fiancé all these years.
   d. the family has moved away from its normal life.

____ 19. Choose the sentence that begins with a participial phrase.
   a. Saying good-bye had never been her favorite thing.
   b. Her family, not surprisingly, praised her courage.
   c. Rising from the chair, she went over and locked the door.
   d. Through the closed window she heard only rain.

____ 20. Which correctly identifies the participial phrase in this sentence?

   She stopped dead, startled by the letter, then moved to pick it up.

   a. She stopped dead
   b. startled by the letter
   c. then moved
   d. to pick it up

Essay Questions

21. Elizabeth Bowen uses World War II as a backdrop for a number of her stories, including "The Demon Lover." Yet she never talks about the Germans or other circumstances of the war directly. Is this a sign of passivity or acceptance? Or do other details in her story express anti-war attitudes? In an essay, take a stand and support it with ideas and details from the story.

22. "The Demon Lover" contains elements of the unnatural and supernatural throughout. In an essay, trace those elements as they appear throughout the story. Indicate why each element is unnatural. Then explain how these elements prepare readers for the final paragraph and the ending of the story.

23. Kathleen Drover is, for the most part, an ordinary person. In what ways do you relate to Mrs. Drover? Have you ever felt uncomfortable in a once-familiar place? Have you ever had a reminder from the past crop up at an unexpected moment? Consider all of Mrs. Drover's feelings and reactions and in an essay discuss those with which you particularly identify. Using examples from the story, how does identifying with Mrs. Drover help you understand her actions in the story as well as your own reactions to the story?

"The Diameter of the Bomb" by Yehuda Amichai
"Everything Is Plundered" by Anna Akhmatova
"Testament" by Bei Dao

Selection Test

Critical Reading

On the line, write the letter of the one best answer.

____ 1. In "The Diameter of the Bomb," the dead young woman came from a city
   a. with two hospitals and a graveyard.
   b. located a hundred kilometers from where the bomb exploded.
   c. in a country far across the sea.
   d. within range of the bomb.

____ 2. The last circle in "The Diameter of the Bomb" refers to
   a. God's compassion.
   b. an infinite void.
   c. communal grieving.
   d. the dropping of another bomb.

____ 3. A central idea in "The Diameter of the Bomb" is that
   a. terrorism destroys one's belief in a benign deity.
   b. terrorism is justified only when the innocent do not suffer.
   c. Israel's suffering from terrorism is unique.
   d. time heals the wounds of terrorism.

____ 4. Amichai intensifies the sense of waste in "The Diameter of the Bomb" by
   a. suggesting that more hospitals were needed.
   b. having the victims come from many different countries.
   c. stressing youth and childhood.
   d. implying the bomb did not destroy its target.

____ 5. In "Everything Is Plundered," the people do not despair because
   a. they know that things cannot get any worse.
   b. they see and feel nature's reviving powers.
   c. death is an end to suffering.
   d. they have become too savage to mourn the loss of civilization.

____ 6. In "Everything Is Plundered," the line that sums up the speaker's disillusionment
   with human behavior is
   a. "Misery gnaws to the bone."
   b. "Everything is plundered, betrayed, sold,"
   c. "something not known to anyone at all,"
   d. "to the ruined, dirty houses—"

____ 7. In "Everything Is Plundered," Akhmatova's personifications of death and misery
   metaphorically turn these forces into
   a. bomber planes.
   b. part of the miraculous.
   c. predatory animals.
   d. giant soldiers.

____ 8. In "Testament," the line "This isn't the year for heroes" suggests that the
   a. forces against the speaker's cause feel overwhelming.
   b. speaker is too young to be heroic.
   c. speaker no longer wants to make sacrifices for his cause.
   d. speaker does not want to endanger his family.

____ 9. Which statement describes the speaker's exact circumstance in "Testament"?
   a. He is witnessing his mother's execution.
   b. He is awaiting death before a firing squad.
   c. He is about to be hanged.
   d. He is dying from a wound suffered in battle.

____ 10. How do all three poets give their protest against war, oppression, and political violence a universal appeal?
   a. by using numbers effectively
   b. by criticizing technology
   c. by making the speaker a political hero
   d. by omitting names, places, and individualizing details

Essay Questions

11. In both "Testament" and "Everything Is Plundered," the first-person speakers are the victims themselves. In "The Diameter of the Bomb," it is less clear who the "I" is. Write an essay speculating on the identity of the speaker in Amichai's poem, and on Amichai's reason for putting the poem into the mouth of an observer rather than a victim.

12. Consider the tone and structure of "The Diameter of the Bomb" and "Testament." In an essay, demonstrate that the emotional impact of both poems depends on their movement from detached, restrained observations to a final impassioned outcry. How do both Amichai and Dao use understatement and detachment to build up to a dramatic spiritual enlightenment?

13. Akhmatova describes a situation in which suffering is overcome in a "miraculous" fashion. Consider all three poems and write an essay demonstrating that "the miraculous" in Akhmatova's "Everything Is Plundered" is affirmed by Dao's "Testament" but denied by Amichai's "The Diameter of the Bomb." How do both Akhmatova and Dao suggest that there are cosmic forces that transcend or subsume social and political chaos?

Part Test, Unit 6, Part 1: Waking From the Dream

Critical Reading

The questions below are based on the following selection.

In the following poem, "Sunday Morning," poet Louis MacNeice gives commentary on the pace of most people's lives by describing Sunday morning.

Down the road someone is practicing scales,

The notes like little fishes vanish with a wink of tails,

Man's heart expands to tinker with his car

For this is Sunday morning, Fate's great bazaar;

[5] Regard these means as ends, concentrate on this Now,

And you may grow to music or drive beyond Hindhead[1]

anyhow,

Take corners on two wheels until you go so fast

That you can clutch a fringe or two of the windy past,

That you can abstract this day and make it to the week of time

[10] A small eternity, a sonnet self-contained in rhyme.

But listen, up the road, something gulps, the church spire

Opens its eight bells out, skulls' mouths which will not tire

To tell how there is no music or movement which secures

Escape from the weekday time. Which deadens and endures.

[1] **Hindhead:** A district in the county of Surrey, England.

On the line, write the letter of the one best answer.

_____ 1. According to the speaker, what are some activities that take place on Sunday morning?
    a. shopping at bazaars and buying cars
    b. writing sonnets and other poems
    c. practicing musical scales and tinkering with cars
    d. fishing and singing

_____ 2. What is the writer's attitude toward Sunday morning?
    a. It is a peaceful time of rest and rejuvenation.
    b. It is a fast-paced, stressful time.
    c. It is a time for work.
    d. It is a sad time.

_____ 3. Why does the speaker call Sunday "Fate's great bazaar"?
    a. On Sunday, people work hard.
    b. On Sunday, people spend time shopping and making big purchases.
    c. On Sunday, people have the time to explore and display interesting aspects of life and themselves.
    d. On Sunday, people often hold large social gatherings.

_____ 4. How might you interpret the speaker's references to music, exploration in a car, and a sonnet?
   a. The speaker is emphasizing the importance of art and travel.
   b. The speaker is emphasizing the beauty and freedom of Sunday morning.
   c. The speaker is criticizing the ways in which people waste time.
   d. The speaker is envious of the activities of others.

_____ 5. What wish does the speaker of this poem express?
   a. a wish to have the peace and beauty of Sunday morning last forever
   b. a wish to drive a faster car
   c. a wish to keep busy and make better use of time throughout the week
   d. a wish to become a skilled musician

_____ 6. Of what is the sound of eight church bells symbolic?
   a. time   c. sonnets
   b. relaxation   d. eternity

_____ 7. How might you best paraphrase the last stanza of the poem?
   a. Church bells ring out the time, reminding people that there is no escape from the deadening pace of weekday time.
   b. Church bells encourage people by alerting them that it is time to relax.
   c. The church bell rings eight times, and people enjoy its movement and musical sound.
   d. People escape from the deadening pace of weekday time by listening to the ringing of the church bells.

_____ 8. How are the last four lines different from the rest of the poem?
   a. They introduce humor.
   b. They are peaceful.
   c. They rhyme.
   d. They are filled with sadness and disappointment.

_____ 9. Which lines best reflect the attitude of Modernism toward modern life?
   a. "Down the road someone is practicing scales, / The notes like little fishes vanish with a wink of tails . . ."
   b. ". . . To tell how there is no music or movement which secures / Escape from the weekday time. Which deadens and / endures."
   c. "A small eternity, a sonnet self-contained in rhyme."
   d. "Regard these means as ends, concentrate on this Now, / And you may grow to music or drive beyond Hindhead . . ."

_____ 10. What is the best description of the theme of "Sunday Morning"?
   a. People must try to be more productive on Sunday mornings.
   b. The peace of Sunday morning is frequently shattered by loud music, fast cars, and church bells.
   c. The peace of Sunday morning is to be cherished, but it is fleeting, as there is no escape from the deadening pace of weekday life.
   d. People endure painfully the boredom of Sunday morning until they are able to return to their everyday lives.

Vocabulary and Grammar

Choose the word or words that best complete each sentence.

_____ 11. We heard all the bells in the valley clanging in a _____ chorus.
   a. paltry   c. clamorous
   b. boreal   d. spectral

_____ 12. The camels were tired and _____, or stubborn.
     a. refractory
     b. despotic
     c. squalid
     d. sequestered

On the line, write the letter of the one best answer.

_____ 13. Which sentence begins with a participial phrase?
     a. At the end of her day in London, Mrs. Drover went to her house.
     b. Walking through her old house, Mrs. Drover felt sad and perplexed.
     c. Mrs. Drover was surprised to find a mysterious letter waiting in the mailbox.
     d. When the rain stopped, Mrs. Drover left the house and climbed into a taxi.

_____ 14. What is the complete noun clause in the sentence?

     He will arise and go to where he can build a cabin and live quietly.

     a. go to where
     b. He will arise and go
     c. where he can build a cabin and live quietly
     d. and live quietly

_____ 15. Which sentence contains a prepositional phrase functioning as an adjectival modifier?
     a. It was a cold and lonely time of the year.
     b. We saw a city street that was muddy.
     c. We heard the men cursing and grumbling.
     d. There were camels walking slowly.

_____ 16. Which sentence demonstrates parallel structure?
     a. The Magi were traveling at night, and they took short naps.
     b. See the withered leaves at your feet; see the newspapers from vacant lots.
     c. Auden says that suffering happens when someone is eating or just walks dully along.
     d. On the day Yeats died, airports were deserted, snow covered public statues, and there were frozen brooks.

_____ 17. In the sentence, what is the nonrestrictive participial phrase?

     Burmans walking with Orwell saw the elephant eight yards from the road, tearing up bunches of grass.

     a. walking with Orwell
     b. eight yards from the road
     c. tearing up bunches of grass
     d. from the road

_____ 18. What is the best meaning of _aperture_ as used in the sentence?

     Through the aperture, Mrs. Drover could see her driver and began to scream.

     a. fog
     b. mirror
     c. tunnel
     d. opening

The questions below consist of a related pair of words in CAPITAL LETTERS followed by four lettered pairs of words. Choose the pair that best expresses a relationship similar to that of the pair in capital letters.

____ 19. DESPOT : TYRANT ::
    a. autocratic : oppressively
    b. constitutional : constitution
    c. liberty : freedom
    d. just : corruption

____ 20. CONVICTION : BELIEVE ::
    a. variation : agreement
    b. disruption : calm
    c. reflection : reflect
    d. comprehension : understanding

Essay Questions

21. The selections in this section are arranged around the theme "Waking From the Dream." Write a short essay about the selection that you feel is most reflective of this theme. How does the piece you choose reflect this theme in its particular way? What dreamlike images does the writer use? What awakening, if any, occurs or is urged in the piece you choose?

22. Symbolism is the use of words, images, or characters to stand for something else. Many writers use symbolism to emphasize the themes of their pieces. In an essay, describe the symbolism of one piece from this section. For example, you might analyze a poem of William Butler Yeats, T. S. Eliot, or Stephen Spender. Describe how the symbolism in the selection you choose reflects the theme of the work.

23. A crucial part of reading and understanding poetry is interpreting images, phrases, and repeated words. When you interpret, you search to find meaning in what you are reading. In an essay, describe the most striking images, phrases, or repeated words in two poems from this section. How did one or more of these elements lead you to meaning in each of the poems?

24. Modernism was a movement of the twentieth century that often used concrete images and musical language to depict a chaotic world. Images in Modernist poetry are often clear and intended to evoke emotion in readers and help readers to find meaning. In an essay, describe a piece from this section that reflects an aspect of Modernism. Give concrete examples from the piece you choose, describing why these examples are Modernist and what meanings they suggest.

25. Through literature, many writers give commentary on some aspect of the human experience. Some writers express anger over a particular aspect of society or human behavior, while other writers express resignation and sadness. Still other writers express hope, and through their pieces urge some type of change or awareness. In an essay, describe the ways in which two pieces from this section examine and comment on some aspect of the human experience. What ideas are expressed in the pieces you choose? In what ways are the pieces both similar to and different from each other?

"The Soldier" by Rupert Brooke
"Wirers" by Siegfried Sassoon
"Anthem for Doomed Youth" by Wilfred Owen
"Birds on the Western Front" by Saki (H. H. Munro)

Selection Test

Critical Reading

On the line, write the letter of the one best answer.

_____ 1. In Rupert Brooke's poem "The Soldier," how is it possible that there could be "some corner of a foreign field / That is forever England"?
   a. Brooke believes totally in England's eventual victory.
   b. England will never yield ground gained at a high price.
   c. The sacrifice of English soldiers lays claim to the land.
   d. His English body will always occupy a part of the earth.

_____ 2. In "The Soldier," the speaker suggests the strength of his patriotism when he
   a. feels blessed by the sun in England.
   b. dreams of exerting an English influence in his afterlife.
   c. assumes his corpse will make richer the soil in which it is buried.
   d. says he wants to die for his country.

_____ 3. Brooke implies in "The Soldier" that he associates England with
   a. ambition.
   b. gentleness.
   c. morbidity.
   d. warfare.

_____ 4. Which word best summarizes Brooke's tone in "The Soldier"?
   a. uncertain
   b. determined
   c. guarded
   d. idealistic

_____ 5. "Wirers" by Siegfried Sassoon is about
   a. men who strung barbed-wire fences on the battlefield.
   b. demolition experts working behind the lines.
   c. the contribution of scientists to munitions work.
   d. bomb-disposal crews defusing unexploded bombs.

_____ 6. In "Wirers," what do these lines suggest?

   Ghastly dawn with vaporous coast
   Gleams desolate along the sky, night's misery ended.

   a. The events in the poem occur on the last night of the war.
   b. Day and night are equally dreadful.
   c. The soldiers are relieved to have survived another night.
   d. Every dawn brings a glimmer of hope.

7. What is the tone in the statement about young Hughes at the end of "Wirers"?

> . . . no doubt he'll die today.
> But *we* can say that the wire's been safely mended.

  a. bitterly ironic
  b. sadly proud
  c. romantically sentimental
  d. naïvely patriotic

8. What is the theme of "Wirers"?
  a. War is dreadful and meaningless.
  b. Soldiers in wartime think only of survival.
  c. Friendship is impossible in the face of death.
  d. Dying is better than confronting horror day after day.

9. Wilfred Owen's "Anthem for Doomed Youth" contrasts the
  a. beauty of life and the pain of pointless death.
  b. tranquility of England to battlefields of France.
  c. customs of death in wartime and peacetime.
  d. peace of life and the peace of death.

10. In "Anthem for Doomed Youth," the "holy glimmers of good-byes" refers to
  a. candles.
  b. prayers.
  c. waves.
  d. tears.

11. In "Anthem for Doomed Youth," what can you infer from this line?

> The pallor of girls' brows shall be their pall;

  a. Families will never know what happened to their loved ones.
  b. The grief of lovers will be the sole memorial service.
  c. There will be no way of honoring those lost.
  d. Memorial services are not held at home for the dead.

12. The theme of "Anthem for Doomed Youth" is
  a. Civilians mourn dead soldiers more than other soldiers do.
  b. The horrors of war do not allow for customary mourning.
  c. Battles do not stop for funeral ceremonies.
  d. Soldiers don't want to be buried in foreign soil.

13. The speaker in Saki's "Birds on the Western Front" is a
  a. minister.   c. soldier.
  b. pilot.   d. biologist.

14. The tone of "Birds on the Western Front"
  a. honors the persistence of natural life in a hazardous environment.
  b. defends the value of understatement and reserve in English patriotism.
  c. satirizes the foolishness of natural instinct in wartime.
  d. contrasts natural life and the absurdity of war.

15. In "Birds on the Western Front," when the narrator notes that "there are always sufficient mice left over to populate one's dugout and make a race course of one's face at night," he is
  a. commenting upon the conditions of life in the trenches.
  b. explaining the war's effect on the balance of nature.
  c. suggesting a decline in the number or efficiency of owls.
  d. accounting for the mice because of the destruction of grain fields.

Vocabulary and Grammar

On the line, write the letter of the one best answer.

_____ 16. Someone who is *stealthy* is
     a. evil.
     b. peculiar.
     c. secretive.
     d. determined.

_____ 17. A *laudable* behavior is
     a. shameful.
     b. comic.
     c. praiseworthy.
     d. wasted.

_____ 18. A person who has been *disconcerted* has been
     a. flustered.
     b. angered.
     c. disappointed.
     d. forsaken.

_____ 19. Which sentence uses the pronoun *who* or *whom* correctly?
     a. Few soldiers still survive whom were in World War I.
     b. Few soldiers who fought in World War I still survive.
     c. Few soldiers who we know of from World War I survive.
     d. Few soldiers fought in World War I whom still survive.

_____ 20. The correct case for *who* or *whom* in an adjective clause is determined by the
     a. function of the clause in the sentence.
     b. function of the noun modified by the adjective clause.
     c. position of the clause in the subject or predicate.
     d. function of the pronoun within the clause.

Essay Questions

21. World War I was different from previous wars in that its size, scale, technology, and tactics changed the idea of combat. The destructiveness profoundly shocked and disillusioned soldiers, civilians, and leaders on both sides. What evidence of the war's tremendous damage do you see in these selections? Write an essay in which you explain inferences one can make about the nature of the war from these selections. Use examples from the literature to explain the inferences.

22. In "The Soldier" and "Wirers," Rupert Brooke and Siegfried Sassoon offer two visions of a soldier's life and death. What views do they express? In an essay, compare and contrast the two poets' visions as shown in their poems. Use examples from the poems to illustrate your points.

23. Saki's "Birds on the Western Front" doesn't say a great deal about the life of a soldier, preferring to talk about bird life instead. How does the tone of the piece carry the message that the essay is not really about birds? Write an essay in which you explain how Saki uses tone to turn an article about birds into a commentary on the human endeavor of war. Use examples from the essay to support your ideas.

"**Wartime Speech**" by Winston Churchill
"**Defending Nonviolent Resistance**" by Mohandas K. Gandhi

Selection Test

Critical Reading

On the line, write the letter of the one best answer.

_____ 1. Churchill's "Wartime Speech" was delivered
    a. on radio.
    b. on television.
    c. to the king.
    d. to Parliament.

_____ 2. What "solemn hour" was Churchill referring to in the opening of his "Wartime Speech"?
    a. the declaration of war
    b. an attack on London
    c. the imminent defeat of France
    d. the transfer of power

_____ 3. The audience for Churchill's "Wartime Speech" speech is the people of
    a. America.   c. Great Britain.
    b. France.   d. Germany.

_____ 4. Which point in "Wartime Speech" supports Churchill's claim that all might not be lost?
    a. the size of the German Air Force
    b. the French gift for counterattack
    c. the unexpected tactics of the Germans
    d. the columns of armor followed by infantry

_____ 5. What is Churchill trying to do for his audience as he first describes the situation in his "Wartime Speech"?
    a. eliminate alarm and confusion
    b. explain the cause of defeat
    c. establish his military authority
    d. deceive the Germans

_____ 6. In "Wartime Speech," why does Churchill say it would be "foolish to disguise the gravity of the hour"?
    a. Overconfidence at this time might be disastrous.
    b. Despite some hope, the situation does not look good.
    c. The High Command must be persuaded to undertake a "furious and unrelenting assault."
    d. Only a very small part of the French Army has been engaged.

_____ 7. In Churchill's "Wartime Speech," what does he say will happen as soon as "stability is reached on the Western Front"?
    a. The battle and the war will have been won.
    b. The oil refineries on which the Germans depend will be damaged.
    c. Holland will be ruined and enslaved within days.
    d. The assault will be turned upon Britain.

8. When Churchill says in "Wartime Speech" that many will feel a pride in "sharing the perils of the Lads at the front," he is preparing his audience for
   a. possible warfare in England itself.
   b. increased efforts to supply munitions.
   c. the need for less waste and more reserves.
   d. an end "bitter or glorious" in France.

9. In Churchill's "Wartime Speech," which point supports the idea that "in that supreme emergency, we shall not hesitate to take every step, even the most drastic" in the war?
   a. Churchill has an administration of every party and every point of view.
   b. Churchill has received sacred pledges that the French will fight to the end.
   c. The "interests of property and hours of labor are nothing compared with the struggle . . ."
   d. This is one of the most "awe-striking periods in the long history of France and Britain."

10. Why does Churchill conclude his "Wartime Speech" with a passage written long ago for Trinity Sunday?
    a. to demonstrate the Germans' disrespect for religious values
    b. to encourage Britons to make a fateful effort as in historic times
    c. to ask for divine help to defeat Nazi Germany
    d. to assure the people that God will not fail them

11. In "Defending Nonviolent Resistance," what is Gandhi's response to the charges against him?
    a. He dismisses them as immoral.
    b. He disputes the interpretation of justice.
    c. He ignores them.
    d. He agrees with them.

12. What is the primary purpose of Gandhi's "Defending Nonviolent Resistance"?
    a. to persuade the judges to resign
    b. to trace the history of British rule in India
    c. to explain why he has become a noncooperator
    d. to force the judges to lighten his sentence

13. Why does Gandhi recount his service to the British Empire in "Defending Nonviolent Resistance"?
    a. to establish himself as a reasonable and credible speaker
    b. to gain the sympathy of the audience for the discrimination he faced
    c. to gain the sympathy of the judge for his efforts
    d. to express his regret at ever having helped the British

14. Which point is *not* support for Gandhi's assertion in "Defending Nonviolent Resistance" that the "British connection had made India more helpless . . ."?
    a. A disarmed India has no power against an aggressor.
    b. Affection cannot be manufactured or regulated by law.
    c. India is so poor that it cannot resist famines.
    d. The cottage industries have been ruined by British policies.

15. In "Defending Nonviolent Resistance," why does Gandhi tell the judge he must either resign or sentence Gandhi to the maximum penalty?
    a. He is trying to win the compassion of the people in the courtroom.
    b. He is trying to make the judge's decision as difficult as possible.
    c. He is rejecting the judge's authority or ability to imprison him.
    d. He is submitting to unjust British law in order to show its injustice.

Vocabulary and Grammar

On the line, write the letter of the one best answer.

____ 16. Parallel structure is the
   a. use of sentences all more or less the same length.
   b. dispersal of thematic elements evenly throughout a work.
   c. balanced arrangement of main points in a speech or essay.
   d. repetition of words, phrases, or grammatical forms.

____ 17. A *formidable* opponent would be one who is
   a. reconciled.
   b. powerful.
   c. reasonable.
   d. deceitful.

____ 18. When Gandhi explains his *disaffection*, he is explaining his
   a. disillusionment.
   b. loyalty.
   c. sincerity.
   d. detachment.

____ 19. Which contains an example of parallel structure?
   a. This is one of the most awe-striking periods in the long history of France and Britain.
   b. Similarly, in 1906, at the time of the Zulu revolt, I raised a stretcher-bearer party and served till the end of the "rebellion."
   c. Our task is not only to win the battle but to win the war.
   d. Nonviolence implies voluntary submission to the penalty for non-cooperation with evil.

____ 20. Circumstances that are *extenuating* are
   a. improving.
   b. protracted.
   c. intolerable.
   d. mitigating.

Essay Questions

21. Gandhi tells the Court that it must either sentence him to a maximum sentence or agree with him that British rule is bad for India, and resign. The audience for the speech was a packed courtroom and the judges who were about to sentence him. Write an essay in which you explain what the purpose of the speech was and how Gandhi suited the contents of the speech to his purpose. Use examples from the speech to support your ideas.

22. Early in his May 19 speech, Churchill points out that if things went well "a sudden transformation of the scene" might occur. He was wrong, and he likely knew it at the time. Within a week the Germans would trap the British on the beaches of Dunkirk, and in a month, all France would be occupied by the Nazis. If Churchill knows France is lost, why give this speech? What is his purpose? Write an essay in which you explain what Churchill's purpose is in this speech, and how he accomplishes it. Use examples from the speech to support your points.

23. Winston Churchill and Mohandas Gandhi were unlike in many respects and differed sharply on the role of the British in India. In fact, Churchill's government imprisoned Gandhi's Indian National Congress during World War II for trying to get the British out of India, which might have helped Japan. What similarities do you see, though, in these two great twentieth-century leaders? Write an essay in which you consider qualities in the speeches of the two leaders that unite them, even though their personalities, speaking style, and politics were different. Use examples from the speeches to support your points.

"The Fiddle" by Alan Sillitoe

Selection Test

Critical Reading

On the line, write the letter of the one best answer.

_____   1. What was the general location of Harrison's Row?
 a. amidst other rows of cottages all alike
 b. far out in the country, amidst fields
 c. at the entrance to the Radford Pit
 d. at the edge of a city

_____   2. What is the main importance of the River Leen to the people in "The Fiddle"?
 a. It threatens them with danger.
 b. Its floods devastate the area.
 c. It is a source of beauty and mystery in their ordinary lives.
 d. It forms a barrier between their houses and the country.

_____   3. The attitude of Jeff Bignal's neighbors toward his fiddling can best be described as
 a. resentful.
 b. indifferent.
 c. envious.
 d. respectful.

_____   4. What setting does Sillitoe describe at the beginning of the story?
 a. ruined cottages
 b. brisk city streets
 c. dark forest land
 d. deep mine shafts

_____   5. What can you predict about the narrator, given what he reveals about himself in this passage?

> In my visions of leaving Nottingham for good—and they were frequent in those days—I never reckoned on doing so by the high road or railway. Instead I saw myself wading or swimming the Leen from Harrison's Row, and setting off west once I was on the other side.

 a. He likely ran away from home when he was a child.
 b. He has visions that foretell the future.
 c. He is likely to leave Nottingham.
 d. He and Jeff Bignal will become good friends.

_____   6. What kind of atmosphere does Sillitoe create in this passage?

> Or they opened the doors and windows so that the sound of his music drifted in, while the woman stayed at the sink or wash-copper, or the man at his odd jobs. Anyone with a wireless would turn it down or off.

 a. serene
 b. hostile
 c. bleak
 d. humble

_____ 7. What effect do the details of this passage have on Jeff Bignal?

> After tea in summer while it was still light and warm he would sit in his back garden playing the fiddle, and when he did everybody else came out to listen.

    a. Jeff hates the mine all the more afterwards.
    b. Jeff allows the neighbors to listen and they, in return, respect his privacy.
    c. People who did not want to listen resented Jeff.
    d. Jeff enjoys a somewhat special status in the neighborhood.

_____ 8. What does the story of Mrs. Deaffy, the stolen cocoa, and Mrs. Atkin reveal about life in Harrison's Row?
    a. It is sometimes casually brutal.
    b. Parents make little effort to control their children.
    c. Crime is a serious problem.
    d. Elderly people are isolated.

_____ 9. Judging from his actions, which of the following seems to be most important to Jeff?
    a. the opportunity to make music
    b. the friendship of his neighbors
    c. a happy marriage
    d. a decent quality of life

_____ 10. Throughout the story, what element of the setting represents the dream of escape?
    a. the chapel on St. Peter's Street
    b. the Denman Street shops
    c. the fields across the Leen
    d. the new high-rise apartments

_____ 11. Which passage evokes a dreary, gloomy atmosphere?
    a. "No one could say that he prospered, but they couldn't deny that he made a living."
    b. "It was virtually true that Jeff saw no daylight, because even on Sunday he stayed in bed most of the day, and if it happened to be dull there was little enough sky to be seen through his front bedroom window."
    c. "Maybe he had a quid or two more knocking around, though if he had it couldn't have been much, but with four quid and a slice of bluff he got enough credit from a wholesaler at the meat market downtown to stock his shop."
    d. "They'd seen how he had got fed up with selling the sweat of his brow."

_____ 12. Jeff starts out as a fiddle-playing miner. He sells the fiddle to become a butcher. What effect does the fiddle have on Jeff?
    a. The fiddle is a form of escape for Jeff, both when he plays it and when he sells it.
    b. The fiddle allows him to express his feelings about being a miner.
    c. The fiddle helps him feel close to the uncle who had taught him to play.
    d. The fiddle is the only reason Jeff is respected; selling the fiddle marks his neighbors' loss of respect.

_____ 13. What happened to Jeff Bignal?
    a. He ran the butcher's shop and watched the neighborhood change.
    b. He moved away when Harrison's Row was condemned.
    c. He resettled in Nottingham with his wife after the war.
    d. He was killed while serving in the army.

_____ 14. Which theme is most central to "The Fiddle"?
    a. the healing powers of music
    b. the difficulty of emerging from poverty
    c. the importance of community sharing
    d. the struggle to achieve privacy within a close community

_____ 15. Which statement best expresses the central idea of "The Fiddle"?
   a. The poor are bound to fail.
   b. Wealth cannot buy happiness.
   c. Poverty leads people to make painful choices.
   d. People need contact with the natural world.

Vocabulary and Grammar

On the line, write the letter of the one best answer.

_____ 16. The rain that caused the flood was *persistent*, meaning
   a. heavy.   c. spotty.
   b. steady.   d. seasonal.

_____ 17. If the city were to *obliterate* the country beyond the Leen, it would _____ the country.
   a. develop   c. mine
   b. destroy   d. exceed

_____ 18. Choose the sentence that begins with a subject.
   a. "To a child it seemed as if the songs lived in the hard collier's muscle."
   b. "On a day that was not too hot, the breeze wafted from the Pennines in Derbyshire."
   c. "Jeff played for himself, for the breeze against his arm, for the soft hiss of the flowing Leen."
   d. "In the middle of the winter Jeff's fiddling was forgotten."

_____ 19. Identify the sentence that begins with an introductory phrase.
   a. "Children living there, and adults as well, had the advantage of both town and country".
   b. "He was not bitter, yet he couldn't help being envious of those still out there in the sunshine."
   c. "Harrison's Row was the last of Nottingham where it met the countryside."
   d. "In that case there was no telling where you'd end up."

_____ 20. What does the sentence begin with?

   Six months after opening the shop he got married.

   a. the subject   c. an introductory phrase
   b. an adverb   d. an introductory clause

Essay Questions

21. Jeff Bignal has a choice to make, and he makes it. What led to his choice? What choice did he make? How did he accomplish his goal? Given the circumstances, did Jeff have any other choices? Answer these questions in an essay.

22. Setting is a vital part of "The Fiddle." If Sillitoe had spent less time on the setting, the story of Jeff Bignal would be slim and ineffective. In an essay, explain how important details of the setting such as the cottages, the Leen, the fiddle, the mine, the 1930's, and World War II all contribute atmosphere and impact to the story.

23. Is this a story about a fiddle? About Jeff Bignal? About a place called Harrison's Row? About the Depression? Why did Sillitoe write this story? Why did he title it "The Fiddle"? In an essay, explain what this story is about, and give evidence from the story to support your points.

"**The Distant Past**" by William Trevor

Selection Test

Critical Reading

On the line, write the letter of the one best answer.

_____ 1. How does Trevor begin "The Distant Past"?
  a. by giving background on the conflict
  b. by suggesting the theme
  c. with a description of the main characters
  d. with vivid descriptions to set the mood

_____ 2. What effect did the Middletons' traditional weekly trips to town have?
  a. The Middletons' presence caused people to harbor resentments against them.
  b. The Middletons' presence caused the tourist business to decline.
  c. The trips allowed the Middletons to keep an eye on who might be conspiring against the British crown.
  d. The Middletons developed friendly relationships with the shopkeepers.

_____ 3. Why did the Middletons drive to town with the union jack displayed in their car window?
  a. to rile up the townspeople
  b. to show their support for the new Queen Elizabeth II
  c. to show respect for their father's beliefs
  d. to protest the green-painted pillar boxes

_____ 4. At the beginning of the story, the line "what sense was there in green-painted pillar boxes" is significant to the story because
  a. the color green is associated with Ireland, and the Middletons scorn Ireland's self-government.
  b. the conservative Middletons resist the self-expressiveness of the Irish.
  c. the Middletons took the green-painted pillar boxes as a militant gesture, and they were afraid.
  d. the green-painted pillar boxes foreshadow the fact that the Middletons will never be accepted.

_____ 5. The townspeople are friendly with the Middletons because
  a. they want to stay on their good side, in case England regains control of Ireland.
  b. they want their business.
  c. they hope to persuade the Middletons to change their loyalties.
  d. the Middletons are likable, although the townspeople consider them odd.

_____ 6. Judging by their actions in the story, with which of the following characteristics of Victorian England do the Middletons most identify?
  a. socialism
  b. patriotism
  c. realism
  d. reformism

_____ 7. While the town thrives following World War II, the Middletons
  a. resent the shopkeepers' success.
  b. age and decline.
  c. stay away to avoid the tourists.
  d. hope their old home will become a tourist attraction.

8. Social conflict is defined as
   a. an argument in public.
   b. a disagreement among people of different social classes.
   c. a struggle between people with opposing views about society.
   d. a struggle over economic issues, as opposed to political issues.

9. What is the main reason behind the townspeople's growing dislike of the Middletons?
   a. the townspeople's hatred of the Irish
   b. the growth of tourism in the town
   c. the reemergence of Irish-English hostilities
   d. a lack of respect for the Queen

10. Why do the Middletons take down the portrait of their father in his Irish Guards uniform?
    a. They feel a sense of regret for lost friendships and for the violence that was occurring in the North.
    b. They fear the townspeople will storm the house and remove the portrait by force.
    c. They question whether their loyalties might have been misplaced all these years.
    d. They don't want even the portrait of their father to become aware of how they are being treated by the townspeople.

11. What effect does the resurgence of the social conflict have on the Middletons' relationship with Fat Driscoll?
    a. Driscoll stops giving them mince for their dog.
    b. Driscoll shows up at Carraveagh with a shotgun.
    c. Driscoll locks his door when he sees them coming.
    d. Driscoll refuses to serve them when they enter his shop.

12. How does Miss Middleton feel about her and her brother's devotion to the distant past?
    a. She never wavers in her loyalty to England and vows to proclaim her loyalty wherever she goes.
    b. She wonders whether it isn't just a game until the effects of it become very real at the end of the story.
    c. She is afraid to tell her brother that she wonders whether they haven't been wrong all these years.
    d. She wishes she could change her loyalties to recover her lost friendships with the townspeople.

13. On whom or on what do the Middletons blame their isolation at the end of the story?
    a. on the decline in tourism
    b. on the distant past
    c. on their father
    d. on the British

14. The climax, or height of action, of "The Distant Past" occurs when
    a. violence breaks out in Northern Ireland.
    b. the townspeople become concerned because of the decline in tourism.
    c. the Middletons realize that their fortune has dwindled to nothing.
    d. people stop speaking to the Middletons because of the family's loyalty to England.

15. The central theme of "The Distant Past" is
    a. the decline of a family fortune.
    b. how political changes can affect relationships among people.
    c. the political tensions between Northern Ireland and Ireland.
    d. how the fall of an empire affects its citizens.

Vocabulary and Grammar

On the line, write the letter of the one best answer.

_____ 16. The Middletons meet with *adversity*, or _____, when they inherit the estate from their father.
   a. hardship
   b. ruin
   c. confusion
   d. shock

_____ 17. The Middletons are considered an *anachronism* because they
   a. have different opinions about England.
   b. are unmarried.
   c. are living off money from their father's estate.
   d. would seem to fit better in a different time period.

_____ 18. What is the italicized phrase in this sentence?

   It was a great day for the Commonwealth of Nations, they replied, a remark *which further amused Fat Driscoll.*

   a. a relative pronoun clause
   b. an adverb clause
   c. a restrictive adjective clause
   d. a nonrestrictive adjective clause

_____ 19. A restrictive adjective clause
   a. is not essential to the meaning of the sentence and is not set off by commas.
   b. is essential to the meaning of the sentence and is not set off by commas.
   c. is not essential to the meaning of the sentence and is set off by commas.
   d. is essential to the meaning of the sentence and is set off by commas.

_____ 20. Which sentence contains a nonrestrictive adjective clause?
   a. Reverend Bradshaw was a younger man who regarded the Middletons as an anachronism.
   b. The Middletons suspected the man and the wife who ran the glove factory to be spies.
   c. The Middletons, who were in their sixties, were resigned to increasing discomfort.
   d. In time he even derived pride from the fact that his parishioners' values were not diminished.

Essay Questions

21. It is helpful when determining meaning to understand cause-and-effect relationships in the action of a story. In an essay, trace the causes and effects of the major events in "The Distant Past." Focus on those events that have an impact on the Middletons' relationship with the townspeople.

22. Discuss the role of social conflict in "The Distant Past" in an essay. What is the conflict between the Middletons and the townspeople? When is the conflict dominant? Under what circumstances do the characters live outside of the conflict? What events or happenings cause the conflict to return to a prominent place in people's minds?

23. Trevor echoes the title phrase, "the distant past," a number of times in the story. What does the phrase indicate about the plot, the characters, and/or the theme? Think of two ways the author uses the title within the story. In an essay, explain what purposes the phrase serves.

"Follower" and **"Two Lorries"** by Seamus Heaney
"Outside History" by Eavan Boland

Selection Test

Critical Reading

On the line, write the letter of the one best answer.

_____ 1. What does the speaker of "Follower" do while the father works with the horse plow?
a. He walks at the front, with the horses.
b. He sits at the edge of the field and watches.
c. He waits at home for the father to return.
d. He follows along behind, stumbling in the furrows.

_____ 2. In "Follower," the line "His shoulders globed like a full sail strung" suggests that the father is
a. bent and aging.
b. expansive and powerful.
c. angry and unpredictable.
d. loud and threatening.

_____ 3. How does the speaker of "Follower" imply how he felt in these lines?

All I ever did was follow / In his broad shadow . . .

a. frustrated   c. lazy
b. neglected   d. useless

_____ 4. How does the diction of this stanza from "Follower" add to the meaning of the stanza?

I stumbled in his hobnailed wake,
Fell sometimes on the polished sod;
Sometimes he rode me on his back
Dipping and rising to his plod.

a. The word *hobnailed* is an especially effective farming term.
b. The repetition of *sometimes* emphasizes the occasional nature of the boy's being in the field with his father.
c. The rhythm of the short, ordinary words creates a sense of the boy's difficulty walking on the uneven ground.
d. The word *plod* brings up images of a horse plodding.

_____ 5. Which is the best summary of "Follower"?
a. I was the follower as a child; now my father follows me.
b. Sometimes I stumbled when I was young; sometimes I rode on my father's back.
c. I could never handle a plow like my father.
d. Sometimes I helped my father when he worked.

_____ 6. In this line from "Follower," what image is the poet invoking?

"I was a nuisance, tripping, falling, / Yapping always"

a. the image of a puppy
b. the image of a clumsy young child
c. the image of a very bothersome child
d. the image of a parent who puts up with a talkative child

____ 7. In "Two Lorries," what does the first lorry driver do?
   a. He dumps his coal in the speaker's yard.
   b. He sweet-talks the speaker's mother, inviting her to a film.
   c. He helps the speaker's mother clean the stove.
   d. He carries explosives in his lorry to deliver to Magherafelt.

____ 8. In what way is the speaker's mother connected with the second lorry in "Two Lorries"?
   a. The second lorry driver flirted with her, just as the first had done.
   b. She is killed in the bus station explosion.
   c. She was in Magherafelt when the bus station exploded, but the speaker only imagines she was hurt.
   d. Because his mother once frequented Magherafelt, the speaker imagines her to have been affected by the explosion.

____ 9. What does the coalman represent, or symbolize, at the end of "Two Lorries"?
   a. the mother's flirtations
   b. death
   c. the explosion
   d. Ireland itself

____ 10. Choose the statement that best summarizes the main idea of this stanza from "Two Lorries."

> To deliver farther on. This time the lode
> Our coal came from was silk-black, so the ashes
> Will be the silkiest white. The Magherafelt
> (Via Toomebridge) bus goes by. The half-stripped lorry
> With its emptied, folded coal-bags moves my mother:
> The tasty ways of a leather-aproned coalman!

   a. My mother is tempted by the coalman's words.
   b. Silk-black coal produces the whitest ashes.
   c. While the coalman was there, the Magherafelt bus went by.
   d. The coalman is tidy about folding his coal-bags.

____ 11. Considering the poet's word choices in "Two Lorries," which statement foreshadows what eventually happens?
   a. The mother being "moved" foreshadows her involvement in the explosion.
   b. The "leather-aproned coalman" foreshadows the other lorry driver.
   c. The ashes, the bus, and the empty bags foreshadow the aftermath of the bus station explosion.
   d. The phrase "To deliver farther on" foreshadows the lorry driver's next delivery.

____ 12. Choose the statement that best describes Heaney's attitude toward violence in Ireland, as expressed in "Two Lorries."
   a. Violence is inevitable.
   b. Violence is furtive and utterly destructive.
   c. Violence is a natural consequence of the people's hatred.
   d. Violence was a part of his childhood, so it must be a part of his adulthood as well.

____ 13. In "Outside History," the speaker claims that stars are outside history because
   a. they have always existed.
   b. what happens to the stars is of no consequence to humans.
   c. their light happened thousands of years before we see it.
   d. there is no intelligent life in outer space.

_____ 14. In "Outside History," the line "And we are too late. We are always too late" probably means
      a. we cannot change history.
      b. life goes on even when we are not paying attention.
      c. we always understand a situation too late to change it.
      d. some events are inevitable.

_____ 15. The imagery in "Outside History"
      a. is completely abstract.
      b. is concrete only when the speaker mentions the stars.
      c. is almost nonexistent as the poet speaks in philosophical terms.
      d. becomes more concrete as the speaker gets involved with the "ordeal."

_____ 16. Which is the best summary of "Outside History"?
      a. The stars witness everything that happens.
      b. The stars have given us light for thousands of years, but eventually they die.
      c. Some choose to keep their distance. I chose to become involved, but I am too late.
      d. There is nothing we can do to save dying people out in the fields and roads.

Vocabulary and Grammar

On the line, write the letter of the one best answer.

_____ 17. The boy was a _nuisance_ because he
      a. caused trouble.
      b. wasn't able to be helpful.
      c. followed his father instead of walking beside him.
      d. was just learning how to plow.

_____ 18. All people are _mortal_ because they
      a. are born.   c. make mistakes.
      b. eventually die.   d. have feelings and emotions.

_____ 19. Choose the item that contains only concrete nouns.
      a. cord, signature, generosity
      b. margin, photograph, mask
      c. attitude, blanket, lake
      d. echo, fear, splash

_____ 20. Which line contains an abstract noun?
      a. "It's raining on black coal and warm wet ashes."
      b. "And films no less! The conceit of a coalman . . ."
      c. "I stumbled in his hobnailed wake,"
      d. "That will blow the bus station to dust and ashes . . ."

Essay Questions

21. In an essay, discuss the style Seamus Heaney uses in "Follower." Include diction, imagery, rhythm, and form in your discussion. Consider, also, the effect of the style on the meaning of the poem. Cite examples whenever you can to support your observations about style.

22. Heaney and Boland express some of their views, at least about Ireland and its "troubles," in the poems "Two Lorries" and "Outside History." In an essay, explain what each poet's views are, using evidence from the respective poems. Then compare their views.

23. In an essay, identify each of the two incidents in the poem "Two Lorries," in literal terms as well as in terms of their personal and psychological impact on the speaker. What, other than the lorry, connects the two incidents or memories in the speaker's mind?

"No Witchcraft for Sale" by Doris Lessing

Selection Test

Critical Reading

On the line, write the letter of the one best answer.

_____ 1. In Doris Lessing's "No Witchcraft for Sale," Gideon is
    a. a herder.
    b. a local medicine man.
    c. the Farquars' cook.
    d. a scientist.

_____ 2. Gideon's attitude toward Teddy as a young child could best be described as
    a. kind but distant.
    b. fond and indulgent.
    c. patient and indifferent.
    d. polite but hostile.

_____ 3. Why was Mrs. Farquar fond of Gideon?
    a. He was affectionate toward Teddy.
    b. He had helped others in the area accept them.
    c. He had a knowledge of native ways.
    d. He was wiser than she.

_____ 4. What effect did Gideon's explanation of the different destinies awaiting Teddy and a young black child have on Mrs. Farquar?
    a. She wondered whether he was being sarcastic.
    b. She objected to his acceptance of this situation.
    c. She recognized that they had a different sense of "God's will."
    d. She felt closer to him because she thought she understood his feelings.

_____ 5. How did Gideon change after Teddy used his scooter to terrorize Gideon's son?
    a. He became distant and formal.
    b. He tried harder to teach Teddy right from wrong.
    c. He became angry and restrained.
    d. He became sad and silent.

_____ 6. How did Teddy respond to Gideon's change after the scooter incident?
    a. He was unaware of the change, not understanding Gideon's words.
    b. He missed Gideon's closeness but began to assume the role of master.
    c. He was determined to receive a full explanation of Gideon's attitude.
    d. He turned to his parents as interpreters of the event.

_____ 7. Teddy's eyes were injured by
    a. a scooter accident.
    b. a venomous insect.
    c. a spitting snake.
    d. sap from a potted plant.

_____ 8. Gideon's remedy for Teddy's eyes
     a. worked because he believed it would.
     b. supplemented the permanganate.
     c. came from a witch doctor.
     d. was a form of native herbal treatment.

_____ 9. The Farquars' response to Gideon after the incident with Teddy's eyes was
     a. to take Gideon's effort for granted.
     b. profound respect.
     c. inexpressible gratitude.
     d. to attempt to profit from the cure.

_____ 10. These sorts of cures
     a. had no scientific validity.
     b. were commonly reported.
     c. were mere legends before this incident.
     d. were usually hoaxes.

_____ 11. The general attitude of the white community toward these cures was
     a. outright disbelief.
     b. shocked discovery.
     c. bemused amazement.
     d. neutrality.

_____ 12. Why did the colonists have so little understanding of this form of medicine?
     a. Technology had not developed for full analysis to be performed.
     b. The colonists were contemptuous and would not investigate adequately.
     c. The native people would not explain the philosophy or details to people who wouldn't understand them.
     d. The native Africans hated the colonists and would not help them.

_____ 13. When the scientist came, why did he shift his approach in discussing the remedy with the Farquars?
     a. He saw they did not really know what had happened.
     b. He saw they did not understand the native people.
     c. He saw they were trying to protect Gideon.
     d. He saw they were uninterested in money.

_____ 14. When the Farquars called Gideon to talk to the scientist, his response was
     a. a clever deceit.
     b. embarrassed humility.
     c. grudging cooperation.
     d. stubborn defiance.

_____ 15. Gideon ultimately gave no help to the Farquars and the scientist about the cure because
     a. he wished to protect the cure and his culture.
     b. he believed his knowledge would be of no value in another culture.
     c. he was interested only in curing people, not in how or why it worked.
     d. he was offended at being embarrassed in front of the scientist.

Vocabulary and Grammar

On the line, write the letter of the one best answer.

____ 16. The word *skeptical* means
    a. careless.
    b. unbelieving.
    c. secretive.
    d. hostile.

____ 17. Something you regard *reverently* is something you think of with
    a. respect.
    b. fear.
    c. anticipation.
    d. nostalgia.

____ 18. Considering the *efficacy* of an action is evaluating its
    a. goal.
    b. history.
    c. cost.
    d. effectiveness.

____ 19. Which sentence is grammatically *correct*?
    a. Like he had suspected, Gideon learned the Farquars didn't understand him.
    b. Mrs. Farquar could just not think like Gideon did.
    c. Gideon could no longer treat Teddy like an innocent child.
    d. Neither could Gideon accept being treated like the scientist would treat him.

____ 20. In the sentence, "He spoke to Mr. Farquar like an unwilling servant," the word *like* is a
    a. preposition.
    b. verb.
    c. subordinate conjunction.
    d. coordinating conjunction.

Essay Questions

21. In "No Witchcraft for Sale," Gideon seems to like and respect the Farquars, and the Farquars like and respect Gideon. Why can't they communicate on some fundamental issues? Write an essay in which you describe and explain the basic conflict, discussing the points of view of the Farquars and Gideon on the events in the story. Use examples from the story to illustrate your ideas.

22. In "No Witchcraft for Sale," the scientist has evidence that something remarkable happened at the Farquars and comes to see about it, although with low expectations. What role does the scientist play in the story? Write an essay in which you explain how Lessing presents the scientist and what the scientist represents in the larger context Lessing is trying to make. Use examples from the story to support your points.

23. In spite of basic differences between cultures, it's clear that Gideon has great affection for the young Teddy. If Gideon is willing to help the colonists by saving the boy, why won't he help them by sharing information about the cure? Write an essay in which you explain the difference between these two actions. Use examples from the story to support your ideas.

"The Rights We Enjoy, The Duties We Owe" by Tony Blair

Selection Test

Critical Reading

On the line, write the letter of the one best answer.

_____ 1. The economic philosophy of the early 1980's, "Get what you can," belonged to the
  a. Labor Party.
  b. liberals.
  c. conservatives.
  d. left.

_____ 2. According to Blair, people's insecurity is at a peak because of
  a. an emphasis on duty and cooperation.
  b. a sense of interdependence.
  c. so many huge changes in family, economy, and technology.
  d. the state's failure to grant people rights.

_____ 3. Blair rejected 10 Downing Street as a home because
  a. Margaret Thatcher had lived there.
  b. it could not house his family comfortably.
  c. he felt obligated to live in a more modest house.
  d. he wanted to "do his own thing."

_____ 4. Blair considers "negative duty"
  a. bureaucratic.
  b. too coercive.
  c. essential for strong and active community.
  d. inadequately passive.

_____ 5. On what does Blair want personal advancement to be based?
  a. birth
  b. technological power
  c. merit
  d. regulation

_____ 6. William Morris, Robert Owen, and William Cobbett were all
  a. mechanical reformers.
  b. Labor Party members.
  c. "fathers" of socialism.
  d. minimal citizens.

_____ 7. Blair's use of a phrase that comes from the Bible, "brother's keeper," is consistent with the Labor Party's
  a. social individualism.
  b. belief in "tyranny of collective coercion."
  c. emphasis on "negative duty."
  d. insistence on moral responsibility.

8. Overall, Blair implies that Margaret Thatcher's government was
   a. egalitarian.
   b. death oriented.
   c. mechanical.
   d. well equipped to meet forces of changes.

9. According to Blair, what elements must be combined in order to achieve social improvement?
   a. bureaucracy and regulation
   b. class structures and rights united with obligations
   c. moral and mechanical reform
   d. powerful collectivist institutions and religion

10. Blair's rejection of "a return to the old hierarchy of deference" sums up his stand against
    a. elitism.
    b. rules.
    c. collective coercion.
    d. enlightened self-interest.

Essay Questions

11. Blair asserts, "People don't want to live in a social vacuum." Write an essay judging whether Blair makes a convincing argument for this claim. How are the individual and society linked, according to Blair? What benefits does he promise to citizens who practice moral responsibility?

12. Toward the end of the selection, Blair quotes G.D.H. Cole's phrase "a socialist society . . . must rest on the widest possible diffusion of power and responsibility." Write a detailed essay demonstrating that Blair himself sees such diffusion as starting with gender and class issues.

13. Consider Blair's praise of the values held by the Labor Party since the mid–nineteenth century in the context of his comment about our insecure era. Write an essay explaining how Blair manages to reconcile his party's traditional principles with the realities of a drastically changing world at the end of the twentieth century. How does he make the principles seem more timely than ever instead of old-fashioned?

Part Test, Unit 6, Part 2: Conflicts Abroad and at Home

Critical Reading

The questions below are based on the following selection.

The following selection is taken from Margaret Drabble's story "A Voyage to Cythera." Cythera is a Greek island near which the Greek goddess of love, Aphrodite, was said to have risen from the sea. In this story, the main character, Helen, is asked by a man on a train to mail a letter. Helen becomes intrigued by the idea of the woman to whom the letter was sent, so she sets out to find the woman's home and catch a glimpse of her. In this excerpt, she is standing outside the woman's window.

But there was no need to knock at the door. Victoria Place, when she reached it, was a short main street of tall terraced houses, either newly recovered or so smart that they had never lapsed: the number 24 was brightly illuminated, shining brightly forth into the gathering darkness. She walked slowly toward it, realizing that she would be able to see whatever there was to see without knocking: realizing that fate had connived with her curiosity by providing a bus stop directly outside the house, so that she could stand there and wait without fear of detection. She took her place at the bus stop, and stood there for a moment before she gathered her courage to turn around, and then she turned. The lights were on in the two lower floors, and she could see straight into the basement, a room which most closely resembled in shape the one where she herself lived. The room seemed at first sight to be full of people, and there was so much activity that it took some time to sort them out. There were two women, and four children; no, five children, for there was a baby sitting in a corner on a blue rug. The larger children were putting up a Christmas tree, and one of the women was laying the table for tea, while the other, her back to the window, one elbow on the mantelpiece, appeared to be reading aloud a passage from a book. It was a large, bright room, with a green carpet, and white walls, and red painted wooden furniture; even the table was painted red. A children's room. It shone, it glittered. A mobile of golden fishes hung from the ceiling, and the carpet was strewn with colored glass and tinsel decorations for the tree.

On the line, write the letter of the one best answer.

_____ 1. What can you infer from the narrator's statement that "there was no need to knock at the door" and from her description of the bus stop?
    a. She is angry that she does not have the courage to knock on the door.
    b. She wishes that she could meet the people inside the house.
    c. She is relieved that she does not have to draw attention to herself.
    d. She hopes that a bus arrives soon.

_____ 2. What does the narrator see inside the house?
    a. women and children socializing in the basement room of the house
    b. a formal dinner
    c. women and children sitting quietly in the basement room of the house
    d. darkness

_____ 3. What can you infer from the fact that the narrator had to "gather her courage" before she could turn to look inside the home?
    a. She is feeling cheerful and without worries.
    b. She is not expecting to see anything inside the home that will interest her.
    c. She is bold and does not care if she is seen.
    d. She is anxious about what she might see and about looking in on the people in the home.

_____ 4. What tone is conveyed as the narrator describes standing outside?
   a. cautiousness
   b. cheerfulness
   c. anger
   d. indifference

_____ 5. From the descriptions of setting, what kind of atmosphere would you say exists in the children's room?
   a. tense and anxious
   b. warm and cheerful
   c. bleak and cold
   d. angry and bitter

_____ 6. What can you infer about the speaker's lifestyle, judging by her statement that the children's room resembles the shape of the room in which she herself lives?
   a. She often holds social gatherings like the one being held in the house.
   b. She lives with many people.
   c. She lives in a single room and does not have as extravagant a lifestyle as the people in the home.
   d. She lives an extravagant life.

_____ 7. What is the speaker's tone in the following passage from the selection?

   > It was a large, bright room, with a green carpet, and white walls, and red painted wooden furniture; even the table was painted red. A children's room. It shone, it glittered.

   a. angry
   b. admiring
   c. mocking
   d. sad

_____ 8. From details provided in this selection, you might best describe the narrator as
   a. curious and wishful.
   b. bitter and angry.
   c. insensitive.
   d. bored.

_____ 9. Why does the narrator contrast the darkness of the street outside with the illuminated children's room?
   a. to show the narrator's connection with the people in the home
   b. to emphasize the unhappiness of the people in the home
   c. to emphasize the narrator's separation from the activities of the home
   d. to help readers understand the events of the story

_____ 10. What effect do you predict the setting of the children's room is likely to have on this narrator?
   a. It is likely to make her more content in her own life.
   b. It is likely to fill her with disgust and a wish to return home.
   c. It is likely to increase her feelings of wishfulness and loneliness.
   d. It is likely to fill her with the Christmas spirit.

Vocabulary and Grammar

The question on the next page consists of a related pair of words in CAPITAL LETTERS followed by four lettered pairs of words. Choose the pair that best expresses a relationship similar to that of the pair in capital letters.

_____ 11. ADVERSITY : MISFORTUNE ::
   a. difficulty : problem
   b. generosity : money
   c. simplicity : complicate
   d. unity : discord

On the line, write the letter of the one best answer.

_____ 12. What is the best meaning of the word *persistent* as it is used in the sentence?

   A persistent autumn rain shower flooded the gardens.

   a. light   c. cold
   b. violent   d. continuing

_____ 13. Which of the italicized nouns in the sentence is abstract?

   Eavan Boland writes about an *ordeal* whose darkness reaches her from various *fields*, *rivers*, and *roads*.

   a. fields   c. rivers
   b. ordeal   d. roads

_____ 14. Rupert Brooke and many of the soldiers with _____ he fought in World War I were people _____ valued England and patriotism.
   a. who, whom   c. whom, who
   b. whom, whom   d. who, who

_____ 15. Which part of the sentence is a nonrestrictive adjective clause?

   To Gideon, the Farquars were like old friends, and he treated Teddy, who was their son, as if he were the most special child in the village.

   a. were like old friends
   b. who was their son
   c. as if he were the most special child
   d. in the village

Essay Questions

16. The selections in this section address the theme of conflict in different ways. Choose the selection that you found most effective, and write a short essay describing how it addresses the theme of conflict. In your essay, answer the following questions: What conflict is highlighted in the selection? What did you find most effective about the selection?

17. Many of the pieces in this section reveal how the human spirit survives under adverse conditions. In this section, you encountered poems that describe the patriotism and loyalty that help soldiers to survive difficult battles; speeches and poems that take important positions in political conflicts; and stories that reveal strong and admirable characters. Write an essay describing how one piece from the section reveals something special about the strength of the human spirit. Provide details from the selection you choose.

18. Writers of poems and stories use specific words and phrases to create tone and atmosphere. Understanding a literary work's tone and atmosphere can help you find meaning in the piece. In an essay, explain how the writers create a specific tone or atmosphere in two pieces from the section. What words and details does each writer use? How do tone and atmosphere reveal meaning in each?

Name _____ Date _____

"The Lagoon" by Joseph Conrad
"Araby" by James Joyce

Selection Test

Critical Reading

On the line, write the letter of the one best answer.

_____ 1. In "The Lagoon," which description of setting symbolically reflects the meaning of the story?
  a. "The churned-up water frothed alongside with a confused murmur."
  b. ". . . tortuous, fabulously deep; filled with gloom under the thin strip of pure and shining blue of the heaven."
  c. "Nothing moved on the river but the eight paddles that rose flashing regularly . . ."
  d. ". . . the slanting beams of sunset touched the broadside of the canoe with a fiery glow . . ."

_____ 2. Why does Conrad fail to characterize the white man fully?
  a. to focus on Arsat and the Malays
  b. to show that the man's life is uninteresting
  c. to reflect the man's rootlessness and detachment
  d. to symbolize human hollowness

_____ 3. Which words best describe the relationship between the white man and Arsat in "The Lagoon"?
  a. unequal but respectful
  b. tender but uncaring
  c. distant but envious
  d. wary but jovial

_____ 4. At several points in "The Lagoon," when Arsat is telling his story, he pauses, listens toward the hut, and continues. At these moments, Arsat is probably
  a. thinking that the white man is bored.
  b. worrying if Diamelen is still breathing.
  c. trying to remember what happens next in his story.
  d. wanting to be alone.

_____ 5. At the end of "The Lagoon," when the white man resumes his posture from the opening scene, Conrad suggests that the man
  a. is unaffected by his experience.
  b. seeks comfort in habit.
  c. is perpetually restless.
  d. fears his steersman.

_____ 6. In "The Lagoon," what is the primary effect of the story within a story?
  a. It illuminates the white man's inner struggle.
  b. It intensifies Arsat's experience.
  c. It explains why the steersman is afraid of Arsat.
  d. It makes Arsat's story seem unreal.

_____ 7. What is the theme of "The Lagoon"?
   a. Cultural differences can be bridged, with enough good will.
   b. People have no business meddling in foreign affairs.
   c. We are ultimately alone with our own consciences.
   d. Western culture offers nothing of value.

_____ 8. What is Joyce's attitude toward the Dubliners in this passage from "Araby"?

   The other houses of the street, conscious of decent lives within them, gazed at one
   another with brown imperturbable faces.

   a. sympathetic
   b. contemptuous
   c. disappointed
   d. sorrowful

_____ 9. What does this passage from "Araby" reveal about the boy's uncle?

   I heard him talking to himself and heard the hallstand rocking when it had received
   the weight of his overcoat. I could interpret these signs.

   a. He is eccentric.
   b. He is lonely.
   c. He is undependable.
   d. He is drunk.

_____ 10. What does the boy in "Araby" feel when he hears his uncle talking to himself?
   a. regret
   b. fear
   c. anxiety
   d. rage

_____ 11. Which word best describes Joyce's attitude toward the boy in "Araby"?
   a. understanding   c. superior
   b. respectful   d. indulgent

_____ 12. Which detail in this passage from "Araby" is the strongest indicator of the boy's inner
   feelings?

   I found myself in a big hall girdled at half its height by a gallery. Nearly all the stalls
   were closed and the greater part of the hall was in darkness.

   a. the hall's height
   b. the gallery that girdles the hall
   c. the stalls
   d. the hall's darkness

_____ 13. At the end of "Araby," the boy experiences anger and sadness because his epiphany
   reveals that
   a. he will never be able to satisfy his desires.
   b. he will have to disappoint Mangan's sister.
   c. he cannot buy someone's love.
   d. he will always fall short of his goals.

_____ 14. In a broad sense, the boy's epiphany in "Araby" reveals the
   a. futility of human pursuits.
   b. indifference of society to individuals.
   c. pervasiveness of self-deception.
   d. pointlessness of religious ceremony.

Vocabulary and Grammar

On the line, write the letter of the one best answer.

____ 15. In "The Lagoon," Arsat discovers that his brother, who is overcome by his pursuers, is not ____.
  a. invincible
  b. august
  c. garrulous
  d. derided

____ 16. The ____ white man shows very little emotion as he listens to Arsat's story.
  a. invincible
  b. propitiate
  c. imperturbable
  d. garrulous

____ 17. Although his uncle ____ him, the boy in "Araby" still wanted to go to the bazaar.
  a. portals
  b. conflagration
  c. litanies
  d. derided

____ 18. Which sentence contains an adverb clause?
  a. "The white man . . . looked back at the shining ripple of the boat's wake."
  b. "Before the sampan passed out of the lagoon into the creek he lifted his eyes."
  c. "Arsat had not moved."
  d. "He stood lonely in the searching sunshine . . . ."

____ 19. In which item is the adverb clause underlined?
  a. <u>She lay still,</u> as if dead; but her big eyes, wide open, glittered in the gloom . . .
  b. She lay still, <u>as if dead;</u> but her big eyes, wide open, glittered in the gloom . . .
  c. She lay still, as if dead; but her big eyes, <u>wide open,</u> glittered in the gloom . . .
  d. She lay still, as if dead; but her big eyes, wide open, <u>glittered in the gloom</u> . . .

____ 20. What word in the sentence is modified by an adverb clause?

When I came downstairs again I found Mrs. Mercer sitting at the fire.

  a. downstairs
  b. I
  c. found
  d. sitting

Essay Questions

21. In both stories, the exterior setting provides clues to the interior lives of the characters. In an essay, explain how envisioning the physical setting and action in either "The Lagoon" or "Araby" leads to revelations about the characters' inner reactions.

22. Conrad and Joyce use different plot devices to strengthen the underlying meaning of their stories. Write an essay in which you analyze each writer's use of a plot device, and explain how its use affects the story. Support your main points with evidence from the stories.

23. As representatives of Modernist literature, what statement do "The Lagoon" and "Araby" make about the individual in the twentieth century? In an essay, consider this question, and draw conclusions about the stories' meaning and the writers' techniques for conveying meaning. Support your opinion with evidence from the selections.

"The Lady in the Looking Glass: A Reflection" by Virginia Woolf
"The First Year of My Life" by Muriel Spark

Selection Test

Critical Reading

On the line, write the letter of the one best answer.

_____ 1. Virginia Woolf most likely wrote "The Lady in the Looking Glass" to
   a. re-create the sensation of a mental breakdown.
   b. examine the philosophical issue of reality.
   c. teach a lesson about upper-middle-class life.
   d. indulge her passion for vivid description.

_____ 2. What question about Woolf's narrator is invited by this passage?

> The house was empty, and one felt, since one was the only person in the drawing room, like one of those naturalists who, covered with grass and leaves, lie watching the shyest animals . . .

   a. Where is the narrator?
   b. Is the narrator a naturalist?
   c. Who is the narrator?
   d. What kind of animals is the narrator watching?

_____ 3. Woolf stylistically re-creates the thought process of the narrator by
   a. allowing ideas to accumulate into long paragraphs.
   b. jumping erratically from subject to subject.
   c. producing a rhythmic, dreamlike effect.
   d. using informal grammatical constructions.

_____ 4. What is Woolf's attitude toward factual information about Isabella?
   a. She finds the facts meaningless.
   b. She ridicules the facts as conventional.
   c. She is overwhelmed by the variety of facts.
   d. She deliberatly ignores the facts.

_____ 5. What does Woolf's narrator suggest by contrasting the outdoor scene and its mirror image as "all changing here, all stillness there"?
   a. The mirror isn't positioned to reflect any action in the garden.
   b. The narrator envies Isabella's composure.
   c. The narrator's thoughts are more turbulent than the outside world.
   d. Time has stopped in Isabella's house.

_____ 6. One of the most striking aspects of a stream-of-consciousness narrative is the relative absence of
   a. conflict.
   b. motivation.
   c. tone.
   d. plot.

____ 7. What is the theme of "The Lady in the Looking Glass"?
   a. Familiarity breeds contempt.
   b. It is impossible to really know and understand another person.
   c. Money can't buy happiness.
   d. Imagination is as important as information gained through the senses.

____ 8. In Muriel Spark's story, what is most significant about the first year of the narrator's life?
   a. The narrator never smiles.
   b. It coincides with the last year of World War I.
   c. The narrator is aware of mourning women.
   d. Her family is amazed at her special talent.

____ 9. Which quotation from "The First Year of My Life" reveals that the story has an omniscient narrator?
   a. "Babies, in their waking hours, know everything that is going on everywhere in the world . . ."
   b. "There were those black-dressed people, females of the species to which I appeared to belong, saying they had lost their sons."
   c. "I woke and tuned into Bernard Shaw who was telling someone to shut up."
   d. "My mother's brother, dressed in his uniform, came coughing."

____ 10. The predominant tone of "The First Year of My Life" is
   a. pessimistic.
   b. bemused.
   c. anxious.
   d. scornful.

____ 11. What question is invited by the following passage from "The First Year of My Life"?

   Now the sentries used bodies for barricades and the fighting men were unhealthy from the start. I checked my toes and fingers, knowing I was going to need them.

   a. How does the narrator know these details about the war?
   b. What role does the narrator expect to play in world affairs?
   c. Why were the fighting men unhealthy?
   d. What does the narrator think of the war?

____ 12. In "The First Year of My Life," what can be inferred from the fact that the narrator does not smile during her first year?
   a. She has found nothing about human affairs that amuses her.
   b. She developed slowly.
   c. She is stubbornly thwarting her family's expectations.
   d. She smiles only when she is alone.

____ 13. Why does Spark interweave the narration of her development with the events of World War I?
   a. to contrast a baby's healthy development with the war's destruction
   b. to distract from the atrocities of war
   c. to balance the story
   d. to condemn Britain's role in the war

____ 14. In the "First Year of My Life," what is the significance of the narrator's smile at the end of the story?
   a. She finally develops a sense of humor.
   b. She finds men more amusing than women.
   c. She is overcome by the absurdity of war.
   d. She loses her ability to tune in to everything in the world.

Vocabulary and Grammar

On the line, write the letter of the one best answer.

____ 15. After World War I, many writers contemplated the ____ quality of modern life, characterized by ____ and a sense of loss.
   a. suffused, omniscient
   b. omniscient, upbraidings
   c. transient, evanescence
   d. reticent, authenticity

____ 16. By peering at Isabella's image in the looking glass, the narrator ____ the woman's true character.
   a. discerned
   b. omniscient
   c. authenticity
   d. suffused

____ 17. A baby who never smiles will probably become a (an) ____ child.
   a. suffused
   b. transient
   c. omniscient
   d. reticent

____ 18. After World War I, there ____ many young men who suffered lung damage from poisonous gas.
   a. is   c. was
   b. are   d. were

____ 19. Which sentence contains correct subject-verb agreement?
   a. From the hallway are sighs and whispers of passersby.
   b. There were the sound of shy animals stepping cautiously into the room.
   c. Here is the shadows of leaves cast by light.
   d. In the garden is traveler's joy and convolvulus.

____ 20. The narrator recalled that on her first birthday, there ____ a birthday cake with one candle.
   a. is
   b. was
   c. are
   d. were

Essay Questions

21. What role do imagination and reality play in these stories by Woolf and Spark? In an essay, explain how each writer views imagination and reality and how the contrasting qualities are presented in their stories. Use examples from the stories to support your main ideas.

22. Woolf and Spark experiment with point of view. How successful are these experiments? In an essay, describe and analyze each writer's technique. Determine what effect each writer achieves and how point of view affects the story's meaning.

23. Both Woolf and Spark create narrators who reveal their thought process in a hodgepodge of ideas and impressions. How does this narrative technique reflect truths about modern life? Write an essay in which you relate Woolf's and Spark's narrative techniques to the modern era.

"The Rocking-Horse Winner" by D. H. Lawrence
"A Shocking Accident" by Graham Greene

Selection Test

Critical Reading

On the line, write the letter of the one best answer.

____ 1. In "The Rocking-Horse Winner," how is Paul's attitude toward luck different from his mother's?
  a. He doesn't believe luck and money are related.
  b. He believes people can create their own luck.
  c. He blames other people for his bad luck.
  d. He relies on luck to make up for recklessness.

____ 2. In "The Rocking-Horse Winner," Paul starts betting on horse races because he
  a. succumbs to Bassett's urgings.
  b. listens to his rocking horse.
  c. hopes to relieve his mother's anxiety.
  d. inherits the family's weakness for gambling.

____ 3. The rocking horse in "The Rocking-Horse Winner" adds to the story's fairy-tale style because it
  a. is used as another character.
  b. ultimately causes Paul's death.
  c. brings Paul and his mother together.
  d. seems to have supernatural powers.

____ 4. In "The Rocking-Horse Winner," the character of Paul is portrayed as
  a. immoral beyond redemption.
  b. victimized by his parents' greed.
  c. spoiled and irresponsible.
  d. passive in the face of opportunity.

____ 5. In "The Rocking-Horse Winner," the reader is meant to interpret Paul's riding his horse as a
  a. harmless pastime.
  b. sign of immaturity.
  c. challenge to his mother.
  d. desperate activity.

____ 6. In "The Rocking-Horse Winner," Paul doesn't reveal the secret of his rocking horse because he
  a. wants to preserve its special powers.
  b. is a deceitful child.
  c. fears ridicule.
  d. has been sworn to secrecy by Bassett.

____ 7. One of Lawrence's themes in "The Rocking-Horse Winner" is the
  a. ways that materialism can warp people psychologically.
  b. power of supernatural forces over people's lives.
  c. need children have for strict discipline.
  d. high cost of taking unnecessary risks.

_____ 8. What is the "shocking accident" of Greene's story?
   a. A spy is shot by secret police.
   b. A pig falls on a man and kills him.
   c. An ostracized boy takes his revenge on his tormentors.
   d. An engaged couple dies in a car accident.

_____ 9. In relation to "A Shocking Accident," what word best describes Jerome's attitude toward his father's memory?
   a. worshipful
   b. conflicted
   c. negative
   d. rejecting

_____ 10. In "A Shocking Accident," why does it pain Jerome to hear his aunt tell strangers the story of his father's death?
   a. He is embarrassed by the story.
   b. He resents his aunt because his father favored her.
   c. He feels his aunt doesn't cherish his father's memory as he does.
   d. He wants to tell the story himself.

_____ 11. Which symbol from "A Shocking Accident" best supports the theme that things are out of place?
   a. the school
   b. the album
   c. the pig
   d. Sally

_____ 12. In reading "A Shocking Accident," a reader identifying with Jerome's dilemma about sharing his father's story with Sally would feel
   a. frustrated.
   b. ambivalent.
   c. amused.
   d. sad.

_____ 13. Sally's question in "A Shocking Accident" about the pig is ironic because
   a. the same question that isolated Jerome from others forms a tighter bond between Jerome and Sally.
   b. no one knows for certain what became of the pig.
   c. she seems to care more about the pig than about Jerome's father.
   d. Jerome has pondered that question since his father's death.

_____ 14. What tone does Greene create in "A Shocking Accident"?
   a. serious   c. judgmental
   b. suspenseful   d. comic

Vocabulary and Grammar

On the line, write the letter of the one best answer.

_____ 15. In "The Rocking-Horse Winner," Paul's ability to predict winning horses is _____.
   a. discreet
   b. brazening
   c. uncanny
   d. remonstrated

____ 16. Despite his mother's objections, Paul ____ refused to stop riding the rocking horse.
    a. careered
    b. obstinately
    c. embarked
    d. intrinsically

____ 17. In "A Shocking Accident," one of the main conflicts involves Jerome's ____ about revealing the details of his father's death.
    a. discreet
    b. brazening
    c. remonstrated
    d. apprehension

____ 18. Uncle Oscar suggests that Paul ____ careful with his money.
    a. is
    b. be
    c. remains
    d. act

____ 19. "If you ____ me and I ____ you," said his mother, "I wonder what we *should* do!"
    a. was, was
    b. were, was
    c. was, were
    d. were, were

____ 20. Jerome is not certain what he would do if Sally ____ to laugh at the story.
    a. is
    b. was
    c. were
    d. weren't

Essay Questions

21. Both Paul in "The Rocking-Horse Winner" and Jerome in "A Shocking Accident" experience difficulties due to events beyond their control. What problems does each character face? What does he feel? As a reader, how do you identify with the character? Focusing on either Paul or Jerome, explore and answer these questions in an essay, incorporating appropriate details from the stories.

22. In "A Shocking Accident," Greene depicts life as unpredictable and bizarre. How accurate is his assessment? Do you agree with his evaluation of modern life? In an essay, explain the view of life expressed in "A Shocking Accident," supporting your points with details from the story. Then critique this view, by stating your opinion and by supporting it with reasonable evidence.

23. In "The Rocking-Horse Winner," symbolism enhances Lawrence's theme. What meaning or meanings does the symbol of the rocking horse have? What theme or themes does it reflect? In an essay, explain how Lawrence uses symbolism to convey theme. Support your ideas with evidence from the story.

"The Book of Sand" by Jorge Luis Borges

Selection Test

Critical Reading

On the line, write the letter of the one best answer.

_____ 1. The Book of Sand is called that because
   a. the stranger bought it in the desert.
   b. it resembles sand in having neither beginning nor end.
   c. it was buried in the plain.
   d. its previous owner did not know how to read.

_____ 2. The narrator calls his new acquisition "the impossible book" because it
   a. belonged to an untouchable.
   b. embodies infinity in a finite object.
   c. should have gone to the British Museum.
   d. could cover the planet with sand.

_____ 3. Along with the book, the narrator also acquires the stranger's
   a. gloomy aura.
   b. love of Stevenson.
   c. handful of rupees.
   d. broken set of *One Thousand and One Nights*.

_____ 4. Why does the narrator decide to leave the Book of Sand in the Argentine National Library?
   a. He can always find it there again.
   b. He wants others to enjoy its unique qualities.
   c. It will disappear into the vast collection there.
   d. He is too weak to go much farther.

_____ 5. What makes the narrator seem monstrous by the end of the story?
   a. his insomnia
   b. his obsession with mastering infinity
   c. his wish to destroy a priceless volume
   d. his inability to locate an illustration twice

_____ 6. One of the narrator's mistaken first impressions is that the stranger is
   a. from Scotland.
   b. old.
   c. an untouchable.
   d. an atheist.

_____ 7. A central idea of the story is that
   a. religious people find reassurance in the idea of infinity.
   b. evil cannot occur in an infinite universe.
   c. evidence of a random universe disturbs the human mind.
   d. geometry is inaccurate.

____ 8. What does the narrator's anxious search for the illustrated anchor he has seen symbolize?

    a. the human need for secure meaning in life

    b. his greed to own the Book

    c. his misanthropy

    d. the importance of Scotland to Argentina

____ 9. Borges makes the encounter between narrator and salesman even more bizarre and fantastic by having the salesman

    a. name a suspiciously low price for the Book.

    b. correct the narrator's love of Hume.

    c. come from Scandinavia.

    d. refuse to speculate on the infinity of time and space.

____ 10. One of the ironic aspects of the ending is that

    a. the library is not a forest.

    b. the narrator never sees the salesman again.

    c. it has nothing to do with the geometric principles at the beginning.

    d. the narrator is so precise about the finite space in which he leaves the infinite book.

Essay Questions

11. The narrator in "The Book of Sand" emerges not only as a bibliophile but also as someone who knows the world only through books. In an essay, discuss this aspect of the narrator and relate it to the fact that he seems somewhat out of touch with reality. Consider how such an identity adds to the story's impact.

12. The line that Borges quotes as the epigraph of this story, "Thy rope of sands . . .," comes from a poem by George Herbert (1633). Herbert's poem dramatizes the option of giving up one's faith in God or religion. In an essay, speculate on why Borges chose this particular line as a focus or clue for his story. Using details from the story, discuss how this epigraph relates to the events of the story.

13. In "The Book of Sand," the narrator's views about several things, including the book itself, are unstable. Starting with his reference to myopia, write a detailed essay about the story's concern with alternate or evolving versions of events/reality. How do these shifts in the first-person narrative relate to the Book of Sand itself?

Part Test, Unit 6, Part 3: Focus on Literary Forms—
The Short Story

Critical Reading

The questions below are based on the following selection.

In "A Dill Pickle" by Katherine Mansfield, two people who had once been in love with each other meet again years after they have parted company. Through their conversation and recollections, the woman remembers both why she once loved the man and why she loves him no more. The following excerpt is taken from the beginning of the story.

And then, after six years, she saw him again. He was seated at one of those little bamboo tables decorated with a Japanese vase of paper daffodils. There was a tall plate of fruit in front of him, and very carefully, in a way she recognized immediately as his "special" way, he was peeling an orange.

He must have felt that shock of recognition in her for he looked up and met her eyes. Incredible! He didn't know her! She smiled; he frowned. She came toward him. He closed his eyes an instant, but opening them his face lit up as though he had struck a match in a dark room. He laid down the orange and pushed back his chair, and she took her little warm hand out of her muff and gave it to him.

"Vera!" he exclaimed. "How strange. Really, for a moment I didn't know you. Won't you sit down? You've had lunch? Won't you have some coffee?"

She hesitated, but of course she meant to.

"Yes, I'd like some coffee." And she sat down opposite him.

"You've changed. You've changed very much," he said, staring at her with that eager, lighted look. "You look so well. I've never seen you look so well before."

"Really?" She raised her veil and unbuttoned her high fur collar. "I don't feel very well. I can't bear this weather, you know."

"Ah, no. You hate the cold. . . . "

"Loathe it." She shuddered. "And the worst of it is that the older one grows . . . "

On the line, write the letter of the one best answer.

_____ 1. What is the significance of the meeting between Vera and the man?
  a. They are in love with each other.
  b. They haven't seen each other for six years.
  c. It is the first time they have met.
  d. The man forgot that he was to meet Vera for lunch.

_____ 2. What does the following exchange reveal about the characters?

  "I don't feel very well. I can't bear this weather, you know."
  "Ah, no. You hate the cold. . . . "

  a. They live in a harsh climate.
  b. They enjoy each other's company.
  c. They know each other well.
  d. They never discuss serious matters.

_____ 3. In this selection, we learn the internal state of only one of the characters. Therefore, what point of view is employed in the selection?
  a. stream of consciousness   c. third-person limited
  b. omniscient   d. first person

____ 4. The selection most likely raises what question?
   a. Where is the action set?
   b. Why is the man dining alone?
   c. What does the man look like?
   d. What is the past relationship between the two characters?

____ 5. Which detail hints at a character's motivation?
   a. "She smiled; he frowned."
   b. "He laid down the orange and pushed back his chair . . ."
   c. "She hesitated, but of course she meant to."
   d. "She raised her veil and unbuttoned her high fur collar."

____ 6. What insight can be gained by envisioning the characters sitting across from each other at the "little bamboo table"?
   a. The characters move in a fast-paced social circle.
   b. The characters know each other well enough to sit in such close proximity to each other.
   c. The characters make an attractive couple.
   d. The author feels disdain for the characters.

____ 7. The selection's point of view
   a. makes the reader focus on Vera's reactions and motivations.
   b. allows the reader to follow the random flow of thoughts in Vera's mind.
   c. reveals the thoughts of both characters to the reader.
   d. alienates the reader from the action.

____ 8. Upon recognizing the man, Vera
   a. feels nervous about speaking with him.
   b. wishes to avoid his glance.
   c. wants to appear interested yet detached.
   d. has no strong feelings about getting the man's attention.

____ 9. When the man remarks that "for a moment" he didn't recognize her, Vera probably feels
   a. delighted.
   b. depressed.
   c. confused.
   d. surprised.

____ 10. What conclusion might reasonably be drawn about the characters?
   a. They are solitary people.
   b. They know very little about each other.
   c. They are mere acquaintances.
   d. They despise each other.

Vocabulary and Grammar

On the line, write the letter of the one best answer.

____ 11. As the man peeled the fruit, the air became _____ with the smell of orange.
   a. discerned
   b. suffused
   c. reticent
   d. imperturbable

____ 12. Gradually, I _____ that the lively man's _____ behavior in public was merely a cover for feelings of insecurity.
   a. embarked, discreet
   b. derided, invincible
   c. remonstrated, brazening
   d. discerned, garrulous

____ 13. For a moment, it seemed as though he _____ going to ignore her.
   a. was
   b. is
   c. were
   d. would

____ 14. There _____ paper daffodils on the table, which looked as if they _____ real.
   a. was, was
   b. were, were
   c. was, were
   d. were, was

____ 15. Which part of the sentence is the adverb clause?

   When he pushed back his chair, she crossed the room and held out her hand to him.

   a. When he pushed back his chair
   b. crossed the room
   c. held out her hand
   d. back his chair

Essay Questions

16. Many of the short stories in this section introduce memorable characters. Choose the one character who most intrigues you, and write an essay explaining why you find the character compelling. Note how you identify with the character to understand his or her feelings and motivations.

17. Most short stories center on a theme. Write an essay in which you compare and contrast the themes of two stories in this section. State the theme of each story, and compare and contrast the ways in which the themes are conveyed.

18. Although all the authors included in this section represent the modern era in British literature, the writers demonstrate varying styles. In your opinion, which story is most modern? What literary devices, themes, subject matter, or other elements make the story modern? Write an essay in which you defend your choice.

"Do Not Go Gentle into That Good Night" and "Fern Hill"
by Dylan Thomas
"The Horses" and **"The Rain Horse"** by Ted Hughes

Selection Test

Critical Reading

On the line, write the letter of the one best answer.

_____ 1. Whom does the speaker in "Do Not Go Gentle into That Good Night" address?
   a. the sun
   b. good men and wild men
   c. his father
   d. death

_____ 2. In "Do Not Go Gentle into That Good Night," the wise men "[d]o not go gentle into that good night" because
   a. they doubt their own wisdom.
   b. they envy those who were less wise.
   c. they are afraid of death.
   d. their wisdom has not inspired others.

_____ 3. Choose the statement that illustrates a reader judging the message of "Do Not Go Gentle into That Good Night."
   a. I don't like this poem.
   b. The line "Rage, rage against the dying of the light" is my favorite.
   c. Thomas uses a three-line stanza with alternating end rhyme.
   d. I think people should be more accepting of death than Thomas is.

_____ 4. The central idea of "Do Not Go Gentle into That Good Night" is that
   a. people die in the same spirit in which they lived.
   b. death always comes too soon and should be resisted.
   c. having regret at the end of one's life is pitiful.
   d. people of all ranks and stations are equal in death.

_____ 5. Which image in "Fern Hill" evokes the idea of natural simplicity and freshness?
   a. ". . . happy as the grass was green . . ."
   b. ". . . the pebbles of the holy streams."
   c. ". . . fire green as grass."
   d. ". . . a wanderer white / With the dew . . ."

_____ 6. In "Fern Hill," what does the poet mean in these lines?

   . . . the spellbound horses walking warm
   Out of the whinnying green stable
   On to the fields of praise.

   a. As a child he felt free only when he was outdoors.
   b. He recalls his boyhood as if it were a dream.
   c. Every day he appreciated the beauty of the farm.
   d. His family gave thanks in prayer each morning.

_____ 7. The line "Though I sang in my chains like the sea" closes "Fern Hill" with a feeling of
   a. bitterness.
   b. frustration.
   c. relief.
   d. triumph.

____ 8. Which statement most accurately describes Thomas's voice in "Fern Hill"?
    a. Thomas uses multiple natural images to evoke the carefree feeling of childhood.
    b. Thomas expresses bitterness that children become "out of grace."
    c. Thomas expresses his belief that children can only thrive if brought up in a natural environment.
    d. Thomas implies that children are thoughtless and "heedless" of the advantages they have.

____ 9. To whom or what does the word *him* refer, in line 45 of "Fern Hill"?

> [43] In all his tuneful turning so few and such morning songs
> Before the children green and golden
> Follow him out of grace.

    a. the farmer   c. the child who is the speaker of the poem
    b. time   d. a parent

____ 10. In "The Horses," the speaker describes
    a. a vivid memory of an early-morning walk in the country.
    b. an experience with a herd of horses that he recently had.
    c. a frightening encounter with a herd of stampeding horses.
    d. a nighttime walk through a dark field.

____ 11. In "The Horses," what does this line mean?

> Slowly detail leafed from the darkness.

    a. The leaves on the trees and bushes came out one by one.
    b. The speaker's eyes became accustomed to the darkness.
    c. Details of the landscape slowly became visible in the growing predawn light.
    d. Some leaves dropped to the ground every now and then as the speaker watched.

____ 12. Readers who are judging the message of "The Horses" might consider
    a. experiences they have had with horses in a horse stable.
    b. their own memories of an experience in a solitary natural setting.
    c. a walk they have taken at sunset.
    d. their recollection of a steamy summer night.

____ 13. In these lines from "The Horses," how does the poet use diction to contribute to the image?

> Huge in the dense gray—ten together—
> Megalith-still . . .

    a. The short phrases stand separately, as if each is a stone-still horse.
    b. The words have a "heavy" sound that contributes to the sense of the word *huge.*
    c. The separation of the phrases slows the speaker down, giving the reader the feeling that he is counting the horses.
    d. The words *huge, gray,* and *megalith* convey the sense that the horses are statues.

____ 14. Choose the best restatement of the basic story line of Hughes's "The Rain Horse."
    a. An old man remembers a time during his boyhood when a farmer's horse threatened him.
    b. A man reconstructs a boyhood experience with a horse in an attempt to analyze the animal's behavior.
    c. A young man trespasses on a farmer's land in an attempt to catch his horse.
    d. A man encounters a horse that seems intent on trampling him.

____ 15. In "The Rain Horse," what similarity is there between the man's feelings about the land and his feelings about the horse?

    a. He is sentimental about the land and the horse, both of which he remembers well from his boyhood.

    b. He is angry at the land because he feels like a stranger, and at the horse for threatening him.

    c. He is annoyed that both the land and the animal have changed since he was in that spot twelve years ago.

    d. He is frightened at being caught on the farmer's land and frightened of the horse.

____ 16. What role does the weather play in "The Rain Horse"?

    a. It adds to the man's discomfort and also tends to blur the reality of the story.

    b. It foreshadows that the man's walk will turn out unhappily.

    c. It is only natural, because the English climate is characteristically rainy.

    d. It adds to the conflict by making it harder for the man to get away from the horse.

Vocabulary and Grammar

On the line, write the letter of the one best answer.

____ 17. The man in "The Rain Horse" is *exasperated* by his situation. *Exasperated* means

    a. "full of anxiety about."   c. "extremely annoyed."

    b. "out of breath."   d. "distracted, bored."

____ 18. The trees in the woods are nondescript saplings, which means they are

    a. without significant identifying characteristics.

    b. very young and unformed.

    c. incapable of being described.

    d. of a variety the narrator cannot identify.

____ 19. Which sentence begins with an adverb clause?

    a. This hill was shaped like a wave, a gently rounded back lifting out of the valley.

    b. As he watched it, the horse ran up to that crest.

    c. All around him the boughs angled down, glistening, black as iron.

    d. Over to his right a thin, black horse was running across the ploughland towards the hill.

Essay Questions

20. In "The Rain Horse," a young man returns to a familiar site from his boyhood. In an essay, explore the following questions: What are his first impressions upon arriving at the top of the hill? How does it feel to be back after twelve years? How has that relationship changed? How does his episode with the horse affect that relationship? Finally, explain whether you think the horse was real or imagined, a thing of the past or of the present.

21. In "Do Not Go Gentle into That Good Night" and "Fern Hill," Dylan Thomas expresses feelings about various stages of life. What are those feelings, as revealed in the two poems? How do Thomas's attitudes about these stages of life fit with your own? Do you agree or disagree, accept or reject his attitudes on the basis of your own experience? In an essay, explain why.

22. In an essay, examine the poet's voice in "The Horses." Consider word choice, rhythm, and diction, which contribute to voice, in addition to looking carefully at the imagery and how Hughes creates it. Characterize the voice in this passage in your own words.

"An Arundel Tomb" and **"The Explosion"** by Philip Larkin
"On the Patio" by Peter Redgrove
"Not Waving but Drowning" by Stevie Smith

Selection Test

Critical Reading

On the line, write the letter of the one best answer.

_____ 1. In "An Arundel Tomb," the effigy shows a
   a. dog.
   b. knight and his armor.
   c. likeness of the sculptor.
   d. husband and a wife.

_____ 2. In this passage from "An Arundel Tomb," what is it that "succeeding eyes" look at, instead of reading?

> How soon succeeding eyes begin
> To look, not read. Rigidly they
> Persisted, linked, through lengths and breadths
> Of time. Snow fell, undated.

   a. the unusual inscription
   b. the earl's hand holding the countess's
   c. the dogs under their feet
   d. the earl's impressive armor

_____ 3. Which would be a strategy for reading and understanding "An Arundel Tomb"?
   a. visualizing falling snow
   b. knowing something about birdcalls
   c. visualizing "bone-riddled ground"
   d. reading in sentences

_____ 4. Choose the item in which the line of iambic tetrameter from "An Arundel Tomb" is correctly scanned.
   a. "Such plainness of the pre-baroque"
   b. "They would not think to lie so long".
   c. "The little dogs under their feet."
   d. "Of smoke in slow suspended skeins"

_____ 5. In "An Arundel Tomb," what is the meaning of these lines?

> . . . The stone fidelity
> They hardly meant has come to be
> Their final blazon . . .

   a. The earl and countess never intended for the sculptor to show them holding hands on their tomb.
   b. The earl and countess never meant for anyone to know about their fidelity.
   c. The earl and countess were not affectionate while alive, yet the affectionate gesture on their tomb is what people remember about them.
   d. The earl and countess wanted to be remembered for something else, not for their fidelity.

_____ 6. In "The Explosion," what is the immediate effect of the explosion?
  a. Normal, above-ground activities are momentarily interrupted.
  b. The wives rush to the entrance to the mine.
  c. The rabbits and larks all hide.
  d. The slagheap collapses.

_____ 7. Which best describes the tone of this stanza from "The Explosion"?

> On the day of the explosion
> Shadows pointed towards the pithead:
> In the sun the slagheap slept.

  a. fearful and mysterious
  b. excited and anticipatory
  c. tense and foreboding
  d. bitter and passionate

_____ 8. Which is a theme of "The Explosion"?
  a. People's memories keep the dead alive.
  b. Death may occur suddenly and unexpectedly.
  c. Disasters are tragic and inevitable.
  d. Grieving is an important process.

_____ 9. Which line from "The Explosion" is in straight trochaic tetrameter?
  a. In the sun the slagheap slept.
  b. One showing the eggs unbroken.
  c. Down the lane came men in pit boots
  d. We shall see them face to face—

_____ 10. In "The Explosion," the poet alters the rhythm of the lines that tell that the explosion occurs. What effect does this have?
  a. The lines sound more like an explosion.
  b. The lines get the reader's attention.
  c. The new rhythm is meant to sound like the speech of the now-dead miners.
  d. The altered rhythm conveys the sense that something "wrong" or unnatural has happened.

_____ 11. In "On the Patio," what scene is the speaker watching?
  a. the gray clouds of a thunderstorm
  b. a wineglass filling up with rainwater
  c. lightning and thunder
  d. paint chipping off a rusty patio table

_____ 12. In "On the Patio," why does the speaker say that the cloud is "crushed into a glass"?
  a. because the water in the glass is reflecting the clouds above
  b. because it is foggy and the cloud surrounds everything thickly
  c. because the wineglass holds the raindrops, which have fallen so far from the cloud above
  d. because the rain has fallen so violently that it has broken the glass

_____ 13. The speaker in "On the Patio" empties the glass because he wants to
  a. fill it up with another cloud.
  b. clean up the mess.
  c. bring the table in out of the rain.
  d. see how much it will rain.

_____ 14. In "Not Waving but Drowning," what is the gesture on which the poem focuses?
  a. a greeting
  b. a gesture of resignation
  c. a plea for help
  d. a farewell

Tomb/Explosion/Patio/Not Waving **287**

_____ 15. Which best describes the voice of the dead man in "Not Waving but Drowning"?
       a. cold   c. violent
       b. frightened   d. remorseful

_____ 16. What sense does the word *cold* have when the dead man in "Not Waving but Drowning" says "it was too cold always"?
       a. The water was always too cold when he swam.
       b. The world was uninviting and unfriendly to him.
       c. The climate never suited him.
       d. It was too cold to have gone swimming in the first place.

Vocabulary and Grammar

On the line, write the letter of the one best answer.

_____ 17. Their fidelity, or _____, is what will be remembered of the earl and countess.
       a. long lives
       b. eccentricity
       c. wealth
       d. faithfulness

_____ 18. An effigy is a (an)
       a. tomb.   c. disguise.
       b. image.   d. copy.

_____ 19. The sense of the verb tense used in the line "Time has transfigured them into / Untruth" is that the action
       a. occurred in the past.
       b. is occurring in the present.
       c. occurred in the past and continues into the present.
       d. occurred in the past before some other event.

_____ 20. What tense should a writer use to express an action or state of being that happened in the past before some other event?
       a. present   c. past
       b. present perfect   d. past perfect

Essay Questions

21. In "Not Waving but Drowning," the poet reveals the thoughts of the dead man. What are those thoughts and what is their message? What is the effect of the comments being made by the other people present? What is the effect of the poet's use of first person when expressing the dead man's thoughts? Write an essay responding to these questions.

22. In an essay discuss the central visual image of "An Arundel Tomb." How does the speaker reveal that image? What is the speaker's attitude toward the tomb? Does he admire it? Scorn it? Or something else? What legacy, according to the speaker, do the earl and countess pass on to us?

23. In the final stanzas of "The Explosion," Larkin alters the trochaic tetrameter in several places. He also makes some important diction decisions having to do with the arrangement of words, particularly in "At noon, there came a tremor; cows / Stopped chewing for a second; sun, / Scarfed as in a heat-haze, dimmed. . . ." In an essay, examine these changes carefully and comment on their effect on the poem. Also, consider the effect of the images, such as the chapels, a coin, the sun, and unbroken eggs, that Larkin creates in the last two stanzas.

Name _____ Date _____

"B. Wordsworth" by V. S. Naipaul

Selection Test

Critical Reading

On the line, write the letter of the one best answer.

_____ 1. The narrator of this story is
   a. an unnamed boy.
   b. B. Wordsworth.
   c. V. S. Naipaul.
   d. the mother of a young boy.

_____ 2. The passage of the story that describes the beggars shows that the narrator's family is
   a. charitable and naive.
   b. stingy and suspicious.
   c. poor but kindly.
   d. artistic and wealthy.

_____ 3. How does the narrator meet B. Wordsworth?
   a. The boy sees Wordsworth perform with calypso singers.
   b. They live on the same block.
   c. Wordsworth is a well-known neighborhood poet.
   d. Wordsworth begs at the boy's home.

_____ 4. Which word best characterizes B. Wordsworth's request to watch bees in the narrator's yard?
   a. typical
   b. friendly
   c. unusual
   d. threatening

_____ 5. B. Wordsworth's pastimes—watching bees, contemplating the stars, deliberating over restaurants— suggest that
   a. beekeepers should be good observers.
   b. poets should be good observers.
   c. children make good poets.
   d. many poets are frauds.

_____ 6. B. Wordsworth refers to the boy as a poet, meaning that he
   a. speaks in rhyme.
   b. is a sensitive person.
   c. is a writer.
   d. speaks in elegant language.

_____ 7. Why does B. Wordsworth call himself Black, brother to White (William) Wordsworth?
   a. He has a split personality and doesn't know who he is.
   b. The brothers have different fathers, one white and one black.
   c. He thinks he is related to the Wordsworth family.
   d. He identifies with the spirit of the famous poet.

_____ 8. What makes this selection a first-person narrative?
   a. It relates an experience from the viewpoint of someone directly involved.
   b. It tells a story from beginning to end.
   c. It relates the experiences of the first person mentioned.
   d. It provides insight into the author's personal views.

_____ 9. Which sentence might be spoken by the first-person narrator?

    I. My mother was angry with me for asking for four cents.

    II. B. Wordsworth was secretly glad to see the young boy.

    III. B. Wordsworth told a story about a girl poet and a boy poet.

    IV. I enjoyed eating the juicy mangoes.

    a. I and IV
    b. I, II, and III
    c. I, III, and IV
    d. all of the above

_____ 10. Which best describes the relationship between B. Wordsworth and the narrator?
    a. teacher and student
    b. father and son
    c. merchant and customer
    d. patron and artist

_____ 11. Which statement summarizes the likeliest reader's response to B. Wordsworth?
    a. He is a smooth-talking bum.
    b. He is a warm man with a talent for wonder, with something pitiable about him.
    c. He is an inspiring model.
    d. He is a vivid warning of the folly of poetry.

_____ 12. The girl whom poet B. Wordsworth describes was most likely
    a. his mother.
    b. the narrator's mother.
    c. his wife.
    d. the woman who came begging at noon.

_____ 13. Why does B. Wordsworth ask the boy to go away and never return?
    a. He knows his home is going to be torn down.
    b. He is afraid the boy will learn that he has lied to him.
    c. He has been angered by the boy.
    d. He doesn't want the boy to watch him die.

_____ 14. By using a first-person narrator, Naipaul emphasizes
    a. B. Wordsworth's unusual behavior.
    b. the young boy's limited knowledge of poetry.
    c. the narrator's growing relationship with B. Wordsworth.
    d. the narrator's all-knowing character.

Vocabulary and Grammar

On the line, write the letter of the one best answer.

_____ 15. What does the word _distill_ mean?
    a. to be very quiet
    b. to obtain the essential part
    c. to comprehend
    d. to distinguish between parts

_____ 16. Which of the following would you feel _keenly_?
    a. bumping into someone
    b. a shoulder massage
    c. a sharp pang of hunger
    d. stepping on a cat's tail

____ 17. Which are related forms of the word *patron*?

  I. patronize

  II. patronage

  III. patrol

  IV. patronizing

  a. I, II, IV
  b. I, II, III
  c. I and IV
  d. all of the above

____ 18. Which sentence from "B. Wordsworth" contains pronouns in a compound construction?
  a. "One day a man called and said he was hungry."
  b. "He spoke very slowly and very correctly, as though every word was costing him money."
  c. "He said, 'That's what I do, I just watch.'"
  d. "He said, 'This is just between you and me, remember.'"

____ 19. Choose the pronoun that correctly replaces the italicized words in the sentence.

  Mr. Wordsworth and *the narrator* watched the stars shine in the sky.

  a. him
  b. he
  c. his
  d. they

____ 20. Which sentence contains an incorrect pronoun case in a compound construction?
  a. Between you and I, that was the juiciest mango I've ever eaten.
  b. The narrator and he took long walks.
  c. They became friends, the poet and he.
  d. Mr. Wordsworth's yard and mango were a secret between him and me.

Essay Questions

21. The young narrator rarely describes his feelings about B. Wordsworth directly. Yet the narrator clearly responds to Wordsworth. In an essay, describe the narrator's response to Wordsworth. Support your response with details from the story.

22. Naipaul's story is written from first-person point of view. The narrator, a young boy who lives in Trinidad, provides information about characters and events from his point of view. In an essay, explain how this story might be different if it were related from an omniscient, or all-knowing, point of view. Furthermore, explain why you do or do not think first-person narration is an effective point of view for relating the story. Support your assertion with several details from the story.

23. Naipaul may be using the character of B. Wordsworth to point out a general truth about what writers are like. Alternatively, he may be making a political point—if William Wordsworth were a black man, this might be his story. In an essay, defend one or the other of these views. Explain what truth Naipaul is expressing, and use details from the story to support your interpretation.

"The Train from Rhodesia" by Nadine Gordimer

Selection Test

Critical Reading

On the line, write the letter of the one best answer.

_____ 1. "The Train from Rhodesia" explores which central idea?
   a. the economic dependence of blacks on the white minority in South Africa
   b. the marketplace economy in South Africa
   c. the varied geography of South Africa
   d. the psychological effects of moving between different cultures in South Africa

_____ 2. Which sentence best summarizes the story's theme?
   a. Do unto others as you would have them do unto you.
   b. A bargain gained at the expense of another is no bargain.
   c. Dignity is the value you place on yourself, not the value others place on you.
   d. Neither a buyer nor a seller should go back on his or her word.

_____ 3. Who are the young man and woman in the story?
   a. professional art collectors   c. journalists
   b. Rhodesians going home   d. tourists

_____ 4. What can be inferred about the old man from this line?

   The old man held [the carved lion] up to her still smiling, not from the heart, but at the customer.

   a. He is eager for the customer to like him.
   b. He takes great pride in his work.
   c. He acts friendly only because he wants to make a sale.
   d. He thinks the customer will try to take advantage of him.

_____ 5. Which is a central conflict in the story?
   a. The prices paid for the crafts will never be equal to their worth.
   b. It is difficult to relate equally to people in an unequal social or economic setting.
   c. The crafts have meaning only in their original cultural context.
   d. No matter how much money the natives get, it will not improve their lives.

_____ 6. Which cultural attitude in South Africa at the time the story was written forms the basis of the story's events?
   a. Whites value the crafts and culture of blacks.
   b. Whites ignore the cultural differences of blacks.
   c. Whites and blacks promote feelings of distrust in each other.
   d. Whites assume that blacks are not their equals.

_____ 7. Which event described in the story might be interpreted as a sign of inequality by an outside observer?
   a. The natives carve wooden animal figures to sell.
   b. The stationmaster's children fetch loaves of bread from the train.
   c. The native children ask tourists for pennies.
   d. The train passengers buy souvenirs during their travels.

_____ 8. By reading between the lines, in which passage can you discover the underlying conflict between blacks and whites in the story?

    a. "The train came out of the red horizon and bore down toward them over the single straight track."

    b. "A stir of preparedness rippled through the squatting native vendors waiting in the dust; the face of a carved wooden animal, eternally surprised, stuck out of a sack."

    c. "A man passed beneath the arch of reaching arms meeting gray-black and white in the exchange of money for the staring wooden eyes, the stiff wooden legs sticking up in the air; . . ."

    d. "Passengers drew themselves in at the corridor windows and turned into compartments to fetch money, to call someone to look."

_____ 9. In this passage from the story, what can be understood about the artists by reading between the lines?

> All up and down the length of the train in the dust the artists sprang, walking bent, like performing animals, the better to exhibit the fantasy held toward the faces on the train. Buck, startled and stiff, staring with round black and white eyes. More lions, standing erect, grappling with strange, thin, elongated warriors who clutched spears and showed no fear in their slits of eyes.

    a. They are proud of their warrior heritage and display this pride through their crafts.

    b. Because of their economic dependence upon whites, they are no longer proud warriors, but vendors of their culture.

    c. They need a creative outlet.

    d. They enjoy performing for the white tourists.

_____ 10. Which word or phrase best describes the relationship between the young man and woman by the end of the story?

    a. distant and strained

    b. affectionate

    c. respectful

    d. angry and vindictive

_____ 11. In which way is the young woman in the story different from her husband?

    a. She more actively treats the South African natives as equals.

    b. She is less interested in buying crafts from South African natives.

    c. She feels more at home amid the culture of South Africa.

    d. She is more sensitive to the dignity of the South African natives.

_____ 12. Why does the old man finally offer to sell the carved lion for "one-and-six"?

    a. He feels the lion isn't worth more.

    b. He needs the money to survive.

    c. He knows the man wanted to surprise his wife.

    d. He does not want the lion to go to anyone else.

_____ 13. What do you discover about the young man's cultural attitudes by reading between the lines of this passage?

> Here, one-and-six baas!—As one automatically opens a hand to catch a thrown ball, a man fumbled wildly down his pocket, brought up the shilling and sixpence and threw them out; the old native, gasping, his skinny toes splaying the sand, flung the lion.

    a. He sees himself as a father figure to the native South Africans.

    b. He reveals his feelings of superiority through his disrespectful treatment of the old man.

    c. He is caught up in a social system that encourages whites to see blacks as unworthy of respect.

    d. He believes whites and blacks should receive equal treatment.

_____ 14. At the end of the story, the man and the woman are in conflict with each other because
   a. the incident has brought to light their different values.
   b. she no longer cares about the carving.
   c. he resents that his wife has changed her mind.
   d. she is more responsive to the old man than to her husband.

Vocabulary and Grammar

On the line, write the letter of the one best answer.

_____ 15. The word _elongated_ means
   a. relieved.   b. lengthened.   c. yearned.   d. enlightened.

_____ 16. The word _atrophy_ contains the prefix _a-_, which means
   a. on top.   b. waste away.   c. negate.   d. without or not.

_____ 17. South African society was ____ into two parts: poor black and rich whites.
   a. impressionistic   b. expressive   c. segmented   d. splayed

_____ 18. Which sentence from "The Train from Rhodesia" contains an absolute phrase?
   a. "The stationmaster was leaning against the end of the train, green flag rolled in readiness."
   b. "The stationmaster went slowly in under the chalet."
   c. "The young man swung in from the corridor, breathless."
   d. "She was pushing it at him, trying to force him to take it."

_____ 19. Which part of this sentence is an absolute phrase?

   Joints not yet coordinated, the segmented body of the train heaved and bumped back against itself.

   a. Joints not yet coordinated
   b. the segmented body of the train
   c. heaved and bumped back against itself
   d. The sentence does not contain an absolute phrase.

_____ 20. Which part of this sentence is an absolute phrase?

   She sat down again in the corner and, her face slumped in her hand, stared out of the window.

   a. She sat down again in the corner and
   b. her face slumped in her hand
   c. stared out of the window
   d. The sentence does not contain an absolute phrase.

Essay Questions

21. In an essay explain the significance of the train's arrival for the local townspeople. How do people respond to the arrival of the train? Why? Use details from the story to support your explanation.

22. In a short story, symbolic elements may work on several levels. They may be used to highlight the story's theme, conflict, or meaning. The carved lion in "The Train from Rhodesia" is one such symbol. In an essay, explain the significance of the lion, relating it to the story's theme, conflict, and meaning.

23. Select a passage from "The Train from Rhodesia" that you think most vividly highlights the inner conflict felt by the young woman as well as the larger conflict central to the story. In an essay, explain the significance of the passage you've chosen.

from *Midsummer*, XXIII and from *Omeros* Chapter XXVIII
by Derek Walcott
"From Lucy: Englan' Lady" by James Berry

Selection Test

Critical Reading

On the line, write the letter of the one best answer.

____ 1. The excerpt from *Midsummer* primarily concerns
  a. the passing of seasons in an English town.
  b. a view of England from a nonwhite perspective.
  c. race riots in England.
  d. the failure of Shakespeare's drama in modern times.

____ 2. Which would help a reader best appreciate Walcott's *Midsummer*, XXIII?
  a. visiting the site of the Brixton riots
  b. watching African actors in Shakespearean productions
  c. visualizing the life cycle of the leaves in the poem
  d. understanding literary allusions and cultural references

____ 3. Which image from *Midsummer*, XXIII is in contrast to the mood of the rest of the poem?
  a. "midsummer's leaves race to extinction like the roar/of a Brixton riot tunneled by water hoses . . ."
  b. ". . . Their thick skulls bled with rancor/when the riot police and the skinheads exchanged quips . . ."
  c. ". . .And, for me, that closes / the child's fairy tale of an antic England—fairy rings, / thatched cottages fenced with dog roses . . ."
  d. "they seethe towards autumn's fire—it is in their nature . . ."

____ 4. In *Midsummer*, Walcott refers to "Caedmon's raceless dew" and "Turner's ships" in order to
  a. show how far the British Empire has fallen.
  b. suggest that past artistic glories are put to shame by the brutality of this age.
  c. hint that these works of British art were never really of value.
  d. imply that the demonstrators have totally missed the point.

____ 5. The speaker in *Midsummer*
  a. understands but is apart from the demonstrators.
  b. opposes actions of the demonstrators that lead to violence.
  c. laments the impending destruction of a great culture.
  d. regards these painful actions as all to the good.

____ 6. The selection from *Omeros* takes as its topic the
  a. destruction of African culture by modern life.
  b. preservation of tradition orally by the griot.
  c. speaker's struggle for his own identity.
  d. dislocation and grief brought by the slave trade.

____ 7. How has the history of Africans enslaved in the West Indies been passed on?
  a. by the griot, who repeats tales orally
  b. through letters sent to the homeland
  c. through messages attached to palm branches set adrift
  d. through the translated poetry of Homer

_____ 8. To what do these lines from *Omeros* refer?

> So there went the Ashanti one way, the Mandingo another,
> the Ibo another, the Guinea. . . .

a. African tribes' unwillingness to adopt one another's customs
b. loss of tribal identity in the New World
c. warring tribal factions in Africa today
d. dispersal of plant seeds from different parts of Africa

_____ 9. Which word best describes the tone of the excerpt from *Omeros*, Chapter XXVIII?
a. hopeful
b. commemorative
c. nostalgic
d. rejoicing

_____ 10. When the speaker of *Omeros* says "remember us to the black waiter bringing the bill," he suggests
a. the destiny of people who have no past.
b. that the griot must support himself with what he can get.
c. the displacement of people who once had a rich identity.
d. that financial gain will compensate for the wrong of slavery.

_____ 11. The "lady" in the title from "From Lucy: Englan' Lady" refers to
a. Lucy.
b. Leela.
c. the queen.
d. the poet's wife.

_____ 12. Given Berry's biography, the speaker of "From Lucy: Englan' Lady" is most likely to be
a. a Jamaican woman.
b. an African American.
c. a Cuban refugee.
d. an Irish woman.

_____ 13. Why does the speaker pity the queen in "From Lucy: Englan' Lady"?
a. She may have an unhappy home life.
b. The monarchy is now an outdated institution.
c. People expect her presence to make them feel happy.
d. She is constantly required to put on a show.

_____ 14. Why would the speaker in "From Lucy: Englan' Lady" likely have such interest in the queen of England?
a. The queen has become an international celebrity.
b. The speaker's homeland was once a British colony.
c. The speaker feels her situation is similar to the queen's.
d. The speaker once met the queen.

_____ 15. Which theme best applies to the three poems by Berry and Walcott?
a. the struggle by displaced people to find a voice
b. the struggle for recognition as a gifted actor or poet
c. honoring one's elders and leaders appropriately
d. appreciating the changing beauty of nature

Vocabulary and Grammar

On the line, write the letter of the one best answer.

____ 16. The word *rancor* means
   a. order.
   b. nobility.
   c. odor.
   d. hostility.

____ 17. Someone or something in *eclipse* is
   a. frightening.
   b. oval.
   c. fading.
   d. joyous.

____ 18. An *antic* behavior is
   a. quirky.
   b. secret.
   c. dangerous.
   d. old-fashioned.

____ 19. Which sentence employs a *correct* use of the word *affect*?
   a. The affect of the procedure is an enhanced life span.
   b. If one is to affect a reversal of events, one may have to reverse one's habits.
   c. A person can massively affect the lives of others without intention.
   d. Some literature, no matter how popular, has little lasting affect.

____ 20. Which sentence employs a *correct* use of the word *effect*?
   a. Using your car's safety equipment will effect your chances of survival in an accident.
   b. The careful researcher will do nothing to effect the integrity of his or her data.
   c. If you would effect the outcome of elections, you could begin by voting.
   d. The effect of long-term high doses of vitamins is not yet clear.

Essay Questions

21. Outside information about the lives of poets and the subjects they write about helps in understanding poems. What information is particularly useful in grasping Berry's and Walcott's poems? Write an essay in which you show how essential background information helps you understand the selections by Walcott and Berry. Use examples from the poems to support your ideas.

22. Walcott and Berry are intimately familiar with English language and culture. They also have an "outsider's" point of view on this tradition. Write an essay in which you explain how Walcott and Berry use this double perspective in their poems. Use examples from the selections to support your points.

23. Both Walcott and Berry use voices and figures that come from outside the tradition of English poetry—voices that might not even understand that tradition. To what extent does their work challenge the value of traditional poetry, and to what extent does their work affirm it? Support your answer with examples from the selection.

Name _____ Date _____

"A Devoted Son" by Anita Desai

Selection Test

Critical Reading

On the line, write the letter of the one best answer.

_____ 1. What does Varma's family celebrate at the beginning of "A Devoted Son"?
  a. Rakesh's admission to college
  b. Rakesh's unexpected return from America
  c. Rakesh's wedding
  d. Rakesh's high marks in an examination

_____ 2. At the beginning of the story, Varma takes most pride in Rakesh's
  a. humility to all around him.
  b. extraordinary accomplishment.
  c. respect for his father.
  d. scholarship to America.

_____ 3. Which choice gives a reasonable evaluation of the family decision to sacrifice for Rakesh's education, considering only the beginning of the story?
  a. reasonable, because they hope to improve the family's prestige and fortunes by it
  b. foolish, because they are too poor to afford it
  c. selfish, because they are only thinking of the money Rakesh will bring them
  d. devoted, because they think only of their son

_____ 4. Rakesh shows that he is a static character by
  a. showing unwavering "devotion" to his father.
  b. changing dramatically once he returns from medical school.
  c. restricting his father's diet, despite his father's complaints.
  d. always getting his own way after his mother dies.

_____ 5. What was most surprising about Rakesh's marriage?
  a. His wife was pretty, plump, and uneducated.
  b. Rakesh followed traditional custom to acquire his bride.
  c. The wedding took place at home in India, not in America.
  d. His wife was good-natured, but lazy.

_____ 6. Rakesh and his wife lived
  a. near the hospital where he worked.
  b. just outside the increasingly shabby colony.
  c. a short drive from the clinic Rakesh founded.
  d. in his father and mother's house.

_____ 7. Rakesh's mother is a
  a. central character.
  b. static character.
  c. rounded character.
  d. dynamic character.

____ 8. What does this passage imply?

> He took his parents in his car . . . to see the clinic when it was built, and the large sign-board over the door on which his name was printed in letters of red, with a row of degrees and qualifications to follow it like so many little black slaves of the regent.

   a. Rakesh was of a rich elite, like colonial rulers.
   b. Rakesh's parents understand the results of his education in traditional terms, as prestige.
   c. Rakesh's clinic was extremely successful financially.
   d. Rakesh's credentials were more important than his medical knowledge.

____ 9. After his wife's death and his own retirement, Varma
   a. grew even closer to his son.
   b. was gratified by his son's attention.
   c. became irritable and fell ill often.
   d. longed for former times.

____ 10. Which statement is a reasonable evaluation of Rakesh's decision to restrict his father's diet?
   a. Rakesh shows courage by doing what is right despite his father's complaints.
   b. Rakesh shows insensitivity in placing medical concerns before his father's happiness.
   c. Rakesh is being spiteful, avenging himself for the way his father tried to run his life when he was young.
   d. Rakesh is being stubborn and just wants to be right all the time.

____ 11. What is the elderly Varma's attitude toward his daughter-in-law?
   a. He feels sorry for her for marrying Rakesh.
   b. He feels she is a perfect wife for Rakesh.
   c. He believes she mocks him with increasing openness.
   d. He believes she is too self-indulgent to be a good mother.

____ 12. The one dynamic character in "A Devoted Son" is
   a. Varma.
   b. Veena.
   c. Rakesh.
   d. Bhatia.

____ 13. Which choice gives a reasonable evaluation of the family decision to sacrifice for Rakesh's education, considering the ending of the story?
   a. The family should have known better than to allow Western ideas to corrupt their son.
   b. The family should not have arrogantly assumed they could better themselves without cost.
   c. The family should have prepared to adjust their traditional thinking to match whatever new attitudes Rakesh adopted.
   d. The family could not have known in advance the true nature of what it was they wished for and eventually received.

____ 14. What was the one remaining pleasure left to the elderly Varma?
   a. meals brought twice a day on a stainless steel tray
   b. *kheer*, a rice pudding served for dessert
   c. having the news read out to him
   d. visits from elderly neighbors

____ 15. Which statement best represents Varma's opinion of Rakesh at the end of the story?
   a. "It was a strange fact, however, that talent and skill, if displayed for too long, cease to dazzle."
   b. "Outwardly, all might be the same but the interpretation had altered: his masterly efficiency was nothing but cold heartlessness. . . ."
   c. "It had to be admitted . . . that Rakesh . . .was not only a devoted son and a miraculously good-natured man who contrived somehow to obey his parents and humor his wife . . ."
   d. "All this was very gratifying to the old man."

Vocabulary and Grammar

On the line, write the letter of the one best answer.

____ 16. Something that is *exemplary* is a
   a. perfect model.
   b. foolish dream.
   c. baffling mystery.
   d. careful plan.

____ 17. One who is *complaisant* is
   a. protesting.
   b. irritable.
   c. obliging.
   d. silent.

____ 18. He could not *fathom* modern technology; he simply could not
   a. admire it.
   b. oppose it.
   c. understand it.
   d. afford it.

____ 19. Writers vary sentences in order to
   a. embed dialogue in critical places.
   b. keep their writing interesting and lively.
   c. withhold plot information until the end.
   d. display their command of language.

____ 20. Which is not a typical technique to provide sentence variety?
   a. varying the length of sentences
   b. varying the structure of sentences
   c. varying the type of sentences
   d. varying the coherence of sentences

Essay Questions

21. In much modern fiction, characters do not see their fondest wishes come true. Yet everything that Varma hopes will happen for Rakesh does so, and Rakesh is "ever a devoted son." How does it all go wrong for Varma? Write an essay in which you trace the changes Varma goes through as Rakesh rises, and explain how Varma's dreams, in coming true, are ruined. Use examples from the story to illustrate your points.

22. In "A Devoted Son," the reader never sees inside Rakesh's thoughts. Write an essay in which you consider why Desai excludes Rakesh's point of view, and give your own version of how he sees things. Use examples from the story to support your assessment.

23. The title "A Devoted Son" is ironic, for though Rakesh may be respectful, his father believes Rakesh treats him poorly. What larger point might Desai be making about the relations between India, and the West? How might Varma's story reflect India's ambivalent (two-sided) attitude towards Western culture?

from "We'll Never Conquer Space" by Arthur C. Clarke

Selection Test

Critical Reading

On the line, write the letter of the one best answer.

_____ 1. What does Clarke predict in his prophetic essay?
   a. Our technology will not allow us to explore space any farther.
   b. Inability to communicate will hinder space travel.
   c. Humans' inability to comprehend space will prohibit us from going beyond the confines of our solar system.
   d. Travel across interstellar space, unlike modern travel on Earth, will always isolate travelers from those left at home.

_____ 2. Which is an example of a memorable phrase Clarke uses to convince readers of his viewpoint?
   a. "The ants have covered the world but have they conquered it . . .?"
   b. "Such a statement may sound ludicrous, now that our rockets are already 100 million miles beyond the moon. . . ."
   c. ". . . radio and light waves travel at the same limited speed of 186,000 miles a second."
   d. "Imagine a vast ocean, sprinkled with islands—some desert, others perhaps inhabited."

_____ 3. What is Clarke's main prophecy?
   a. We don't have the technology to conquer space.
   b. The vastness of space prevents us from conquering it.
   c. Humans are intimidated by the vastness of space.
   d. Our concept of the vastness of space is limited.

_____ 4. Why does Clarke mention the time lag caused by communicating on a planetary or stellar basis?
   a. to show how inadequate our technology is
   b. to emphasize the vastness of space
   c. to make a point about the speed of radio and light waves
   d. to convey how isolated space travelers would be from Earth

_____ 5. What does Clarke mean by this statement?

   Because we have annihilated distance on this planet, we imagine that we can do it once again.

   a. Distance no longer means anything to us.
   b. We will be able to move from planet to planet as quickly as we can get around on Earth.
   c. Since people travel incredible distances on Earth without disrupting their lives, they think they will be able to do the same in space.
   d. Our planet seems small and insignificant to us.

_____ 6. What would prevent instantaneous communication with a person on another planet?
   a. inferior communications technology
   b. the time transmissions take to cross such distances
   c. radio wave interference
   d. difference in time between one planet and the other

_____ 7. In addition to making his own prediction in his prophetic essay, Clarke is also
a. displaying his technical knowledge.
b. recounting the history of space exploration.
c. painting a picture of humanity's place in the universe.
d. casting doubt on the existing laws of physics.

_____ 8. When Clarke compares space to a "vast ocean sprinkled with islands," he makes the point that
a. there are too many planets to be explored.
b. the distances between stars are so great that exploration would be impossible.
c. current space technology is as primitive as a dugout canoe.
d. the distances between stars would forever separate space travelers from Earth, just as island residents were separated from their original culture.

_____ 9. Which does Clarke assume as an unchangeable fact?
a. Nothing can move faster than the speed of light.
b. Telephone technology is at its peak.
c. Spaceflight technology may improve some, but not much.
d. Humans will never comprehend a number like 10^9.

_____ 10. Clarke asks us to picture an object five feet away, with nothing around it for 1,000 miles. He uses this image to illustrate the
a. difference between travel on earth and travel in space.
b. distance to our moon versus the distance to the sun.
c. difference between our nearest star and the next galaxy.
d. distance to the nearest planet as opposed to the distance to the nearest star.

_____ 11. Given his use of the word _might_, what is Clarke doing in this statement?

> This achievement [harnessing nuclear energy for spaceflight], which will be witnessed within a century, might appear to make even the solar system a comfortable, homely place, with such giant planets as Saturn and Jupiter playing much the same role in our thoughts as do Africa or Asia today.

a. He is partially agreeing to the opposing viewpoint for persuasive effect.
b. He is stating when nuclear-powered spaceflight will be achieved.
c. He is creating a picture of how we would view our solar system.
d. He is guessing about the consequences of nuclear-powered spaceflight.

_____ 12. How should a critical reader respond when seeing the word _never_ in an essay?
a. Accept this as a fact.
b. Assume that the writer is using the term loosely.
c. Be suspicious of an overgeneralization.
d. Assume that the writer researched the issue and is correct.

_____ 13. How would a reader best challenge this statement?

> These suns are on the average five light-years apart; in other words, we can never get from one to the next in less than five years.

a. Are our measurements of the distances between the suns accurate?
b. This assumes that faster-than-light travel is not possible. Is this a valid assumption?
c. This assumes we can even get to the first sun. How far away is it?
d. Are the suns habitable?

____ 14. Which sentence expresses Clarke's prediction about what would happen if humans colonize space?
   a. "For the universe has two aspects—its scale, and its overwhelming, mind-numbing complexity."
   b. "Before such numbers, even spirits brave enough to face the challenge of the light-years must quail."
   c. "We have left the realm of human comprehension in our vain effort to grasp the scale of the universe; so it must always be, sooner rather than later."
   d. "So it will be with us as we spread outwards from Mother Earth, loosening the bonds of kinship and understanding."

____ 15. Why does Clarke say humans will never venture back from Vega of the Lyre, "the brightest star of the northern skies"?
   a. It is so pleasant that people would not want to leave.
   b. Given the average human life span, it is unlikely someone could make a round trip.
   c. We will never have the technology to go there.
   d. It is uninviting and uninhabitable.

Vocabulary and Grammar

On the line, write the letter of the one best answer.

____ 16. Clarke maintains that a time lag in communication between Earth and the stars would be *inevitable*, or
   a. intolerable.
   b. tolerable.
   c. unavoidable.
   d. conquerable.

____ 17. Clarke identifies 61 Cygni as an *enigma*, meaning that it
   a. is unlike any other star.
   b. was only recently discovered.
   c. is unapproachable because it is so far away.
   d. poses a perplexing riddle.

____ 18. Identify the sentence that contains a linking verb.
   a. "Self-contained cosmic arks . . . may be another solution . . ."
   b. "Imagine a vast ocean, sprinkled with islands."
   c. "But the messages will take minutes . . . on their journey . . ."
   d. "Returning messengers could report what had happened on the nearest colony—five years ago."

Essay Questions

19. What, exactly, does Clarke predict in his essay? Why does he believe as he does? What arguments does he put forth in support of his prediction? As you summarize Clarke's argument in an essay, cite any particularly notable evidence or examples Clark uses to support his prediction.

20. Do you accept the ideas Clarke puts forth in "We'll Never Conquer Space"? What rings true? What doesn't? In an essay, challenge his assertions, stating what you agree and disagree with, and why. As you challenge the text, make note of assumptions Clarke makes and whether they are valid.

21. Clarke makes three statements about the "size" of the Earth. He writes that "we have annihilated distance on this planet," that we "have abolished space here on the little earth," and that "there are no longer any remote places on earth." What does Clarke mean by these statements? Do you agree with him? Do you think people in different nations and of different cultures have other attitudes about earth's distances? In an essay, explain why.

Part Test, Unit 6, Part 4: From the National to the Global

Critical Reading

The questions below are based on the following selection.

The selection includes the first and second stanzas of "Shore Woman," a poem by Seamus Heaney. In these lines, the speaker reflects on her contrasting experiences on land and at sea.

Man to the hills, woman to the shore.

Gaelic proverb

I have crossed the dunes with their whistling bent
Where dry loose sand was riddling round the air
And I'm walking the firm margin. White pocks
Of cockle, blanched roofs of clam and oyster

[5] Hoard the moonlight, woven and unwoven
Off the bay. At the far rocks
A pale sud comes and goes.
Under boards the mackerel slapped to death
Yet still we took them in at every cast,

[10] Stiff flails of cold convulsed with their first breath.
My line plumbed certainly the undertow,
Loaded against me once I went to draw
And flashed and fattened up towards the light.
He was all business in the stern. I called

[15] "This is so easy that it's hardly right,"
But he unhooked and coped with frantic fish
Without speaking. Then suddenly it lulled,
We'd crossed where they were running, the line rose
Like a let-down and I was conscious

[20] How far we'd drifted out beyond the head.
"Count them up at your end," was all he said
Before I saw the porpoises' thick backs
Cartwheeling like the flywheels of the tide,
Soapy and shining. To have seen a hill

[25] Splitting the water could not have numbed me more
Than the close irruption of that school,
Tight viscous muscle, hooped from tail to snout,
Each one revealed complete as it bowled out
And under.

On the line, write the letter of the one best answer.

_____ 1. What effect does the epigraph "Man to the hills, woman to the shore" have on the poem?
a. It serves as the poem's title.
b. It reveals the poet's purpose.
c. It establishes the poem's context.
d. It suggests contrasting points of view.

____ 2. What change occurs from the first stanza to the second stanza?
   a. a shift in speaker
   b. a shift in setting
   c. an absence of context
   d. a change from past to present tense

____ 3. What conflict does the speaker face?
   a. She struggles with her fear of the unknown.
   b. She argues with the man in the boat.
   c. She feels torn between a life spent on land and a life at sea.
   d. She must learn a new trade.

____ 4. The lines from "Shore Woman" are examples of free verse because they
   a. have a regular rhythm.
   b. contain end rhyme.
   c. contain varying line lengths and rhythms.
   d. are arranged in stanzas of equal length.

____ 5. The mood reflected in the first stanza is
   a. tense and anxious.   c. cautious yet hopeful.
   b. energetic and confident.   d. calm and contemplative.

____ 6. Why does the speaker become afraid when she sees porpoises in the water?
   a. She fears the man will kill them.
   b. She fears they will hit or attack the boat.
   c. She has never been in a boat.
   d. She believes they will scare away the mackerel.

____ 7. Read these lines in sentences, and choose the best paraphrase.

   He was all business in the stern. I called
   "This is so easy that it's hardly right,"
   But he unhooked and coped with frantic fish
   Without speaking . . .

   a. The speaker calls out to the man that he is "all business," but the man continues working.
   b. The speaker comments that the fishing seems too easy, but the man continues working silently.
   c. The man is occupied with unhooking fish.
   d. The fish don't speak.

____ 8. What effect do the rhythmic, short phrases "woven and unwoven" and "comes and goes" in the first stanza have on the poem?
   a. They echo the sound of the waves hitting the shore.
   b. They create suspense.
   c. They establish context.
   d. They create a regular rhythm throughout the poem.

____ 9. What background information would be best applied to a reading of "Shore Woman"?
   a. knowledge of boating rules
   b. interpretations of Gaelic proverbs
   c. information about porpoise behavior
   d. statistics about the Irish fishing industry

____ 10. Which word best summarizes Heaney's voice?
   a. clipped   c. smooth
   b. rushed   d. plodding

Vocabulary and Grammar

Write the letter of the one best answer on the line.

____ 11. The word most nearly *opposite* in meaning to *atrophy* is
     a. *thrive.*
     b. *revive.*
     c. *deteriorate.*
     d. *fast.*

____ 12. The word most nearly *opposite* in meaning to *keenly* is
     a. *intensely.*
     b. *quickly.*
     c. *dully.*
     d. *underhandedly.*

____ 13. The word most nearly *opposite* in meaning to *complaisant* is
     a. *reluctant.*
     b. *argumentative.*
     c. *cooperative.*
     d. *forgetful.*

____ 14. I find it difficult to _____ the vastness of the universe.
     a. eclipse
     b. distill
     c. patronize
     d. fathom

____ 15. _____ with the long wait for seating and the poor service, I vowed never to _____ the restaurant again.
     a. Grieved, distill
     b. Exasperated, patronize
     c. Inducted, atrophy
     d. Elongated, eclipse

____ 16. The inventor's _____ behavior made him a(n) _____ in the town.
     a. antic, enigma
     b. malevolent, effigy
     c. nondescript, rogue
     d. ludicrous, zenith

____ 17. The lecturer explained the physiological _____ of space travel to my classmates and _____.
     a. effects, I
     b. affects, I
     c. effects, me
     d. affects, me

____ 18. Which phrase identifies the underlined portion of the sentence?

    When the train suddenly stopped, everyone was thrown forward.

     a. tense shift
     b. absolute phrase
     c. subject complement
     d. adverb clause

____ 19. Which part of the sentence is an absolute phrase?

The old native, gasping, his skinny toes splaying the sand, flung the lion.

a. The old native

b. gasping

c. his skinny toes splaying the sand

d. flung the lion

____ 20. Which sentence contains a linking verb and a subject complement?

a. "This was the view he had been thinking of."

b. "I walked along Alberto Street a year later, but I could find no sign of the poet's house."

c. "Man will never conquer space."

d. "Their thick skulls bled with rancor. . . . "

Essay Questions

21. Several of the selections in this section contain characters who face conflicts and make difficult decisions. Which character left the strongest impression on you? What struck you about the character? Did you sympathize with the character, or were you angered or disturbed by the character's behavior? Write an essay in which you explain your choice and evaluate the character's actions and decisions.

22. Although many modern poems employ free verse, some contemporary poets still use regular meter and rhyme. Choose two poems (one in free verse and one in another form) from this part, and in an essay compare and contrast the use of free verse and traditional verse form. How does the chosen form interact with the poem's meaning?

23. Each poet featured in this part has a distinct voice. Choose two poets, and compare and contrast their voices in an essay. Note how each poet forms a distinctive voice through sound devices, rhythm, word choice, pace of speaking, and other techniques.

24. Many of the writers represented in this section have been influenced by the effects of British imperialism. Write an essay in which you explain how history has influenced the work of at least one writer from this section.

25. Disillusionment is a common theme in many of this section's selections. Write an essay in which you explore the theme of disillusionment in three selections. Explain how each work incorporates this theme, and make connections, where applicable, among the selections.

ANSWERS
Unit 1: From Legend to History (449–1485)

"The Seafarer,"
translated by Burton Raffel
"The Wanderer,"
translated by Charles Kennedy
"The Wife's Lament,"
translated by Ann Stanford

Selection Test (p. 1)

Critical Reading/Vocabulary and Grammar

1. a 2. d 3. c 4. c 5. b 6. d 7. d 8. b 9. a
10. c 11. b 12. a 13. b 14. c 15. c 16. a
17. a 18. d 19. b 20. a

Questions are classified in these categories:
Comprehension 2(E), 9(A), 11(C)
Interpretation 4(E), 6(A), 7(A), 13(C), 14(C)
Literary Analysis 1(E), 8(E), 10(C), 15(A)
Reading Strategy 3(A), 5(A), 12(C)
Vocabulary 16(A), 18(A), 19(A)
Grammar 17(E), 20(A)
E = Easy, A = Average, C = Challenging

Essay Questions

21. (Easy) *Guidelines for student response:*
Students should tell how migration and
leaving one's home was a common occur-
rence at this time, and knowing this can
help them understand and appreciate the
poems. Students may use examples of
exile on the sea in "The Seafarer," exile
from home and companions in "The
Wayfarer," and exile from home and the
one you love in "The Wife's Lament."

22. (Average) *Guidelines for student response:*
Students may respond that in each case,
the subject of the poem accepts what
fate has dealt to him or her. In "The
Seafarer," the sailor accepts that the sea
will always call him and that he will
always follow the call. In "The Wanderer,"
the man accepts that his life with his lord
and friends is over, and that he will never
find such friends or sense of belonging
again. In "The Wife's Lament," the wife
accepts that her husband now hates her
and has exiled her, even though she did
nothing to deserve this.

23. (Challenging) *Guidelines for student
response:* Students may respond that
the use of kennings provides interesting
descriptions that are easy to remember
and repeat. The caesura helps establish
the rhythm, as well as providing a
natural pause. Students should provide
examples from the selections to illustrate
these points.

from *Tristia* by Ovid
"Far Corners of Earth" by Tu Fu

Selection Test (p. 4)

Critical Reading

1. b 2. b 3. a 4. c 5. b 6. b 7. c 8. a
9. b 10. d

Questions are classified in these categories:
Comprehension 3(E), 5(A), 6(A), 8 (E)
Interpretation 1(C), 2(A), 4(C), 7(C), 9(C),
10 (A)
E = Easy, A = Average, C = Challenging

Essay Questions

11. (Easy) *Guidelines for student response:*
Students should identify separation from
familiar things (loved ones, one's home,
etc.) and being excluded from society as
the two main consequences of exile.
Students may judge Tu Fu's poem more
powerful in its evocation of despair, or
they may prefer Ovid's poem because
of its fuller explanation of the situation
of exile.

12. (Average) *Guidelines for student response:*
Students should point out the dual
meaning of clouds: something that
blocks out the sun, and therefore a
symbol of the dark mood of gloom and
despair that accompanies the poet on his
wandering. Students could make similar
analyses of the mountains, the endless
road (on the one hand a long road, on the
other symbolic of his lack of hope to ever
return home), and the wasted highway.

from *Tristia* by Ovid
"Far Corners of Earth" by Tu Fu
(continued)

Students might further analyze the "geography" of exile contained in the image of the "far corner," contrasting the place of exclusion and separation ("far") to what is familiar ("near").

13. (Challenging) *Guidelines for student response:* Students should point out at least two passages as especially critical of local mores and customs, such as Ovid's comment about those who "think it is shameful to live without plundering men," the "unjust justice . . . enforced with a rigid sword blade," or his criticisms of the manner of dress and speaking of the local inhabitants. Students should point out that Ovid's pose of wounded pride, writing as someone whose nobility contrasts with the barbarity of his surroundings. Students should identify Ovid's criticisms as pointed and scornful, not characteristics that would endear him to his targets.

Part Test, Unit 1, Part 1: Earthly Exile, Heavenly Home (p. 6)

Critical Reading/Vocabulary and Grammar

1. c 2. b 3. d 4. a 5. b 6. d 7. b 8. a 9. d 10. c 11. a 12. d 13. c 14. b 15. b

Questions are classified in these categories:
Comprehension 1(C), 6(A), 8(A)
Interpretation 2(A), 7(A)
Literary Analysis 3(C), 5(C), 9(A), 10(C)
Reading Strategy 4(C)
Vocabulary 13(C)
Grammar 11(A), 12(A), 14(C), 15(A)
E = Easy, A = Average, C = Challenging

Essay Questions

16. (Easy) *Guidelines for student response:* Students' essays should give a clear, thorough picture of the speaker of the poem, based on passages from the text. For example, students might note the speaker's honesty ("there isn't a man on earth . . . so brave . . . that he feels no fear as the sails unfold"), bravery and fortitude ("my feet were cast in icy bands . . ."),

and self-dramatization ("Who could understand, in ignorant ease, what we others suffer as the paths of exile stretch endlessly on?").

17. (Average) *Guidelines for student response:* Students' essays should clearly explicate the meaning of the wife's statement about bearing the anger of her beloved. For instance, students could cite lines 18–20 as evidence that the beloved's anger is directed not at his wife—but rather at a worldly foe. Of course, this situation fueled by this anger affects the wife directly and "cruelly" by separating her from her beloved; what she bears is the separation brought on by the anger (or military responsibilities) of her husband.

18. (Challenging) *Guidelines for student response:* Students' essays should provide a clear, thoughtful exploration of the effect of exile on an individual. For instance, they might cite text—such as "I had few loved ones in this land or faithful friends" ("The Wife's Lament"), "whirled in sorrow, alone in a world blown clear of love" ("The Seafarer"), or "a heart that is frozen, earth's winsomeness dead" ("The Wanderer")—to demonstrate the pointed emotional and physical stresses of exile.

from *Beowulf,*
translated by Burton Raffel

Selection Test (p. 9)

Critical Reading/Vocabulary and Grammar

1. c 2. b 3. d 4. a 5. b 6. c 7. d 8. a 9. d 10. d 11. b 12. c 13. d 14. a 15. c 16. c 17. c 18. b 19. c 20. a

Questions are classified in these categories:
Comprehension 2(E), 6(A), 10(E)
Interpretation 4(E), 5(A), 7(A), 11(E), 17(A)
Literary Analysis 1(A), 3(A), 14(A), 20(C)
Reading Strategy 9(A), 15(E), 19(C)
Vocabulary 8(E), 12(A), 18(A)
Grammar 13(C), 16(C)
E = Easy, A = Average, C = Challenging

Essay Questions

21. (Easy) *Guidelines for student response:* Students who agree may refer to themes

that always are relevant to human life: good *vs.* evil; the glorification of generous rulers who try to do good for others; the importance of dedication, bravery, and fairness. Those who disagree may say that the emphasis on the forces of good winning by physical strength and violence should not be relevant to today's world, that the battle of good *vs.* evil is too simplistic, or that heroes of Beowulf's perfection are implausible and irrelevant.

22. (Average) *Guidelines for student response:* Students should realize that one of Beowulf's main goals is to win glory by killing Grendel. His deeds have given him a reputation for heroism and support from his people to help the Danes. When he goes into the lake to fight Grendel's mother, the bystanders fear he has lost his life—and fame: here, death equals defeat equals loss of glory. Even when old, Beowulf wants to seek fame by fighting the dragon. He doesn't wish to die at the end, but when he sees that it is inevitable, he asks his warriors to build a tower that will keep his name alive in memory.

23. (Challenging) *Guidelines for student response:* Students may mention such virtues as bravery (*e.g.*, He faces death at the hands of three monsters fearlessly.); fairness (He fights Grendel bare-handed.); responsibility (He feels it's his duty to help the Danes.); concern for others (He saves the communities the monsters ravage.); piety (He thanks God for his victories.); ambition (He wants to earn fame by his deeds.); loyalty (He's good to his subjects.); and intelligence (He plans how he will battle Grendel and the dragon.).

"The Prologue" from *Gilgamesh,*
translated by David Ferry
from *The Iliad* by Homer

Selection Test (p. 12)

Critical Reading

1. c 2. c 3. b 4. d 5. a 6. c 7. d 8. b 9. c
10. a

Questions are classified in these categories:
Comprehension 1(E), 2(A), 3(C), 6(A), 7(A), 8(E)
Interpretation 4(A), 5(A), 9(C), 10(C)
E = Easy, A = Average, C = Challenging

Essay Questions

11. (Easy) *Guidelines for student response:* For both heroes, students should point out that whereas their abilities are extraordinary, their achievements are not beyond "normal" human beings. For example, Gilgamesh traveled the world, built a city, defeated enemies, created maps ("measured the world"), etc. Achilleus is a great warrior, but not an immortal. In that connection, students might suggest that "great" humans inevitably seem like gods to people of lesser ability. Students might see their deeds as godlike, but their emotions (Gilgamesh: heartbroken, reconciled; Achilleus: consumed by revenge) as human.

12. (Average) *Guidelines for student response:* Students should point out that the stories depicted here were considered history, and thus directly connected to ancient society. On a more personal level, the behavior of epic heroes provided examples of how to deal with strong emotions and formidable obstacles. Students may suggest that if the history is less relevant today, the struggle to deal with basic human emotions is as much or more so.

13. (Challenging) *Guidelines for student response:* Students should point out that both selections delay actions in various ways. Students should note, for example, that tension builds while Achilleus and Hektor talk about what they will do to each other before they do it. Students should also point out that the purpose of a prologue is to delay the main action while giving enticing details that pique the audience's interest. Students might note that the prologue to *Gilgamesh* also addresses the audience with imperatives ("study," "climb," "see," "open"), literally

"The Prologue" from Gilgamesh,
translated by David Ferry
from The Iliad by Homer
(continued)

commanding attention. Also, the fact the participants are heroes and gods, and not mere mortals, adds to their attraction. Students should compare one of the selections to a contemporary work, noting similarities and differences.

Part Test, Unit 1, Part 2: Focus on Literary Forms— The Epic (p. 14)

Critical Reading/Vocabulary and Grammar

1. c 2. b 3. b 4. a 5. d 6. c 7. a 8. b 9. d
10. c 11. b 12. a 13. a 14. d 15. a

Questions are classified in these categories:
Comprehension 1(E), 8(E)
Interpretation 2(A), 6(A), 10(A)
Literary Analysis 3(C), 5(A), 9(A)
Reading Strategy 4(A), 7(A)
Vocabulary 13(C)
Grammar 11(A), 12(C), 14(C), 15(C)
E = Easy, A = Average, C = Challenging

Essay Questions

16. (Easy) *Guidelines for student response:* Students should give a clear, considered explanation of Beowulf's character as revealed through his initial speech to the Danish king. For instance, students might cite specific words and phrases that indicate how Beowulf's words demonstrate personal qualities such as an instinct for leadership, boldness and forthrightness, responsiveness to his people, confidence and calmness in the face of conflict, and even a sense of humility (before God) about his fate.

17. (Average) *Guidelines for student response:* Students should provide a reasoned explanation of the way in which the battle between Beowulf and Grendel represents the battle between good and evil. For example, students could choose textual details such as "bearing God's hatred," "forever joyless," "mankind's enemy," and explicit phrases like "the shepherd

of evil" to support the idea that Grendel symbolizes evil; they might cite other details—Beowulf's selfless response to news of Grendel's destruction, as well as descriptions such as "greater and stronger than anyone anywhere in the world" or "I, alone and with the help of my men, may purge all evil from this hall"—as evidence that Beowulf represents good.

18. (Challenging) *Guidelines for student response:* Students should make clear, logical arguments about the appropriateness of the term *Dark Ages*. For example, they could focus on the apparent lack of culture, learning, and art to support the idea that humanity was "dark" or "unenlightened" in the early Middle Ages. Others might use details showing Beowulf's belief in God—and the epic's portrayal of good's triumph over evil—to support the idea that the early Middle Ages were not truly dark.

from A History of the English Church and People by Bede
from The Anglo-Saxon Chronicle,
translated by Anne Savage

Selection Test (p. 17)

Critical Reading/Vocabulary and Grammar

1. b 2. c 3. a 4. c 5. d 6. c 7. a 8. a 9. b
10. b 11. a 12. c 13. d 14. a 15. d 16. c
17. d 18. c 19. b 20. c

Questions are classified in these categories:
Comprehension 3(C), 4(E)
Interpretation 1(E), 2(A), 6(A), 7(C), 8(A)
Literary Analysis 5(A), 9(E), 11(A), 13(A)
Reading Strategy 10(E), 12(C), 14(A)
Vocabulary 16(A), 17(A), 19(A)
Grammar 15(C), 18(A), 20(E)
E = Easy, A = Average, C = Challenging

Essay Questions

21. (Easy) *Guidelines for student response:* Students may suggest that historical literature can provide a guide by which we may learn from the mistakes of the past. They may cite documents such as the Declaration of Independence and the

Constitution and important speeches by leaders such as Abraham Lincoln and Martin Luther King, Jr.

22. (Average) *Guidelines for student response:* Students may respond that depending on oral tradition could lead to inaccuracies; reasons for this could be faulty memory on the part of the storyteller, a tendency to change the truth to make it more interesting or its characters more heroic, and so on. They may also say that ancient manuscripts, no matter how carefully preserved, can be destroyed over time by such factors as weather, poor handling, and so on.

23. (Challenging) *Guidelines for student response:* Students may say that Bede's interest in science and the natural world is seen in his careful description of the geography of Britain: "It extends 800 miles northwards, and is 200 in breadth . . . the coastline . . . extends to 3,675 miles." Bede's scientific interests are also seen in his description of Britain's natural resources, including marine life, cockles that can be used to make dye, hot springs, and mineral mines. In their essays, students should distinguish between scientific facts and fanciful folklore, such as the tales of burning jet driving away snakes or Irish books curing snakebites.

The Prologue from *The Canterbury Tales* by Geoffrey Chaucer

Selection Test (p. 20)

Critical Reading/Vocabulary and Grammar

1. b 2. d 3. b 4. a 5. d 6. d 7. b 8. d 9. c 10. a 11. d 12. c 13. d 14. c 15. c 16. b 17. c 18. c 19. b 20. d

Questions are classified in these categories:
Comprehension 4(A), 7(E)
Interpretation 6(C), 8(C), 13(C), 14(A)
Literary Analysis 1(E), 2(A), 3(C), 10(A), 12(A)
Reading Strategy 5(E), 9(A), 11(A)
Vocabulary 15(A), 17(E), 20(C)
Grammar 16(C), 18(E), 19(E)
E = Easy, A = Average, C = Challenging

Essay Questions

21. (Easy) *Guidelines for student response:* Students should support their conclusions about the nature of the character they have chosen to write about with details of appearance, behavior, and speech as well as any direct statement Chaucer's narrator makes about the nature of that individual's personality.

22. (Average) *Guidelines for student response:* Students should realize that Chaucer has a fairly cynical attitude toward the church and religious practitioners, viewing most of them as corrupt and as given to self-serving and so-called "sinful" behavior as the people for whom they supposedly set an example. To illustrate this, students might point to his characterizations of the Nun, the Monk, the Friar, the Summoner, and/or the Pardoner—and, in particular, what these characters say about how they spend their time and what they're willing to overlook or pardon in exchange for gifts.

23. (Challenging) *Guidelines for student response:* Students should realize that Chaucer's narrator has a naive, straightforward personality. To illustrate this, students might point to the fact that he seems to be impressed by people's titles, clothes, and other possessions and tends to take what they say about themselves as being true. They might further support this impression with the narrator's direct statement about himself, made in an apology in line 766, "I'm short of wit as you will understand."

"The Nun's Priest's Tale" and "The Pardoner's Tale" from *The Canterbury Tales* by Geoffrey Chaucer

Selection Test (p. 23)

Critical Reading/Vocabulary and Grammar

1. c 2. b 3. a 4. b 5. b 6. a 7. a 8. a 9. c 10. b 11. d 12. c 13. b 14. a 15. d 16. c 17. d 18. a 19. a 20. d

"The Nun's Priest's Tale" and "The Pardoner's Tale" from *The Canterbury Tales* by Geoffrey Chaucer *(continued)*

Questions are classified in these categories:
Comprehension 1(A), 3(A), 6(A), 10(E), 13(E)
Interpretation 2(A), 8(E), 11(A), 14(C)
Literary Analysis 4(C), 5(C), 12(A)
Reading Strategy 7(A), 9(C)
Vocabulary 15(E), 18(A), 20(E)
Grammar 16(E), 17(C), 19(A)
E = Easy, A = Average, C = Challenging

Essay Questions

21. (Easy) *Guidelines for student response:* Most students will probably say that they would have enjoyed the tale less if the characters were human, explaining that it is the contrast between the heroic descriptions of the characters and events and the fact that these characters are actually barnyard animals that makes this tale so amusing and charming.

22. (Average) *Guidelines for student response:* Students should realize that both Chanticleer and the fox are undone by their own pride and by their need to boast, or show off. They may, therefore, devise a moral to the tale such as "Pride goeth before a fall." The incidents they use to support this moral may vary but should include how Chanticleer is duped by the fox as well as how the fox is duped by Chanticleer.

23. (Challenging) *Guidelines for student responses:* Students may have varying opinions about the old man in the story, although most will recognize him as either an ally of Death's, or Death itself. They should use examples from the text to show how the old man ultimately pointed the three rioters to their deaths. Students also may make the argument that since Death was everywhere, the rioters could not avoid it.

"Elizabeth II: A New Queen," *The London Times*

Selection Test (p. 26)

Critical Reading

1. c 2. b 3. a 4. d 5. c 6. c 7. d 8. b
9. b 10. d

Questions are classified in these categories:
Comprehension 1(A), 2(E), 6(C), 7(E), 8(A), 9(A)
Interpretation 3(C), 4(A), 5(C), 10(A)
E = Easy, A = Average, C = Challenging

Essay Questions

11. (Easy) *Guidelines for student response:* In terms of qualities and preparation, students should note Elizabeth's seriousness of purpose, her graceful manner, her education, and her public speaking experience. Students should note that while Elizabeth is described as vigorous, youthful, and full of vitality, these qualities do not seem as important as her seriousness and commitment to duty.

12. (Average) *Guidelines for student response:* Students may argue against the monarchy, suggesting that the attention, energy, and money paid to the royal family could better be used elsewhere; that rather than uniting the nation the royal family merely distracts it from solving real problems; that the idea of royalty is undemocratic and most royals seem out of touch with the people. Students may argue in favor of the monarchy, suggesting that despite personal problems, the monarchy remains a lightning rod for public opinion by which it may still contribute to a sense of community and purpose for all of society. Students might suggest that royalty has lost its luster in the wake of increased public appetite for scandal, fed by the many incidents surrounding the royal family, including the death of Diana, Princess of Wales, in a car crash in 1997.

13. (Challenging) Guidelines for student response: Students should point out that the media is willing to cover things that they would have left in private in the

1950s. Students might argue that the media attention unfairly focuses on scandals within the royal family, or, on the contrary, that the royal family brings media attention to itself through its inability to avoid scandal. Students may suggest that the categories of "royalty" and "celebrity," once distinct, have become intertwined, with the result that "royalty" has lost its position of unquestioned respect. Students might suggest that constant media attention has broken down the barriers separating the people from the royals, showing the royals to be no better than other people, which in turn destroys faith in the monarchy.

Part Test, Unit 1, Part 3: A National Spirit (p. 28)

Critical Reading/Vocabulary and Grammar

1. c 2. a 3. a 4. d 5. c 6. a 7. c 8. d 9. d
10. b 11. c 12. a 13. b 14. c 15. c

Questions are classified in these categories:
Comprehension 1(E)
Interpretation 2(A), 7(A), 8(A)
Literary Analysis 3(A), 5(C), 10(A)
Reading Strategy 4(A), 6(A), 9(C)
Vocabulary 13(C)
Grammar 11(C), 12(A), 14(A), 15(A)
E = Easy, A = Average, C = Challenging

Essay Questions

16. (Easy) *Guidelines for student response:* Students should make a clear decision about whether they would find a visit to medieval Britain interesting or appealing, and their essays should give telling explanations about why they feel as they do.

17. (Average) *Guidelines for student response:* Students' essays should take account of the wide diversity of character and occupation in the Prologue. They should also note that Chaucer expects his audience to be able to laugh at familiar types, to respect virtues such as the Knight's, and to be familiar with the stories and lore satirized in "The Nun's Priest's Tale."

18. (Challenging) *Guidelines for student*

response: Using references to the texts, students should provide lucid and thoughtful explanations of what the Anglo-Saxons found important. For example, from the numerous references to military battles, it can be inferred that war was an important element of life. Similarly, the inclusion of the names of distinguished Danish and Anglo-Saxon leaders indicates that society was stratified.

from *Sir Gawain and the Green Knight,* translated by Marie Borroff
from *Morte d'Arthur* by Sir Thomas Malory

Selection Test (p. 31)

Critical Reading/Vocabulary and Grammar

1. b 2. c 3. d 4. a 5. b 6. d 7. c 8. b 9. c
10. d 11. a 12. c 13. c 14. b 15. d 16. b
17. c 18. b 19. d 20. c

Questions are classified in these categories:
Comprehension 2(A), 7(E), 13(C)
Interpretation 4(E), 8(C), 9(A), 10(A), 11(A), 14(A)
Literary Analysis 3(A), 5(A), 10(A), 12(A)
Reading Strategy 1(A), 6(E), 15(C)
Vocabulary 16(E), 19(A), 20(C)
Grammar 17(A), 18(E)
E = Easy, A = Average, C = Challenging

Essay Questions

21. (Easy) *Guidelines for student response:* Students should indicate at least one example of vivid realism, one of magic or the supernatural, and one of religious sentiment for both selections. Examples in *Sir Gawain and the Green Knight* include the following: vivid realism—the description of Sir Gawain beheading the Green Knight; magic or the supernatural—the Green Knight carrying about his own head; religious sentiment—evoking God's name and blessing to reinforce what Sir Gawain says to the Green Knight. Examples in *Morte d' Arthur* include the following: vivid realism—the description of King Arthur killing Sir Mordred; magic or the super

from _Gawain and the Green Knight,_ translated by Marie Borroff
from _Morte d'Arthur,_ by Sir Thomas Malory
(continued)

natural—King Arthur's prophetic dream; religious sentiment—Sir Gawain's warning to King Arthur not to battle Sir Mordred the following day is underscored with religious references.

22. (Average) _Guidelines for student response:_ Students should realize that the character of King Arthur is portrayed consistently in the two stories. They might point out that King Arthur shows he is supportive when he encourages Sir Gawain to enter the contest with the Green Knight, brave when he attacks Mordred, wise when he listens to the message in his dreams, shrewd when he tells his men to be ready to attack if one of Mordred's men draws a sword, and honorable because he truly appreciates the loyalty of his knights.

23. (Challenging) _Guidelines for student response:_ Developed by feudal nobles, the chivalric code combined Christian values and the virtues of being a warrior. Knights were to be brave, honest, and loyal; to right wrongs and selflessly defend the weak. Students' responses will vary depending upon which characters they select but should reflect the code of chivalry. They should note that Gawain's self-protectiveness and Sir Belvidere's less-than-unquestioning loyalty both lead them to violate the code; the Green Knight's and Arthur's forgiveness, and the fact that the knights eventually "get it right," resolve the conflict.

Letters of Margaret Paston
"Lord Randall," "The Twa Corbies,"
"Get Up and Bar the Door,"
and "Barbara Allan," Anonymous

Selection Test (p. 34)

Critical Reading/Vocabulary and Grammar

1. c 2. b 3. a 4. a 5. c 6. b 7. b 8. c 9. c
10. d 11. c 12. a 13. b 14. c 15. d 16. c

17. d 18. d 19. b 20. b

Questions are classified in these categories:
Comprehension 2(A), 3(A), 4(E), 5(E)
Interpretation 8(A), 9(A), 13(E), 14(A), 15(C)
Literary Analysis 1(A), 6(A), 10(C)
Reading Strategy 7(C), 11(C), 12(A)
Vocabulary 16(A), 19(C), 20(C)
Grammar 17(E), 18(E)
E = Easy, A = Average, C = Challenging

Essay Questions

21. (Easy) _Guidelines for student response:_ Students should note that each of these ballads is a narrative poem that was written to be sung. Each uses four-line stanzas called quatrains, in which the second and fourth lines rhyme. All of these ballads have refrains or use repetition. Students should note that regular rhythm and rhyme make them suitable for singing. The use of dialogue, and the choice of the tragic or the humorous side of love as a subject, would help keep the attention of listeners.

22. (Average) _Guidelines for student response:_ Students should realize that Lord Randall's trust turns to heartbreak when he discovers he's been poisoned. They should also see that Barbara Allen's trust in Sir John changed to mistrust because she thought he had ignored her, but that she comes to regret her mistrust. Students should conclude that trust leads to death for Lord Randall and that a lack of trust leads to death for Barbara Allen.

23. (Challenging) _Guidelines for student response:_ Students should mention some of the following disadvantages to learning history through personal letters: the writer may mention events or people without explaining their significance because he or she assumes the correspondent is familiar with them; the writer may use a dialect that is difficult to understand; if only one half of a correspondence is available, the reader will probably never see answers to the writer's questions. Perhaps most important, the writer's bias or incomplete understanding of facts can distort the truth. Some of the

advantages that students might mention include the following: letters can be dramatic and interesting; they give eyewitness accounts of events such as wars and political struggles. Students should realize that a writer's bias affects the way he or she interprets events.

"How Siegfried Was Slain" from *The Nibelungenlied,*
translated by A. T. Hatto

Selection Test (p. 37)

Critical Reading

1. d 2. a 3. b 4. a 5. c 6. c 7. b 8. a
9. d 10. a

Questions are classified in these categories:
Comprehension 3(A), 4(A), 5(E)
Interpretation 1(C), 2(A), 6(A), 7(A), 8(C), 9(A), 10(C)
E = Easy, A = Average, C = Challenging

Essay Questions

11. (Easy) *Guidelines for student response:* Students should point out Siegfried's physical prowess, loyalty, trusting nature, and ability to love as essential qualities of the tragic hero. Students should note that tragic heroes are almost entirely good, but come to a bad end as a result of a single character flaw. In Siegfried's case, his overly trusting nature and large ego (inability to resist a challenge) lead to his downfall. Without the flaw, the character would be too perfect. The imperfection makes him sympathetic.

12. (Average) *Guidelines for student response:* Students should describe the various omens and foreshadowing, starting with Kriemhild's dreams, and including the hunt itself (in which the hunters pursue not just game, but Siegfried), as well as Siegfried's killing of the bear (which symbolizes Siegfried's complicity in his own death, since as the strongest and most feared animal in the woods, the bear stands as a double of Siegfried himself). Students should suggest that each of these details contributes to a sense of foreboding and inevitability in the selection.

13. (Challenging) *Guidelines for student response:* Students should identify the interconnectedness of the four categories, noting that Siegfried's love for Kriemhild and his innate sense of honor keep him from suspecting Hagen's treachery. Furthermore, students should note that despite her love for Siegfried, Kriemhild has effectively betrayed him by passing on knowledge of his weak spot. Also, Hagen's betrayal of Siegfried stems from Brunhild's seeking revenge for her own spurned love. Given all these facts, students may suggest that love is the main emotion from which all other acts derive. Students probably will argue that human nature has not changed much since the tale was composed.

Part Test, Unit 1, Part 4: Perils and Adventures (p. 39)

Critical Reading/Vocabulary and Grammar

1. b 2. c 3. a 4. a 5. a 6. c 7. d 8. b 9. c
10. d 11. a 12. c 13. d 14. b 15. c

Questions are classified in these categories:
Comprehension 1(E), 5(A), 7(A), 8(A)
Interpretation 2(A), 6(A)
Literary Analysis 3(A), 9(A), 10(C)
Reading Strategy 4(C)
Vocabulary 13(C), 14(A)
Grammar 11(E), 12(A), 15(A)
E = Easy, A = Average, C = Challenging

Essay Questions

16. (Easy) *Guidelines for student response:* Students' essays should clearly and thoroughly explain the events in one of the four ballads. For example, the events in "Lord Randall" are expressed through a dialogue in which a son answers his mother's questions about recent events. He tells her that he went out in "the wild wood" and ate eels for dinner with his "true-love," and that his bloodhounds "swell'd" and died; he repeats that he is tired and would like to lie down. Hearing her son's words, she expresses her fear that he has been poisoned. The implication is that his love may have poisoned

him; a larger implication is that love itself may be compared to a mortal illness.

17. (Average) *Guidelines for student response:* Students should note that the Duke can use the law as a weapon against the Pastons (he has their supporters arrested) and that the Pastons must ultimately depend on themselves for the protection of their property. Students should note that Gawain's obligation to the Green Knight is purely a matter of honor—it is enforced primarily by his own conscience. In calling in the debt, the Green Knight shows another side of chivalry: he is merciful. By contrast, the modern idea of law

demands protection of property by an impartial, central authority; contracts, not debts of honor, are an important form of relationships.

18. (Challenging) *Guidelines for student response:* Students' essays should effectively explain the failure of chivalry portrayed in one of the selections. For example, in "The Twa Corbies", a knight is shown in a most un-chivalric light: as carrion for two ravens. The ballad demonstrates the idea that ultimately chivalry matters little, as its practitioners come—like everyone else—only to dust. Students may point out, though, that his death would not be as affecting if his ideals had not been set high.

Unit 2: Celebrating Humanity (1485–1625)

Sonnets 1, 35, and 75
by Edmund Spenser
Sonnets 31 and 39 by Sir Philip Sidney

Selection Test (p. 43)

Critical Reading/Vocabulary and Grammar
1. b 2. b 3. c 4. c 5. b 6. b 7. d 8. b 9. b
10. a 11. b 12. d 13. a 14. c 15. a 16. a
17. a 18. a 19. c 20. b
Questions are classified in these categories:
   Comprehension 2(E), 7(A), 9(A)
   Interpretation 5(C), 6(C), 11(A), 12(A), 15(A)
   Literary Analysis 3(A), 4(A), 10(E), 13(E)
   Reading Strategy 1(C), 8(C), 14(C)
   Vocabulary 16(E), 20(E), 19(C)
   Grammar 17(A), 18(E)
   E = Easy, A = Average, C = Challenging

Essay Questions
21. (Easy) *Guidelines for student response:* Students should choose images that convey the theme of hopeless and painful love and explain how each contributes to the theme. For example, they might select the image of "sleep, the certain knot of peace" that Sidney longs for to bring him some relief from his pain, or love as the "busy archer" with his "sharp arrows" as the

cause of that pain. They might also mention Spenser's likening his eyes to Narcissus's gaze that nothing but the sight of his beloved can satisfy.

22. (Average) *Guidelines for student response:* In their essays, students should select examples that reflect the conventions of the fair but unresponsive lady and the faithful suffering lover. For example, students may respond that in Sonnet 1, Spenser conveys his beloved's beauty by referring to her "lily hands" and likening her to an angel. He, on the other hand, suffers and envies the "leaves," "lines," and "rhymes" of his poem, because his beloved will give them more attention than she will him. They might also refer to Sidney's Sonnet 31, in which the poet identifies with the moon, who has the wan and languishing look of a lover. In questioning the moon about love "above," Sidney presents a portrait of the beloved as a proud beauty who loves to be loved, but scorns her lover.

23. (Challenging) *Guidelines for student response:* Student responses should analyze each of the sonnets and then describe the overall impression made by the three taken together. For example, students

might mention that Sonnet 1 addresses the poet's own poems and pictures them with envy in the hands of his beloved, perhaps pleasing her as he, in person, cannot. Sonnet 35 concentrates on the lover's "hungry eyes," that are only satisfied by the sight of the beloved. Sonnet 75 deals with the immortality conveyed by poetry which outlives flesh and blood. Together, the poems convey the suffering and unfulfilled love of the poet and the overwhelming effect that the beloved has on him. The poems are seen as the poet's main way of approaching his love and the means to make that love live on.

Sonnets 29, 106, 116, and 130
by William Shakespeare

Selection Test (p. 46)

Critical Reading/Vocabulary and Grammar

1. d 2. c 3. c 4. a 5. b 6. d 7. c 8. d 9. b
10. a 11. a 12. a 13. b 14. b 15. c 16. b
17. c 18. d 19. d 20. a

Questions are classified in these categories:
Comprehension 1(E), 3(A), 6(C)
Interpretation 4(C), 5(A), 7(A), 8(A), 9(A)
Literary Analysis 10(A), 11(A), 13(C)
Reading Strategy 2(A), 12(A), 14(C)
Vocabulary 15(A), 16(A), 17(A)
Grammar 18(E), 19(A), 20(A)
E = Easy, A = Average, C = Challenging

Essay Questions

21. (Easy) *Guidelines for student response:*
Students should explain how love is treated in each sonnet. For example, they may make some of these points in their answers: in Sonnet 29, love is an antidote to jealousy and self-pity; in Sonnet 106, love grows out of beauty; in Sonnet 116, true love is represented as unchanging; a mature notion of love, unencumbered by idealized fantasies, is conveyed in Sonnet 130. Students may select any poem as the truest depiction of love as long as they support their points. They might, for instance, choose Sonnet 130 because of its recognition that love is based on more than physical perfection.

22. (Average) *Guidelines for student response:*
In their essays, students should distin-

guish between the endings of Sonnets 29 and 130 and explain how each is effective. For example, students may suggest that in Sonnet 29, the couplet effectively and triumphantly drives home the point of the preceding quatrains by summarizing them: that love makes the speaker accept himself and his lot. In Sonnet 130, in contrast, students should recognize that the couplet presents a twist. After implying in the quatrains that his love is not the incredible goddess of beauty usually presented in such poetry, the poet says in the couplet that yet she is just as "rare" to him as anyone who might be considered more beautiful.

23. (Challenging) *Guidelines for student response:* In their essays, students should contrast the concepts of time presented and show how time and beauty are related in the poem. They might, for example, suggest that Sonnet 106 emphasizes the difference between time past, when people had the skill to praise beauty eloquently, and time present, when people can recognize exceptional beauty but lack the skill to immortalize it. The sonnet implies that poetry preserves beauty from the ravages of time. The idea of time presented in Sonnet 116, in contrast, is that of the destroyer, which alters the physical features—"rosy lips and cheeks"—we call beauty, yet cannot destroy true love.

Sonnets 18 and 28
by Francesco Petrarch
Sonnets 69 and 89 by Pablo Neruda

Selection Test (p. 49)

Critical Reading

1. b 2. b 3. a 4. c 5. b 6. b 7. c 8. a 9. b
10. d

Questions are classified in these categories:
Comprehension 2(C), 4(C), 5(A), 9(E), 10(A)
Interpretation 1(A), 3(E), 6(C), 7(C), 8(A)
E = Easy, A = Average, C = Challenging

Essay Questions

11. (Easy) *Guidelines for student response:*
Students should point out the concrete nature of Neruda's vision of love vs. the abstractness of Petrarch's; that is, Neruda

Sonnets 18 and 28 by Francesco Petrarch
Sonnets 69 and 89 by Pablo Neruda
(continued)

loves a real woman but Petrarch is in love with the state of being in love. Students might note that Neruda often uses the pronoun "we," suggesting a two-sided affair, but Petrarch seems to be the only actor in his own sonnets, suggesting his interest as much in his own emotions as in any particular woman. Students should find similar or contrastive elements in a modern text of their own choosing.

12. (Average) *Guidelines for student response:* Students should compare the natural setting in Sonnet 18 (desert glade, mountains, wood and plain, river) to the wind, light, wheat, rosebush, etc. in Neruda's Sonnets 69 and 89. Students should note that for Petrarch nature seems to be a retreat from love or a place to express himself without fear of rejection, misunderstanding, or ridicule. For Neruda, on the other hand, nature completely envelops his love. Students should point out that Neruda's nature imagery makes his poetry more tactile and sensual than Petrarch's, whose expressions of love are more introverted and psychological.

13. (Challenging) *Guidelines for student response:* Students should note that West describes a side of love that, instead of promising harmony and joy, causes pain, suffering, and sadness. Students should point out that neither Neruda nor Petrarch descend to such a pragmatic level described by West. Nevertheless, both poets do address the sorrow of separation, as well as feelings of melancholy, "woe," or "nothingness" at loving but not being loved in return.

Part Test, Unit 2, Part 1: Lovers and Their Lines (p. 51)

Critical Reading/Vocabulary and Grammar

1. b 2. b 3. d 4. c 5. d 6. a 7. b 8. c 9. d 10. b 11. a 12. c 13. b 14. d 15. a

Questions are classified in these categories:
Comprehension 1(A), 5(A)
Interpretation 4(A), 9(E), 10(A)

Literary Analysis 3(A)
Reading Strategy 2(A), 6(A), 7(A), 8(E)
Vocabulary 13(C), 14(A), 15(A)
Grammar 11(A), 12(C)

Essay Questions

16. (Easy) *Guidelines for student response:* Students' essays should analyze a single author's portrayal of friendship and explain why they find this portrayal especially interesting. For example, in Sonnet 29, Shakespeare's speaker professes his love and friendship to a person who gives his life profound meaning. This friendship allows the speaker to transform feelings of despair and envy into feelings of contentment.

17. (Average) *Guidelines for student response:* Students' essays should clearly and thoroughly analyze the symbolic presentation of nature in a poem. For instance, in "The Passionate Shepherd to His Love" nature represents all that is beautiful, simple, wholesome, and true in the world.

18. (Challenging) *Guidelines for student response:* Students' essays should concisely and completely analyze a poem's imagery and explain how this imagery influences the work's total effect. For instance, in addition to imagery relating to the natural world—plants, animals, details of terrain and bodies of water—Christopher Marlowe employs images of clothing. Although most of the images are based on the sense of sight, Marlowe also involves the reader's sense of hearing ("birds sing madrigals"), smell ("a thousand fragrant posies"), and touch ("lined slippers for the cold"). The imagery creates the impression of an ideal world in which love may flourish.

from *Utopia* by Sir Thomas More
Elizabeth's Speech Before Her Troops by Queen Elizabeth I

Selection Test (p. 54)

Critical Reading/Vocabulary and Grammar

1. b 2. c 3. a 4. d 5. b 6. a 7. a 8. a 9. d 10. c 11. a 12. c 13. c 14. a 15. d 16. b 17. d 18. c 19. c 20. b

Questions are classified in these categories:
  Comprehension 1(E), 10(E), 14(E)
  Interpretation 2(C), 3(C), 5(C), 11(A), 13(C)
  Literary Analysis 4(A), 7(A), 9(C)
  Reading Strategy 6(E), 8(C), 12(A)
  Vocabulary 15(A), 17(A), 18(A)
  Grammar 16(E), 19(A), 20(C)
  E = Easy, A = Average, C = Challenging

Essay Questions

21. (Easy) *Guidelines for student response:*
Students' answers should be logical and
supported by examples from the speech.
Many students will say that the queen's
speech is persuasive and moved them.
Elizabeth presents a kind and caring face
to her subjects. She tells them they are
trustworthy and that she'd die for them.
This is the stuff of persuasive speech-
making that causes a strong, favorable
reaction in an audience, especially when
their lives are being threatened by a
despised enemy.

22. (Average) *Guidelines for student response:*
Students should realize that More's views
of what a ruler should be are more realistic
and less idealistic than those of Elizabeth's.
The queen speaks in terms of laying down
her life for her kingdom, but More focuses
on a monarch who simply cares for his
subjects, albeit before himself, by tending
to poverty, curbing crime, and allowing
for the pleasures of life. Students may
note that the queen's speech is based on
a far more pressing issue—the threat of
war—and the language she uses creates
greater distance between herself and her
listeners, constructing a larger-than-life
sense of leadership.

23. (Challenging) *Guidelines for student response:* Students should note that *utopia*
today means an ideal place or state with
perfect laws. They should realize that the
title of More's book indicates an ideal he
wants monarchs to strive for, but exists
in "no place," or is unattainable. He is not
saying that this utopia has been achieved.
Students should note the many examples
from the selection that point to the king's
failings as evidence that a utopia doesn't
exist. Accept reasonable theories about
why More felt he had to invent a new word
to title his book.

from The King James Bible

Selection Test (p. 57)

Critical Reading/Vocabulary and Grammar

1. b 2. d 3. c 4. a 5. c 6. c 7. a 8. a 9. b
10. c 11. b 12. d 13. a 14. d 15. d 16. c
17. c 18. b 19. d 20. b

Questions are classified in these categories:
  Comprehension 6(A), 11(E), 12(E)
  Interpretation 1(A), 2(C), 9(A), 13(A), 15(E)
  Literary Analysis 3(C), 4(C), 7(E), 14(A)
  Reading Strategy 5(A), 8(C), 10(C), 16(E)
  Vocabulary 17(A), 20(A)
  Grammar 18(A), 19(C)
  E = Easy, A = Average, C = Challenging

Essay Questions

21. (Easy) *Guidelines for student response:*
Students should describe the relationship
that they infer and give examples from the
psalm. For example, they may infer that
God cares for, protects, and nurtures
human beings, just as a shepherd takes
loving care of his sheep in his flock or as a
good host who "preparest a table before"
his guests and makes sure they have
everything they need.

22. (Average) *Guidelines for student response:*
Students should explain the message
about the relationship of God and humans that they think the parable presents. They may state, for example, that it
means God is quick to forgive those who
have broken his commandments, even
though they have wasted their talents or
their lives, and he will joyously welcome
them back if they return to a relationship
with him. They may suggest that the role
of the other son shows God also loves and
will abundantly reward those who have
remained faithful to him.

23. (Challenging) *Guidelines for student response:* In their responses, students should
describe how animals help convey the
message in each of the selections, using
specific examples. For instance, students
might mention the inference that people
are like sheep or lambs, in Psalm 23, which
shows that God cares for them as a shepherd cares for his flock. In "The Parable of
the Prodigal Son," the association of the
prodigal son with a swine implies how deep

into degradation he had fallen; the fatted calf symbolizes abundance, generosity, and celebration. In the "Sermon on the Mount," the image of the "fowls of the air" is used to demonstrate how God cares for even the smallest creatures, and thus how he will care for his people.

from *A Man for All Seasons*
by Robert Bolt

Selection Test (p. 60)

Critical Reading

1. c 2. c 3. b 4. d 5. a 6. c 7. d 8. b 9. c 10. a

Questions are classified in these categories:
  Comprehension 2(A), 3(E), 5(E), 6(A), 7(A), 10(E)
  Interpretation 1(A), 4(C), 8(C), 9(A)
  E = Easy, A = Average, C = Challenging

Essay Questions

11. (Easy) *Guidelines for student response:* Students should identify the significant pressures of absolute authority, including the isolation that accompanies total responsibility for one's actions and the direction of the country. Students may see the power to do good as among the pros, and the temptation to abuse one's power as among the cons. Students should sense that Henry is not sincere in his desire to escape his duties, but rather is power hungry above all else.

12. (Average) *Guidelines for student response:* Students should point out that More was unwilling to betray his personal beliefs for the sake of Henry's whims. Students may note that More is not opposed in principle to absolute power, but believes rather that power must be measured by wisdom, morality, and reason. More's refusal to give in to Henry threatens the monarchy by providing an example for other people to follow.

13. (Challenging) *Guidelines for student response:* Students should note that among the constraints on absolute power are a sense of honor, duty, tradition, and

conscience, as well as the need to convince subjects to carry out orders. An absolute ruler cannot exercise his power without the support of a wide range of bureaucrats or other servants. In Henry's case, students may also point to the opposition of a moral authority, such as the Pope, which hinders, if not prevents, Henry from carrying out his wishes.

Part Test, Unit 2, Part 2: The Story of Britain—The Influence of the Monarchy (p. 62)

Critical Reading/Vocabulary and Grammar

1. c 2. a 3. b 4. a 5. d 6. c 7. b 8. a 9. c 10. c 11. b 12. d 13. a 14. c 15. b

Questions are classified in these categories:
  Comprehension 1(C), 5(A), 8(E)
  Interpretation 9(A), 10(C)
  Literary Analysis 3(A), 7(C)
  Reading Strategy 2(A), 4(A), 6(C)
  Vocabulary 11(C), 12(A)
  Grammar 13(A), 14(A), 15(C)

Essay Questions

16. (Easy) *Guidelines for student response:* Students' essays should offer clear, logical reasons why Psalm 23 might offer consolation or comfort to some people after the death of a loved one. For instance, students might mention the informal, personal tone, the gentle and accessible phrases characterizing death, and the use of imagery that conjures typical daily life.

17. (Average) *Guidelines for student response:* Students' essays should clearly and concisely compare and contrast the techniques employed in the two selections. For example, the speaker of the sermon uses an authoritative—even harsh—tone to offer archetypal examples proving his point about God's ultimate power; the speaker of the parable uses numerous details of a single narrative to instruct his audience.

18. (Challenging) *Guidelines for student response:* Students' essays should provide a clear and thorough picture of possible social and political conditions in early sixteenth-century England. For example, it is relatively easy to infer that England may have been ruled by a monarch who

was out of touch with his or her citizens' poverty, misery, and swelling feelings of resentment and willingness to create public disorders.

The Tragedy of Macbeth, Act I,
by William Shakespeare

Selection Test (p. 65)

Critical Reading/Vocabulary and Grammar
1. c 2. a 3. c 4. c 5. d 6. d 7. b 8. a 9. b
10. c 11. b 12. c 13. b 14. c 15. c 16. d
17. c 18. a 19. d 20. a

Questions are classified in these categories:
Comprehension 7(A), 8(C), 10(A)
Interpretation 1(A), 3(C), 5(E), 6(A), 12(E)
Literary Analysis 2(A), 4(C), 12(A), 15(C)
Reading Strategy 9(A), 11(A), 13(A)
Vocabulary 18(A), 19(E), 20(A)
Grammar 16(C), 17(C)
E = Easy, A = Average, C = Challenging

Essay Questions
21. (Easy) *Guidelines for student response:* Students should select several stage directions and explain what they mean and how they help the reader understand the play. For example, they might say that the stage direction [*Aside*] means that the actor is to speak the character's words aloud to the audience, but not to any other character. Lines introduced by [*Aside*] express the character's inner thoughts and are unheard by others in the scene. Students might suggest that this device allows the audience or reader to understand a character's motives. They may refer to Macbeth's lines "If chance will have me King, why, / Chance may crown me, / Without my stir," and "The Prince of Cumberland! That is a step / On which I must fall down, or else o'erleap. . . ."

22. (Average) *Guidelines for student response:* In their responses, students should interpret these lines and tell how they relate to Lady Macbeth's character in the first act. For example, students might say that Lady Macbeth is talking herself into the deed that she wants done. She wants to change her feminine nature to one she perceives as masculine—more violent and

less liable to being ruled by conscience. As is apparent, she needs this power to prevent Macbeth from backing down from his stated desire. Students might point out that later in the scene, Lady Macbeth seems to have been granted her wish for "unsexing" as she says that she would have killed her own child, if she had sworn to do it as Macbeth has sworn to do away with Duncan.

23. (Challenging) *Guidelines for student response:* Students should compare and contrast Banquo and Macbeth, using examples to illustrate their ideas. They might suggest, for example, that both are noblemen, courageous in battle, and loyal to the king as the play opens. Both are thought to be honest and upright. Students will probably point out that the differences between them start to become obvious in their first scene with the witches: Banquo sees the witches' premonitions as evil—Macbeth simply sees them as profitable for himself. Later when Macbeth speaks to the king, he refers in an aside to the fact that Malcolm is an obstacle. In the same meeting, Banquo pledges his allegiance to the king. As Macbeth plots, Banquo remains loyal and true.

The Tragedy of Macbeth, Act II,
by William Shakespeare

Selection Test (p. 68)

Critical Reading/Vocabulary and Grammar
1. c 2. b 3. b 4. a 5. c 6. b 7. a 8. c 9. a
10. c 11. a 12. c 13. a 14. b 15. b 16. d
17. b 18. c 19. d 20. c

Questions are classified in these categories:
Comprehension 5(A), 6(A), 8(A)
Interpretation 1(E), 3(A), 7(C), 11(C), 12(C)
Literary Analysis 2(C), 4(A), 13(E)
Reading Strategy 9(A), 10(A), 14(A)
Vocabulary 16(A), 18(C), 19(E)
Grammar 15(C), 17(E), 20(E)
E = Easy, A = Average, C = Challenging

Essay Questions
21. (Easy) *Guidelines for student response:* Students should explain how Macbeth's imagination works, giving examples from

the act to support their ideas. For example, they might mention the dagger he imagines, which actually seems to lead him on to do the deed and in a sense helps him go through with it. They might also mention the voice he imagines after the murder saying that "Macbeth does murder sleep," as his guilty conscience asserts itself and ensures that he will suffer more after the deed than before; it frightens him so much that he cannot complete the final details of the plot.

22. (Average) *Guidelines for student response:* Students should discuss the meaning of these lines and explain the effects of Macbeth's moral suffering. For example, students could say that the lines mean Macbeth's guilty conscience over his evil deed will prevent him from ever enjoying the relaxing and revitalizing effects of sleep. They might suggest that Shakespeare portrayed Macbeth as conscience-stricken because he is in part a good man. This is what makes him a tragic character; he has very far to fall. If Macbeth were wholly without conscience, the audience could not identify with him and would not care about him. As it is, it is as if someone we know and like had committed murder. The fact that Macbeth feels his guilt makes him more human.

23. (Challenging) *Guidelines for student response:* Students should recognize the contrast between Macbeth and Lady Macbeth in the scenes of Act II. Students might say, for example, that although Macbeth's imagination runs wild before he commits the murder, he is able to carry it out, but not really deal rationally with the details of the plot. Details are left to Lady Macbeth, who makes it all work by drugging the guards, readying their daggers for Macbeth, and planting the false evidence afterwards. She is much more rational, confident, and fearless than her husband. Students might suggest that Macbeth begins to grow into the role of successful assassin when he murders the supposedly guilty guards near the end of the scene.

The Tragedy of Macbeth, Act III,
by William Shakespeare

Selection Test (p. 71)

Critical Reading/Vocabulary and Grammar

1. c 2. d 3. b 4. d 5. c 6. b 7. a 8. a 9. b
10. c 11. b 12. d 13. c 14. a 15. b 16. d
17. b 18. a 19. b 20. c

Questions are classified in these categories:
Comprehension 1(E), 4(E), 7(A)
Interpretation 2(C), 5(A), 9(C), 10(A), 12(A)
Literary Analysis 6(A), 13(A), 15(E)
Reading Strategy 3(A), 8(C), 11(C), 14(A)
Vocabulary 17(A), 18(E), 20(A)
Grammar 16(E), 19(C)
E = Easy, A = Average, C = Challenging

Essay Questions

21. (Easy) *Guidelines for student response:* Students should explain what this soliloquy reveals about Lady Macbeth's situation and state of mind. For example, they may say that Lady Macbeth is not as happy about her husband's being king as she had expected. She knows they are still in a dangerous situation. Killing Duncan brought them their desire (power), but it did not make them "content" or bring them "safety." Students may also note that her claim that it is safer to be destroyed than to destroy and feel insecure shows how upset Lady Macbeth is.

22. (Average) *Guidelines for student response:* Students should discuss the statement considering the similarities and differences in the murders and explaining the changes in Macbeth revealed by the plot to murder Banquo. For example, students may point out as similarities that Macbeth is responsible for both murders, commits them for power, and pretends to honor both men even as they are being executed. As differences, students could say that Duncan was a mighty king, while Banquo is Macbeth's peer and friend. Macbeth kills Duncan with his own hand but has henchmen murder Banquo. Students may suggest that Macbeth is more calm and organized in his plan to murder Banquo. He almost carefully plans the crime so that it won't reflect on him without the fears that

plagued him at the death of Duncan. He is more used to such evil.

23. (Challenging) *Guidelines for student response:* Students should point out in their responses examples of characters using masks in Act III. For example, they might mention that characters such as Banquo and Lennox mask their suspicions of Macbeth for good reasons: survival and the hope of freeing their nation from tyranny. Macbeth and his wife wear evil masks: to keep his power, Macbeth pretends to be Banquo's friend, cheerfully welcomes his banquet guests after the murder, and conceals the nature of his upset from them; Lady Macbeth joins her husband in his lies and betrayals and even conceals from him her own feelings about the insecurity of their position.

The Tragedy of Macbeth, Act IV,
by William Shakespeare

Selection Test (p. 74)

Critical Reading/Vocabulary and Grammar

1. c 2. b 3. a 4. d 5. b 6. c 7. a 8. b 9. a
10. c 11. d 12. c 13. d 14. a 15. d 16. b
17. d 18. a 19. d 20. a

Questions are classified in these categories:
Comprehension 4(A), 5(A), 9(A)
Interpretation 1(A), 2(A), 3(A), 6(C), 7(C)
Literary Analysis 8(E), 10(A), 13(A)
Reading Strategy 11(C), 12(C), 14(C)
Vocabulary 15(E), 17(E), 20(E)
Grammar 16(E), 18(A), 19(A)
E = Easy, A = Average, C = Challenging

Essay Questions

21. (Easy) *Guidelines for student response:* Students should discuss Macbeth's crime in this act, suggest reasons for it, and tell how it differs from his previous crimes. For example, students might point out that in having Macduff's family murdered in Act IV, Macbeth for the first time commits a crime against completely innocent and defenseless people whose lives have little impact on his political power. This makes it an even more vicious crime than his previous murders. They might mention that his motive seems cloudy and paranoid, but Macbeth probably fears

Macduff's line because of the warning to "Beware Macduff!"

22. (Average) *Guidelines for student response:* Students should tell how Macbeth's presence is felt in each of the two scenes. For example, they might state that Lady Macduff's anger and fear in Scene ii, though directed at her absent husband, are really produced by the atmosphere of insecurity created by Macbeth's tyranny, and that the family's murders were ordered by Macbeth. Students may also mention that the meeting between Malcolm and Macduff grows from the need to save Scotland from Macbeth; Malcolm's suspicions and testing of Macduff are a direct result of the state of fear and distrust to which Macbeth has reduced everyone in Scotland.

23. (Challenging) *Guidelines for student response:* In their essays, students should evaluate each scene in Act IV, explaining how dramatically effective each is and how it contributes to plot development. They might find the first scene effective because of its frightening, otherworldly quality. They might suggest that the scene gives Macbeth more knowledge of his situation and shows the audience how brazen he has become. Students might find Scene ii effective because it gives us a view of Lady Macduff and her son that ensures we will feel pity for them and horror at the deed. Scene iii shows Macduff's and Malcolm's true natures as good men deeply saddened by Scotland's state. The testing of Macduff and the report that his family has been murdered are compelling. Of course, the scene sets the opposition to Macbeth in motion.

The Tragedy of Macbeth, Act V,
by William Shakespeare

Selection Test (p. 77)

Critical Reading/Vocabulary and Grammar

1. b 2. a 3. a 4. b 5. c 6. a 7. d 8. d 9. d
10. d 11. b 12. c 13. a 14. a 15. c 16. c
17. b 18. a 19. b 20. a

Questions are classified in these categories:
Comprehension 1(A), 2(A), 11(C)
Interpretation 5(A), 10(A), 12(C), 13(E), 14(E)
Literary Analysis 3(E), 4(A), 6(C), 7(C)

The Tragedy of Macbeth, Act V,
by William Shakespeare
(continued)

Reading Strategy 8(A), 9(A)
Vocabulary 16(A), 19(A), 20(E)
Grammar 15(A), 17(A), 18(E)
E = Easy, A = Average, C = Challenging

Essay Questions

21. (Easy) *Guidelines for student response:* Students may choose to defend either point of view in their essays as long as they support it with examples. For example, students who agree that the villains get what they deserve will say that nothing except death is a worthy penalty for cruel murderers who tear their own country apart. In contrast, some students might feel that because Lady Macbeth chooses to end her own life and Macbeth's death is quick and brave, these villains do not suffer enough for their crimes. Students might say that the fate of the Macbeths would be the same even today and that in many parts of the world today systems of checks and balances help keep rulers from becoming dictators.

22. (Average) *Guidelines for student response:* In their essays, students should apply the remark to both Lady Macbeth's condition and to the situation of Macbeth's realm. For example, in discussing Lady Macbeth, they might feel that her murderous deeds and cold-blooded attitude are unnatural and so produce her unnatural sleep walking. As far as the condition in Macbeth's realm is concerned, students might say that the unnatural murder of Duncan and the unnatural succession of Macbeth to the throne can only be followed by further unnatural acts of tyranny.

23. (Challenging) *Guidelines for student response:* Students should give their interpretation of this passage and relate it to Macbeth's situation, telling why it has fascinated readers. For example, students might mention that in the speech, Macbeth recognizes the inevitability of death, regardless of how great or evil a person is. They may note that Macbeth is also taking the position that life in general with all its ambitions and deeds is essentially meaningless. At this point, he has given up. Students may feel the speech is fascinating

because it is an eloquent and vivid summation of an unpleasant, but perhaps not uncommon, feeling about life.

from *Oedipus, the King* by Sophocles
Selection Test (p. 80)

Critical Reading

1. c 2. b 3. a 4. d 5. c 6. c 7. d 8. b 9. b 10. d

Questions are classified in these categories:
   Comprehension 2(E), 3(A), 5(E), 6(A)
   Interpretation 1(A), 4(C), 7(A), 8(C), 9(C), 10(A)
   E = Easy, A = Average, C = Challenging

Essay Questions

11. (Easy) *Guidelines for student response:* Students should point out that despite his great qualities and achievements, Oedipus was never as blessed as he seemed. Students should note the intense tone of despair in the ending, which suggests that Sophocles viewed life as a hard and bitter struggle. Students should suggest that Sophocles values the struggle above all else, seeing in the struggle (not in the circumstances of one's life) the true determination of character.

12. (Average) *Guidelines for student response:* Students should point out that Sophocles never questions fate or laments the circumstances of misfortune surrounding Oedipus. Instead, Sophocles is interested in how, given certain circumstances, a person can be expected to react. Thus, on any level the interaction of fate and free will remains paradoxical. On the one hand, Oedipus cannot escape his destiny. On the other, this does not matter, as the free choices he makes reveal and change his character, even if they do not alter the outcome.

13. (Challenging) *Guidelines for student response:* Students should point out that Oedipus's ignorance of his true identity sets events in motion. Students should see Oedipus's struggles as a journey of self-discovery. Students might see Oedipus's self-blinding as fitting retribution for a man who has been blind to a number of facts throughout. Conversely, students may see in his journey a demonstration of fierce honesty, courage, integrity, and the

workings of a powerful self will. Showing his willingness to accept a just punishment, Oedipus reaches a new level of self-awareness and humanity.

Part Test, Unit 2, Part 3: Focus on Literary Forms— Drama (p. 82)

Critical Reading/Vocabulary and Grammar

1. c 2. a 3. c 4. b 5. d 6. b 7. d 8. c 9. b
10. b 11. d 12. c 13. a 14. c 15. b 16. c
17. a 18. d 19. c 20. c

Questions are classified in these categories:
  Comprehension 1(A), 5(A), 9(A)
  Interpretation 2(A)
  Literary Analysis 3(A), 7(C), 10(A)
  Reading Strategy 4(A), 6(A), 8(A)
  Vocabulary 11(A), 12(A), 13(A), 14(A), 15(A)
  Grammar 16(A), 17(A), 18(A), 19(A), 20(C)
  E = Easy, A = Average, C = Challenging

Essay Questions

21. (Easy) *Guidelines for student response:* Students' essays should take the form of obituaries and concisely and clearly summarize the life of a character and manner of death—as well as indicating key personality traits. For example, an obituary of Lady Macbeth might allude to her nobility, her marriage to her husband, her brief motherhood, and her death in a haze of madness in her bed—and indicate that her character was marked by political ambition, moral corruption, and finally, madness.

22. (Average) *Guidelines for student response:* Students' essays should clearly and thoroughly analyze the character traits of King Duncan and explain this figure's importance to the total effect of the play. Students

may note Duncan's kindness, fairness, politeness, warmth, and generosity. The horror of his murder is only increased by the goodness of the man himself.

23. (Average) *Guidelines for student response:* Students' essays should accurately and clearly analyze the imagery in a soliloquy from the play. For instance, in Macbeth's soliloquy at the start of Act I, Scene vii, Shakespeare utilizes imagery involving the human body (*bloody, naked newborn babe, eye, tears*), animals and nature and the spirit world (*horsed, sightless couriers of the air, wind, angels, cherubin*), and possible implements of murder (*poisoned chalice, knife*) to make vivid Macbeth's murderous thoughts.

24. (Average) *Guidelines for student response:* Students' essays should clearly and vividly compare and contrast two important characters from *The Tragedy of Macbeth*. For instance, Macbeth and Macduff are both courageous men who have a strong bent of kindness; yet one can vividly contrast Macbeth's lack of self-control and wild ambition (which lead him to a violent, immoral act) with Macduff's evenhandedness, integrity, and "moral" use of violence.

25. (Challenging) *Guidelines for student response:* Students' essays should clearly explain the role of the witches and their prophecies in the play's plot and themes. For instance, the witches and their prophecies impel Macbeth's actions at the beginning of the play, and his actions set the entire plot in motion. Similarly, Banquo's sense of ambition is also stirred by the witches, although he keeps this sense in check. However, in both cases, the men themselves—and not the supernatural world—are responsible for their actions.

Unit 3: A Turbulent Time (1625–1798)

Works of John Donne

Selection Test (p. 86)

Critical Reading/Vocabulary and Grammar

1. a 2. d 3. b 4. c 5. d 6. b 7. d 8. b 9. a
10. b 11. c 12. a 13. b 14. d 15. c 16. b
17. b 18. c 19. a 20. d

Questions are classified in these categories:
  Comprehension 4(E), 10(E)
  Interpretation 1(E), 6(A), 11(A), 12(A), 14(A)
  Literary Analysis 8(C), 9(C), 13(C)
  Reading Strategy 2(A), 3(C), 5(A), 7(A)
  Vocabulary 15(A), 16(E), 17(C)
  Grammar 18(A), 19(A), 20(E)
  E = Easy, A = Average, C = Challenging

Works of John Donne
(continued)

Essay Questions

21. (Easy) *Guidelines for student response:* Students should choose one paradox from "Meditation 17," discussing it in terms of its apparent contradiction and the sense behind it. They should explain how the conceits they choose are appropriate. For example, students might choose to explain the paradox that "affliction is a treasure," saying that affliction—usually considered something to be avoided—brings people closer to God. As conceits, students might note the comparison of mankind to a book, which is appropriate because it empha-sizes the relationship of individuals to each other and is used to give a view of death. They might also choose the comparison of mankind to a continent that is diminished if one clod of earth is washed away.

22. (Average) *Guidelines for student response:* Students should cite several special char-acteristics of the love between the speaker and his beloved, illustrating them with references to the text. For example, they might mention that the couple's love is more spiritual than physical, and there-fore greater, as evidenced by the compari-son with "Dull sublunary lovers" in "A Valediction." Students might also say that this love involves a total sharing of all emotions, so that the unhappiness of one lover ("When thou sighest . . . ") has a destructive effect on the other, as shown in "Song." Students could note Donne's idea of love as a sharing of souls, which makes physical separation not "A breach, but an expansion" ("A Valediction: Forbidding Mourning").

23. (Challenging) *Guidelines for student re-sponse:* Students should give accurate definitions of conceits and paradoxes and then provide good explanations for why each is especially appropriate to religious writings and love poetry, supporting their ideas with examples from Donne. Stu-dents might suggest that such religious beliefs as life after death can only be ex-pressed as paradoxes, while conceits allow the religious writer to explore concepts that may be difficult to illuminate in more straightforward language. The use of the image of a book for the relationship of men to each other and to God is an example. Students might note that love involves paradoxical and mysterious notions that are best explained by unusual images like the "compass conceit."

"On My First Son," "Song: To Celia," and "Still to be Neat" by Ben Jonson

Selection Test (p. 89)

Critical Reading/Vocabulary and Grammar

1. a 2. b 3. b 4. d 5. d 6. c 7. c 8. d 9. a
10. c 11. b 12. d 13. b 14. a 15. b 16. d
17. b 18. a 19. b 20. b

Questions are classified in these categories:
    Comprehension (3A), 10(C), 12(C)
    Interpretation 1(E), 2(A), 6(E), 8(A), 11(A)
    Literary Analysis 4(A), 5(E0, 9(A), 15(E)
    Reading Strategy 7(E), 13(C), 14(A)
    Vocabulary 16(C), 19(C), 20(A)
    Grammar 17(A), 18(A)
    E = Easy, A = Average, C = Challenging

Essay Questions

21. (Easy) *Guidelines for student response:* Students should mention that the poem "On My First Son" is addressed to the poet's deceased son; "Song: To Celia" is addressed to a lady whom the speaker loves; "Still to Be Neat" is addressed to a lady, but the speaker's relationship to her is unclear. Students may state that the first stanza of the poem "Song: To Celia" would be dramatically different if written in the third person. The poet could not use the image in the first four lines ("Drink to me only with thine eyes . . .") without altering them, losing the grace and balance of the lines. "On My First Son" gains much of its emotional power from the direct address of the speaker to his son, especially in lines 1–2 and lines 9–10. Much of this intense emotion would be lost if the poem were written in the third person.

22. (Average) *Guidelines for student response:* Students should cite specific characteris-tics of Jonson's work such as clarity, grace,

and balance. They should support their essay with specific details from the poems. For example, they may mention carefully chosen words and phrases such as "sweet neglect," "Drink to me only with thine eyes," and "makes simplicity a grace."

23. (Challenging) *Guidelines for student response:* Students should mention that the brevity of an epigram forces the poet to compress emotion into a few lines, making it all the more intense. Students may cite lines 1–2 and lines 9–10 as examples of how Jonson powerfully expresses his grief. Students may mention that while a longer poem might include more details about the boy, the intensity of emotion expressed by Jonson may become watered down.

"To His Coy Mistress"
by Andrew Marvell
"To the Virgins, to Make Much of Time" by Robert Herrick
"Song" by Sir John Suckling

Selection Test (p. 92)

Critical Reading/Vocabulary and Grammar

1. b 2. c 3. a 4. c 5. d 6. c 7. c 8. a 9. b
10. b 11. b 12. d 13. c 14. a 15. a 16. d
17. c 18. b 19. c 20. a

Questions are classified in these categories:
    Comprehension 1(A), 3(A), 8(A)
    Interpretation 2(E), 5(A), 7(A), 9(A), 10(A)
    Literary Analysis 12(C)
    Reading Strategy 4(C), 11(A), 13(A)
    Vocabulary 14(A), 15(E), 16(E), 17(E)
    Grammar 18(A), 19(A), 20(A)
    E = Easy, A = Average, C = Challenging

Essay Questions

21. (Easy) *Guidelines for student response:* Students should recognize that each of these poets uses the *carpe diem* theme for different purposes. The speaker in "To His Coy Mistress" is urging his mistress to stop being coy and to live and love for the moment. The speaker in "To the Virgins, to Make Much of Time" is not writing to a mistress, but to two or more virgins. His purpose is to urge them not to waste their lives waiting for the perfect love because their beauty will fade. Suckling's poem is

the least like the other two. His speaker is talking to a friend who is sick with unrequited love. The speaker is urging his friend not to waste his youth being wan and mute for someone who doesn't love him. Get on with your life, he says.

22. (Average) *Guidelines for student response:* Students should state that each poet clearly displays his wit and facility with language in each poem. "To His Coy Mistress," is clearly lighthearted. Marvell's speaker uses exaggeration to put down his mistress's wish to be coy. He describes at length the slow, deliberate ways in which he would love her and insists, "Nor would I love at lower rate." Of course, he adds in subsequent verses that there's just no time for all that. In "To the Virgins, to Make Much of Time," Herrick draws clever metaphors using the rosebuds and the sun. He plays with words, as with *marry* in the last verse, which could mean "to marry," "for goodness' sake," or "to be merry." Suckling enjoys chiding his subject by repeating questions in the form of "Prithee, why so pale?" and "Prithee, why so mute?" He plays with the words *move, make,* and *take*. For example, in the final verse, he insists his listener's actions "cannot take her" so the "devil take her!"

23. (Challenging) *Guidelines for student response:* Students should recognize that both Marvell and Herrick use images to develop their poems, but Suckling does not. Marvell's poem is loaded with images. Many of them are brief references, but several, as the image of the bird of prey, are better developed. Some of Marvell's images, such as the reference to the conversion of the Jews, are somewhat obscure and require special knowledge or footnotes to understand. Herrick uses just a few metaphors that are each developed in an entire stanza. His images are easily accessible. Special knowledge is not required, for example, to understand the image of the rose or the sun. Students will probably conclude that the images are effective in communicating emotions and ideas that would be difficult to explain directly.

"Freeze Tag" by Suzanne Vega
"New Beginning" by Tracy Chapman

Selection Test (p. 95)

Critical Reading

1. b 2. b 3. a 4. c 5. b 6. b 7. c 8. a 9. b
10. d

Questions are classified in these categories:
   Comprehension 2(E), 4(A), 6(E), 7(E)
   Interpretation 1(A), 3(C), 5(A), 8(C), 9(C),
      10(A)
   E = Easy, A = Average, C = Challenging

Essay Questions

11. (Easy) *Guidelines for student response:*
   Students should recognize that
   Chapman's philosophy is directly opposed
   to Santayana's. Students might prefer
   Chapman's approach, arguing that historical memory has caused suffering
   as often as it has prevented it. Students
   may see Santayana's philosophy as more
   practical and Chapman's as more idealistic. Students should relate one of the
   two philosophies to a contemporary
   social problem.

12. (Average) *Guidelines for student response:*
   Students should identify the everyday details (numerous variations on the motifs
   of "cold" and "game"), the juxtaposition of
   which creates metaphors of indecision
   and role-playing (as opposed to genuine
   action). Students should see the everyday
   picture of a schoolyard in winter as a
   metaphor for the entropy which can
   envelop relationships.

13. (Challenging) *Guidelines for student response:* Students should note the
   "utopian" aspects of Chapman's song,
   suggesting that the mere desire for change
   may yield few results without a concrete
   plan of action. Students may view Chapman as arguing for a spiritual makeover,
   from which concrete social changes might
   then occur. Students should see that
   Vega's song describes a spiritual rut
   people can fall into, one that prevents
   them from making changes. Chapman's
   song addresses global and even political
   concerns, while Vega's is more intimate
   and personal. Students might suggest
   that changes are more easily made on the

personal than on the social level, or that
the two levels are inextricably connected.

Part Test, Unit 3, Part 1: The War Against Time (p. 97)

Critical Reading/Vocabulary and Grammar

1. a 2. c 3. d 4. b 5. b 6. c 7. a 8. d 9. b
10. d 11. a 12. a 13. c 14. d 15. b

Questions are classified in these categories:
   Comprehension 1(C), 5(C), 9(A)
   Interpretation 2(A), 6(A), 8(C), 10(C)
   Literary Analysis 3(A), 7(C)
   Reading Strategy 4(A)
   Vocabulary 11(A), 12(A), 13(A)
   Grammar 14(A), 15(C)
   E = Easy, A = Average, C = Challenging

Essay Questions

16. (Easy) *Guidelines for student response:*
   Students' essays should identify the
   specific object of the poet's gentle (or
   sharp) barbs—and explain how the poet
   goes about making fun of this aspect of
   romantic love. For example, Sir John
   Suckling pokes fun at some lovers'
   tendency to affect (or fall prey to) a sense
   of physical ailment and despondency in
   order to win the heart of a lover.

17. (Average) *Guidelines for student response:*
   Students' essays should compare and
   contrast Jonson's and Herrick's poetic
   styles in these two poems and explain how
   their styles relate to the subject of death.
   For example, Herrick's relatively sunny
   imagery (*rosebuds, a-flying, flower, smiles*)
   and his use of rhythm and rhyme create a
   light, songlike effect, which is appropriate
   in light of his subject—the eventual death
   of (all) young women (and men). In contrast, Jonson's topic—the death of his
   seven-year-old son—is more sober and personal. Fittingly, his imagery is largely color-
   less (*sin, hope, fate, flesh's rage, misery*),
   and the poem's rhythm and rhyme underscore the speaker's serious, grieving tone.

18. (Challenging) *Guidelines for student response:* Students' essays should clearly
   explain how one poet addresses themes of
   life and death. For instance, by personifying and directly addressing death, John
   Donne's speaker lessens the sense of overwhelming dread and fear that so often

imbues poems about death. The speaker unapologetically sets out the reason—God's promise of eternal life—why death's treachery is illusion.

Poetry of John Milton

Selection Test (p. 100)

Critical Reading/Vocabulary and Grammar

1. b 2. d 3. a 4. d 5. c 6. b 7. a 8. a 9. a
10. b 11. c 12. b 13. c 14. b 15. d 16. a
17. d 18. c 19. b 20. c

Questions are classified in these categories:
  Comprehension 6(A), 12(C)
  Interpretation 1(A), 5(A), 7(A), 8(E), 9(E), 14(A)
  Literary Analysis 4(A), 11(C)
  Reading Strategy 2(A), 3(C), 10(A), 13(A), 15(C)
  Vocabulary 16(E), 17(E), 18(E)
  Grammar 19(A), 20(A)
  E = Easy, A = Average, C = Challenging

Essay Questions

21. (Easy) *Guidelines for student response:* Students should explain whether they do or do not think that Milton was working through personal issues in these poems. Most students will conclude that he was. They may cite, for example, his worry that his blindness is preventing him from using his talents to serve God. They may point out that a concern over the passage of years is an issue that most people must deal with sooner or later. They may also point out that *Paradise Lost* was written after the Restoration when Milton's hopes for the Protestant government were crushed. In dealing with defeat and victory and the ongoing fight between good and evil in this epic, he may have been sifting through his feelings toward events in England during his lifetime.

22. (Average) *Guidelines for student response:* Students will point out that the civil war in England is paralleled by the poem's civil war in heaven. They may say that there were definite winners in the battle between Satan and God, but that God's victory did not bring peace and calm. Students should give examples from the poem to support their responses.

23. (Challenging) *Guidelines for student response:* Students should identify and analyze the salient aspects of Satan's character. They should then explain how these character traits help make him a powerful and interesting central figure. Students will probably point out that Satan is clearly an evil force in this book. He is also a charismatic leader who appears to have the absolute confidence of his followers. These attributes make Satan interesting. Students will probably say he is also a sympathetic character and may give as reasons, such as his downcast state, his courage in facing his diminished state, and his determination to continue the fight as reasons for their sympathy. They may also cite the reasons he gives for his rebellion, such as his opposition to the "tyranny of heav'n," as additional cause for sympathy.

from "Eve's Apology in Defense of Women" by Amelia Lanier
"To Lucasta, on Going to the Wars" and "To Althea, from Prison"
by Richard Lovelace

Selection Test (p. 103)

Critical Reading/Vocabulary and Grammar

1. a 2. d 3. b 4. b 5. c 6. d 7. c 8. d 9. b
10. a 11. b 12. b 13. d 14. c 15. d 16. d
17. c 18. b 19. c 20. a

Questions are classified in these categories:
  Comprehension 1(E), 8(C)
  Interpretation 6(C), 9(A), 10(A), 11(A), 12(A), 13(A)
  Literary Analysis 3(C), 7(C), 14(E)
  Reading Strategy 2(A), 4(A), 5(A)
  Vocabulary 15(A), 16(E), 17(E)
  Grammar 18(A), 19(E), 20(E)
  E = Easy, A = Average, C = Challenging

Essay Questions

21. (Easy) *Guidelines for student response:* Students should accurately describe the general historical context of Lovelace's poems, including the poet's siding with the king during a civil war. His feelings of honor and duty toward the king are evident in "To Lucasta, on Going to the Wars." Students might also mention that Lovelace was twice imprisoned by the

from "Eve's Apology in Defense of Women"
by Amelia Lanier
"To Lucasta, on Going to the Wars" and
"To Althea, from Prison" by Richard Lovelace
(continued)

Puritans. In "To Althea, from Prison," he says his ideals keep him free even though his body is confined.

22. (Average) *Guidelines for student response:* Students should present their interpretations of "Eve's Apology in Defense of Women" using examples from the poem to support their ideas. For example, students may mention Lanier's opening statement that Adam "was most to blame." Students might make connections between the unfair treatment of Eve and the continued treatment of women as second-class citizens.

23. (Challenging) *Guidelines for student response:* Students should present their interpretations of either "To Lucasta, on Going to the Wars" or "To Althea, from Prison" or both, supported by specific details from the poems. Students might say that Lovelace believes in the chivalric values of love, honor, and loyalty. Students might say that Lovelace holds honor above romantic love, and that he would not believe himself worthy of love if he did not perform his duty. Regarding "To Althea, from Prison," students might mention all of the images that Lovelace uses—such as love, loyalty, and hope—as ideals that set him free even in his imprisonment.

Part Test, Unit 3, Part 2: The Story of Britain—A Nation Divided (p. 106)

Critical Reading/Vocabulary and Grammar

1. b 2. d 3. a 4. c 5. a 6. d 7. c 8. b 9. a
10. b 11. c 12. c 13. a 14. b 15. d

Questions are classified in these categories:
Comprehension 1(E), 5(A), 9(A)
Interpretation 2(C), 6(C), 8(C)
Literary Analysis 3(A), 7(C), 10(A)
Reading Strategy 4(C)
Vocabulary 11(A), 12(C), 13(A)
Grammar 14(A), 15(C)
E = Easy, A = Average, C = Challenging

Essay Questions

16. (Easy) *Guidelines for student response:* Students' essays should describe in detail how Lovelace's poem would affect them if they were its intended audience. For instance, students might note that they would feel anger, fear, or sadness when reading that Lovelace's speaker loved "honor more" than themselves.

17. (Average) *Guidelines for student response:* Students' essays should clearly and thoroughly explain how Lovelace expresses both grief and praise in a single poem. For example, Lovelace's speaker praises his lover, Althea, with images evoking her physical beauty ("I lie tangled in her hair"), as well as her loyalty and spirit. He grieves for his lost liberty—yet he believes that because his love for Althea is so profound and alive, he is essentially free even in prison.

18. (Challenging) *Guidelines for student response:* Students' essays should analyze a sonnet carefully in order to explain how Milton treats the issue of free will. For example, in Sonnet VII Milton's speaker asserts quite explicitly ("It shall be still in strictest measure even / To that same lot . . . Toward which time leads me, and the will of Heaven") that his life is directed by God.

from *The Diary* by Samuel Pepys
from *A Journal of the Plague Year* by Daniel Defoe

Selection Test (p. 109)

Critical Reading/Vocabulary and Grammar

1. d 2. b 3. b 4. a 5. c 6. b 7. d 8. a 9. b
10. a 11. c 12. d 13. d 14. a 15. d 16. b
17. a 18. b 19. a 20. c

Questions are classified in these categories:
Comprehension 3(E), 8(E)
Interpretation 1(A), 2(A), 6(C), 7(C), 9(E), 13(C)
Literary Analysis 4(C), 5(E), 10(A), 11(A)
Reading Strategy 12(A), 14(A)
Vocabulary 19(A), 17(E), 20(A)
Grammar 16(C), 18(A), 19(A)
E = Easy, A = Average, C = Challenging

Essay Questions

21. (Easy) *Guidelines for student response:* Students' essays should identify details that illustrate what it might have been like to live in London during the plague. For example, Defoe's narrator notes that while walking down the street, he constantly hears cries of mourning.

22. (Average) *Guidelines for student response:* Students' essays should examine the structures of the excerpts by either Pepys or Defoe or both. Pepys primarily writes about events in chronological order, offering little reflection or background information. Defoe writes about one ongoing event in chronological order, but the rest of his account provides background information, facts and statistics, and reflection. Pepys also is clearly writing at the time that the events occurred, while Defoe's narrator appears to be writing some years later.

23. (Challenging) *Guidelines for student response:* Students' essays should examine the qualities of either Pepys or the narrator of Defoe's *Journal,* or both. Pepys's response to the plague is to continue to do his job as a civil servant as well as he can, while the response of Defoe's narrator seems to be to indulge his curiosity about what is happening. But both characters have feelings of compassion for the plague victims.

from *Gulliver's Travels*
by Jonathan Swift

Selection Test (p. 112)

Critical Reading/Vocabulary and Grammar

1. a 2. c 3. c 4. a 5. b 6. a 7. d 8. a 9. b
10. d 11. a 12. c 13. c 14. a 15. d 16. c
17. d 18. d 19. b 20. c

Questions are classified in these categories:
  Comprehension 4(A), 9(E), 10(A)
  Interpretation 3(A), 7(C), 8(C), 13(C), 14(A)
  Literary Analysis 5(A), 6(A), 11(A)
  Reading Strategy 1(A), 2(A), 12(C)
  Vocabulary 15(A), 16(A), 17(E)
  Grammar 18(E), 19(A), 20(A)
  E = Easy, A = Average, C = Challenging

Essay Questions

21. (Easy) *Guidelines for student response:* Students' essays should present their findings supported by specific details from the selection, for example, Swift's satire of human nature as reflected by the petty acts of the ruling class. Students could also cite the emperor of Lilliput's reaction when Gulliver refuses to use his physical might to ruin the kingdom of Blefuscu. The emperor takes this as a personal slight and begins scheming to rid Lilliput of Gulliver. Students might find other examples in the conflict between the two egg-cracking factions, which satirizes religious conflicts, specifically the one between Catholic France and Protestant England.

22. (Average) *Guidelines for student response:* Students' essays should show that, within the excerpts in this selection, Swift is mainly addressing the intertwined topics of politics and religion. Students should use specific examples, such as the political situation between the Blefuscudians and the Lilliputians, a thinly veiled reference to the religious conflicts of Swift's day. They might also mention the king of Brobdingnag's assessment of English politics and Gulliver's nationalism.

    Another possibility is to draw the connection between the satire of Swift and his experience (loss of his career in politics due to his religion, and the turnaround in his political fortunes when he converted).

23. (Challenging) *Guidelines for student response:* Students' essays should provide examples of Swift's cutting satire regarding, for example, the pride of the emperor of Lilliput, the scheming among the Lilliputian ministers, and the patronizing attitudes of the king and court of Brobdingnag. They should also note Swift's love of the individual spirit, as evidenced by the king of Brobdingnag's intelligence and sensitivity.

from *An Essay on Man* and from *The Rape of the Lock*
by Alexander Pope

Selection Test (p. 115)

Critical Reading/Vocabulary and Grammar

1. b 2. d 3. b 4. b 5. c 6. d 7. b 8. d 9. c
10. a 11. a 12. c 13. d 14. c 15. b 16. d
17. c 18. c 19. b 20. c

Questions are classified in these categories:
Comprehension 12(E)
Interpretation 1(E), 2(C), 7(C), 10(A), 11(A)
Literary Analysis 9(A), 13(A), 14(C)
Reading Strategy 4(A), 5(A), 6(A), 8(A)
Vocabulary 15(E), 16(E), 17(E)
Grammar 18(A), 19(A), 20(A)
E = Easy, A = Average, C = Challenging

Essay Questions

21. (Easy) *Guidelines for student response:* Students may point out that the poet introduces gods, goddesses, and spirits that have a hand in what happens in the poem. This conceit deflects blame for the silly behavior away from Belinda and her cohorts and onto nonhuman creatures. The poet also presents the characters as overly grand rather than ordinary; their deeds are described as heroic rather than petty. Pope could just as easily have written an embittered, brutal attack. Instead he simply points out absurdities by exaggerating the situation until it becomes comic.

22. (Average) *Guidelines for student response:* Students may say that because Pope was not allowed into the court, he was able to view it more objectively and therefore see the humor and irony in what took place there. Having to work all his life to make a living from his writing, he must have found the leisure classes he lampoons in *The Rape of the Lock* very silly indeed. Perhaps his illness kept him from mixing with others, giving him an outsider's clear-eyed, or perhaps somewhat jealous, view.

23. (Challenging) *Guidelines for student response:* Students may note that most people tend to take their problems (even petty ones) very seriously, just as the people in *The Rape of the Lock* do. Students may also note the universality of the struggles between the sexes, as shown by the war fought over the taking of a lock of Belinda's hair. They may mention the universal aspects of mankind put forth in *An Essay on Man:* for example, doubt, ignorance, passion, confusion, and so on. The idea that mankind is at once amazing and ridiculous is one that has traveled down through the ages.

from *The Preface to A Dictionary of the English Language* and from *A Dictionary of the English Language* by Samuel Johnson
from *The Life of Samuel Johnson*
by James Boswell

Selection Test (p. 118)

Critical Reading/Vocabulary and Grammar

1. d 2. c 3. c 4. b 5. c 6. d 7. a 8. a 9. b
10. c 11. a 12. d 13. a 14. b 15. a 16. d
17. b 18. d 19. b 20. a

Questions are classified in these categories:
Comprehension 3(A), 10(E), 12(E)
Interpretation 1(A), 2(E), 11(A), 13(A), 14(A)
Literary Analysis 4(A), 9(C), 15(E)
Reading Strategy 5(A), 6(A), 7(A), 8(C)
Vocabulary 16(C), 17(E), 18(A)
Grammar 19(A) 20(C)
E = Easy, A = Average, C = Challenging

Essay Questions

21. (Easy) *Guidelines for student response:* Students should point out the chief differences in Johnson's dictionary; for example, the subjective quality of the definitions, the emphasis on literary examples, and the lack of phonetic and etymological information. They should show awareness of Johnson's great achievement in standardizing English usage. They might conclude that, in spite of his reservations about his work in "The Preface," Johnson brought order and authority to the English language, two goals he had set for himself.

22. (Average) *Guidelines for student response:* Students should describe Johnson's contradictory traits as set forth in the biography. In evaluating these qualities, they might point out that his literary and intellectual achievements, high moral standards, kindness, and benevolence toward

others outweigh, by far, his occasional rudeness and sarcasm.

23. (Challenging) *Guidelines for student response:* Students should describe Boswell's character as inferred from his statements about Johnson in the biography. For example, they might identify Boswell's insight into human nature when he describes the contradictory qualities in Johnson and how such qualities are exaggerated in a man of brilliance.

"Elegy Written in a Country Churchyard" by Thomas Gray
"A Nocturnal Reverie" by Anne Finch, Countess of Winchilsea

Selection Test (p. 121)

Critical Reading/Vocabulary and Grammar

1. c 2. c 3. b 4. a 5. c 6. a 7. b 8. d 9. d
10. b 11. a 12. d 13. a 14. b 15. b 16. d
17. c 18. b 19. d 20. c

Questions are classified in these categories:
Comprehension 5(A), 7(E), 9(C), 11(A)
Interpretation 4(E), 6(A), 8(C)
Literary Analysis 2(A), 10(E), 12(C), 13(C)
Reading Strategy 1(E), 3(A), 14(A)
Vocabulary 15(E), 16(E), 17(A)
Grammar 18(E), 19(A), 20(A)
E = Easy, A = Average, C = Challenging

Essay Questions

21. (Easy) *Guidelines for student response:* Students can point to the end of the poem, which states that the calm of the night will soon give way to the confusion of the day. The speaker wishes to remain wrapped in the mysterious wonderment of the night. There she finds that she is content with wordless musings, that her "rage" is "disarmed." She also mentions that with daylight comes the pursuit of pleasures that are seldom reached.

22. (Average) *Guidelines for student response:* Students may note that night has long been associated with mystery and unknowable things, concepts that fascinated both Gray and Finch. Darkness and night can also be used as metaphors for death. In Gray's "Elegy," the dusk is associated with a melancholy that "marked him for its own." In Finch's

"Reverie," the darkness brings with it a deep sense of peace, an appreciation for the natural world and all its intricacies, and an escape from the confusion and unfairness of daylight pursuits.

23. (Challenging) *Guidelines for student response:* Students may cite Gray's background and lifestyle as components that set him apart from his rural subjects. He stands apart from them by virtue of the fact that he is obviously educated and wealthy enough that he has no need to engage in manual labor. In short, he displays a certain detachment from the people, as shown by his references to them as "rude forefathers," "rustic moralists," and "unlettered Muse."

from *The Analects* by Confucius
from The Declaration of Independence by Thomas Jefferson

Selection Test (p. 124)

Critical Reading

1. c 2. b 3. a 4. d 5. c 6. c 7. d 8. b 9. c
10. d

Questions are classified in these categories:
Comprehension 3(A), 6(A), 8(E), 9(C)
Interpretation 1(C), 2(C), 4(A), 5(A), 7(C), 10(A)
E = Easy, A = Average, C = Challenging

Essay Questions

11. (Easy) *Guidelines for student response:* Students should see the dialogue form of *The Analects* as a means of making Confucius and his philosophy seem alive and relevant. Students may suggest that the dialogue form shows Confucius thinking and acting, and it encourages the reader to engage with the text as a living philosophy, not simply as received wisdom.

12. (Average) *Guidelines for student response:* Students should note that the central principle of the Declaration of Independence is the right of self-determination. In justifying independence, Jefferson faults the king of England for serving his own desires rather than the needs of his people. Confucius had denounced such behavior centuries

from *The Analects* by Confucius

from The Declaration of Independence by Thomas Jefferson
(continued)

earlier. Jefferson and Confucius agree that service to the people is the guiding principle of just government. Though Confucius does not mention democracy, he believes, as Jefferson does, that the only rational form of government is one that is just and moral.

13. (Challenging) *Guidelines for student response:* Students should identify Confucius's emphasis on moral behavior as the cornerstone of his conception of moral government. They may also be able to link this idea to the justifications put forth by Jefferson for declaring independence, and point out that both writers place great emphasis on morality in the conduct of government.

Part Test, Unit 3, Part 3: The Ties That Bind (p. 126)

Critical Reading/Vocabulary and Grammar

1. b 2. a 3. d 4. b 5. c 6. b 7. c 8. a 9. b
10. d 11. c 12. d 13. a 14. a 15. b 16. c
17. a 18. b 19. c 20. a

Questions are classified in these categories:
Comprehension 1(E), 5(A)
Interpretation 2(A), 6(E), 9(C), 10(A)
Literary Analysis 3(A)
Reading Strategy 4(A), 7(C), 8(E)
Vocabulary 11(C), 12(A), 18(A), 19(C), 20(C)
Grammar 13(A), 14(C), 15(A), 16(A), 17(A)
E = Easy, A = Average, C = Challenging

Essay Questions

21. (Easy) *Guidelines for student response:* Students' essays should use one example to explain how Pope uses grand language to make his subject appear ridiculous. For example, Pope uses words such as *aerial guard*, *rank*, *ancient race*, *kings in majesty revered*, *expressive emblem*, and *halberts in their hand* to describe a simple card game.

22. (Average) *Guidelines for student response:* Students' essays should identify a handful of elements of society that Swift ridicules—as well as judge his satire light

or bitter. For instance, students might note that Swift takes aim at human affectation, political and legal corruption, injustice, and war. Swift's satire tends toward the dark, bitter, and unsparing, although it does not lack humor.

23. (Average) *Guidelines for student response:* Students' essays should clearly and effectively discuss what Gray's speaker actually mourns. For instance, students should note that the speaker mourns all of humanity, as well as his own eventual death.

24. (Average) *Guidelines for student response:* Students' essays should comprise four or five dictionary entries written in the style of Samuel Johnson in his *Dictionary of the English Language*. For example: *musician, n.* One who skillfully elicits tones or melodies from an instrument such as a violin or harpsichord. At the king's entrance, the musician began to play a grand march.

25. (Challenging) *Guidelines for student response:* Students' essays should discuss concisely and clearly the relationship between Boswell and Johnson as it is detectable in the biographical excerpt. For example, students may note that Boswell greatly admires his subject, though he can be critical of some of Johnson's habits. Though Boswell's view is biased, some students may still argue that his portrait is "true."

"On Spring" by Samuel Johnson
from "The Aims of the Spectator" by Joseph Addison

Selection Test (p. 130)

Critical Reading/Vocabulary and Grammar

1. c 2. b 3. a 4. c 5. d 6. c 7. c 8. a 9. b 10. c
11. a 12. b 13. b 14. d 15. d 16. c 17. a 18. b
19. d 20. a

Questions are classified in these categories:
Comprehension 1(A), 7(A)
Interpretation 3(A), 5(A), 6(C), 10(A), 11(A)
Literary Analysis 4(C), 8(A), 9(C), 12(E)
Reading Strategy 2(E), 13(E), 14(A)
Vocabulary 15(A), 16(A), 17(E)
Grammar 18(E), 19(A), 20(C)
E = Easy, A = Average, C = Challenging

Essay Questions

21. (Easy) *Guidelines for student response:* Students should present their interpretations of "On Spring" with support from specific details from the essay. For example, they may say that Johnson sees springtime as a time of hope, and more importantly as a time to take pleasure in and commune with nature. They may cite Johnson's criticism of people who enjoy only social pleasures and not the pleasures of solitary walks in the outdoors. They might also find a recommendation for enjoying nature in the writer's passages describing natural beauty and the gifts that are to be found in nature.

22. (Average) *Guidelines for student response:* Students should interpret their views of Addison's attitudes using examples and specific details from the essay. For example, they might say that Addison's attitude toward the "well-regulated families" is positive and that he believes *The Spectator* will provide a healthy dose of news and wisdom. Alternatively, students might say that Addison's attitude toward the "fraternity of spectators" is also positive, and that *The Spectator* will provide such people a greater insight into the workings of people and the world. Students may also say that Addison is highly critical of people who are interested only in trivial things. They may also write that Addison is not critical of women, but that he is critical of the constraints that society places on women and on their ability to better themselves and their minds.

23. (Challenging) *Guidelines for student response:* Students should interpret the meaning and significance of the scholar's quote using examples from the essay to support their ideas. Students may cite Johnson's mention of men "who cannot bear [their] own company," or people who must "divert their thoughts by cards, or assemblies, a tavern dinner, or the prattle of the day," or "those whom sorrow incapacitates to enjoy the pleasures of contemplation," or some other specific quote that describes a frailty from Johnson's point of view. Students might also mention that Johnson does not condemn these traits but only finds them sad given the opportunities that nature affords for pleasant solitude and reflection on the wonders of nature.

"Homeless" by Anna Quindlen

Selection Test (p. 133)

Critical Reading

1. b 2. b 3. a 4. c 5. b 6. b 7. c 8. a 9. b 10. d

Questions are classified in these categories:
  Comprehension 2(E), 5(C), 6(E), 9(A), 10(C)
  Interpretation 1(C), 3(A), 4(A), 7(A), 8(A)
  E = Easy, A = Average, C = Challenging

Essay Questions

11. (Easy) *Guidelines for student response:* Students should suggest that the informal essay achieves an immediacy that a formal genre may lack. Students may or may not find the writer's approach appropriate. Nonetheless, they should point out that Quindlen's informality acts as a lure, drawing readers in and persuading them to consider her point of view. Although a factual, objective text might give more information, Quindlen's informal essay conveys a better sense of what homelessness means in widely understandable terms.

12. (Average) *Guidelines for student response:* Students should be able to repeat Quindlen's definition of home as a place of "certainty, stability, predictablity, and privacy." Students should note that Quindlen does not desire this type of "home" for herself alone, but for her family as well. Students should note that Quindlen's sense of place, which propels her interest in homelessness, derives from a family relationship (her grandfather). Students should further point out that the loosening of family bonds over the years has gone hand in hand with the deterioration of the concept of "home."

13. (Challenging) *Guidelines for student response:* Students might agree that Quindlen offers no concrete solutions, or they might contend that her "start with

"Homeless" by Anna Quindlen
(continued)

something small" approach is really the only way to conquer the problem. Students should note that Quindlen does not state any specific goals, though they might suggest something like "a house for every person." Students should suggest some policy of their own as a way to address homelessness.

Part Test, Unit 3, Part 4: Focus on Literary Forms— The Essay (p. 135)

Critical Reading/Vocabulary and Grammar

1. d 2. b 3. c 4. a 5. d 6. b 7. a 8. c 9. d
10. d 11. c 12. b 13. d 14. d 15. c

Questions are classified in these categories:
  Comprehension 1(A), 5(C), 9(A)
  Interpretation 2(E), 6(A), 10(A)
  Literary Analysis 3(C), 7(A)
  Reading Strategy 4(A), 8(A)
  Vocabulary 11(C), 12(E), 13(A)
  Grammar 14(C), 15(C)
  E = Easy, A = Average, C = Challenging

Essay Questions

16. (Easy) *Guidelines for student response:* Students' essays should explain the specifics of Addison's target audience. For example, in the excerpt he identi-

fies "well-regulated families," gentlemen with nothing to do, men with few original ideas, and females. These people could be interested in anything from social gossip to business affairs to philosophy.

17. (Average) *Guidelines for student response:* Students' essays should explain their interpretation of the statement and offer their opinions about its accuracy and overtones. For example, Johnson seems to be saying that few people are attuned to the natural wonders around them as they take a walk. One might speculate that being good at taking a walk would mean that a person was sensitive to the sights, sounds, smells, textures, and tastes around him or her while walking.

18. (Challenging) *Guidelines for student response:* Students' essays should identify and discuss ways in which Johnson treats a common subject with freshness. For example, he begins his essay on what he later calls "the smile of nature" by focusing on an easily recognizable, anxiety-ridden habit of human nature— and offers details on how a somewhat eccentric acquaintance of his uses the prospect of spring to ease his mental burdens.

Unit 4: Rebels and Dreamers (1798–1832)

"To a Mouse" and **"To a Louse"**
by Robert Burns
"Woo'd and Married and A'"
by Joanna Baillie

Selection Test (p. 138)

Critical Reading/Vocabulary and Grammar

1. b 2. c 3. a 4. d 5. c 6. b 7. d 8. b 9. b
10. c 11. b 12. a 13. a 14. c 15. d 16. a
17. d 18. b 19. c 20. c

Questions are classified in these categories:
  Comprehension 1(E), 11(E), 12(A)
  Interpretation 3(A), 4(C), 6(A), 8(C), 13(A)
  Literary Analysis 2(E), 7(A), 14(A)
  Reading Strategy 5(C), 9(A), 10(E), 15(A)
  Vocabulary 16(A), 17(E), 18(E)
  Grammar 19(A), 20(A)

E = Easy, A = Average, C = Challenging

Essay Questions

21. (Easy) *Guidelines for student response:* Students' essays should compare the use of the louse and the mouse in Burns's two poems. For example, students should note that the speaker is sympathetic to the mouse but not the louse. The mouse symbolizes the fragility of life and the impossibility of predicting and controlling the future. The louse symbolizes human flaws that are common to everyone.

22. (Average) *Guidelines for student response:* Students' essays should identify strong similarities in the three poems. For example, all are written about everyday subjects and use conversational language

that contains a strong Scottish dialect. Both poets use clear rhyme schemes, dialogue, and direct address.

23. (Challenging) *Guidelines for student response:* Students' essays should identify characteristics that might have made Burns's poetry popular in Scotland. For example, students might point out that the use of Scottish dialect could give readers the sense that Burns understood the lives of uneducated workers. The image of a farmer plowing in the fall might be familiar to many. Lice would have been familiar to all Scots of Burns's day, and the theme of "To a Louse," which declares that all people are the same, probably touched a common chord in his readers.

"The Lamb," "The Tyger," "The Chimney Sweeper," and "Infant Sorrow" by William Blake

Selection Test (p. 141)

Critical Reading/Vocabulary and Grammar

1. c 2. d 3. a 4. d 5. b 6. a 7. c 8. b 9. c 10. c 11. d 12. c 13. a 14. b 15. c 16. d 17. a 18. b 19. b 20. c

Questions are classified in these categories:
  Comprehension 3(A), 9(E), 13(A)
  Interpretation 2(A), 6(E), 7(A), 12(E)
  Literary Analysis 1(C), 5(A), 10(A), 11(E)
  Reading Strategy 4(C), 8(E), 14(A)
  Vocabulary 15(A), 16(E), 17(C)
  Grammar 18(A), 19(C), 20(A)
  E = Easy, A = Average, C = Challenging

Essay Questions

21. (Easy) *Guidelines for student response:* Students should interpret the ideas and images in the poem in relation to the Industrial Revolution and its impact on society. They might, for example, point out the poverty of the children and the fact that the father "sold" the speaker when he was just a baby. They might also point out the theme of early death, which is significant in the poem.

22. (Average) *Guidelines for student response:* Students should present their interpretations and comparisons of "The Lamb"

and "The Tyger" supported by specific details from the poems. For example, they may say that the lamb and the tyger symbolize the opposite sides of human nature and of human experience. Also, students might say that the peaceful streams and vales in which the lamb lives stand opposite the dark and chaotic wood in which the tyger lives. Students may also mention that although the lamb and the tyger are set up as opposites, there is a similarity between them. According to Blake, they were both made by the Creator.

23. (Challenging) *Guidelines for student response:* Students should make their interpretations using examples from the two poems they chose to support their ideas. Students may mention that the lamb symbolizes not only innocence, but also the Creator. They might also mention that the tiger represents experience and worldliness. In the cases of both "The Lamb" and "The Tyger," students might mention the significance of the settings described in each poem. If students choose "The Chimney Sweeper" or "Infant Sorrow," they might mention the symbols of heaven and the creator in "The Chimney Sweeper" and the symbol of confinement in "Infant Sorrow."

Introduction to *Frankenstein* by Mary Wollstonecraft Shelley

Selection Test (p. 144)

Critical Reading/Vocabulary and Grammar

1. c 2. c 3. d 4. c 5. a 6. b 7. d 8. b 9. c 10. a 11. a 12. c 13. b 14. a 15. c 16. b 17. c 18. a 19. d 20. a

Questions are classified in these categories:
  Comprehension 2(E),
  Interpretation 1(A), 4(A), 8(E), 10(A), 11(C)
  Literary Analysis 3(A), 5(A), 13(A), 14(A)
  Reading Strategy 6(C), 7(C), 9(E), 12(A)
  Vocabulary 15(A), 16(E), 17(E)
  Grammar 18(A), 19(C), 20(A)
  E = Easy, A = Average, C = Challenging

Introduction to *Frankenstein*
by Mary Wollstonecraft Shelly
(continued)

Essay Questions

21. (Easy) *Guidelines for student response:*
Students' essays should identify traits
that make *Frankenstein* a classic example
of Gothic literature. For example,
Frankenstein contains a supernatural
being, and the story is intended to be sinister and scary.

22. (Average) *Guidelines for student response:*
Students' essays should compare
Frankenstein with a contemporary work
that explores the theme of technology
used for the wrong purposes. For example, students might compare *Frankenstein*
with *Jurassic Park*, a novel and movie that
explores the possibility that scientists
might find a way to clone dinosaurs from
dinosaur DNA. If so, students might note
that just as *Frankenstein* was inspired by
public interest in the experiments of Dr.
Erasmus Darwin, *Jurassic Park* was inspired by scientific attempts to clone one
animal from the cell of another animal.

23. (Challenging) *Guidelines for student response:* Students' essays should identify
characteristics of the Gothic novel that
make it a part and product of the Romantic Age. For example, Gothic literature
grew out of the Romantic denial of the Age
of Reason's claim that everything could be
explained scientifically.

"The Oval Portrait" by Edgar Allan Poe

Selection Test (p. 147)

Critical Reading

1. c 2. c 3. b 4. d 5. a 6. c 7. d 8. b 9. c
10. a

Questions are classified in these categories:
Comprehension 1(E), 3(A), 5(C), 6(E), 10(C)
Interpretation 2(A), 4(C), 7(A), 8(C), 9(E)
E = Easy, A = Average, C = Challenging

Essay Questions

11. (Easy) *Guidelines for student response:*
Students should point to various explicit
descriptions that create an atmosphere
of foreboding: gloom, deep shade, deep

midnight, and so on. They should observe
that it is particularly the darkness and
the remoteness or isolation of the turret
room that we find in both frame and
frame story: The obvious possibility is
that the painter and the bride once lived
in this same chateau; another more complex possibility is that the narrator
dreams the history of the portrait in
accordance with the setting in which he
finds himself. They might go on to comment on the way the gloomy setting reflects the artist's dark moral impulse.

12. (Average) *Guidelines for student response:*
Students should note that the story plays
up the artist's self-absorption while everyone else notices the wife's decline. The
"hour" of her first sight, love, and marriage
to the artist is described as "evil." The
phrase "dreading . . . untoward instru-
ments" seems to imply that he is torturing
her, while the term *would* rather than
could suggests his willful excess in trans-
fusing her life force onto his canvas. He
seems especially cruel or inhuman because she is so fresh and flourishing at the
beginning (just ripening into womanhood,
"frolicksome as the young fawn," "full of
glee") and so passive and vulnerable.

13. (Challenging) *Guidelines for student response:* Students should note that the
presence of a valet suggests an upper-
class, educated narrator whose interest in
and assessment of the chateau and its art
work become credible. The narrator's need
of his valet's help also underlines his
"desperately wounded condition," which
in turn leads to his delirium. The delirium, the wound, and his sleepiness all
combine to suggest that possibly the narrator dreams or hallucinates the portrait
and/or its history. The first-person narration emphasizes his subjectivity and his
inner state. It might occur to students
that he imagines life draining out of the
bride because of his own mortal danger
from his wound.

Part Test, Unit 4, Part I: Fantasy and Reality (p. 149)

Critical Reading/Vocabulary and Grammar

1. c 2. a 3. d 4. b 5. a 6. b 7. a 8. d 9. b
10. c 11. b 12. c 13. d 14. a 15. c

Questions are classified in these categories:
Comprehension 1(E)
Interpretation 2(E), 3(A), 7(A), 8(E)
Literary Analysis 9(A), 10(C)
Reading Strategy 4(E), 5(C), 6(A)
Vocabulary 12(A), 15(A)
Grammar 11(A), 13(E), 14(C)
E = Easy, A = Average, C = Challenging

Essay Questions

16. (Easy) *Guidelines for student response:* Students' essays should focus on the details of one selection from the section and how these details reflect reality and fantasy. For example, students writing about "Introduction to *Frankenstein*" might describe how the realistic discussions of Lord Byron and Percy Shelley about life and the experiments of Charles Darwin inspired Mary Shelley's supernatural fantasy *Frankenstein*. Students writing about "To a Mouse" might describe how Robert Burns combines realistic details about people and a mouse with his imaginative descriptions of the mouse's feelings.

17. (Average) *Guidelines for student response:* Students' essays should focus on the dark, sinister elements of any two pieces from the section. For example, some students might focus on Mary Shelley's description of the monstrous consequences of a person's attempt to reach beyond the acceptable limits of human knowledge and power. In describing this piece, they might describe the scientist's frightening discovery of his "horrid" creation. Some students might also focus on Blake's poem "Infant Sorrow," which gives a cold and painful view of an infant's first moments in the world. In describing this poem, they might focus on the details of the struggling, helpless child bound in blankets and the description of the world as "dangerous." Other strong choices include Blake's "The Tyger" and "The Chimney Sweeper."

18. (Challenging) *Guidelines for student response:* Students should show a thorough understanding of the symbolism of any two selections from the section. For example, some students might focus on Mary Shelley's symbolic monster, which symbolizes the danger of humans' trying to "mock the stupendous mechanism of the Creator of the world." Students should explain that Shelley's monster is a reaction to the discussions about life and science she hears her husband and Lord Byron having. Some students might discuss the symbolism of Blake, such as the innocence, gentleness, and purity of the lamb in "The Lamb" or the evil and primitive nature of the tyger in "The Tyger." Students should recognize that these symbols represent the good and evil aspects of the world.

Poetry of William Wordsworth

Selection Test (p. 152)

Critical Reading/Vocabulary and Grammar

1. b 2. a 3. d 4. c 5. d 6. b 7. a 8. c 9. a 10. d
11. b 12. a 13. a 14. a 15. d 16. b 17. c 18. b
19. c 20. b

Questions are classified in these categories:
Comprehension 3(A), 6(E), 9(A)
Interpretation 1(A), 4(A), 5(A), 11(A), 12(E)
Literary Analysis 7(E), 8(A), 14(A)
Reading Strategy 2(C), 10(C), 13(C)
Vocabulary 15(E), 16(A), 17(C)
Grammar 18(A), 19(E), 20(C)
E = Easy, A = Average, C = Challenging

Essay Questions

21. (Easy) *Guidelines for student response:* Students should mention that Romantic poetry frequently dealt with nature, and they should cite the nature imagery of "Tintern Abbey" or the concern expressed in "The World Is Too Much With Us" that people have turned away from nature. They should also mention the importance that Romanticism attaches to emotions and to the individual, citing the personal emotional reactions expressed in "Tintern Abbey" and/or the excerpt from *The Prelude*.

22. (Average) *Guidelines for student response:* Students should describe Wordsworth's concern that people had come to be too much involved with society and making money and did not appreciate life and

nature enough. They may cite such examples as his statement that he'd rather worship Greek nature gods than ignore nature the way others of his time did. Student opinions will vary, but many will probably agree that these concerns are as relevant to our own time as they were to Wordsworth's.

23. (Challenging) *Guidelines for student response:* Students should describe the change in the narrator's feelings at Tintern Abbey from the carefree wildness of a young boy to the more sober reflections of a grown man. They should also describe the change in Wordsworth's own feelings regarding the French Revolution—from believing it to be a change for the better to the realization that the new regime was at least as bad as the old. The two works are similar in that they describe changes that come with age and experience, but they are different in that "Tintern Abbey" evokes a more general, universal experience while the selection from *The Prelude* is very specific and personal.

"The Rime of the Ancient Mariner" and "Kubla Khan"
by Samuel Taylor Coleridge

Selection Test (p. 155)

Critical Reading/Vocabulary and Grammar

1. d 2. a 3. c 4. d 5. a 6. c 7. b 8. c 9. a 10. c 11. b 12. c 13. c 14. b 15. a 16. c 17. d 18. b 19. d 20. c

Questions are classified in these categories:
   Comprehension 5(A), 10(A), 13(A)
   Interpretation 2(E), 6(A), 7(C), 9(C)
   Literary Analysis 1(A), 3(A), 8(A), 12(A)
   Reading Strategy 4(C), 11(A), 14(A)
   Vocabulary 15(E), 16(C), 17(E)
   Grammar 18(E), 19(C), 20(A)
   E = Easy, A = Average, C = Challenging

Essay Questions

21. (Easy) *Guidelines for student response:* Students should note that in both poems, the forces of nature are unpredictable, contain supernatural elements, and lie far beyond the modest powers of humankind. In each case, nature inspires awe and exhibits the power to overwhelm human beings. Students might also note, however, that in "Kubla Khan," nature helps to create a majestic (if disturbing) fantasy, whereas in "The Rime of the Ancient Mariner," nature is the scene of a horrible nightmare.

22. (Average) *Guidelines for student response:* Students should describe the elements of fantasy that Coleridge ascribes to Xanadu, pointing to such details as the spirit of the "woman wailing for her demon lover" and the vision of the Abyssinian maid "singing of Mount Abora." Students may also point out that a love of the exotic is naturally suited to the Romantic temperament, which revels in the mystery of the unknown and all that lies outside the realm of everyday experience.

23. (Challenging) *Guidelines for student response:* Students' answers should note that these lines explain why the Mariner's voyage became so disastrous after he killed the albatross—the Polar Spirit was taking revenge on him. Some students may note that the Mariner's problems, created by the Polar Spirit's love for the albatross, can only be resolved when the Mariner himself begins to feel love for the natural world. Students should identify the assonance created by the *i* sound in the first line and the simple repetition of words in the third line (*loved . . . loved*). The stark simplicity of these lines produces a lonely tone that, some students may suggest, implies that lack of appreciation for nature results in loneliness and disconnectedness.

"She Walks in Beauty," from *Childe Harold's Pilgrimage* and **from *Don Juan*** by George Gordon, Lord Byron

Selection Test (p. 158)

Critical Reading/Vocabulary and Grammar

1. b 2. a 3. c 4. d 5. c 6. b 7. a 8. b 9. b 10. c 11. c 12. b 13. d 14. a 15. c 16. a 17. b 18. b 19. d 20. c

Questions are classified in these categories:
   Comprehension 4(E), 14(C)
   Interpretation 1(A), 7(C), 8(A), 9(C), 13(A)

Literary Analysis 3(A), 6(A), 10(A), 12(A)
Reading Strategy 2(E), 5(A), 11(C)
Vocabulary 18(A), 19(A), 20(C)
Grammar 15(A), 16(E), 17(E)
E = Easy, A = Average, C = Challenging

Essay Questions

21. (Easy) *Guidelines for student response:*
Students may compare the speaker's
approach to life as a young man and at age
thirty, or they may focus on his approach
at age thirty. They should mention the
main lesson the speaker claims to have
learned, that fame is not as rewarding as it
appears to be, but they should also note
that the speaker still appears to seek fame.

22. (Average) *Guidelines for student response:*
Students' essays should identify traits of a
person that the speaker attributes to the
ocean. For example, the speaker states
that the ocean hates the destruction that
humans wreak on land.

23. (Challenging) *Guidelines for student response:* Students' essays should compare
the ways in which the speakers of "She
Walks in Beauty" and *Childe Harold's
Pilgrimage* elevate their subjects with the
ways in which the speaker of *Don Juan*
makes fun of himself. For example, the
speakers of the first two poems compare
their subjects to things that are eternal—
night and "the Almighty"—while the speaker
of *Don Juan* compares his life to something
that is easily and quickly used up—money.

"Ozymandias," "Ode to the West Wind," and "To a Skylark"
by Percy Bysshe Shelley

Selection Test (p. 161)

Critical Reading/Vocabulary and Grammar

1. c 2. b 3. d 4. b 5. a 6. a 7. c 8. b 9. a
10. c 11. b 12. d 13. a 14. a 15. c 16. b
17. c 18. d 19. a 20. d

Questions are classified in these categories:
Comprehension 2(E), 6(A), 10(A)
Interpretation 1(A), 5(C), 7(A), 12(A), 14(C)
Literary Analysis 3(C), 4(E), 9(A), 13(E)
Reading Strategy 8(A), 11(A), 15(E)
Vocabulary 16(A), 18(C), 19(E)
Grammar 17(A), 20(C)
E = Easy, A = Average, C = Challenging

Essay Questions

21. (Easy) *Guidelines for student response:*
Students' essays should note that in these
three poems, Shelley depicts nature as better and more powerful than humans and
as having something to teach humanity.
For example, "Ozymandias" shows that
nature is more enduring than a human
kingdom, and "To a Skylark" depicts the
skylark as being able to exist without
emotions such as hate, pride, and fear.

22. (Average) *Guidelines for student response:*
Students' essays should note that the
speaker admires the destructive force of
the West Wind because it makes new be-
ginnings possible, and that Shelley seems
to be suggesting that death is a necessary
part of life. For example, the wind carries
seeds to their cold graves, but in the
spring, the seeds will sprout and grow.

23. (Challenging) *Guidelines for student response:* Students' essays should identify
the speaker's problem as a kind of writer's
block. The speaker is frustrated with his
work and hopes for the wind to help scatter
his "dead thoughts" and produce the conditions that are necessary for him to have a
creative "Spring." For example, the speaker
asks the wind to make him its lyre.

Poetry of John Keats

Selection Test (p. 164)

Critical Reading/Vocabulary and Grammar

1. c 2. d 3. b 4. a 5. d 6. a 7. c 8. a 9. d
10. a 11. c 12. b 13. c 14. d 15. a 16. b
17. c 18. b 19. b 20. d

Questions are classified in these categories:
Comprehension 2(A), 8(A), 9(A)
Interpretation 1(A), 5(A), 6(C), 7(A), 15(A)
Literary Analysis 10(E), 11(E), 12(A)
Reading Strategy 3(C), 4(A), 13(C), 14(E)
Vocabulary 16(E), 17(C), 18(C)
Grammar 19(E), 20(A)
E = Easy, A = Average, C = Challenging

Essay Questions

21. (Easy) *Guidelines for student response:*
Students should discuss the significance of
one emotion invoked in at least two of the
four poems by Keats. For example, they

Poetry of John Keats
(continued)

may write about the sadness in "When I Have Fears That I May Cease to Be" and "Ode to a Nightingale" or the excitement found in "On First Looking Into Chapman's Homer" and "Ode on a Grecian Urn." They might also write about the sense of wonderment that runs throughout all four poems. Students should refer to specific examples from the text to support their discussion.

22. (Average) *Guidelines for student response:* When comparing the two odes, students should refer to passages and details from the text to support their arguments. They may note that he considers the figures painted on the urn to be free of some human constraints, but the nightingale has earthly cares, sickness, and even death. The figures on the urn are free from the stealing, punishing passage of time. The eternal youth and springtime of the urn painting, however, seem to inspire him to ecstatic admiration, whereas the nightingale causes him to reflect heavily on his own mortality and cares.

23. (Challenging) *Guidelines for student response:* Students may note that Keats regards immortality with wonderment and admiration, and that the enduring quality of art and literature probably plays an important role in his appreciation of them. His own mortality, on the other hand, is a source of worry and sorrow. In "On First Looking Into Chapman's Homer," for example, students might point out that while he does not speak directly of immortality, he is impressed by the grandeur of Homer as expressed by Chapman; Homer's greatness has lasted for centuries, and Keats's exposure to this literature expands his own horizons on a universal level. Students might then note that "When I Have Fears That I May Cease to Be" shows Keats's great fear that he will not live long enough to write everything he wants to write. It may seem to them that to leave behind great works represents his only chance at immortality.

"The Lorelei" by Heinrich Heine
Haikus by Bashō, Yosa Buson, and Kobayashi Issa

Selection Test (p. 167)

Critical Reading

1. c 2. c 3. b 4. d 5. a 6. c 7. d 8. d 9. c 10. a

Questions are classified in these categories:
Comprehension 2(A), 5(A), 8(E), 10(A)
Interpretation 1(C), 3(C), 4(A), 6(C), 7(A), 9(C)
E = Easy, A = Average, C = Challenging

Essay Questions

11. (Easy) *Guidelines for student response:* Students should link gold/golden with value, warmth, the sun, etc., to establish its positive connotations. Then they need to note that the twilight cool and the setting sun frame the gold in a rather ominous way. In fact, the Lorelei's position high up on a mountain links her to the setting sun and therefore to coming darkness, death. Students might be familiar with literary uses of gold for symbolizing immortality or eternity and therefore see irony in the boatman's fate in pursuing the golden vision.

12. (Average) *Guidelines for student response:* Students should establish that a haiku is a short, simple, and concentrated form of three lines, creating a clear picture to arouse an emotion or express a spiritual insight. A haiku offers more suggestive power because it has less development of images and ideas (fewer words!) than most other poems; it also has more observation and less symbolism. Nature figures crucially in most haiku. Regarding structure, students might note that Basho and Buson seem to favor starting with an image from nature and then moving out to its effect/meaning or to human nature ("The Cuckoo," "Summer grasses" and Buson's "Spring Rain"); Issa prefers moving *to* an image that supplies or narrows down the context for the first two lines ("Far-off mountain peaks," "With bland serenity," "Beautiful, seen through holes").

13. (Challenging) *Guidelines for student response:* Students should notice how both poems use the word *vision* to suggest perilous quests. The boatman's and the soldiers' respective aspirations—a perfect melody/beauty and freedom/glory—reveal the insignificance of individual human desires when confronted with natural forces: the boatman is absorbed by the river; the soldiers' battlefield yields to seasonal indifference. The greater detail and the brooding commentator in Heine's lyric open up more room for ambivalence than we find in Basho's approach.

Part Test, Unit 4, Part 2: Focus on Literary Forms— Lyric Poetry (p. 169)

Critical Reading/Vocabulary and Grammar

1. c 2. b 3. d 4. a 5. b 6. c 7. b 8. a 9. c
10. d 11. c 12. a 13. d 14. b 15. c 16. a
17. d 18. b 19. c 20. b

Questions are classified in these categories:
Comprehension 2(E), 6(E)
Interpretation 8(A)
Literary Analysis 3(A), 4(A), 5(A), 7(C), 9(A)
Reading Strategy 1(A), 10(C)
Vocabulary 11(C), 12(E), 15(A), 18(E), 20(E)
Grammar 13(C), 14(E), 16(E), 17(A), 19(A)
E = Easy, A = Average, C = Challenging

Essay Questions

21. (Easy) *Guidelines for student response:* Students should be able to give a detailed description of the imagery in one poem from the section and describe how the imagery relates to meaning. For example, some students might focus on Percy Bysshe Shelley's images of the wind in "Ode to the West Wind." They should understand how these images relate to thenatural changes that are part of the cycle of life, and how the speaker turns to the changes in the wind for spiritual rejuvenation.

22. (Average) *Guidelines for student response:* Students should be able to describe nature imagery from two poems in the unit. For example, students might write strong essays that focus on two of the poems of Percy Bysshe Shelley. They might describe Shelley's images of the wind in "Ode to the West Wind" or images of the spirited skylark in "To a Skylark." Students might also focus on Lord Byron's images of nature in "She Walks in Beauty" or the selection from *Childe Harold's Pilgrimage.* Students should be able to present concrete details and explain how these details of nature reveal the writer's feelings toward nature and his subject.

23. (Average) *Guidelines for student response:* Students' essays should reveal an understanding of poetic devices such as alliteration, consonance, assonance, and internal rhyme. Students should show that they can recognize poetic devices in a poem from the section and describe what effect these devices create. For example, some students might focus on the rhyme in "The Rime of the Ancient Mariner" and how this device gives the poem a musical feel, or how assonance in the same poem suggests the howling of wind.

24. (Average) *Guidelines for student response:* Students' essays should reveal an understanding of at least one poem from the selection that presents a type of social criticism. For example, some students might describe the details and theme of "The World Is Too Much With Us," or "London, 1802"—both by William Wordsworth. Other students might focus on "Ozymandias" or "To the Skylark" by Percy Shelley.

25. (Challenging) *Guidelines for student response:* Students should show a clear understanding of important ideals of Romanticism—such as the admiration of nature and the belief in emotion over reason. To illustrate their definitions, they should present concrete details from any two poems in the section. They should be able to explain how each of their poems reflects the ideals of Romanticism. For example, strong essays might be written about the work of Wordsworth or two of the poems of Keats or Shelley.

"Speech to Parliament: In Defense of the Lower Classes"
by George Gordon, Lord Byron
"A Song: 'Men of England'"
by Percy Bysshe Shelley
"On the Passing of the Reform Bill"
by Thomas Babington Macaulay

Selection Test (p. 173)

Critical Reading/Vocabulary and Grammar

1. c 2. b 3. c 4. d 5. b 6. a 7. c 8. d 9. a
10. b 11. c 12. c 13. d 14. b 15. b 16. b
17. a 18. c 19. b 20. d

Questions are classified in these categories:
  Comprehension 1(A), 6(C), 10(C)
  Interpretation 2(A), 3(C), 7(A), 11(A)
  Literary Analysis 4(A), 8(C), 12(A), 14(A)
  Reading Strategy 5(E), 9(E), 13(E)
  Vocabulary 15(E), 16(C), 17(E)
  Grammar 18(A), 19(A), 20(A)
  E = Easy, A = Average, C = Challenging

Essay Questions

21. (Easy) *Guidelines for student response:*
    Students' essays should discuss how
    money informs the disparate conditions of
    the working and ruling classes. Students
    will probably base their explanations on
    the idea that money allows people to ac-
    quire basic necessities. In addition, often
    money begets personal confidence, social
    influence, and political power.

22. (Average) *Guidelines for student response:*
    Students should make a considered judg-
    ment about the images' effectiveness and
    explain why they are more or less appro-
    priate in Byron's speech. For instance, to
    support the idea that Byron's images of
    food and war are crucial to the success of
    his speech, a student might argue that
    the weavers' hunger was literal and real—
    and that the force of laws protecting mere
    property ought to pale in contrast with
    human starvation.

23. (Challenging) *Guidelines for student re-
    sponse:* Students should make a clear
    statement about what they deem the ap-
    propriate relationship between art and
    politics. The view that politics and art are
    rightly mixed could be supported, for in-
    stance, by citing evidence of Shelley's not
    sacrificing artistic quality while enlighten-

ing his audience and inciting social
change. Students who hold the view that
politics and art are best kept separate
might support their idea with references
to Byron's "Speech to Parliament: In Defense of the Lower Classes." By using ora-
torical and rhetorical devices (rather than
poetic devices oriented toward aesthetics),
Byron makes the most forceful political
argument possible.

"On Making an Agreeable Marriage"
by Jane Austen
from *A Vindication of the Rights of Woman* by Mary Wollstonecraft

Selection Test (p. 176)

Critical Reading/Vocabulary and Grammar

1. d 2. a 3. d 4. b 5. c 6. a 7. b 8. c 9. a
10. d 11. a 12. b 13. b 14. c 15. d 16. b
17. b 18. d 19. c 20. d

Questions are classified in these categories:
  Comprehension 1(A), 8(A), 9(A)
  Interpretation 2(C), 6(C), 10(E), 14(E)
  Literary Analysis 3(C), 5(A), 7(C), 13(C)
  Reading Strategy 4(C), 11(E), 12(C)
  Vocabulary 15(A), 16(E), 17(E)
  Grammar 18(E), 19(A), 20(A)
  E = Easy, A = Average, C = Challenging

Essay Questions

21. (Easy) *Guidelines for student response:*
    Students may mention Austen's gentle
    style and her modesty about what she
    tells her niece. They may also mention
    Austen's enthusiasm and depth of insight
    in praising Fanny's boyfriend's many fine
    qualities while holding fast to the good-
    sense issues of marrying a man who has
    money and a position. Austen also sheds
    light on the human problem of fickleness
    by pointing out that once Fanny had won
    her young man she became indifferent to
    him. However, at the end of the letter
    Austen warns her niece against marrying
    someone without the benefit of affection,
    which ends up being the main, heart-
    warming message of the letter.

22. (Average) *Guidelines for student response:*
    Students' essays may compare such
    things as Austen's mention of the need to
    marry "the eldest son of a Man of Fortune"

with Wollstonecraft's assertion that the only way a woman could rise in the world was through marriage. They may make use of more subtle comparisons, such as Austen's mention of her recently married friend, Anna. Austen states that she is glad Anna doesn't parade her happiness and behave in a silly manner over her marriage. Wollstonecraft spends much of her essay addressing women's silly behavior over men and over life in general. The two authors' styles are in stark contrast with each other. Students should contrast Austen's gentleness of manner and her coaxing style with Wollstonecraft's strong assertions and more instructive style.

23. (Challenging) *Guidelines for student response:* Students may or may not feel that Wollstonecraft's style is blunt by today's standards. Whichever answer they choose, their essays should provide support for their point of view.

from the Screenplay of *Sense and Sensibility* and Diaries
by Emma Thompson

Selection Test (p. 179)

Critical Reading

1. d 2. d 3. c 4. a 5. b 6. d 7. a 8. c 9. d
10. b

Questions are classified in these categories:
   Comprehension 1(E), 6(E), 8(A), 10(E)
   Interpretation 2(A), 3(A), 4(C), 5(C), 7(A), 9(C)
   E = Easy, A = Average, C = Challenging

Essay Questions

11. (Easy) *Guidelines for student response:* Students should point out how Edward's mother is concerned with status symbols while Edward himself wants quality of life. To reject power, prestige, and money, he opposes meaningful occupation and moral growth. Edward's kindness to Margaret, his sense of humor, his mildness in criticizing his mother, and Elinor's attraction to him are among the factors that endorse his choices.

12. (Average) *Guidelines for student response:* Students should note that Edward and Elinor initially bond over his kindness to her sister, then move on to more personal

disclosures. We see that they share a sense of humor as well as of social constriction. For example, she is ready to correct his comment, and he accepts and even admires "her boldness." The screenplay's direction for arm-in-arm walking also signals their growing closeness. At the same time, Edward's mildness, his snobbish mother's influence over him, and Elinor's bold honesty (note his shock) could become obstacles in a courtship.

13. (Challenging) *Guidelines for student response:* Students should consider Margaret's actual tree house and her imaginings about China and pirates as signs that she is still enjoying a child's freedom to express herself. Once older, she will learn that adults must put propriety above honesty and that society prohibits average ("normal") middle-class ladies from heading expeditions, traveling unchaperoned, and climbing trees. Part of the comedy in the scene stems from her unawareness, and Edward and Elinor's amused tolerance, of her deviation from adult gender norms.

Part Test, Unit 4, Part 3: The Reaction to Society's Ills
(p. 181)

Critical Reading/Vocabulary and Grammar

1. a 2. b 3. c 4. a 5. d 6. a 7. b 8. c 9. c
10. d 11. c 12. a 13. b 14. c 15. b

Questions are classified in these categories:
   Comprehension 2(E)
   Interpretation 1(A), 3(C), 8(A), 9(C)
   Literary Analysis 4(A), 10(A)
   Reading Strategy 5(A), 6(E), 7(A)
   Vocabulary 11(A), 12(A), 13(C)
   Grammar 14(A), 15(A)
   E = Easy, A = Average, C = Challenging

Essay Questions

16. (Easy) *Guidelines for student response:* Students' essays should identify one selection with a compelling message. Students must clearly explain the selection's message and support their opinions of the message with reasonable evidence. For instance, students might praise Austen's assessment of the state of marriage and cite Austen's wit and humor as engaging vehicles for her message.

17. (Average) *Guidelines for student response:* Students' essays should identify two separate selections: one that makes political commentary and one that makes social commentary. Students should infer connections between political and social ills. For example, students might point out that the subjugation of the working class by the ruling class, described in Shelley's poem, parallels the subjugation of women that Wollstonecraft details.

18. (Challenging) *Guidelines for student response:* Students' essays should identify one selection in which the writer uses a combination of direct and indirect commentary or reveals such commentary consciously or unconsciously. For example, students might compare and contrast Byron's direct remarks about the "squalid wretchedness" of his country with his indirect criticism implied through imagery such as "gibbets" and "Sherwood Forest."

Unit 5: Progress and Decline (1833–1901)

from "In Memoriam, A.H.H.," "The Lady of Shalott," "Ulysses," and from *The Princess:* "Tears, Idle Tears" by Alfred, Lord Tennyson

Selection Test (p. 184)

Critical Reading/Vocabulary and Grammar

1. a 2. c 3. d 4. b 5. c 6. a 7. c 8. b 9. b 10. d 11. a 12. c 13. d 14. a 15. a 16. d 17. b 18. c 19. b 20. d

Questions are classified in these categories:
Comprehension 1(E), 8(A), 12(A)
Interpretation 4(C), 5(E), 6(A), 10(A), 14(C)
Literary Analysis 3(E), 7(A), 13(C), 15(C)
Reading Strategy 2(A), 9(A), 11(C)
Vocabulary 18(E), 19(A), 20(C)
Grammar 16(A), 17(E)
E = Easy, A = Average, C = Challenging

Essay Questions

21. (Easy) *Guidelines for student response:* Student essays should identify two main areas in which the Lady's life is like an artist's. First, as a weaver, she makes things. Secondly, she is socially isolated. In the case of the Lady, this is represented as a curse, but many artists view the world differently and feel isolated. Like the Lady, artists are observers of life, and the nature of their personalities often prevents them from engaging the world naturally and freely.

22. (Average) *Guidelines for student response:* Students should note that the type of heroism proposed by Tennyson is a heroism of effort rather than of accomplishment. Tennyson's Ulysses is no longer beautiful, young, strong, or hopeful. He has accomplished what one can accomplish and lists the accomplishments, including pride in his son. His heroism lies in making attempts, not what he is attempting, and to that end he will "sail beyond the sunset . . . until I die."

23. (Challenging) *Guidelines for student response:* Students should note that these four sections of the poem represent a progression from total grief to a kind of faith. Sections 1 and 7 illustrate the bleak impact of loss. Section 7 illustrates pain itself, as the speaker stands grieving in front of the house of his lost friend in the rain after a sleepless night. By Section 82, the speaker accepts death as an "Eternal process moving on." He indicates a surviving faith by describing A.H.H. as a "ruined chrysalis." A chrysalis is ruined by an emerging butterfly; therefore, death leads to a more beautiful form of life. In Section 130, the speaker's acceptance of death has merged with his affection and faith. He believes that he will not lose his faith or his friend "though I die."

"My Last Duchess," "Life in a Love," and "Love Among the Ruins"
by Robert Browning
Sonnet 43 by Elizabeth Barrett Browning

Selection Test (p. 187)

Critical Reading/Vocabulary and Grammar

1. c 2. d 3. a 4. a 5. b 6. d 7. c 8. b 9. b
10. b 11. c 12. d 13. d 14. a 15. d 16. c
17. b 18. c 19. a 20. c

Questions are classified in these categories:
  Comprehension 1(E), 7(E), 11(A)
  Interpretation 3(C), 8(A), 9(C), 13 (A), 14(A)
  Literary Analysis 4(A), 5(E), 10(A)
  Reading Strategy 2(A), 6(A), 12(C)
  Vocabulary 15(A), 16(E), 17(A)
  Grammar 18(A), 19(C), 20(A)
  E = Easy, A = Average, C = Challenging

Essay Questions

21. (Easy) *Guidelines for student response:*
Students should recognize that all three
of Robert Browning's poems are dramatic
monologues; they each feature a single
character who reveals his personality
through his words to a silent listener.
For example, students might note that
the speaker in "My Last Duchess" directly
reveals his pride by boasting about the
painting to the Count's agent. Indirectly,
the speaker also reveals his arrogance,
jealousy, and temper with his remarks
about his deceased wife.

22. (Average) *Guidelines for student response:*
Some students may contend that the
speaker in "My Last Duchess" reveals
the most because the Duke, intent on
winning over the Count's agent, probably
alienates him with what he says about his
dead wife. In saying that his wife had "A
heart—how shall I say?—too soon made
glad," the Duke reveals that his own heart
is cold and hardened.

23. (Challenging) *Guidelines for student response:* Students should note that both
speakers believe love is the most valuable
of all human endeavors. The speaker of
Sonnet 43 describes her love openly and
expressively, but her ideas about the value
of love must be inferred. In "Love Among
the Ruins," the speaker dwells mostly on

the scene of the ruins and its past glory,
devoting relatively little time to his beloved.
However, the speaker ends his ruminations
with the definitive statement "Love is best."

"You Know the Place: Then"
by Sappho
"Invitation to the Voyage
by Charles Baudelaire

Selection Test (p. 190)

Critical Reading

1. d 2. d 3. c 4. b 5. b 6. a 7. c 8. a
9. b 10. d

Questions are classified in these categories:
  Comprehension 1(E), 3(A), 6(C), 7(A), 8(E),
  9(A)
  Interpretation 2(C), 4(C), 5 (A), 10(C)
  E = Easy, A = Average, C = Challenging

Essay Questions

11. (Easy) *Guidelines for student response:*
Students should note that though
Baudelaire opens "Invitation to the Voyage"
with an address to "my child, my sister,"
the only individualizing traits he ascribes
to the addressee are "treacherous eyes . . .
shining through their tears." The rest of
the poem describes less a relationship
than a condition of the poet's existence—
one that makes for melancholy reverie
rather than the fevered anticipation and
desire expressed by Sappho.

12. (Average) *Guidelines for student response:*
Students should reiterate Sappho's imagery, including pleasant groves, incense
smoke, dill scents, sleek horses, cold
streams murmuring (combination of
touch and sound), and so on. Students
should suggest that the accumulation of
imagery creates a sensual depiction of
strong, vibrant, physical love. The overall
mood of the poem is joyous, whereas
Baudelaire's imagery evokes a sense of
languor and quiet reflection. Baudelaire's
lyric voice is resigned, whereas Sappho's
is expectant.

13. (Challenging) *Guidelines for student response:* Students should contrast the
natural setting of Sappho's poem with
the more modern world illustrated by

"You Know the Place: Then" by Sappho
"Invitation to the Voyage
by Charles Baudelaire
(continued)

Baudelaire (still infused by nature, but including a drawing room and sailing ships). Students might note the ideal nature of the setting in both poems. They should further point out that Sappho's speaker seems already to inhabit the world she describes, while the place described by Baudelaire exists primarily in the speaker's imagination ("dream / how sweet all things would seem").

Part Test, Unit 5, Part 1: Relationships (p. 192)

Critical Reading/Vocabulary and Grammar

1. d 2. b 3. a 4. b 5. c 6. a 7. b 8. c 9. d
10. a 11. c 12. a 13. b 14. a 15. d

Questions are classified in these categories:
Comprehension 3(E), 6(A)
Interpretation 2(A), 7(C), 16(E)
Literary Analysis 5(A), 8(A), 18(C)
Reading Strategy 1(E), 4(C), 9(A), 10(A), 17(A)
Vocabulary 11(A), 12(E)
Grammar 13(E), 14(A), 15(A)
E = Easy, A = Average, C = Challenging

Essay Questions

16. (Easy) *Guidelines for student response:* Students' essays should compare the views of romantic love in two of the poems. For example, students might identify the "all for love" quality of the Lady of Shalott's love, the possessive nature of love in "My Last Duchess," the ironic view of love in "Life in a Love," the idealistic "love is better than anything" view in Sonnet 43.

17. (Average) *Guidelines for student response:* Students' essays should focus on a single poem. For example, students might say that the all-encompassing, almost obsessive love expressed in Elizabeth Barrett Browning's Sonnet 43 is consistent with a person who eloped and moved to a foreign land.

18. (Challenging) *Guidelines for student response:* Students may focus on the journey through the speaker's grief in "In Memoriam, A.H.H.," the Lady of Shalott's journey, the hero's desire for a journey in "Ulysses," or the Duke's journey from his former wife to a new wife in "My Last Duchess."

from *Hard Times* by Charles Dickens
from *Jane Eyre* by Charlotte Brontë

Selection Test (p. 195)

Critical Reading/Vocabulary and Grammar

1. c 2. a 3. c 4. b 5. b 6. d 7. c 8. b 9. b
10. d 11. b 12. a 13. c 14. d 15. c 16. c
17. d 18. c 19. a 20. a

Questions are classified in these categories:
Comprehension 1(E), 3(E), 9(E), 13(A)
Interpretation 5(C), 7(E), 10(A), 12(A), 14(A), 15(C)
Literary Analysis 4(A), 8(C), 16(C)
Reading Strategy 2(A), 6(A), 11(A)
Vocabulary 18(A), 20(A)
Grammar 17(A), 19(A)
E = Easy, A = Average, C = Challenging

Essay Questions

21. (Easy) *Guidelines for student response:* Students should say that Helen and Jane discuss their lives at Lowood. The conversation reveals that Helen is humble, passive, and critical of herself. Any troubles that she encounters at the school, she blames on herself. She also forces herself to forgive her enemies. Jane, on the other hand, feels much more inclined to fight back and demand her rights. Helen's philosophy of life is that one must be passive, understanding, and forgiving. Any injustices in this life will be corrected in the next life. Jane, on the other hand, is not passive and lives much more in the present.

22. (Average) *Guidelines for student response:* Students should say that Sissy Jupe is a quiet girl who has not learned to conform to the rigid ideas of her classroom. Bitzer, on the other hand, is an eager student who promptly tells the teacher what he wants to hear. He gives a complete definition of the horse, sticking only to the facts. Lacking in his definition, however, are any images that relate the beauty of a horse. Dickens focuses on these characters to show a contrast between people

caught up in fact and people who still have imagination and innocence.

23. (Challenging) *Guidelines for student response:* Students should understand that both novels examine institutions that attempt to smother individuality. *Hard Times* focuses on a classroom in which children are referred to as numbers, run by a man who places value only on facts and who reprimands people for having thoughts related to imagination. *Jane Eyre* focuses on a boarding school for girls of low social standing. At the school, girls are always cold and underfed, and they are constantly criticized for not conforming to standards of behavior put forth by severe teachers. They have very little time to focus on their own interests and thoughts. Brontë is calling attention to injustices felt by poor people who are tucked away in institutions and the ways in which these institutions rob people of self-respect.

from *War and Peace* by Leo Tolstoy

Selection Test (p. 198)

Critical Reading

1. c 2. c 3. d 4. c 5. b 6. b 7. c 8. c 9. c
10. d

Questions are classified in these categories:
  Comprehension 1(E), 3(A), 5(E), 7(A), 9(A)
  Interpretation 2(A), 4(C), 6(A), 8(C), 10(C)
  E = Easy, A = Average, C = Challenging

Essay Questions

11. (Easy) *Guidelines for student response:* Students should demonstrate that, according to Tolstoy, the theory of the *grand homme* argues for the leading role of individual decision makers in the unfolding of history. In contrast with Napoleon, who believed in his own powers, Kutuzov is portrayed as modest and ordinary, never hypocritical or false to himself. Kutuzov's patience and understanding of the true course of events led him to believe that the best action was often no action at all. His faithfulness to Russia and his ability to submit his own will to that of "divine providence" make Kutuzov truly great in Tolstoy's eyes. Students should suggest someone from their own experience and

compare the person with Tolstoy's definition of a great man.

12. (Average) *Guidelines for student response:* Students should identify Kutuzov's abandoning of Moscow and his willingness to simply follow events as evidence of Tolstoy's theory of history in this selection. Students should note that, according to Tolstoy, history moves in a way that remains a mystery to the vast majority of people (such as Napoleon and the historians). Judging from Kutuzov's example, students should see Tolstoy as arguing that history results from a vast number of ordinary, interrelated events that no one man (such as Napoleon) can direct or control.

13. (Challenging) *Guidelines for student response:* Students should note that Tolstoy dismisses historians with such emotionally charged words and phrases as "dull-witted," "flunkey," and "hatred and contempt of the crowd." Tolstoy portrays Kutuzov's opponents as hypocrites with a false sense of their own importance. Tolstoy is fierce in his defense of Kutuzov and scathing in his denunciation of everyone else. His tone is didactic and moralizing.

Part Test, Unit 5, Part 2: Focus on Literary Forms— The Novel (p. 200)

Critical Reading/Vocabulary and Grammar

1. d 2. c 3. d 4. a 5. b 6. c 7. d 8. a 9. a
10. b 11. d 12. b 13. c 14. c 15. a

Questions are classified in these categories:
  Comprehension 1(A), 5(A)
  Interpretation 2(E), 6(C)
  Literary Analysis 3(A), 7(E), 10(C)
  Reading Strategy 4(C), 8(E), 9(A)
  Vocabulary 11(E), 12(A), 13(C)
  Grammar 14(A), 15(A)
  E = Easy, A = Average, C = Challenging

Essay Questions

16. (Easy) *Guidelines for student response:* Students' essays should identify one selection from Part 3 and describe the commentary on society the selection makes. They should cite details that explain how the selection's events create an attitude of

social comment. Examples might include the numbing and irrelevant curriculum in *Hard Times*, the mean-spirited cruelty of those supposed to care for children in *Jane Eyre*, or society's contempt for a general who cares more for the lives of his troops than for fame in *War and Peace*.

17. (Average) *Guidelines for student response:* Students should identify a selection and summarize its comment on one of society's institutions. Essays should explain how the author reveals the attitude. In each selection, the author criticizes institutions by telling stories of people involved with them, and making central characters the victims of the institutions' flaws. For example, in *Hard Times*, Dickens mocks the curriculum and ridicules the faculty with names like Gradgrind and M'Choakumchild and exposes their insensitivity in interactions with students.

18. (Challenging) *Guidelines for student response:* Students should identify a selection and a central issue about which societal attitudes compete with the author's attitude. In *Hard Times*, for example, two views of education of children appear, one utilitarian, one imaginative. Dickens wants children to be children, and Sissy Jupe wins the debate about flowers. The competing attitudes in *War and Peace* are about leadership: The model modern European hero is flashy, political, ambitious, and well spoken. Kutuzov is none of these things. He lacks the heartlessness required to sacrifice lives for conquest and is thus a greater hero in Tolstoy's view.

"Dover Beach" by Matthew Arnold
"Recessional" and "The Widow at Windsor" by Rudyard Kipling

Selection Test (p. 203)

Critical Reading/Vocabulary and Grammar

1. c 2. a 3. d 4. b 5. b 6. c 7. d 8. a 9. c
10. a 11. b 12. d 13. c 14. a 15. b 16. d

17. a 18. c 19. a 20. b

Questions are classified in these categories:
Comprehension 1(A), 7(E), 12(E)
Interpretation 2(A), 5(C), 8(A), 9(A), 14(E), 15(C)
Literary Analysis 4(A), 6(C), 10(C), 16(A)
Reading Strategy 3(E), 11(E), 13(A)
Vocabulary 17(E), 18(A)
Grammar 19(E), 20(A)
E = Easy, A = Average, C = Challenging

Essay Questions

21. (Easy) *Guidelines for student response:* Students should state that the message of the poem is a warning to nations as well as to people who hold power. The repeated phrase "Lest we forget" is a reminder that power and glory come at a price and are ultimately transient.

22. (Average) *Guidelines for student response:* Students should acknowledge that although Kipling's poems include a message of caution, they are not anti-imperialist. The speaker in "Recessional" does not imply that having "dominion over palm and pine" is a bad thing. He just asks for guidance in that dominion. In "The Widow at Windsor," the speaker, a soldier, has a healthy respect for "Missis Victorier," although he also expresses a healthy dose of sarcasm about the job that she sends him out to do. He is not rebellious, though, just accepting of the reality of his lowly, dirty job for the sake of the Empire.

23. (Challenging) *Guidelines for student response:* Students should recognize that although Arnold fills the first two stanzas with a natural setting, it is a setup for the poet's real message, which comes later in the poem. Arnold's nature is neither hostile nor beneficent. It is simply there. It is neither cause nor carrier of the sadness the speaker laments. Nature is an inert force in the poem, in spite of the action the poet so skillfully creates in the second stanza. It is unconscious but active, just like the "ignorant armies" that "clash by night."

"Condition of Ireland,"
The London Illustrated News
"Progress in Personal Comfort"
by Sydney Smith

Selection Test (p. 206)

Critical Reading/Vocabulary and Grammar

1. c 2. a 3. d 4. b 5. c 6. b 7. c 8. b 9. c
10. d 11. c 12. a 13. c 14. b 15. d 16. c
17. d 18. a 19. b 20. d

Questions are classified in these categories:
Comprehension 1(E), 2(A), 7(A), 9(E), 13(E)
Interpretation 4(C), 5(A), 6(C), 12(E), 14(C), 15(C)
Literary Analysis 8(A), 10(A)
Reading Strategy 3(A), 11(A)
Vocabulary 16(A), 18(A), 20(A)
Grammar 17(A), 19(A)
E = Easy, A = Average, C = Challenging

Essay Questions

21. (Easy) *Guidelines for student response:* Students should say that informative language is needed when the piece addresses specific legislative issues and specific ideas about how the resources in Ireland might be used more effectively. Emotive language increases the effectiveness of the piece when the writer describes the beauty of Ireland and the hardships faced by people in Ireland. Emotive language also helps the reader to understand the writer's attitude toward Britain's policies in Ireland.

22. (Average) *Guidelines for student response:* Students should understand that "Condition of Ireland" is a serious journalistic essay that examines problems and injustices in Ireland and brings forth ideas to remedy these problems. It is written in the voice of a person standing on the outside of the problem looking in—as a witness or a judge. Because the writer of the essay is unhappy with the way in which the British government handled matters in Ireland, the facts are presented to emphasize the error of British policy and the plight of Irish citizens. "Progress in Personal Comfort" is a light essay that celebrates the ways in which progress has brought personal comfort to people. The piece is written in the voice of a person

who is thrilled and amazed by changes in the world. The piece reflects the writer's enthusiasm, and the examples of progress presented reflect the writer's own interests and ideas about how changes occur.

23. (Challenging) *Guidelines for student response:* Students should understand that "Condition of Ireland" conveys the idea that progress will truly be made if the government confronts and then attempts to correct its mistakes. The article also conveys the idea that progress will be achieved if people end the suffering in Ireland and make reasonable use of the resources there. During the Irish famine, the British government placed a great deal of importance on progress in economic theory. They felt that the measures they took in Ireland would increase economic prosperity and progress in their own country. In "Progress in Personal Comfort," Mr. Smith values progress that has made his life easier and more comfortable.

"Opening Statement for the Inaugural Session of the Forum for Peace and Reconciliation"
by Judge Catherine McGuinness

Selection Test (p. 209)

Critical Reading

1. b 2. b 3. a 4. c 5. b 6. b 7. c 8. d 9. b
10. a

Questions are classified in these categories:
Comprehension 1(E), 3(A), 6(E), 7(A), 9(E)
Interpretation 2(A), 4(C), 5(C), 8(C), 10(A)
E = Easy, A = Average, C = Challenging

Essay Questions

11. (Easy) *Guidelines for student response:* Students should comment on McGuinness's use of the Presbyterian minister Armour and the republican-socialist Connolly as two very different sources of wisdom or insight regarding Irish identity. They should also consider how McGuinness's own background pulls together different cities, counties, and classes. The last paragraph invites views from a range of parties or traditions.

12. (Average) *Guidelines for student response:*

"Opening Statement for the Inaugural Session of the Forum for Peace and Reconciliation"
by Judge Catherine McGuinness
(continued)

Students should realize that McGuinness wants a balance between enough pride in the past so that each group feels valued in Ireland, but not so much that each group sees its own traditions as the only, or most, Irish ones. It is important, also, for every group to accept responsibility for its share in the wrongs of the armed conflict, for its share of destructive nationalism.

13. (Challenging) *Guidelines for student response:* Students should note that Connolly's comment criticizes working for abstract ideals at the cost of human connection. If a country isn't its people, then what is it? McGuinness's third-from-last paragraph unites people in the universality of their responses to life, suggesting that thoughtful patriotism thinks in larger, human terms and works for peace and economic stability. True patriotism pools resources (is inclusive—like the Forum) rather than tears a country apart.

Part Test, Unit 5, Part 3: The Story of Britain—The Empire and Its Discontents (p. 211)

Critical Reading/Vocabulary and Grammar
1. c 2. b 3. d 4. c 5. a 6. b 7. d 8. a 9. b
10. c 11. d 12. a 13. c 14. b 15. d

Questions are classified in these categories:
Comprehension 1(A), 7(E)
Interpretation 2(A), 6(E)
Literary Analysis 3(A), 8(C), 9(A)
Reading Strategy 4(A), 5(C), 10(E)
Vocabulary 11(A), 12(E)
Grammar 13(A), 14(E), 15(C)
E = Easy, A = Average, C = Challenging

Essay Questions
16. (Easy) *Guidelines for student response:* Students should focus on just one selection and its particular commentary. For example, they may note the gentle criticism of Arnold's "Dover Beach," citing the "ignorant armies" line, or they may describe the supportive warning from Kipling in "Widow."

17. (Average) *Guidelines for student response:* Students should point out that the purpose of a journalistic essay is to provide perspectives on current events or trends, not to explore one essayist's experience or ideas. Journalistic essays may be judgmental, as is the Ireland article, or simple commentary, as is the essay on progress.

18. (Challenging) Guidelines for student response: Students should conclude that using emotive language turns a political issue into an emotional one for readers. Once an issue becomes an emotional one, people may be more easily persuaded to think a certain way or to act. For example, Arnold uses emotive language in "Dover Beach" in his description of lost faith. The Ireland essayist uses emotive language in his vivid description of the empty, uncultivated land on which the starving people are not allowed to plant gardens.

"Remembrance" by Emily Brontë "The Darkling Thrush" and " 'Ah, Are You Digging on My Grave?' " by Thomas Hardy

Selection Test (p. 214)

Critical Reading/Vocabulary and Grammar
1. d 2. c 3. a 4. b 5. c 6. a 7. b 8. d 9. b
10. c 11. d 12. b 13. a 14. c 15. c 16. a
17. b 18. d 19. a 20. a

Questions are classified in these categories:
Comprehension 2(A), 6(E), 11(E)
Interpretation 1(C), 5(A), 7(A), 9(A), 14(C)
Literary Analysis 4(A), 8(E), 13(A)
Reading Strategy 3(A), 10(A), 12(A)
Vocabulary 15(A), 16(E), 17(A)
Grammar 18(C), 19(C), 20(A)
E = Easy, A = Average, C = Challenging

Essay Questions
21. (Easy) *Guidelines for student response:* Students should recognize that each stanza conveys an idea or creates a mood. The first stanza of "The Darkling Thrush," for example, sets the mood for the poem, and subsequent stanzas reinforce the mood. Students should also see the stanzas as parts of a whole. For instance, the individual stanzas of "Remembrance" describe the speaker's struggle with her loss; when

taken as a whole, the stanzas convey the deeper meaning of the poem: Life cannot be lived in a state of constant grieving.

22. (Average) *Guidelines for student response:* Students should briefly describe the poem's stanza structure and explain the expectations it creates. For instance, in "Ah, Are You Digging on My Grave?" the repetition of the speaker's question in the first line of every stanza creates the expectation that someone will grieve for the speaker. When the speaker discovers that not even her dog grieves for her, the reader's expectations are shattered. Likewise, Brontë's speaker expresses her grief in a regular pattern of four-line stanzas. In the last few stanzas, however, Brontë uses the same stanza structure to introduce the speaker's radical decision to forget her love, an ironic ending to the poem.

23. (Challenging) *Guidelines for student response:* Students might contend that Brontë's poem is atypical of Romanticism. While it begins with a rush of strong emotion, the poem ends with the speaker's resignation toward her loss. "The Darkling Thrush" seems more Romantic than Naturalistic; the final mood of the poem is cautiously optimistic, with the speaker daring to hope that the new century will usher in good rather than ill will. However, "Ah, Are You Digging on My Grave?" is a good representative of Hardy's naturalistic beliefs; he refuses to give in to the sentimentality that the speaker professes.

"God's Grandeur" and "Spring and Fall: To a Young Child"
by Gerard Manley Hopkins
"To an Athlete Dying Young" and "When I Was One-and-Twenty"
by A. E. Housman

Selection Test (p. 217)

Critical Reading/Vocabulary and Grammar
1. b 2. b 3. c 4. a 5. d 6. c 7. b 8. c 9. d
10. a 11. c 12. b 13. d 14. a 15. c 16. b
17. b 18. d 19. d 20. a

Questions are classified in these categories:
Comprehension 1(A), 5(E), 6(A), 13(C)
Interpretation 7(A), 8(C), 10(A), 11(C), 12(E),

14(E)
Literary Analysis 2(A), 3(A), 15(E)
Reading Strategy 4(E), 9(C), 12(E)
Vocabulary 18(E), 19(A), 20(A)
Grammar 16(A), 17(A)
E = Easy, A = Average, C = Challenging

Essay Questions

21. (Easy) *Guidelines for student response:* Student essays should reflect the understanding that Housman has chosen an athlete to represent humanity at the pinnacle of positive experience in the world. An athlete represents this height in the following ways: Athletic victory is visible and measurable, and all recognize victory in athletic competition. Athletic competition is limited in scope, so its successes are clear-cut. The virtues of athletes are measured only by their skill. Athletes are generally regarded as attractive, young, and strong. All these qualities symbolize humanity at the summit of its optimism, and it is from these heights that years drag us down.

22. (Average) *Guidelines for student response:* Students should recognize that Hopkins clearly regards humanity as a spoiler of the beauty of nature, not a part of it. In "God's Grandeur", he explicitly states that "men do not now" understand, that "all is seared with trade; bleared, smeared with toil; and wears man's smudge and shares man's smell" and even humanity's feet do not feel "being shod." This may represent humankind's fallen state as dictated by Hopkins' theology, which is implicitly expressed in "Spring and Fall: To a Young Child." The child as she grows will "come to such sights colder" "nor spare a sigh" at the destruction of nature. This is the "blight man was born for." Hopkins sees humans not in the natural landscape, but outside it, and apart from it, and as unworthy of its beauty.

23. (Challenging) *Guidelines for student response:* Experience is a painful process in almost all of Housman's poetry. In "To an Athlete Dying Young," life inevitably degrades. Housman calls the

"God's Grandeur" and **"Spring and Fall: To a Young Child"** by Gerard Manley Hopkins
"To an Athlete Dying Young" and **"When I Was One-and-Twenty"** by A. E. Housman
(continued)

dead youth "Smart lad" to escape the fate of others whom he calls a "rout" of those who outlive their honor. Triumph and joy cannot endure in life. In "When I Was One-and-Twenty," experience is still painful but not meaningless. Because the lesson in love's disappointment is rendered trivial and is certainly not fatal, the lesson is less harsh than in "To an Athlete Dying Young."

"Eternity" by Arthur Rimbaud

Selection Test (p. 220)

Critical Reading
1. a 2. a 3. d 4. b 5. a 6. a 7. b 8. d 9. a
10. c

Questions are classified in these categories:
    Comprehension 1(A), 5(C), 10(E)
    Interpretation 2(A), 3(E), 4(C), 6(C), 7(A),
        8(A), 9(C)
    E = Easy, A = Average, C = Challenging

Essay Questions
11. (Easy) *Guidelines for student response:* Students should discuss how Rimbaud makes the final stanza circle back to the first, enacting the "recovery" mentioned in lines 1 and 21. This cycle echoes the way the sun twice touches the sea daily, at sunrise and sunset. With Stanza 5 suggesting a painful relapse into reality, Stanza 6 begins another high moment of eternity.

12. (Average) *Guidelines for student response:* Students should link "the sun," "the fiery day," "ardor," and "embers," discussing their interrelationship and the degrees of light / heat at different points in the poem. Ideally, students would go on to mention that light is associated with the good, the heavenly, and that heat suggests intensity.

13. (Challenging) *Guidelines for student response:* Students should observe the way that lines 7–8 suggest day breaking upon or following night. They might observe

that the soul's soaring parallels the upward motion of the rising sun and then the images of embers and exhaling seem more associated with sunset. In fact, Rimbaud's leaving it ambiguous, implying both possibilities, helps make the poem all the more cyclical.

Part Test, Unit 5, Part 4: Gloom and Glory (p. 222)

Critical Reading/Vocabulary and Grammar
1. a 2. d 3. c 4. a 5. b 6. c 7. d 8. b 9. b
10. c 11. d 12. b 13. a 14. c 15. a

Questions are classified in these categories:
    Comprehension 1(E)
    Interpretation 2(A), 5(E), 10(C)
    Literary Analysis 3(E), 4(A), 7(C)
    Reading Strategy 6(A), 8(C), 9(A)
    Vocabulary 11(E), 12(A), 13(C)
    Grammar 14(E), 15(A)
    E = Easy, A = Average, C = Challenging

Essay Questions
16. (Easy) *Guidelines for student response:* Students' essays should identify the selection that they find bleakest and explain why, focusing on details in the poem that express that view. For example, students might cite the dead love in "Remembrance"; the forgotten, dead love in "Ah, Are You Digging on My Grave?"; the dismal hopelessness of the setting of "The Darkling Thrush"; the lost chances of "To an Athlete Dying Young" or "When I Was One-and-Twenty"; or human fate itself in "Spring and Fall: To a Young Child." Responses should include specific elements that indicate the pain or pessimism.

17. (Average) *Guidelines for student response:* Students' essays should focus on ironic lines or actions in the poem chosen, showing how they reverse or comment upon an expectation. For example, "Ah, Are You Digging on My Grave?" is ironic in its repeated proof of human forgetfulness, stanza by stanza, even to the faithful, hungry dog. "Remembrance" is gently ironic in its determination to forget lest one not survive remembering. The two Housman poems are ironic in their contrast between innocence and experience, as is Hopkins's "Spring and Fall: To a

Young Child," contrasting youth's naiveté with humanity's destiny.

18. (Challenging) *Guidelines for student response:* Students' essays should identify a poem and discuss how memory is transformed through expression in the poem, focusing on particular ideas or lines that show the mind working on its experience. For example, Housman's analysis of the transience of youth expresses itself in aching comment. Brontë explores a strategy for dealing with the memory of loss in "Remembrance." Hardy finds consolation in a chance bird call in "The Darkling Thrush" but sears memory with the scorching "Ah, Are You Digging on My Grave?" In each case, students should explain the elements of the poem that allude to memory, and the message the poet states with those elements.

Unit 6: A Time of Rapid Change (1901–Present)

Poetry of William Butler Yeats

Selection Test (p. 225)

Critical Reading/Vocabulary and Grammar

1. b 2. a 3. c 4. a 5. d 6. b 7. c 8. d 9. c
10. d 11. a 12. b 13. b 14. a 15. c 16. c
17. b 18. d 19. a 20. c

Questions are classified in these categories:
   Comprehension 1(E), 6(E), 8(A), 10(C)
   Interpretation 2(A), 3(C), 4(A), 9(A), 13(A)
   Literary Analysis 7(E), 12(A), 14(C)
   Reading Strategy 5(A), 11(E), 15(C)
   Vocabulary 16(E), 17(C), 18(A)
   Grammar 19(A), 20(A)
   E = Easy, A = Average, C = Challenging

Essay Questions

21. (Easy) *Guidelines for student response:* Student essays should clearly identify something longed for in each of the three poems and give examples from chosen poems to indicate evidence of that longing. For example, in "When You Are Old," the speaker longs for unrequited love and the missed opportunity it held. In "The Lake Isle of Innisfree," Yeats explicitly longs for peace. In "The Wild Swans at Coole," the speaker longs for a world that does not change, for in the "nineteenth autumn" of his watching, he recalls when he trod "with a lighter tread."

22. (Average) *Guidelines for student response:* Students should identify symbols in three of the poems in the selection and describe what each represents in the poem and the world beyond it. For example, in "When You Are Old," the fictional old woman symbolizes the future and lost opportunity in love. The "stars" where love has hidden symbolize artistic endeavor. In "The Lake Isle of Innisfree," the isle and everything described on it symbolize a place of peace, either in itself or made from artistic effort. In "The Wild Swans at Coole," the obvious symbols are the swans, who represent unchanging nature, even as they fly away.

23. (Challenging) *Guidelines for student response:* Students must discuss the idea of nature in three poems of their choosing. For example, Yeats often contrasts the un-self-conscious beauty of nature and the conscious work of the human mind. In "When You Are Old," both the woman's beauty and time serve as enemies of the true union of souls the speaker had sought. In "The Lake Isle of Innisfree," the most traditional use of nature is apparently made, with the idyllic natural setting offering peace. In "The Wild Swans at Coole," the speaker laments the unchanging change that occurs in nature, for he will no longer witness the swans, though they will be somewhere. In all of the poems, Yeats sees humans as bound by the rules of nature but wishes the mind were not subject to them.

"Preludes," "Journey of the Magi," and "The Hollow Men" by T. S. Eliot

Selection Test (p. 228)

Critical Reading/Vocabulary and Grammar

1. c 2. a 3. c 4. b 5. b 6. d 7. a 8. b 9. c
10. b 11. d 12. b 13. d 14. b 15. c 16. b
17. a 18. d 19. b 20. d

Questions are classified in these categories:
Comprehension 1(E), 2(A), 14(A)
Interpretation 4(A), 5(C), 6(E), 8(C), 9(A), 10(C)
Literary Analysis 3(A), 11(C), 13(A)
Reading Strategy 5(A), 7(E), 12(A)
Vocabulary 15(E), 16(A), 17(A)
Grammar 18(E), 19(A), 20(A)
E = Easy, A = Average, C = Challenging

Essay Questions

21. (Easy) *Guidelines for student response:* Students should understand that the journey of the Magi is long and difficult. It is important to them because, despite hardships, difficult people, and self-doubt, they press onward. Students should name specific images of the journey's hardships, such as "The ways deep and the weather sharp," the "sore-footed camels," and the "cities hostile and the towns unfriendly." The journey changes their lives in that it affirms their faith and helps them to anticipate change in the world around them. They are no longer at ease with the "old dispensations," or belief systems, of people.

22. (Average) *Guidelines for student response:* Students should understand that both poems contain images that reveal an ugly, sad world that is spiritually lacking. In the images from "Preludes," the dirtiness of the city is emphasized. People are described only as "muddy feet" who gather each morning for masquerades. The use of the word *masquerade* and the description of people as anonymous, muddy feet imply that there is emptiness or untruthfulness in the lives of people. They lack self-awareness and a spiritual connection to themselves and one another. They are fragmented and lost in their daily routines. In "The Hollow Men," the description of people with heads full of grass and quiet, meaningless voices implies the same kind of detachment and emptiness.

The image of rats and broken glass implies the same ugliness and painful despair that is found in the opening lines of "Preludes."

23. (Challenging) *Guidelines for student response:* Both poems represent a break from traditional types of verse in that they convey meaning through simple but meaningful images intended to have a powerful emotional effect. These images reflect the Modernist view of the world in their depiction of chaos, spiritual emptiness, and dirtiness. In "Preludes," the poet describes a rainy, cold city in which people—described as only hands and feet—are fragmented and lost. In daylight, people walk around without direction and in masquerade. At night, they are haunted by a thousand sordid images. At the end of the poem, Eliot expresses the hope that the human spirit can rise above and beyond the sordid circumstances of their lives. In "The Hollow Men," Eliot expresses the meaningless, repetitive behaviors people display in modern life. They are inhibited by corruption, disillusionment, and an inability to connect to their spiritual selves. These themes are emphasized by images of sightlessness, images of a tired, broken, world, and images of people being paralyzed and unable to save themselves.

"In Memory of W. B. Yeats" and "Musée des Beaux Arts" by W. H. Auden
"Carrick Revisited" by Louis MacNeice
"Not Palaces" by Stephen Spender

Selection Test (p. 231)

Critical Reading/Vocabulary and Grammar

1. a 2. a 3. d 4. c 5. a 6. c 7. b 8. c 9. b
10. c 11. d 12. b 13. b 14. d 15. d 16. b
17. d 18. a 19. c 20. a

Questions are classified in these categories:
Comprehension 2(A), 9(E), 12(E)
Interpretation 1(A), 5(C), 6(A), 7(A), 14(C)
Literary Analysis 4(A), 8(A), 11(C)
Reading Strategy 3(C), 10(A), 13(E)
Vocabulary 15(A), 16(E), 17(A)
Grammar 18(E), 19(A), 20(A)
E = Easy, A = Average, C = Challenging

Essay Questions

21. (Easy) *Guidelines for student response:*
    Students should offer paraphrases for several sections of the poem and use them to draw conclusions about the poem's meaning. For instance, a possible paraphrase for stanza three in "Carrick Revisited" might read: "Seeing a place we know from memory is like hearing but not understanding. We can't know precisely how our past has shaped us." Students must explain how their paraphrases helped them understand the poem's meaning. For instance, the paraphrase of stanza three might lead students to identify the poem's theme of the origins of artistic identity.

22. (Average) *Guidelines for student response:*
    Students must focus on two poems. Statements of theme must be supported with relevant lines from the poems. For example, students might note that the theme of "Musée des Beaux Arts" is that tragedy matters only to those who are affected by it. Students should realize that Auden states the theme both directly and indirectly. Lines 1–4, which note that human suffering takes place while ordinary events happen, state this theme directly. Auden's detached tone and word choice—"walking dully along," "innocent," and "leisurely," for example—convey the theme indirectly.

23. (Challenging) *Guidelines for student response:* Students must state the views of two poets and compare and contrast them. For example, students might feel an affinity with Auden's view that "poetry makes nothing happen" and contrast it with Spender's fervent belief that poetry can rally people toward a "purpose which the wind engraves."

"Shooting an Elephant"
by George Orwell

Selection Test (p. 234)

Critical Reading/Vocabulary and Grammar

1. b 2. d 3. c 4. d 5. a 6. c 7. c 8. a 9. b
10. c 11. b 12. b 13. a 14. d 15. c 16. d
17. a 18. d 19. a 20. b

Questions are classified in these categories:
   Comprehension 7(E), 8(C), 14(A)
   Interpretation 3(A), 5(C), 6(A), 12(E), 13(A)
   Literary Analysis 4(A), 9(A), 11(C)

Reading Strategy 1(A), 2(A), 10(C)
Vocabulary 15(E), 16(A), 17(A)
Grammar 18(A), 19(A), 20(E)
E = Easy, A = Average, C = Challenging

Essay Questions

21. (Easy) *Guidelines for student response:*
    Students should recognize that the real motives Orwell names are the fear of appearing weak or foolish and the desire to impress the subjugated. Students might cite examples such as Orwell's self-consciousness in front of the crowd, his realization that he is an "absurd puppet," his fear of being laughed at, and the contradiction in killing an animal that is no longer a threat.

22. (Average) *Guidelines for student response:*
    Students should focus their essays on the conflicting attitudes Orwell expresses in the essay. He begins by voicing his objections to imperialism but soon reveals his frustration with the ill treatment he receives from the Burmese. His comment that most officials share his ambivalence toward imperialism but will only admit to it "off duty" demonstrates his feeling of being "stuck between" his official role and his moral position. Other examples of this dilemma include his quandary about shooting the elephant and his conflicting attitudes toward the death of the coolie.

23. (Challenging) *Guidelines for student response:* Students should note that Orwell primarily uses irony of situation in his essay. The inherent assumption behind Orwell's statement is that tyrants destroy the freedom of those they control. The irony, therefore, is that the tyrants destroy their own freedom as well, in an attempt to maintain an appearance of authority, power, and control. Orwell's disillusioning knowledge that he must act as the crowd expects him to act—as a representative of imperialism—conveys this loss of freedom. As a member of the ruling class, he presumably has freedom of choice. However, from the moment he is called to investigate the problem, he becomes part of a chain of events seemingly beyond his control.

"The Demon Lover"
by Elizabeth Bowen

Selection Test (p. 237)

Critical Reading/Vocabulary and Grammar

1. d 2. b 3. a 4. c 5. c 6. a 7. b 8. c 9. d
10. b 11. c 12. a 13. b 14. a 15. b 16. b
17. b 18. d 19. c 20. b

Questions are classified in these categories:
Comprehension 1(E), 8(A), 9(C)
Interpretation 2(C), 3(A), 10(A), 12(E), 14(E)
Literary Analysis 4(C), 5(A), 7(A), 15(C)
Reading Strategy 6(A), 11(E), 13(A)
Vocabulary 16(E), 17(A), 18(C)
Grammar 19(E) 20(A)
E = Easy, A = Average, C = Challenging

Essay Questions

21. (Easy) *Guidelines for student response:* Some students may choose to state that Bowen uses the war to create tension in her stories, to serve as the unhappy background for unhappy people. They may interpret this as opportunism, perhaps therefore acceptance. Or they may say that because Bowen experienced the war herself, its events don't seem noteworthy or interesting to her. Other students may note that all of the strangeness in the story is the result of Mrs. Drover's family being "dislocated" from their normal life as a result of the bombings. The unhappiness and tension that exist in Mrs. Drover are Bowen's way of showing how war breaks people down.

22. (Average) *Guidelines for student response:* Students should point out the "queerness" of Mrs. Drover's street. Mrs. Drover is "perplexed" by being in her own home. The presence of the letter, as well as its message, is disturbing. The circumstances of her long-ago meeting with her fiancé were a bit odd, as were her years of "dislocation" afterward. She cannot remember his face. She feels a draft of cold air from downstairs. The taxi seems to be waiting for her and starts up without her instructions. All of these "unnatural" elements serve to build suspense so that the reader is expecting catastrophe but still taken by surprise when the taxi speeds off with the screaming

Mrs. Drover.

23. (Challenging) *Guidelines for student response:* Students should "identify with" at least two incidents in the story, and explain *how* they identify with them. For example, a student may remember an odd feeling of surprise and confusion upon receiving a letter from someone he or she hadn't heard from or thought about for years. Students' own feelings or experiences should lead them to express increased understanding of Mrs. Drover's actions and responses.

"The Diameter of the Bomb" by Yehuda Amichai
"Everything Is Plundered" by Anna Akhmatova
"Testament" by Bei Dao

Selection Test (p. 240)

Critical Reading

1. b 2. b 3. a 4. c 5. b 6. b 7. c 8. a 9. b
10. d

Questions are classified in these categories:
Comprehension 1(A), 2(A), 5(E), 9(C)
Interpretation 3(A), 4(C), 6(A), 7(C), 8(C), 10(E)
E = Easy, A = Average, C = Challenging

Essay Questions

11. (Easy) *Guidelines for student response:* Most basically, students could conclude that an observer makes sense because the victims of the bomb are dead or incapacitated. Additionally, students should comment on Amichai's choice of an impersonal, scientific opening that builds to the emotional outrage of the ending (speaker finally uses "I"). The observer could be a journalist or a doctor trying to restrain emotions while reporting facts. Or possibly the speaker is any Israeli ironically using statistics to shame the world into caring what happens "only" in his distant country. Finally, students might suggest that if no God is watching, then there needs to be another witness who sees the full horror of the event.

12. (Average) *Guidelines for student response:* Students should trace how Amichai's pre-

cise measurements and statistics lead up to a fierce rejection of God while Dao's catalogue of his minimal needs and actions ends in a declaration of faith. Amichai uses concrete "geometric" terms to describe incalculable human suffering and only releases his horror in the last four lines. In Dao's structure, the third line in each stanza is more emotionally suggestive than the first two. Students might observe that both Amichai and Dao create a climax by saving the most poetic language (the strongest figurative imagery) for the closing lines.

13. (Challenging) *Guidelines for student response:* Students should relate the "miraculous" in Akhmatova's poem to nature and to its regenerative powers. The summer reawakens the people's instinct to come to life and feel pleasure. Both Akhmatova and Dao receive courage and hope from nature, especially from the sky. The imagery of the last stanza of "Testament" (stars, dawn) suggests a cycle like Akhmatova's (darkness-light, winter-summer). By contrast, students should note that Amichai does not situate his poem in a cyclical natural world but in a cosmic void. In Amichai's poem no natural beauty or vital forces offset the human destruction.

Part Test, Unit 6, Part 1: Waking From the Dream (p. 242)

Critical Reading/Vocabulary and Grammar

1. c 2. a 3. c 4. b 5. a 6. a 7. a 8. d 9. b 10. c 11. c 12. a 13. b 14. c 15. a 16. b 17. c 18. d 19. c 20. c

Questions are classified in these categories:
Comprehension 1(E)
Interpretation 3(C), 5(A), 8(A)
Literary Analysis 6(A), 9(C), 10(A)
Reading Strategy 2(A), 4(E), 7(A)
Vocabulary 11(A), 12(A), 18(C), 19(E), 20(C)
Grammar 13(A), 14(E), 15(C), 16(E), 17(A)
E = Easy, A = Average, C = Challenging

Essay Questions

21. (Easy) *Guidelines for student response:* Students' essays should reveal a clear understanding of the section's theme and should identify one piece from the section that is reflective of this theme. In describ-

ing the selection they choose, they should be able to recall concrete details that show how the selection reflects the theme in its own particular way. For example, in "The Demon Lover," a writer describes the dreamlike atmosphere of war and how it makes things from everyday life seem strange and out of place. In Yeats's "The Wild Swans at Coole," the speaker focuses on dreamlike serenity of natural images and an awakening to the passage of time; W. H. Auden's poem "Musée des Beaux Arts" attempts to awaken readers to the realities of human existence.

22. (Average) *Guidelines for student response:* Students should reveal an understanding of symbolism and be able to identify symbolism and its meaning in one piece from the section. For example, a strong essay might be written about the "indignant desert birds" of Yeats's "The Second Coming" or the word *monuments* in the Yeats poem "Sailing to Byzantium." Other students might write essays about the bleak city images in Eliot's poem "Preludes" or the hollow men in the poem "The Hollow Men."

23. (Average) *Guidelines for student response:* Students' essays should focus on the imagery and language of two poems from the section. Students should be able to identify significant images and words and interpret these elements to find meaning and theme in each poem. For example, students writing about "The Hollow Men" by T. S. Eliot might describe the repetition of words such as *hollow, stuffed,* and *broken* and explain how these words reflect Eliot's attitude toward the lives of the hollow men and life in the modern world. Students writing about Yeats's "The Second Coming" might focus on the images of the falcon or the desert birds and explain what these images reveal about theme.

24. (Average) *Guidelines for student response:* In their essays, students should reveal a clear understanding of aspects of Modernism discussed in the section. They should be able to identify a poem that reflects the ideas of Modernism, giving concrete examples from the poem. For example, a strong essay might be written about T. S. Eliot's poem "Preludes."

Students writing about this poem might describe the poem's bleak images of modern life in a city, which reveal the chaos and directionlessness of the modern world. Students might also explain that these images are clear snapshots and that they evoke specific emotions in readers.

25. (Challenging) *Guidelines for student response:* Students' essays should focus on two selections that present some type of commentary on the human experience. Students should be able to describe details and themes from these pieces and also compare and contrast the pieces. For example some students might focus on the bleak depictions of modern life in T. S. Eliot's poems "Preludes" and "The Hollow Men." Other students might discuss Auden's view of the human condition in "Musée des Beaux Arts" or Spender's view and suggestions to humankind in "Not Palaces." Some students might also focus on the experience of the narrator in George Orwell's "Shooting an Elephant," and what this reveals about a person's inability to overcome pressures from a crowd to do what he knows is right.

"The Soldier" by Rupert Brooke
"Wirers" by Siegfried Sassoon
"Anthem for Doomed Youth" by Wilfred Owen
"Birds on the Western Front" by Saki (H. H. Munro)

Selection Test (p. 246)

Critical Reading/Vocabulary and Grammar

1. d 2. c 3. b 4. d 5. a 6. b 7. a 8. a 9. c
10. d 11. b 12. b 13. c 14. d 15. a 16. c
17. c 18. a 19. b 20. d

Questions are classified in these categories:
Comprehension 1(A), 5(E), 9(C)
Interpretation 2(A), 6(C), 8(E), 10(A), 12(A)
Literary Analysis 4(E), 7(A), 13(E), 14(C)
Reading Strategy 3(A), 11(C), 15(A)
Vocabulary 16(A), 17(E), 18(A)
Grammar 19(A), 20(C)
E = Easy, A = Average, C = Challenging

Essay Questions

21. (Easy) *Guidelines for student response:* The experience of World War I totally dominates existence in all these selections. There is no sense of seeing beyond war's end. Even the speaker in Brooke's poem, the only idealist, assumes he will die. In "Wirers," peril and death numb both speaker and reader; the final lines bitterly call into question the purpose of the wirers' activities and the war. Owen's "Anthem for Doomed Youth" also describes the experience of total war constantly waged, contrasting it with remembered civility. Saki uses an ironic and absurd tone of normalcy in an extremely abnormal situation, and his cheerful commentary on natural life amid mass destruction underscores the permanent presence of unnatural death in a ravaged landscape.

22. (Average) *Guidelines for student response:* The only similarity between "The Soldier" and "Wirers" is that both seem to assume no other fate than death for a soldier. The fundamental difference between the two is in whether the cause is worth the sacrifice: to Brooke it is; to Sassoon it's not. Brooke focuses on the beauty of English life that prepares him for this sacrifice, that the "pulse in the eternal mind" bear more of an English rhythm. Sassoon's "Wirers", by contrast, sets grim images of exhausted men stumbling in terror beside a matter-of-fact attitude about death. The death of young Hughes gains only a wire "safely mended," which will need to be mended again.

23. (Challenging) *Guidelines for student response:* Saki's tone comes from two primary factors: a cheerful voice making casual comments and a faintly bizarre topic interspersed with details about the real scenery. Focusing on bird behavior, the narrator still points out "a wealth of ruined buildings" or notes he had "occasion to throw myself abruptly on my face." These off-center descriptions of destruction and danger point to the absurd nature of the topic. The tone of normalcy in the most abnormal of situations implies a contrast between war and normal life. The detailed description of bird behavior in these conditions also implies a contrast

between the natural life of the inhabitants and that of the combatants.

"Wartime Speech" by Winston Churchill
"Defending Nonviolent Resistance" by Mohandas K. Gandhi

Selection Test (p. 249)

Critical Reading/Vocabulary and Grammar

1. a 2. c 3. c 4. b 5. a 6. b 7. d 8. a 9. c
10. b 11. d 12. c 13. a 14. b 15. d 16. d
17. b 18. a 19. c 20. d

Questions are classified in these categories:
Comprehension 1(E), 7(A), 11(C)
Interpretation 2(A), 6(E), 8(E), 15(C)
Literary Analysis 3(A), 5(C), 10(E), 13(A)
Reading Strategy 4(A), 9(C), 12(E), 14(A)
Vocabulary 17(E), 18(A), 20(A)
Grammar 16(A), 19(A)
E = Easy, A = Average, C = Challenging

Essay Questions

21. (Easy) *Guidelines for student response:* The purpose of the speech is a clear explanation of the causes and goals of Gandhi's actions against British rule. First, he traces the rise of his disaffection with British rule by citing incidents of racism and repression, although noting service to the Empire. Second, he points to the current condition of the Indian people under British rule, who are powerless, weak, and poor. Third, he states the principle that it is a virtue to oppose a government that has caused the damage he has already cited, a "sin to have affection" for such a system. The credibility of the first two points makes the logic of the third seem ironclad, and so he considers it a "precious privilege" to oppose such authority. In agreeing to the charges on grounds of morality, he reinforces the notion that the government that makes the laws is immoral.

22. (Average) *Guidelines for student response:* Churchill's purpose in the speech is to meet the emotional needs of his audience by addressing what the situation is and preparing Britons for what it will be. First, he reports facts, acknowledging what people already know, that France is in trouble, and thus seems in touch and in control.

Second, he further calms a troubled audience by noting the efforts and qualities of the French and British troops. Third, he offers limited hope, suggesting ways things could turn out well and what it might take, although noting it would be "foolish to disguise" what will probably happen. Then he shifts to preparing for war alone and calls on the nation to prepare and produce for the "battle for our island" in the name of "right and freedom." He closes by invoking centuries of British valor and history to emphasize the like nature of this moment.

23. (Challenging) *Guidelines for student response:* Although Churchill and Gandhi differed in almost every personal respect, their speeches reveal several similar traits. Both are fearless in difficult circumstances: Neither hedges nor offers compromise, although neither has any real control over his fate. Both understand the needs of their audience: Churchill rallies and prepares his people with patriotic appeals for a solitary struggle, and Gandhi states his principle of continuation, courage to hearten his supporters and impress his foes. Both are clear explainers of their positions, and both are inspiring speakers who look beyond the moment to the larger issues of their struggles: Churchill invokes history past and future to place the current battle in the context of all of British history, and Gandhi is unconcerned with his particular case in pursuit of the larger cause of Indian independence.

"The Fiddle" by Alan Sillitoe

Selection Test (p. 252)

Critical Reading/Vocabulary and Grammar

1. d 2. c 3. d 4. a 5. c 6. a 7. d 8. a 9. d
10. c 11. b 12. a 13. d 14. b 15. c 16. b
17. b 18. c 19. d 20. c

Questions are classified in these categories:
Comprehension 1(E), 3(A), 13(A), 15(E)
Interpretation 2(A), 8(C), 9(A), 10(C), 14(A)
Literary Analysis 5(A), 7(C), 12(C)
Reading Strategy 4(E), 6(A), 11(A)
Vocabulary 16(E), 17(A)
Grammar 18(E), 19(A), 20(C)
E = Easy, A = Average, C = Challenging

"The Fiddle" by Alan Sillitoe
(continued)

Essay Questions

21. (Easy) *Guidelines for student response:* Students should identify Jeff's choice as whether to continue to be a miner or to effect some change in that existence. His poverty and his dislike for the mine work lead to his choice. He sells his fiddle, which gives him enough money to purchase a new occupation. Jeff gave up the only thing he liked about his life to remedy the part of his life that was absolutely intolerable. Given the circumstances, there was little else Jeff could have done to release himself from working in the mine, aside from simply becoming unemployed, like Blonk.

22. (Average) *Guidelines for student response:* Students should identify the cottages as a shabby backdrop for the story. The Leen lends a pleasant air to the neighborhood, except when it floods and must be avoided. It is pleasant because it comes from somewhere else and goes somewhere else. It doesn't have to stay, as the people do. The fiddle is a release and an escape, when it is being played as well as when it is sold. The mine oppresses and hangs over Jeff. The 1930s setting lends futility and hopelessness to the story, for the whole world suffered during that time. And World War II brings inevitable destruction and death to the story.

23. (Challenging) *Guidelines for student response:* Students may state that the story is about the difficulty of a man's life due to his circumstances—living in the 1930s, working as a miner, being poor. The man chooses to make a difficult decision to change his circumstances. That decision centers on the fiddle, which *had* been the man's one source of comfort in life. The fiddle serves as a symbol of the man's escape, both temporary and permanent, as it turns out. The other elements of the story—the many aspects of the setting—serve to enrich the plot and provide atmosphere.

"The Distant Past" by William Trevor

Selection Test (p. 255)

Critical Reading/Vocabulary and Grammar

1. c 2. d 3. b 4. a 5. d 6. b 7. b 8. c 9. c
10. a 11. a 12. b 13. b 14. d 15. b 16. a
17. d 18. c 19. b 20. c

Questions are classified in these categories:
Comprehension 1(A), 7(E), 9(E), 12(C)
Interpretation 4(C), 5(A), 13(E), 14(A), 15(A)
Literary Analysis 6(C), 8(E), 11(C)
Reading Strategy 2(A), 3(E), 10(C)
Vocabulary 16(E), 17(A)
Grammar 18(E), 19(E), 20(E)
E = Easy, A = Average, C = Challenging

Essay Questions

21. (Easy) *Guidelines for student response:* Students may identify the Middletons' Protestantism, which they inherited from their family. The effect of this is to place them in opposition—religiously and politically—to many of their neighbors. The "lock-up" incident during the Middletons' childhood was caused by these differing opinions. The effect was to isolate the Middletons from the townspeople. The eccentric oddness of the Middletons was caused by their lifestyle and loyalties. The effect of it was to endear them to the townspeople. The recurrence of violence in the North was caused by opposing viewpoints that could not be laid to rest. The effect was the resurgence of suspicions and resentments that had been put aside for many years.

22. (Average) *Guidelines for student response:* Students should identify the conflict between the Middletons and the townspeople as one of differing opinions about their society. The conflict is dominant when the political situation is hot, such as when the Middletons were locked in their house. When the characters accept, more or less, the status quo, and when the political climate, in general, cools down, they are able to be friends and neighbors without resentment. The escalation of hostilities in the North causes the conflict to return to the fore of the Middletons' lives.

23. (Challenging) *Guidelines for student response:* Students should recall that the Middletons talk about the distant past with the shopkeepers, who accept their comments though they don't share their opinions. When the townspeople begin to be cool, the "talk there had been in the distant past" arises, suggesting that suspicions and accusations creep into people's conversations. Finally, Miss Middleton's final thoughts reveal that because of the distant past they will die friendless. The phrase refers as much to time past as to a *different* time, when English rule existed and was not contested. The time when the Middletons were friends with the townspeople is overshadowed by the distant past.

"Follower" and "Two Lorries"
by Seamus Heaney
"Outside History" by Eavan Boland

Selection Test (p. 258)

Critical Reading/Vocabulary and Grammar

1. d 2. b 3. d 4. c 5. a 6. a 7. b   8. d 9. b
10. a 11. c 12. b 13. c 14. a 15. d 16. c
17. a 18. b 19. b 20. b

Questions are classified in these categories:
  Comprehension 1(E), 7(A), 8(C), 13(A)
  Interpretation 2(A), 3(A), 9(E), 12(C), 14(A)
  Literary Analysis 4(C), 11(A), 15(A)
  Reading Strategy 5(A), 6(E), 10(E), 16(C)
  Vocabulary 17(E), 18(A)
  Grammar 19(A), 20(A)
  E = Easy, A = Average, C = Challenging

Essay Questions

21. (Easy) *Guidelines for student response:* Students should be able to relate to the poem's informal, conversational style well enough to recognize it as such. The story-telling quality and the many concrete nouns add to the friendliness of the poem. The imagery, too, is concrete and accessible. Readers can see the horse, the plow, the strong man working, the young boy stumbling, the rough dirt opened up behind the plow, then the old man following the now-grown boy. Students should be able to recall that alternating lines rhyme in each stanza. The form is traditional four-line stanzas.

22. (Average) *Guidelines for student response:* In "Two Lorries," once the second lorry is introduced, everything in the poem becomes death and ashes. Heaney's image implies that the violence is deceitful—who would expect a lorry to be doing anything but delivering things? He also finds the violence particularly destructive—the only thing that reemerges from the explosion, as it were, is the "driver," who may represent death, violence, or terrorists in general. In "Outside History," Boland refers to "that ordeal" as a darkness that is clogging the roads and rivers with dead bodies. Her feeling that "we are always too late" implies that the violence will go on in spite of efforts to stop it. Students should conclude that Heaney and Boland express similar views on Ireland's troubles.

23. (Challenging) *Guidelines for student response:* Students should be able to label the first incident as a boyhood memory of a delivery man flirting with his mother. Such an incident—outside of the everyday norm—would have made a huge impact on a young boy. The second incident is that of an explosive-laden lorry blowing up a bus station. This event happens years after the first. In a sort of "look what the world has come to" mode, the speaker imagines that his mother, already dead, could have been in that bus station, perhaps with the lorry driver who had flirted with her all those years ago. In addition to the lorry, memories of his mother link the two incidents, although her connection with the second incident is only a working of the speaker's imagination.

"No Witchcraft for Sale"
Doris Lessing

Selection Test (p. 261)

Critical Reading/Vocabulary and Grammar

1. c 2. b 3. a 4. d 5. a 6. b 7. c 8. d 9. b
10. b 11. c 12. d 13. d 14. a 15. b 16. b
17. a 18. d 19. c 20. a

Questions are classified in these categories:
  Comprehension 1(E), 7(A), 13(C)
  Interpretation 2(A), 3(E), 9(E), 12(C)
  Literary Analysis 4(C), 5(A), 11(C), 14(E)
  Reading Strategy 6(A), 8(E), 10(A), 15(C)

"No Witchcraft for Sale" Doris Lessing
(continued)

Vocabulary 16(E), 17(A), 18(A)
Grammar 19(E), 20(C)
E = Easy, A = Average, C = Challenging

Essay Questions

21. (Easy) *Guidelines for student response:*
Student essays should reflect that they
understand the conflict of cultures. The
Farquars see themselves as masters who
run things. Mrs. Farquar rewards Gideon
with money, in keeping with his status.
Teddy assumes a ruling status after terror-
izing a black child. However kind they
choose to be, the world is a place they run.
Gideon wishes not to run the world but live
peacefully in it. His comments on the separate cultures reveal sadness, and he is disappointed but not surprised at Teddy's
acts. The fundamental misunderstanding
of his healing art offends him, for the
knowledge is not a trick; it is integrally
linked to him and his people and he refuses
to separate it. Their view is disrespectful to
him and they cannot understand.

22. (Average) *Guidelines for student response:*
The scientist bluntly represents the
colonists' way of thinking. To a European,
the world is an empirical place where
everything must have an explanation. The
Farquars accept this philosophy, but the
scientist embodies it explicitly. He is polite, but merely in form, and not in true
respect. He is cynical enough to try what
works, first on the Farquars, for whom he
must shift tactics when money isn't appealing. Then he offers Gideon a gift, a
cheap barter that would offend Gideon. It
may be that the scientist means no harm,
but his understanding, which is limited
merely to proof, is too shallow to grasp the
gap between the kinds of understanding
he knows and the kind of knowledge
Gideon has. His approach to knowledge
will fail in Gideon's culture.

23. (Challenging) *Guidelines for student response:* Gideon cured the child because
he cared for him, because it was an emergency, and because he knew he could do
so. The motivation was never use of or
demonstration of his power. When the

Farquars and the scientist ask him how
he did it, they are offending him because
in so doing they call into question his motivation and his skill. It should be enough
that a good thing happened. He has
sought no reward. Neither has he anything to prove and is offended to be asked
to do so. He is surrounded, he feels, by
"yelping dogs," who have little sense of
who he is. Under no circumstance will he
allow his culture or himself to be invaded
and his art taken away.

"The Rights We Enjoy, The Duties We Owe" by Tony Blair

Selection Test (p. 264)

Critical Reading

1. c 2. c 3. b 4. d 5. c 6. c 7. d 8. c 9. c
10. a
Questions are classified in these categories:
  Comprehension 1(A), 2(A), 3(E), 5(E), 6(A),
  9(C)
  Interpretation 4(A), 7(A), 8(C), 10(C)
  E = Easy, A = Average, C = Challenging

Essay Questions

11. (Easy) *Guidelines for student response:*
Students should mention that according
to Blair, citizens in a morally responsible
society receive the respect necessary for
healthy individuality. Such citizens also
have an equal chance at achievement despite birth status. What Blair calls a "decent society" provides its members with a
sense of shared purpose and fellowship,
which in turn makes them well-adjusted.

12. (Average) *Guidelines for student response:*
Students should identify Blair's explicit
gender/class comments: Great Britain
does "not want women chained to the
sink" or "old class structures back."
Women, who are already half of the work
force, and those of lower birth status, deserve equal opportunities in a society to
which they contribute.

13. (Challenging) *Guidelines for student response:* Essays should discuss how Blair
stresses that the modern world makes people more interdependent than ever, so that
working together is a tool for surviving and
thriving in the twenty-first century. Moral

rules, he suggests, are anchors of order in a constantly shifting landscape—they provide direction and a sense of community. Even if religion has been eroded, cooperative support of certain ethical principles (such as human brotherhood) will stabilize the contemporary world.

Part Test, Unit 6, Part 2: Conflicts Abroad and at Home
(p. 266)

Critical Reading/Vocabulary and Grammar

1. c 2. a 3. d 4. a 5. b 6. c 7. b 8. a 9. c
10. c 11. a 12. d 13. b 14. c 15. b

Questions are classified in these categories:
Comprehension 2(E)
Interpretation 8(E)
Literary Analysis 4(A), 5(A), 7(A)
Reading Strategy 1(A), 3(A), 6(A), 9(A), 10(C)
Vocabulary 11(C), 12(E)
Grammar 13(A), 14(A), 15(A)
E = Easy, A = Average, C = Challenging

Essay Questions

16. (Easy) *Guidelines for student response:* Students should be able to explain in a thorough way how one selection from the section deals with conflict effectively. For example, a student writing about Saki's "Birds on the Western Front" might describe the theme of war in the piece and the effects war has on innocent wildlife found in battle areas. Students writing about William Trevor's "The Distant Past" might focus on how the story addresses political conflict and the effects it has on people's relationships within a country. Students should support their ideas and opinions with concrete details from the chosen selection.

17. (Average) *Guidelines for student response:* Students should be able to focus on one piece from the section that reveals something about the strength of the human spirit. They should explain their ideas, using concrete details from the piece they choose. For example, some students might describe the patriotism and loyalty expressed by Rupert Brooke in "The Soldier" or the experiences of soldiers in the poems by Siegfried Sassoon or Wilfred Owen. Other students might focus on the beliefs

expressed in the speeches of Winston Churchill or Mohandas Gandhi, or the protectiveness of Gideon toward his culture in Doris Lessing's "No Witchcraft for Sale."

18. (Challenging) *Guidelines for student response:* Students should reveal a thorough understanding of tone and atmosphere and be able to identify specific words and phrases that create tone and atmosphere in two pieces from the section. For example, students might give details to show the patriotic, wistful tone of Rupert Brooke's "The Soldier" or details that reveal Wilfred Owen's tone in describing death on the battlefield. Students might also describe atmosphere in "The Fiddle."

"The Lagoon" by Joseph Conrad
"Araby" by James Joyce

Selection Test (p. 269)

Critical Reading/Vocabulary and Grammar

1. b 2. c 3. a 4. b 5. a 6. b 7. c 8. b 9. d
10. c 11. a 12. d 13. a 14. a 15. a 16. c
17. d 18. b 19. b 20. c

Questions are classified in these categories:
Comprehension 1(A), 5(A), 7(E)
Interpretation 2(C), 3(A), 8(C), 9(A), 11(A)
Literary Analysis 6(A), 13(C), 14(A)
Reading Strategy 4(E), 10(A), 12(C)
Vocabulary 15(A), 16(C), 17(E)
Grammar 18(A), 19(E), 20(A)
E = Easy, A = Average, C = Challenging

Essay Questions

21. (Easy) *Guidelines for student response:* Students analyzing "The Lagoon" should recognize that the dark and isolated setting of the lagoon provides clues to Arsat's mental state; he has chosen to "live amongst the spirits that haunt the places abandoned by mankind." The dying fire by which Arsat tells his tale symbolizes Arsat's burning passion for Diamelen, a passion that soon fades in the face of Arsat's terrible choice. Students analyzing "Araby" should note that the grim Dublin setting weighs heavily against the boy and his chances to succeed. The boy lives on a "blind," or dead-end street, and by the end of the story he comes to realize that his life is a dead end as well.

"The Lagoon" by Joseph Conrad
"Araby" by James Joyce
(continued)

22. (Average) *Guidelines for student response:* Students should note that Conrad uses a story within a story and that Joyce uses an epiphany. In analyzing Conrad's plot device, students might explain that placing Arsat's tale within a larger framework provides a meaningful context and allows the reader to make connections between Arsat's inner struggle, which the character articulates, and the white man's inner struggle, which is left unspoken. Students might point out that Joyce's use of epiphany strikes a stronger emotional chord than merely stating a lesson learned or summarizing a moral. The boy's sudden, painful revelation conveys anger, humiliation, frustration, and resignation all within a single moment.

23. (Challenging) *Guidelines for student response:* Students might conclude that these works demonstrate an introspection and isolation peculiar to the individual in Modernist literature. Students should provide evidence from the stories as well as analyze the writers' styles and techniques. For example, in "The Lagoon," both the white man and Arsat are isolated from humanity—the rootless man travels aimlessly on the river, while Arsat sequesters himself at the lagoon. Conrad underscores this isolation through the lagoon's isolated and forbidding setting. Both Conrad and Joyce imply the introspective states of their characters—Arsat in "The Lagoon" is tortured by his ruminations, and, similarly, the boy in "Araby" lives in a world of illusions that he voices to no one.

"The Lady in the Looking Glass: A Reflection" by Virginia Woolf
"The First Year of My Life" by Muriel Spark

Selection Test (p. 272)

Critical Reading/Vocabulary and Grammar

1. b 2. c 3. a 4. a 5. d 6. d 7. d 8. b 9. c
10. b 11. b 12. a 13. a 14. c 15. c 16. a
17. d 18. d 19. a 20. b

Questions are classified in these categories:
Comprehension 4(A), 7(A), 8(E)
Interpretation 1(A), 5(C), 10(A), 12(A), 14(A)
Literary Analysis 3(C), 6(E), 9(A)
Reading Strategy 2(E), 11(C), 13(A)
Vocabulary 15(C), 16(A), 17(A)
Grammar 18(A), 19(A), 20(E)
E = Easy, A = Average, C = Challenging

Essay Questions

21. (Easy) *Guidelines for student response:* Most of Woolf's story is consumed with imagination. The narrator wants to determine Isabella's true character and tries to do so by imagining what her belongings reveal about her. However, when Isabella appears in front of the looking glass, the illusion the narrator has created disappears and the reality of Isabella's emptiness is exposed. Spark bases her story on the imaginative supposition that babies are completely omniscient. With this premise, Spark seems to suggest that only imagination can filter the grim reality of war.

22. (Average) *Guidelines for student response:* Through stream-of-consciousness narration, Woolf forces the reader to question perceptions of reality. For example, the narrator assumes that the "masklike indifference of [Isabella's] face" reveals greater passion. When Isabella is eventually unmasked, the narrator's judgment is exposed as mere fancy. Spark also wants readers to question reality. Her omniscient narrator reduces human activity to two categories—meaningful or irrelevant. What many assume to be meaningful—the baby's development—is irrelevant in the face of the war's horrors. In the end, the reality behind the narrator's smile is not contentment or amusement but contempt for those who cannot accept reality.

23. (Challenging) *Guidelines for student response:* Students might note that Woolf stresses the difference between reality and our perception of it. This idea is echoed in modern psychological theories, as well as in the changing nature of social structures. For example, the narrator imagines that Isabella's superficial dinner conversation belies a "profounder state of being." However, such assumptions are proved

false. Spark's narrator, who knows everything happening everywhere, brings to mind modern systems of communication and the instantaneous dispersal of news. In the modern era, facts are equated with reality when, in actuality, very few people seem willing to interpret facts for themselves; instead, they accept someone else's view of reality as the partygoer accepts Asquith's assessment of the war.

"The Rocking-Horse Winner"
by D. H. Lawrence
"A Shocking Accident"
by Graham Greene

Selection Test (p. 275)

Critical Reading/Vocabulary and Grammar

1. b 2. c 3. d 4. b 5. d 6. a 7. a 8. b 9. a 10. c 11. c 12. b 13. a 14. d 15. c 16. b 17. d 18. b 19. d 20. c

Questions are classified in these categories:
    Comprehension 1(A), 2(A), 8(E)
    Interpretation 5(C), 6(A), 9(E), 13(C), 14(C)
    Literary Analysis 3(A), 7(A), 11(A)
    Reading Strategy 4(A), 10(A), 12(C)
    Vocabulary 15(A), 16(A), 17(E)
    Grammar 18(A), 19(A), 20(E)
    E = Easy, A = Average, C = Challenging

Essay Questions

21. (Easy) *Guidelines for student response:* Paul is deeply affected by his parents' materialism. He senses their anxiety about money and status and assumes the responsibility of resolving it. His anxiety, desire to please, and fierce sense of loyalty make him an easy character to identify with. Jerome, too, is affected by an event beyond his control—the bizarre details of his father's death. The reader seems to feel more sympathy for Jerome because he doesn't view himself as a pitiable person—he thinks the circumstances of his father's death "were still part of the mystery of life." Jerome's main discomfort and unhappiness arise from his inability to view the world as others around him do. The reader hopes that Jerome will find peace or understanding with another person.

22. (Average) *Guidelines for student response:* Students should recognize that Greene strongly aligns himself with the notion of unpredictability through his story's main premise—a boy's life is drastically altered by the bizarre circumstances of his father's death. By ending the story with the bizarre question from the story's beginning—"What happened to the pig?"— Greene reconfirms his view. Jerome does not escape the unpredictability; rather, he finds comfort, or at least familiarity, in it. Students who share Greene's opinion might point to the incident in which Jerome earns the nickname "Pig"; such labeling and ridicule are an unfortunate part of life. Students who disagree with Greene's view might argue that Jerome, with his oblivious approach to the circumstances of his father's death, seems more of a literary invention than a reflection of the state of existence.

23. (Challenging) *Guidelines for student response:* Students should identify the rocking horse as the primary symbol in Lawrence's story and realize that it conveys several meanings. For instance, its stationary form symbolizes the futile struggle of materialism; Paul's mother creates a frenzy over money but gets nowhere. Paul's fierce attachment to the rocking horse, even after he outgrows it, echoes his mother's unrealistic attachment to the ideals of wealth and status. Through this symbolism, Lawrence condemns the superficiality of the British elite and highlights the psychological damage wrought by materialism.

"The Book of Sand"
by Jorge Luis Borges

Selection Test (p. 278)

Critical Reading

1. b 2. b 3. a 4. c 5. b 6. b 7. c 8. a 9. b 10. d

Questions are classified in these categories:
    Comprehension 1(E), 3(A), 4(E), 6(A), 9(E)
    Interpretation 2(A), 5(A), 7(C), 8(C), 10(C)
    E = Easy, A = Average, C = Challenging

"The Book of Sand"
by Jorge Luis Borges
(continued)

Essay Questions

11. (Easy) *Guidelines for student response:* Students should discuss the narrator's expertise, his book collection, his love of Scotland through Scottish authors, and his library job. The narrator's misanthropy seems related to the bibliophilia, especially when he mentions fear of having his latest acquisition stolen. Among other things, his obsessiveness adds to the impact of his disposal of the book.

12. (Average) *Guidelines for student response:* Students should note the Biblical context of the story and move on to the idea that the narrator exchanges his Bible for the "devilish" Book of Sand, which, despite its resemblance to a Bible, actually suggests a random, arbitrary universe without a presiding God. The book seems monstrous and obscene because it tempts the narrator to lose his faith in a benign universe.

13. (Challenging) *Guidelines for student response:* Students should note that the narrator revises his views or first impressions of several things and uses phrases like "Only later was I to realize," which suggests the fallibility or incompleteness of human perception. Such shifts reflect the shifting nature of the Book of Sand. The narrator's myopia symbolizes human limits in relating to both reality and the infinite. Some students might note that the narrator even changes his mind about how to start the story after the first paragraph.

Part Test, Unit 6, Part 3: Focus on Literary Forms— The Short Story (p. 280)

Critical Reading/Vocabulary and Grammar

1. b 2. c 3. c 4. d 5. c 6. b 7. a 8. c 9. d
10. a 11. b 12. d 13. c 14. b 15. a

Questions are classified in these categories:
Comprehension 1(E)
Interpretation 2(A), 8(A), 10(C)
Literary Analysis 3(A), 7(A)
Reading Strategy 4(A), 5(C), 6(A), 9(A)
Vocabulary 11(A), 12(C)

Grammar Skill 13(A), 14(C), 15(E)
E = Easy, A = Average, C = Challenging

Essay Questions

16. (Easy) *Guidelines for student response:* Students' essays must identify one character from one of the stories and clearly explain why the character is intriguing. For example, students might explain that Arsat in "The Lagoon" is the most compelling because of his tortured inner struggle. Students might identify with his feelings of isolation or regret. Students might find Jerome in "A Shocking Accident" most compelling because of his absurd situation and unusual approach to it.

17. (Average) *Guidelines for student response:* Students' essays must identify the theme in two separate stories and the literary devices used to convey each theme. For example, students might compare and contrast Lawrence's "The Rocking-Horse Winner" with Joyce's "Araby." Students should note that Lawrence conveys theme mainly through symbolism and that Joyce conveys theme mainly through one character's epiphany.

18. (Challenging) *Guidelines for student response:* Students' essays must focus on one story and explain why it is modern, supporting the opinion with strong, convincing evidence. Students might name "The Lady in the Looking Glass: A Reflection" because of Woolf's stream-of-consciousness point of view. They might choose Conrad's "The Lagoon" or Greene's "A Shocking Accident," noting that although the narrative form is more traditional, the theme in each story mirrors or comments upon the psychological state of modern life.

"Do Not Go Gentle into That Good Night" and "Fern Hill" by Dylan Thomas "The Horses" and "The Rain Horse" by Ted Hughes

Selection Test (p. 283)

Critical Reading/Vocabulary and Grammar

1. c 2. d 3. d 4. b 5. a 6. c 7. d 8. a 9. b
10. a 11. c 12. b 13. a 14. d 15. b 16. a
17. c 18. a 19. b

Questions are classified in these categories:
Comprehension 1(E), 2(C), 9(E), 10(E), 14(A)
Interpretation 4(A), 5(A), 6(A), 7(C), 11(A), 15(C), 16(A)
Literary Analysis 8(C), 13(C)
Reading Strategy 3(A), 12(A)
Vocabulary 17(E), 18(A)
Grammar 19(E)
E = Easy, A = Average, C = Challenging

Essay Questions

20. (Easy) *Guidelines for student response:* Students should recall that the man's initial response is nothingness, boredom. He had apparently spent time here as a boy hunting rabbits and apparently knew his way around well. As the episode develops with the horse, his anger at the strangeness of the land is transferred to the horse as he tries to outsmart it and get away from it. Students may conclude that the horse *did* appear on this day and serves as a symbol or sign that the man no longer "belongs" there. Other students may argue that the incident with the horse happened twelve years ago and the man simply relives the whole thing, including the final scene in the farmer's shed. Or, perhaps because of his long absence and detachment from the land, the man had *never* met a horse in that field, and he imagined the whole thing, again symbolizing that he no longer belonged.

21. (Average) *Guidelines for student response:* In "Do Not Go Gentle," Thomas urges resistance to dying. People should not accept death willingly but should fight against it. In "Fern Hill," Thomas expresses a fondness for childhood as a "green and golden" time. He also expresses regret at its passing. Students may or may not accept Thomas's attitudes about the "golden" nature of childhood, citing lack of similar "natural" or pleasurable, free experiences such as Thomas describes. Students may agree or disagree with Thomas's attitudes toward death. Students should focus on the attitude of the *dying* toward death, not of the survivors.

22. (Challenging) *Guidelines for student response:* The simple language of the work helps communicate the silence, broken

only by the curlew's tear. The phrase "detail leafed from the darkness" expresses the gradual clarification of objects in the predawn. The hard consonant sounds in "to its core tore" express the rending of the grayness by the sun's rays. Students should be able to conclude that Hughes's voice is respectful and reverent in this passage.

"An Arundel Tomb" and "The Explosion" by Philip Larkin
"On the Patio" by Peter Redgrove
"Not Waving but Drowning" by Stevie Smith

Selection Test (p. 286)

Critical Reading/Vocabulary and Grammar
1. d 2. b 3. d 4. a 5. c 6. a 7. c 8. b 9. c
10. d 11. b 12. c 13. a 14. c 15. d 16. b
17. d 18. b 19. c 20. d

Questions are classified in these categories:
Comprehension 1(E), 6(A), 11(E), 14(E)
Interpretation 2(A), 5(C), 7(A), 8(A), 12(C), 13(A), 15(A), 16(E)
Literary Analysis 4(C), 9(A), 10(C)
Reading Strategy 3(E)
Vocabulary 17(E), 18(A)
Grammar 19(A), 20(A)
E = Easy, A = Average, C = Challenging

Essay Questions

21. (Easy) *Guidelines for student response:* Students should recognize that the central idea of the poem is that this person has felt like an outsider all his life. He has felt "much too far" outside the company of other people and has been waving to try to get their attention. They didn't notice, just as they didn't notice him waving when he was out in the water. "They" in the poem talk about the dead man as if he weren't there; they apparently ignored him when he was alive as well. The use of first person for the dead man's thoughts makes readers feel closer to him than to the other persons and makes them sympathize with the dead man.

22. (Average) *Guidelines for student response:* Students should recognize that the central visual image is the effigy on the tomb of an

"An Arundel Tomb" and "The Explosion"
by Philip Larkin
"On the Patio" by Peter Redgrove
"Not Waving but Drowning" by Stevie Smith
(continued)

earl and a countess. Most importantly, the effigy shows the earl fondly holding the countess's hand. The speaker reveals this, at the end of the second stanza, with apparent surprise, as if he is sharing his initial discovery of the fact with readers. The speaker feels that this small detail, created by a sculptor, is the only detail that later generations will notice. He says the gesture, the "fidelity" is an untruth, preserved by the sculptor, but latched onto by viewers as truth because they want to believe that love survives.

23. (Challenging) *Guidelines for student response:* Students should be able to recognize the altered meter that serves to communicate the unreality of the image and of the whole event, as far as the wives are concerned. In the displayed lines, the altered meter, combined with the single syllable that hangs at the end of each, creates a jarring effect as the world is interrupted by the "tremor." The images the wives imagine in the last two stanzas are vivid, yet unreal; the husbands' forms are visible but not distinct, as if seen on a coin or against the backdrop of the sun (much like the flash of an explosion).

"B. Wordsworth" by V. S. Naipaul

Selection Test (p. 289)

Critical Reading/Vocabulary and Grammar

1. a 2. c 3. d 4. c 5. b 6. b 7. d 8. a 9. c
10. a 11. b 12. c 13. d 14. c 15. b 16. c
17. a 18. d 19. b 20. a

Questions are classified in these categories:
  Comprehension 1(E), 3(E)
  Interpretation 2(A), 6(A), 7(C), 10(A), 12(A)
  Literary Analysis 8(A), 9(C), 14(C)
  Reading Strategy 4(E), 5(A), 11(C), 13(A)
  Vocabulary 15(E), 16(A), 17(E)
  Grammar 18(A), 19(A), 20(C)
  E = Easy, A = Average, C = Challenging

Essay Questions

21. (Easy) *Guidelines for student response:* Students may note any number of events or details to show the narrator's response to Wordsworth, including the fact that he is comforted by the poet, his desire to see the poet again, and his sadness as the poet ages. Students should conclude that the narrator is full of affection for the poet and is quite impressed by his personality and by what he says.

22. (Average) *Guidelines for student response:* Students should note that if "B. Wordsworth" were written from an omniscient point of view, information about specific characters and events would not be limited. For example, an omniscient narrator would relate what other characters, specifically B. Wordsworth, see, hear, think, imagine, and assume. Students will probably conclude, however, that the story is effective written in first person because, through the wondering and thoughtful mind of the young narrator, the reader empathizes with his experience, from which he grows.

23. (Challenging) *Guidelines for student response:* Students who argue that B. Wordsworth is an image of writers in general should note his wonderment in everyday events, such as watching bees, gazing at stars, and deliberating over which cafe to patronize. They may note that he is a bit of a failure; Naipul may be showing that poetry is related to lack of success in life. Those who argue that Naipul is making a political point should note that B. Wordsworth's impracticality and poverty lead him to beg and cause an encounter with the police. No one around him besides the boy responds to his talent. White Wordsworth, students may speculate, had better opportunities to have his vision recognized.

"The Train from Rhodesia"
by Nadine Gordimer

Selection Test (p. 292)

Critical Reading/Vocabulary and Grammar

1. a 2. b 3. d 4. c 5. b 6. d 7. c 8. c 9. b
10. a 11. d 12. b 13. c 14. a 15. b 16. d
17. c 18. a 19. a 20. b

Questions are classified in these categories:
Comprehension 1(A), 3(E), 12(A)
Interpretation 4(C), 6(A), 7(C), 10(E), 11(C)
Literary Analysis 2(A), 5(A), 14(A)
Reading Strategy 8(A), 9(C), 13(C)
Vocabulary 15(E), 16(A), 17(A)
Grammar 18(A), 19(C), 20(C)
E = Easy, A = Average, C = Challenging

Essay Questions

21. (Easy) *Guidelines for student response:* Students must understand the train's arrival signals the arrival of wealthy white tourists who provide the townspeople with the money they need for economic survival. Therefore, people gather at the station as if expecting a big event. Students may note that it is due to the colonization of Africa that Africans, at the time of this story, are no longer economically independent. By selling their handmade crafts and begging, native South Africans show their desperate dependence upon whites for economic survival.

22. (Average) *Guidelines for student response:* Students may interpret the lion as a representative of the African continent—itself bought and sold as if an object at the train station. In the lion's "open jaws, the pointed teeth, the black tongue," students may see the silent, terrible roar of Africa—her land and people, formerly independent and fierce, now dependent upon a life of meager change thrown from the windows of departing trains.

23. (Challenging) *Guidelines for student response:* Whichever passage students select, they must explain how it highlights the inner conflict felt by the young woman as well as the larger conflict central to the story. Students will most likely select a passage from the story's ending, where these conflicts are directly experienced by the young woman.

from *Midsummer*, XXIII and from *Omeros* from Chapter XXVIII
by Derek Walcott
"From Lucy: Englan' Lady"
by James Berry

Selection Test (p. 295)

Critical Reading/Vocabulary and Grammar

1. b 2. d 3. c 4. b 5. a 6. d 7. a 8. b 9. b
10. c 11. c 12. a 13. d 14. b 15. a 16. d
17. c 18. a 19. c 20. d

Questions are classified in these categories:
Comprehension 1(A), 6(A)
Interpretation 3(A), 5(C), 9(A), 11(E), 13(C)
Literary Analysis 10(E), 14(A), 15(A)
Reading Strategy 2(A), 4(C), 7(E), 8(C), 12(A)
Vocabulary 16(A), 17(E), 18(A)
Grammar 19(A), 20(A)
E = Easy, A = Average, C = Challenging

Essay Questions

21. (Easy) *Guidelines for student response:* Both Berry and Walcott are people of color raised in West Indian culture, a culture that is defined by economic, historical, and cultural ties to England. This fact may influence their choices of topic and of perspective. Walcott applies the conventions of the epic, passed to him through a British-style education, to West Indian history in *Omeros*. He gives an outsider's view of English culture in *Midsummer*. Berry offers a Jamaican woman's view of Britain's queen. These poets' West Indian background both distances them from and links them to things British.

22. (Average) *Guidelines for student response:* Both Berry and Walcott mix British and West Indian traditions. Walcott ironically turns to Shakespeare to understand the fate of English blacks (who some whites say cannot "do" Shakespeare). His vision is complicated by the fact that he has a foot in both worlds and a home in neither. Berry uses the down-home patterns of Jamaican speech to tell a simple human truth about England's queen. Students' examples should point up the areas in these selections in which the viewpoints of the West Indian, of the British-educated person, and of the "outsider" intersect.

from *Midsummer*, XXIII and **from** *Omeros*
from Chapter XXVIII by Derek Walcott
"From Lucy: Englan' Lady" by James Berry
(continued)

23. (Challenging) *Guidelines for student response:* Students might point to Walcott's Calibans, to his griot and the images of palm trees he uses, and to Berry's Jamaican speaker as instances of voices and figures from outside the tradition of English poetry. In *Midsummer*, Walcott challenges the value of traditional poetry, to the extent that he contrasts "Caedmon's raceless dew" (the origin of English poetry) with the brutality of present-day life in racially divided England. He also affirms poetry's value, since he uses references to that tradition to help us understand the riots in Brixton. Berry's poem suggests that it takes a plainspoken, unsophisticated person to see through the pomp of the queen's life and see the underlying human truth. Students may note, though, that we only receive the benefit of her wisdom through Berry's poem, which fits traditional ideas of poetry.

"A Devoted Son" by Anita Desai

Selection Test (p. 298)

Critical Reading/Vocabulary and Grammar

1. d 2. c 3. a 4. a 5. b 6. d 7. b 8. b 9. c
10. b 11. c 12. a 13. d 14. d 15. b 16. a
17. c 18. c 19. b 20. d

Questions are classified in these categories:
    Comprehension 1(A), 6(E), 9(E), 14(C)
    Interpretation 2(E), 5(A), 8(C), 11(A), 15(A)
    Literary Analysis 4(A), 7(A), 12(E)
    Reading Strategy 3(C), 10(A), 13(C)
    Vocabulary 16(E), 17(A), 18(A)
    Grammar 19(E), 20(A)
    E = Easy, A = Average, C = Challenging

Essay Questions

21. (Easy) *Guidelines for student response:* Students should trace the progression in Varma's life based on changes his ambitions for his son bring about. Although Rakesh shows outward signs of devotion, his modern ways cause his father's unhappiness. Varma moves from pride, through complaining, to defiance, to a kind of realization of what his son is, to a final outburst of protest.

22. (Average) *Guidelines for student response:* Student essays should indicate that Desai does not show us Rakesh's "insides," because she uses him as a foil to show effects of time and cultural conflict on Varma. Students may show that in each case where Rakesh seems to defy his father, he is acting reasonably, though not perhaps from love.

23. (Challenging) *Guidelines for student response:* Students may note that Desai shows that Indians are tempted to incorporate Western ideas into a traditional context, but that this blending often causes unhappiness. Students should point out that, in the story, Western medicine appears first as a route to traditional goals—increased prestige and income for the family. It is only when Rakesh begins to apply his medical knowledge to the care he gives his father that the conflict between Western and Indian ways comes to light. Students should provide examples showing how Rakesh's use of Western ideas in an Indian context—his attention to his father's diet, for instance—is both consistent with and destructive of tradition.

from "We'll Never Conquer Space" by Arthur C. Clarke

Selection Test (p. 301)

Critical Reading/Vocabulary and Grammar

1. d 2. a 3. b 4. d 5. c 6. b 7. c 8. d 9. a
10. d 11. a 12. c 13. b 14. d 15. b 16. c
17. d 18. a

Questions are classified in these categories:
    Comprehension 6(E), 10(A), 15(A)
    Interpretation 4(A), 5(C), 8(A), 9(E)
    Literary Analysis 1(E), 2(A), 3(C), 7(C), 14(A)
    Reading Strategy 11(C), 12(E), 13(A)
    Vocabulary 16(E), 17(A)
    Grammar 18(E), 19(A), 20(C)
    E = Easy, A = Average, C = Challenging

Essay Questions

19. (Easy) *Guidelines for student response:* Students should recognize that Clarke

predicts [that] solar and stellar space will never be "easily" traversed as are distances—even great distances—on Earth. He argues that the vastness of space prohibits reasonable communication. He assumes that the laws of physics, as we know them, will not change, and that we will never be able to travel faster than the speed of light. This barrier will prevent colonists from sharing a common life or history with those back home.

20. (Average) *Guidelines for student response:* Students may take the stand that Clarke sells humans short by assuming we won't come up with the technology to bridge interstellar distances. We have done other things that no one ever thought we could do, so why should mastering space travel be any different? Or students may conclude that Clarke's assertions about the vastness of space are valid and convincing. Without changing the laws of physics and the barrier set by the speed of light, mastering interstellar distances seems unlikely.

21. (Challenging) *Guidelines for student response:* Students should recognize that Clarke is referring to the fact that air travel allows us to get just about anywhere within a day. Instant communication via telephone, computer, and satellite is more or less a global phenomenon, and video communication is continuing to be more common. We can see real-time images of people on the other side of the world, instead of reading old news about them. Students may point out that cultural differences still separate people. Students should acknowledge that people in developing countries, who have little or no access to—or use for— these technologies, would have very different attitudes about the Earth.

Part Test, Unit 6, Part 4: From the National to the Global
(p. 304)

Critical Reading/Vocabulary and Grammar

1. d 2. b 3. a 4. c 5. d 6. b 7. b 8. a 9. c
10. c 11. a 12. c 13. b 14. d 15. b 16. a
17. c 18. d 19. c 20. a

Questions are classified in these eategories:
Comprehension 2(A)
Interpretation 1(A), 5(A), 6(C)
Literary Analysis 3(A), 4(E), 8(C), 10(A)
Reading Strategy 7(A), 9(A)
Vocabulary 11(A), 12(A), 13(C), 14(E), 15(A), 16(A)
Grammar Skill 17(C), 18(A), 19(A), 20(A)
E = Easy, A = Average, C = Challenging

Essay Questions

21. (Easy) *Guidelines for student response:* Students' essays must name one character, identify his or her conflict, and evaluate the character's actions. For example, students might sympathize with the father, Varma, in Desai's "A Devoted Son." They might identify with his struggle against changing roles and admire his stand for himself. In contrast, the actions of the young man in Hughes's "The Rain Horse," might anger students who disapprove of the character's violent reactions.

22. (Average) *Guidelines for student response:* Students' essays must identify one poem written in free verse and one written in another form. For example, students might compare and contrast Berry's "From Lucy: Englan' Lady" and Larkin's "An Arundel Tomb." Students might discuss Berry's varying line lengths and rhythms and his irregular stanza structure. They might contrast it with Larkin's use of end rhyme and regular rhythm. They should go on to note that Berry's free verse complements the rhythms of his speaker's distinctive voice, while Larkin's formal approach mirrors the formal quality of the statue he is questioning and the serious, philosophical nature of the questions he poses.

23. (Average) *Guidelines for student response:* Students' essays must compare and contrast two poets and provide evidence from each poet's work to support their conclusions. Students might compare and contrast Dylan Thomas and Derek Walcott. Points of comparison might include both poets' sophisticated word choice and use of sound devices. Points of contrast might include Walcott's inclusion of "spoken words," as in the excerpt

from *Midsummer*, or Thomas's rushed pace in "Fern Hill."

24. (Average) *Guidelines for student response:* Students' essays should focus on at least one writer and demonstrate the effects of British imperialism on the writer's work. Students might explain that in his two poems, Derek Walcott makes connections between the colonial slave trade and injustices faced by West Indians in modern times. Other students might examine Gordimer's "The Train from Rhodesia" or Naipul's "B. Wordsworth."

25. (Challenging) *Guidelines for student response:* Students' essays must explore the theme of disillusionment in three selections. For example, students might note disillusionment with nature in Hughes's "The Rain Horse," disillusionment with one's society or personal relations in Gordimer's "The Train from Rhodesia," and disillusionment with technology in Clarke's "We'll Never Conquer Space."